CW00429636

A Bold and
Ambitious Enterprise

A Bold and Ambitious Enterprise

THE BRITISH ARMY IN THE LOW COUNTRIES, 1813–1814

Andrew Bamford

Frontline Books
London

A Bold and Ambitious Enterprise:
The British Army in the Low Countries, 1813–1814
This edition published in 2013 by Frontline Books,
an imprint of Pen & Sword Books Ltd,
47 Church Street, Barnsley, S. Yorkshire, S70 2AS
www.frontline-books.com

ISBN: 978-1-84832-685-9

CIP data records for this title are available from the British Library

For more information on our books, please visit
www.frontline-books.com, email info@frontline-books.com
or write to us at the above address.

Printed and bound by CPI Group (UK) Ltd, Croydon, CR0 4YY

Typeset in 10.8/13.8 point Minion Pro

Contents

Plates

Maps

Maps

Introduction

LATE IN THE AFTERNOON OF 13 MARCH 1814, Major the Hon. James Stanhope of the 1st Foot Guards arrived in London and immediately waited upon the Earl of Bathurst, Secretary of State for War and the Colonies. Like many other weary and travel-stained officers who had arrived in the capital during the course of the previous two decades, Stanhope brought despatches from a British commander overseas, with news of a recent battle. But whilst London had become accustomed to hearing of a succession of victories, won in Portugal, Spain and France by the armies of Lord Wellington, Stanhope came from Holland and bore news of a defeat. Four days earlier, on the night of 8–9 March, British troops from the army commanded by Sir Thomas Graham had attempted to seize the French-held fortress of Bergen-op-Zoom by a coup de main: after an initial success, they had been counter-attacked by the rallied garrison and the assault had collapsed. Half of the attacking forces were killed, wounded or taken prisoner.

Notwithstanding the ill nature of the news that he bore, Stanhope was immediately taken on to see the Prince Regent, who was gracious enough to concede that the gallantry shown in the attack went no small way to compensate for its failure, and that no blame should be accorded to Graham. Bathurst took a similar line, to the extent that Stanhope was even able to persuade the Secretary of State to arrange for him to receive a brevet lieutenant colonelcy, quite as if he had brought news of a victory. On the face of things, this seemed an unusually forgiving line for both the Regent and his minister to take: with the Napoleonic Wars seemingly at last approaching their conclusion, thoughts were already turning to the settlement of the peace and any blow to British arms and prestige at such a juncture could only lead to a reduction of influence within the Sixth Coalition. But those same factors also help explain why the news of Graham's defeat was met with such understanding: when Bathurst read in Graham's despatches of how the general had been let down by his troops and his subordinates, the Secretary of State surely had cause to remember that it was he, Bathurst, who had had the greatest hand in organizing the dispatch of

Graham's little army and who bore no small part of the responsibility for the fact that its means were never commensurate with the mission he had assigned it. James Stanhope's promotion, perhaps, owed something to the guilty conscience of the man responsible for directing Britain's war effort.

But there was more to it than that, for the failed attack did not mark the failure of the campaign, nor the end of the mission on which Graham had been sent. That an attack on a second-rate fortress had been repulsed was unfortunate, and the level of casualties incurred to be regretted, but it was not in order to capture Bergen-op-Zoom that Graham and his army had been sent to Holland. Rather, their presence there was part of a far more ambitious scheme, aimed at ensuring that Britain was able to fulfil a key war aim that had been a cornerstone of its foreign policy since the 1790s and before. At stake were both the political future of the Low Countries and the matrimonial future of the heiress to the British throne. Standing against Britain were not only the forces of Napoleonic France, still grimly fighting for their Emperor even as his empire collapsed around him, but also Britain's allies in the Sixth Coalition, who, if they could not oppose Britain's goals by military means, could certainly do their best to impede them politically as they, too, sought to attain their own war aims. As if this were not enough, Britain was already heavily committed both to the main struggle against Napoleon – heretofore carried out by its Army in the Peninsula, its Navy across the oceans, and its gold wherever it could be spent to subsidize the fight – and to the growing struggle in North America where the United States still sought to capture Canada whilst Britain's back was turned. Under the circumstances, it was hardly surprising that the forces that could be spared to open a third front were frequently deficient in quantity, quality or both.

This, then, is the story of that third front: of the politics that led to its opening, of the conflicting objectives that plagued it, of the double-dealing and broken promises that soured relations between the Allied powers, and of the soldiers who fought and died as a result. Military success was only ever partial, and Britain found itself out-manoeuvred both by its allies and by its erstwhile Dutch client state. Under these circumstances, it is easy for the more successful elements of the campaign – notably the two actions fought around the village of Merxem – to be forgotten. Even where eventual success came as a result of political manoeuvring rather than military action, this would never have been possible without the presence of British redcoats on the ground.

Under the circumstances, then, it remains surprising that the campaign has not been covered in greater detail before. Sir John Fortescue emphasized the importance of the campaign, and his treatment of it is better than most, but it forms only a few pages within the many hundreds he devoted to the Napoleonic Wars as a whole, and two-thirds of his narrative focuses on Bergen-op-Zoom.[1] Even more heavily focussed on the failed storm is the chapter in a staff history with the unpromising title of *British Minor Expeditions*,[2] and a similar bias may be found amongst the biographers of Sir Thomas Graham, although at least in this case there is some justification in the need to account for the less than distinguished end to the subject's active military career. Despite their focus, none of these accounts satisfactorily explain Graham's motives for ordering the attack, nor the reasons for its failure.[3] We might even wonder whether some of their authors even had access to Graham's public and private correspondence relating to the campaign, whilst Delavoye, who certainly did have access since he quotes extensive passages verbatim, offers little by way of analysis of its contents.

By contrast, this account draws extensively on Graham's correspondence with Bathurst and with the Under-Secretary of State, Colonel Henry Bunbury, as well as the official and semi-official papers of two of Graham's key subordinates: Major General Herbert Taylor and Lieutenant Colonel James Carmichael Smyth. Not only do these sources reveal several shortcomings in the existing brief published accounts of the campaign, but they also flesh them out with a far greater level of detail. Perhaps their greatest value, however, is the insight they give into the thinking of their authors. Much of this correspondence deals with still-born schemes that were overtaken by events even as they were first committed to paper, reminding the reader of the intelligence blackout in which the main participants in the campaign were operating and warning against the overzealous use of hindsight in judging their actions. Judgements of a different kind – ranging from military matters on the one hand to the qualities of Dutch women and Dutch gin on the other – may be found in the surprisingly large number of first-hand accounts that exist of the campaign. To these, we need also add the anonymous publication entitled *Letters from Germany and Holland*, which, on the face of it, consists of just that from an officer serving in an unspecified capacity under Gibbs in the Baltic and Graham in the Low Countries. Upon closer perusal, however, the work reads more like a history of those campaigns in epistolary form: that it remains useful as such is undeniable, and it is clear that the letters themselves are genuine enough since they lack the hindsight inherent in the after-the-fact accounts, but the deliberate anonymity of both author and editor suggest that, at the same time, they are not quite all they purport to be.

This book is a history of the operations of the British Army, and I make no apology for the fact that the bulk of the eyewitnesses whose testimony

I have used to back up the official records are also British. Several excellent general histories exist of the military and diplomatic events of the Sixth Coalition, and my purpose here is not to supplant them but rather to flesh out the hitherto limited coverage of Britain's military involvement in northern Europe. It is nevertheless important to consider the actions and motives of Britain's allies, and it is particularly fortunate in this regard that Michael Leggiere's *The Fall of Napoleon*, dealing with the first phase of the 1814 campaign, draws so heavily on the papers of the Prussian General-leutnant Friedrich-Wilhelm von Bülow, whose Prussian corps was extensively involved in operations alongside Graham in the Low Countries.[4] Anglo-Dutch diplomatic relations during the period are also well set out in G. J. Renier's, *Great Britain and the Establishment of the Kingdom of the Netherlands*, which is still valid despite being over eighty years old,[5] but accounts of the Dutch military involvement in this stage of the war are still lacking. In part, this may well reflect the limited active role played by the newly raised Dutch Army, but individuals within that army did play a vital part in this campaign and none more so than engineer officer Jan van Gorkum, who provides an essential account of his involvement in both the planning and execution of the failed attack on Bergen-op-Zoom.[6] In that my Dutch is all but non-existent, I am extremely grateful to Ellie Wout for her translation of this text: those passages from van Gorkum that are quoted in this work, though referenced to the Dutch original, are all Ellie's translations.

The names of many of the towns and villages that were fought over or marched through in 1813 and 1814 have since changed, as borders have shifted over the intervening two centuries. On the whole, I have used the modern place name unless I believe that doing so would be confusing, usually if there are multiple modern variants or if an older alternative is extensively used in the primary sources that I have quoted. The usual British arrogance in renaming places to suit our own tongue means that I have consistently referred to Antwerp, Brussels and The Hague rather than Antwerpen, Bruxelles and Den Haag, and I have also kept the anglicised Merxem for the village – now a suburb of Antwerp – that was twice captured by Graham's troops. I have also made a point of using the name Holland to refer to the country that is today known as the Netherlands: this may seem odd, but I have done so deliberately since in the period covered by this book 'The Netherlands' could viably be used to refer to the whole of the Low Countries and, more specifically, was linked to the concept of a United Netherlands ruled by the House of Orange. Established after the peace, this eventually took the form of a shotgun union of what is now Belgium, which during the Napoleonic period had originally been the Austrian Netherlands and then been directly annexed to France, with what is now the Netherlands but which during the Napoleonic period was successively the United Provinces, the Batavian Republic and the Kingdom of Holland, before also being annexed to France. Holland, in any case, is what nearly all British accounts call the area they were fighting in, although by rights much of the action actually took place in Zeeland and Brabant.

There are several individuals to whom I must extend my particular thanks for their contributions to this project. The staff at the British Library, The National Archives, and the Prince Consort's Military Library were all extremely helpful, as was Lieutenant Colonel George Latham at the Highlanders' Museum. Carole Divall, who has written two excellent books on the 30th Foot during the Napoleonic Wars, was extremely generous in sharing her research notes on the 2/30th and passing on to me her copies of the journals of Surgeon Elkington and Volunteer McCready. Keith Hollick likewise made available his notes and transcripts on the Royal Marines. As ever, the contributors to the Napoleon Series website and discussion forum were extremely helpful in answering queries and pointing me to the location of additional source material: I should extend my particular thanks to Steven H. Smith, Oscar Lopez, Ron McGuigan, Dominique Timmermans and Bas de Groot. Elsewhere, I must also thank Dave Brown, Andy Burbidge, Kevin Linch and John White for their various contributions along the way. In putting the book together, the advice and patience of Michael Leventhal, Stephen Chumbley, and Donald Sommerville at Frontline Books was invaluable.

Special thanks go to my father, Mick Bamford, for again volunteering to proof-read a manuscript for me, and to my wife, Lucy, who has also read through the whole piece and drawn out the base maps which have then been annotated by our local IT guru, Dave Beckford. Finally, I should end by extending my great thanks to two great friends, Vic James and Ellie Wout, with whom Lucy and I travelled to visit some of the sites that feature in this narrative. Ellie, of course, has in addition provided the translation of van Gorkum's memoirs, but both parties have been steadfast in support of this project from the outset. Would that the politicians of 1814 had managed to construct as solid an Anglo-Dutch alliance as these two.

Chapter I

'Not at Present in a Fit State'

THE LARGE-SCALE SHIFT in the political and military balance of Europe between autumn 1812 and summer 1813 took Britain somewhat by surprise, presenting both problems and opportunities and necessitating a rethink of old strategic priorities. Since 1809 and the collapse of Austria and Spain, Britain had been playing a long game. Its was the only major military force still in the field against the French, and it was clear that it could only operate on the peripheries, most notably the Iberian Peninsula where, with the aid of the Portuguese and a slowly resurgent Spain, the upper hand had been gained by the end of 1812. In the meantime, naval and colonial superiority meant that in economic terms Britain was ahead of France, whose Continental System, designed to hamper British commerce, was palpably failing. Nevertheless, success still came with a price, since a high-handed approach towards the United States had embroiled Britain in a new transatlantic war as the young republic sought to protect its seagoing trade and bag Canada into the bargain. All this meant that, in the immediate aftermath of the collapse of Napoleon's Russian adventure, Britain was poorly placed to capitalize on the opportunities afforded. The British Army and Navy were already thinly stretched, and the former was largely committed to what was now, as the focus of war again shifted to Northern Europe, a secondary theatre. With a potential end to the great struggle with France at last in sight, Britain would need a rethink if its share of the peace settlement was to be commensurate with the money and blood that had been expended since 1793.[1]

Britain had not entirely neglected the powers of Northern Europe, whose fate, due to their location if nothing else, was of considerable importance to it. In 1811 consignments of arms had been sent to the Baltic in hopeful expectation of a Prussian revolt against Napoleon, and British diplomacy and subsidies helped turn Sweden from a nominal French ally to an active – if unreliable member – of the allied coalition. This latter achievement was all the more impressive when it is recalled that Crown Prince Karl Johan of Sweden, the effective head of state due to the incapacity of King Karl XIII, had until 1810 been better known as Marshal Jean-Baptiste Bernadotte.[2] But the erstwhile French marshal had always had his eye on the main chance, and, having been invited to assume the Swedish throne in eventual succession to its childless and infirm incumbent, he quickly realigned his personal goals for aggrandisement with those of his new country by reversing Sweden's old foreign policy in order to seek conquests at the expense of Denmark rather than Russia. Being the first power to heed Britain's siren call for European allies, Sweden would do better than most when it came to the first round of subsidies, and would be able to secure concessions from Britain that would allow it a favoured status during any peace negotiations. Only later did it become clear that the unprincipled and untrustworthy Crown Prince had been playing his own game throughout the events of 1812–14. This, in turn, would cause serious problems when, as commander of the allied Army of the North, he would have nominal control over British troops.

In contrast to Sweden's willingness to accept British gold, Russia's relations with Britain during 1812 were limited and remained so for some time. The largely notional state of warfare that had existed between the two powers as a result of Russia's alignment with France was swiftly brought to a close, along with that between Britain and Sweden, in two treaties signed at Orebro on 18 July 1812. In order to cement Anglo-Russian relations, General Viscount Cathcart was sent to St Petersburg as ambassador, but, with the Emperor Alexander absent with his armies, Cathcart was initially unable to exert much influence. There was, in any case, some doubt within Russia, never mind outside, as to whether its war with Napoleon would continue beyond the eviction of the frostbitten remnants of the Grande Armée from its soil; only after Alexander overruled his generals did it become clear that, for the Emperor at least, this was to be a fight to the finish and that the Russian advance would therefore continue into Poland and Germany. This decision had the effect of finally forcing the hand of Prussia, where a strong nationalistic clique within the Army had, until now, been kept in check by the cautious and vacillating monarch, Friedrich Wilhelm III. Because of its obligations as a French client state, Prussia had had to provide a sizeable corps for the Grande Armée, which had operated on the far left wing along the Baltic and thus had survived the campaign relatively intact. Now, with the Russians posed to advance into Prussian territory, the Prussian field commander, Yorck, concluded a convention that neutralized his corps and ensured that Alexander's forces would enter Prussia as liberators not conquerors. Friedrich Wilhelm initially disavowed Yorck's actions, but, with the defiant general now throwing aside the pretence of neutrality and actively organizing East Prussia to fight alongside the

Russians, the king was eventually compelled to face the facts and align himself with Russia.

Thus, by spring 1813, Russia and Prussia were preparing their forces for a continued drive into Germany, where Napoleon's client states in the Confederation of the Rhine were beginning to grow uneasy about their alignment with apparently failing French fortunes. Sweden was slowly mobilizing too, but as yet with few troops in the field and with the Crown Prince's gaze still focussed primarily on Danish-held Norway rather than the struggle in Germany. On the sidelines sat Austria, which had successfully extracted its own auxiliary corps from Russia, where it had fought on the far right of Napoleon's forces, and which was now maintaining a careful neutrality whilst its wily Chancellor, Klemens von Metternich, assessed the potential consequences of events in Germany. Traditionally France's oldest continental foe, but now with a Habsburg archduchess as Empress of France, Austria had a foot in both camps and Metternich intended to keep things that way until it became clear who was going to come out on top. His caution was entirely justified, for Napoleon had employed phenomenal energy in the raising of a new army, calling in conscripts and drafting the Garde Nationale wholesale into the line in order to replace men lost in Russia. As a result of these measures, Napoleon was able to achieve numerical superiority when the armies clashed for the first time at Lützen on 2 May, although in the event not all his forces were engaged: the same mistake was not, however, repeated in the second and last major battle of spring 1813, when Napoleon was able to converge 115,000 troops against 96,000 Russians and Prussians at Bautzen. In a two-day battle fought on 20–21 May, the Allies were heavily defeated and forced to retreat, prompting Austria to intervene and mediate an armistice.[3] Both sides saw this primarily as a temporary cease-fire, but the Allied readiness to open negotiations – which neither Cathcart, nor his counterpart at the Prussian court, Lieutenant General Sir Charles Stewart, were able to influence – suggested that an end to the war through the out-and-out defeat of Napoleon was by no means a foregone conclusion. In this uncertain situation, Britain was compelled to tread carefully if it wished to exert its influence and work towards a peace that would satisfy its own war aims as well as those of its new-found allies.

Although profoundly opposed to the excesses of the French Revolution, Britain had not gone to war back in 1793 on purely ideological grounds. Indeed, at first, there had been plenty who welcomed the apparent self-destruction of the nation's oldest foe, and it was not until the excesses of the Terror, and the declared desire to export Revolution across Europe, that it became clear that the threat from France had grown rather than receded. It was the French invasion of the Austrian Netherlands, however, that brought matters to a head, since by seeking to exert its influence in the Low Countries France's new government had done one of the things best calculated to incur British ire. Nor was this ire without reason, for it had long been a cornerstone of British foreign policy that France should be kept away from the coast of Northern Europe and that the powers there should be friendly to – or, better still, clients of – Britain. Whereas Britain's southern coastline was defensible enough, with the anchorages at Portsmouth, Plymouth and Torbay providing bases for a fleet to counter any aggressive move up the English Channel, the eastern coastline was far more vulnerable. It was from this direction that the Dutch had come in 1667 to force the Medway and Thames and burn or carry away the great ships of the bankrupt Charles II, and it was from Dutch ports too that the last successful invasion of England had sailed in 1688. In the aftermath of that year's Glorious Revolution, the United Provinces had become an ally, and, into the eighteenth century, this had remained the case, although as Dutch power and prestige waned it had become imperative that other continental powers take on part of the burden of securing the Low Countries against France. Since 1713 this thankless task had fallen to Austria, although the Habsburgs had sought throughout the century to trade the Austrian Netherlands for territory contiguous with the rest of their Empire. Britain, meanwhile, continued to maintain effective relations with the Austrians and Dutch, even giving up conquests in Canada and India in order to ensure that the 1748 Treaty of Aix-la-Chapelle, ending the War of the Austrian Succession, included the return of French conquests in the Low Countries.

In more recent years, things had gone less well. Austria had become a French ally for a time in the mid-eighteenth century, as both powers sought to curb Fredrician Prussia, and the constant Anglo-Dutch rivalry over trade had flared into war for a fourth and last time in 1780 when the United Provinces joined the growing list of European powers hoping to achieve gains whilst Britain's attentions were diverted by events in America. Although the Dutch fleet gave the British North Sea squadron a bloody nose in the drawn Battle of the Dogger Bank in 1781, little was changed by these brief hostilities. Nevertheless, Britain watched with some concern as the Dutch fell prey to internal crises during the mid-1780s, and was therefore all the more concerned when Revolutionary France took up the old objective of Bourbon foreign policy and began aggressively to push France's frontier eastwards towards the Rhine. Thus, when Britain went to war in 1793 its two primary goals, as indicated by the dispatch of its two largest military forces, were the conquest of France's colonies and the security of the Low Countries.

Twenty years later Britain had secured the first goal twice over – having given most of the captured islands back in the 1802 Treaty of Amiens only to begin the process again when hostilities resumed a year later – but the second remained as illusory as ever.

This was certainly not for want of trying. Between 1793 and 1795 an army eventually totalling some 27,000 British troops, reinforced by Hanoverians and other Germans for a total of around 40,000, had served in the Low Countries under the command of the Duke of York. Initially this force cooperated – if the term can be stretched that far – with the Austrians and, later, as the campaign moved northwards, with the Dutch. Although there were successes at a tactical level, the campaign as a whole was badly managed and eventually ended in the complete collapse of Allied logistics during the final retreat to the Weser, from where the British contingent was evacuated in April 1795.[4] It was from this campaign that the future Duke of Wellington 'learnt what one ought not to do',[5] and its aftermath left France in control of the full extent of the Netherlands coast; this in turn made the threat of invasion very real, since the French had gained control of the Dutch fleet and began the construction of invasion craft in Dutch ports.

An attempt to impede the movements of the latter led to the 1798 raid on Ostend, wherein a brigade-sized force landed with the objective of destroying the sluices of the canal there; the objective was successfully achieved, but rising seas prevented the re-embarkation of the troops, who were eventually compelled to surrender.[6] Whilst the Ostend operation had been small-scale, the following year saw a return to the Low Countries in force, with a rather more ambitious objective. Taking advantage of the disaffected state of the Dutch fleet in the Texel, an army of 24,000 British and 11,000 Russian troops, again under the Duke of York, was landed at the Helder with the objective of liberating the Low Countries as part of a grand Allied offensive in conjunction with Austro-Russian offensives in Germany, Switzerland and Italy. In the event, Dutch and French alike fought hard to resist the invasion, and, after a vicious series of battles amongst the sand dunes, York was unable to break out of the Helder peninsula and instead found himself under attack by the reinforced Franco-Dutch under the future Marshal Brune. It was only after a convention was negotiated with the French that the Allied forces were able to re-embark unmolested, and the failure of the campaign left the Dutch provinces, reorganized since 1795 as the Batavian Republic, firmly within the French strategic orbit.[7]

The events of 1799 had raised questions over Dutch loyalties and indicated the vulnerability of the Texel as a fleet base, so that when Napoleon began to increase his naval build-up after hostilities resumed in 1803 it was

Antwerp that became the focus for his building plans: eventually, nineteen large warships were constructed there, and the growing fleet loomed large in British considerations during the last decade of the war.[8] The threat was not now from small craft for an invasion attempt but from ships of the line, mounting 74 or 80 guns apiece and intended to restore France's naval fortunes in the aftermath of Trafalgar. Antwerp and its fleet formed the primary objective of Britain's so-called Grand Expedition of summer 1809, although the operation was wrapped up in the wider politics of the Fifth Coalition and partially intended as a diversion in favour of Austria. Some 40,000 men under Lieutenant General the Earl of Chatham were landed on Walcheren and surrounding islands, but although they were able to capture Middelburg and Flushing, Antwerp proved too tough a nut to crack. With men dropping like flies from the effects of Walcheren Fever, further operations were abandoned and the bulk of the troops were soon withdrawn: the last garrison forces would be gone by November.[9] Thereafter, no further direct moves were made against the Low Countries, although the Antwerp fleet remained under blockade. Nevertheless, this did not for a minute indicate that the British government had lost its interest in the area; the fate of the Low Countries remained a primary concern for the makers of British policy.

In the meantime, however, Britain had contracted several additional obligations, which now also needed to be taken into account when defining objectives in the spring of 1813. For the time being, at least, sheer pragmatism meant that these newer objectives assumed a greater significance than the old, and when Foreign Secretary Viscount Castlereagh outlined British war aims in a manifesto of July 1813 the Low Countries were not accorded first priority. Instead, British aims were categorized within a sliding scale, with the first level – those issues without whose resolution a peace would not be acceptable – devoted to the claims of those nations that had continued the fight alongside Britain: Portugal, Spain and Sicily. To this trio was also added Sweden, thanks to promises made as a result of the Crown Prince's adroit diplomatic moves during the negotiations to bring the country over to the Allied camp. These countries were all either wholly or partially free of French forces, and the settlement of their claims was therefore already some way to being achieved. The Low Countries instead formed part of the second category, which Castlereagh deemed almost as essential, along with the complete restoration of Hanover and the strengthening of Austria and Prussia as a safeguard against future French aggression. However, the manifesto called only for the restoration of an independent Holland and said nothing about the former Austrian

Netherlands, which had been ceded to France – albeit under duress – as part of the 1797 Treaty of Campo Formio. In that it potentially left Antwerp in French hands, and said nothing about a barrier power between France and Holland, this was by no means a full version of Britain's hopes for this part of the world. In a third category of aims, considered desirable but not essential, was the political restructuring of Germany and Italy, again with a view to limiting French influence. From the limited nature of these aims, and the fact that it was expected that concessions would need to be made, it is clear that Castlereagh was still thinking in terms of a negotiated settlement that would leave Napoleon in power in France.[10] Under these circumstances, giving the fate of the Low Countries so high a priority, even in a truncated form relating only to Holland, indicates the importance that Britain accorded to this point.

It was one thing to define aims, however, but quite another to secure them. In the first place, with Napoleon preparing to reopen the campaign in Germany at the head of some 450,000 men, an Allied victory did not seem by any means a foregone conclusion. Furthermore, even if France were to be defeated, would Britain's allies share its goals? Similarly, would they be prepared to offer concessions in the right direction if the war was apparently won through their exertions rather than Britain's? Suddenly, the deployment of so great a proportion of the British Army to the Iberian Peninsula seemed to be far less of an asset than had once been the case. As early as mid-1812, Wellington had been authorized to conduct negotiations towards a convention by which the French would evacuate Spain; this, if implemented, would have freed some 40,000 British troops to take the field in Northern Europe. But the French were able to launch a counter-offensive in the autumn of 1812, and the New Year of 1813 saw Wellington back on the Portuguese border. Proposals would continue throughout the next year-and-a-half that would have removed all or part of the British contingent from the Peninsula, but nothing ever came of them. Wellington was steadfast in his opposition to such a policy, and, indeed, continued throughout to seek reinforcements for his own army at the expense of other theatres. But even without Wellington's opposition, any major British withdrawal from the Peninsula would not have become even remotely viable until the spring of 1814, and by then it was far too late for it to matter. But with the cream of its Army in the Peninsula, and a growing commitment to the war in Canada, the question remained in mid-1813 of how best Britain might exert its military power in Northern Europe in such a way as to gain a credible voice in any peace settlement.

One way, of course, was through money. British gold had financed the first five coalitions against France, and the new Sixth Coalition would be no exception. Sweden, having got in first, obtained the lion's share and received an initial payment of £1 million as a result of its adroit change of sides. Prussia, meanwhile, received cannon, small arms and uniforms in the immediate aftermath of its defection from France, and along with Russia would share a further £2 million to finance the spring campaign of 1813. Additional money was earmarked to pay for the upkeep of Russian warships that had taken refuge in British ports, and to pay for the Russo-German Legion that had been raised out of prisoners taken from Napoleon's allied contingents during the 1812 campaign. Yet more cash was promised once it became clear that the armistice would soon end in renewed and expanded hostilities, with Austria being offered £500,000 as a lump sum on joining the Allies and the same again in monthly payments of £100,000 a time thereafter. Sweden also obtained similar monthly payments, but these were to continue until the end of the war. Russia and Prussia continued to be subsidized largely in kind, receiving 200,000 muskets between them, along with over a hundred cannon: total value of the stores shipped to the two powers amounted to over £1 million, with a further £300,000 in specie. More of the same would follow in 1814, allowing Castlereagh to claim that, in terms of the numbers of men Britain was bankrolling, his country's contribution was equal to that of any of the major land powers; certainly, it was indispensable to the continued prosecution of the war. But creditors are rarely popular, and once a subsidy was paid the potential leverage that could be obtained from it was gone. What it came down to, at the finish, was the need to have British redcoats present on the continent, fighting alongside the other Allied powers, and this was simply not possible in the sort of numbers required to make the point.

Notwithstanding its commitments elsewhere, Britain was fairly quick in sending troops to North Germany once the circumstances permitted, but this initial contingent was small and its primary mission not overtly warlike. Nevertheless, since the bulk of these troops would ultimately find their way to the fighting in the Low Countries, it is worth following their story from the outset. That troops were sent at all was as a result of the continued wrangling needed to get the Crown Prince to commit the Swedish Army actively to the war in Germany. Although Swedish troops had landed in Pomerania during the spring of 1813, they had not played any part in the fighting before the armistice. Now, as preparations were made for the renewal of hostilities in August, the Crown Prince had been accorded command of one of the three main Allied armies, to be known as the Army of the North and composed of substantial numbers of Prussian and Russian troops in addition to his Swedes. Throughout the campaign, the Crown Prince would display a marked disinclination towards activity, delaying his movements and favouring allied troops for dangerous tasks rather than his Swedish corps. From a personal point of view, this made perfect sense. In his current position as Crown Prince of Sweden, the political credibility of Jean-Baptiste Bernadotte relied on his military reputation, which he was unprepared to risk in battle if it could at all be avoided; at the same time, neither did he wish to burn all his bridges with France – not least since Emperor Alexander had already spoken of him as a potential successor to Napoleon – and so did not wish to be seen to be actively engineering the defeat of France's forces in the field.[11] Thus, even before the campaign began, the excuses and *gasconnades* justifying Swedish delays began to mount and the Allies found themselves repeatedly compelled to chivvy the Army of the North into action. One such excuse was the need to garrison the ports through which supplies were being sent from Britain, and here, at least, the bluff could be called and a British garrison furnished for the main supply port of Stralsund in order to free Swedish troops for active operations.

Under normal circumstances, finding the men needed for a foreign mission of this nature would have simply added to the growing manpower problems faced by the British Army; on this occasion, however, the nature of the task in fact furnished an opportunity to improve the situation. Since 1803 the infantry of the British Army, which provided the backbone of any military force, had begun to adopt an organization based on a two-battalion regiment. Within this system, the 1st battalion would undertake active duty overseas whilst the 2nd battalion processed recruits and carried out home-defence duties. This was well and good in theory, but in practice not all regiments were able to organize a 2nd battalion, and many of those that were raised found themselves being sent overseas anyway. From the beginning of the Peninsular War, 2nd and 3rd battalions had been required to make up the number of troops required, and this demand was increased in 1809 when the simultaneous deployment of troops both to Portugal and Walcheren led to a period of military overstretch. By 1813 things had improved, but there were still insufficient troops to go round. However, there were units in Britain – mostly junior battalions that had not yet seen foreign service, or single-battalion regiments recalled from the colonies – that were reaching a point where they could be considered for active duty. The best of these units were earmarked for the Peninsula, where Wellington continued to demand reinforcements, but others, less fit to go into the field immediately, remained available for the Baltic. Thus, a virtue could be made of necessity and a

garrison found for Stralsund without drawing on troops who could otherwise have been actively employed elsewhere. At the same time, serving in
such a garrison role would allow the units in question to complete their
training and organization, such that, in the future, they might be redeployed
in a more active capacity elsewhere.[12]

The man chosen to command the Stralsund garrison was Major General
Samuel Gibbs, a veteran of considerable colonial service. Gibbs had entered
the Army as an ensign in 1783, and subsequently jumped from regiment to
regiment in the usual manner as he worked his way up through the ranks.
In 1798, as a major in the 11th Foot, he took part in the disastrous Ostend
Expedition and was taken prisoner, but was soon exchanged and continued
to serve with his regiment in the West Indies where he won promotion to
lieutenant colonel. Shortly after hostilities resumed he transferred to the 59th
Foot, commanding the 1st Battalion of that regiment at the capture of the
Cape of Good Hope, in the Travancore War, and at the capture of Java. In
1810 he was breveted a full colonel, having already been employed as a
brigade commander, and on 4 June 1813, less than a month before his
appointment to the Baltic, became a major general.[13] Having spent much of
the Napoleonic Wars on the colonial sidelines, Gibbs is not one of the
conflict's better-known generals, but his reputation was evidently recognized
at the time, and remarked upon favourably by the anonymous author of
Letters from Germany and Holland who welcomed the news of his appointment after it was first rumoured that the troops would be placed under the
more senior, but less dashing, Major General James Dunlop.[14]

Gibbs's instructions made it clear that he was being placed directly under
the orders of the Crown Prince, who might in turn subordinate him to
whomever he chose to appoint as governor of Stralsund, and emphasized
that the security of the place was a matter of great importance to Sweden,
and thus to Britain. Nevertheless, it was evidently counter-productive for
the Swedes to supply the British troops when they themselves were being
supplied by Britain and Gibbs was provided with his own commissariat. As
Sir Charles Stewart pointed out in his account of the war, even this arrangement required some negotiation, with the Crown Prince needing to be
convinced that the British did not seek to control Stralsund themselves; it
was nevertheless made clear to the Swedes that the interior management of
the British force was to remain entirely with its own officers, which further
helped justify the need to set up an independent commissary organization.[15]
Gibbs's instructions also emphasized the limitations of the battalions that
would form his command, with Bathurst stressing that they were 'not at
present in a fit state for active service in the field'. As a result, Gibbs was not

'authorised on any representation to engage your troops in advance in any active operations in the field, but [to] confine them to the immediate defence of Stralsund'.[16] Having first tied Gibbs down, however, Bathurst's somewhat mercurial temperament led to a change of heart, as communicated in a supplementary note to the initial instructions:

> If during the time you continue at Stralsund an opportunity should present itself of undertaking an enterprise the success of which would be highly advantageous to the common cause, and add lustre to His Majesty's arms, and the failure of which would not in your judgement endanger the safety of Stralsund, to the defence of which you are primarily to attend, you may consider yourself as authorized to undertake it, if called upon so to do; provided that the enterprise be one not calculated either by the length of the march or any other cause to expose the health of the British forces, and provided also that the chief command of such an expedition be entrusted to you.[17]

Gibbs, as we shall see, would make creative use of this authorization, stretching the permission rather further than Bathurst was likely to have envisaged.

Gibbs was assigned a total of six battalions, of which four were ready for immediate service and two were to join later. As it happened, the 33rd was also able to sail with the initial expedition, with the two transports with that battalion embarked joining those bearing the 2/25th, 54th, 2/73rd and 2/91st in Hoseley Bay on 4 July, in company with the frigate HMS *Amphion* with Gibbs and his staff on board. After being held for several days by contrary winds, the convoy finally set out on the evening of 12 July.[18] Gibbs's final battalion, the 4/1st, was still not ready and would join later. In the ranks of the 2/73rd, embarked aboard the transport *Saragossa*, was Private Thomas Morris, who would later write a rare and valuable account of service under Gibbs and Graham from his position at the bottom of the military hierarchy.

At a time when, as he himself pointed out, many men were seeking to avoid the ballot that might compel them to serve in the militia, the young Morris was inspired by stories of the doings of Wellington's troops in Spain deliberately to seek a military career. As a youth of only sixteen he joined a Volunteer regiment in 1812, but close proximity with the 2/73rd, in which his brother was already serving, led him to feel 'at times almost ashamed to be only half a soldier'. These feelings induced him to seek to join his brother's battalion, which was already under orders for active service, but his brother forbade it and the battalion marched off to embark at Harwich. After thinking things over, Morris decided that, notwithstanding his brother's objection, and the distress it would undoubtedly cause his parents, he would enlist anyway and in this he was aided by a soldier of the battalion who, having been on furlough, had missed its departure and was now on the way to catch up. Morris accompanied him from London to the regimental depot at Colchester and presented himself to Major Dawson Kelly, who accepted him as a recruit and sent him for a medical examination. The sergeant who conducted him to the surgeon, upon learning that Morris was only seventeen, advised him to add an extra year when he formally enlisted in order to avoid spending a year consigned to the boy service, which Morris willingly did. He was not, however, so enthused with the life of a regular soldier – having already witnessed two brutal floggings – to sign on for life, and wisely elected instead to take the option of a seven-year enlistment.

Morris was now in, although Kelly, on seeing his proficiency at drill, at first suspected him to be a deserter from another corps and had to be convinced that the zealous recruit had truly reached such a high standard as a member of the oft-derided Volunteers. Having been addressed by the major, and convinced him that he was what he purported to be, Morris took the opportunity to persuade Kelly to include him in a reinforcing draft that was about to join the rest of the battalion at Harwich. The major refused, but did permit him a furlough to visit his brother before the expedition sailed: on reaching Harwich, Morris promptly persuaded the battalion's commander, Lieutenant Colonel William Harris, to allow him to accompany it. With a note bearing Harris's permission, Morris hurried back to Colchester and was included in the 150-man reinforcing draft under Kelly, finding himself aboard the *Saragossa* transport alongside his brother.[19]

The voyage out was an eventful one, with the convoy initially being delayed by storms in the North Sea and then later becalmed for a time in the entrance to the Baltic. The rumoured threat of prowling American frigates, and the very real threat posed by Danish gunboats, ensured that the transports had a strong escort for this most dangerous part of the passage, which came in handy when the ships came under fire from Danish batteries. The author of *Letters from Germany and Holland*, meanwhile, missed the excitement after his transport became detached from the rest and did not arrive off Stralsund until 12 August, three days behind the rest of the expedition, by which time the rest of the force was safely ashore.[20]

The Crown Prince was present at Stralsund in person to welcome the new arrivals, although his presence there doubtless had more to do with the impending arrival from the United States of Jean-Marie-Victor Moreau, the exiled French general having been tempted back to Europe to assist in the defeat of his old rival Napoleon. The Crown Prince nevertheless found time for an audience with Gibbs, treating him with his usual cordiality, before he and Moreau set off to join the armies in the field and left the garrison to settle into its new home. From the outset it was clear that much needed to be done, for when the French had evacuated the place they had done their best to slight the fortifications which now required reconstruction to enable Stralsund to be put in a state of defence. Although the main French forces were operating in Saxony under Napoleon's direct command, a strong corps was based on Hamburg under the command of Marshal Davout, who had orders to advance eastwards towards the Baltic and threaten the rear of the Crown Prince's army.[21] Accordingly, the Swedish Governor, Engelbrecht, put the whole populace to work in defence of the place, forming the men of the middle classes into a home guard and conscripting the lower classes by the thousands to work on the fortifications alongside Gibbs's troops. The Governor was seemingly something of a figure of fun for the British officers – 'much broader than he is long' and a 'surly old fellow' disinclined to be welcoming to his new allies – but there was no denying his energy.[22]

For Morris, wielding pick and shovel in the ranks, there was less opportunity to see the funny side of things, although the fact that the conscripted workers included a thousand or so of the country women did allow for mutual flirtations. The attractions, however, cannot have been that great: the women had been issued male workmen's attire, as a result of which, as Morris put it, 'some ludicrous mistakes took place with some of our men, who [. . .] were not always able to distinguish the women from the men'.[23] Such contretemps aside, Gibbs's men had little time to acquaint themselves with their surroundings due to the punishing regime. Morris implies that the work began immediately on landing, whilst other accounts suggest a day or two's respite, but either way it was heavy and fatiguing whilst it lasted, with long hours and little rest. It was a hard introduction to the regular service, and the young Morris on one occasion found himself succumbing to sleep whilst on guard duty; a fortuitous nightmare woke him shortly before the grand guard made its rounds, saving him detection in what could have been counted as a capital offence.

Once the work was finished, Gibbs was better able to take stock of the qualities of his battalions, and, judging by the formal reports that he would submit that autumn as part of the Army's biannual cycle of inspections, much of what he saw did not impress him. The 2/91st was surely the worst of the lot, with Gibbs characterizing their rank and file 'as a body of men very bad, with the exception of about two hundred stout able men'; the junior leadership was also dubious, as 'the sergeants with the corps[,] not sufficient for the Regimental Duties[,] are neither respectable or well-looking and very bad Sergeants. The Corporals rather better but not good Non Commissioned Officers.'[24] Things were rather better in the 54th, which had been rebuilt after returning from a long spell in the West Indies, the battalion being described as 'a very good serviceable body of men with very few young boys',[25] but there was again a shortage of good NCOs and the battalion was numerically quite weak with only 423 rank and file upon landing.[26] This lack of numbers was in part because one company had been left behind on Jamaica, and a second had remained in Britain with the depot leaving only eight companies to embark with Gibbs.[27] Also weak was the 2/25th, the smallest of all Gibbs's units with only 350 men in the ranks. No inspection report survives for this battalion, nor for the 33rd, which had had only a short spell in Britain following fifteen years' service in India; like the 54th, the 33rd had largely been rebuilt from scratch following its return home in 1812. Perhaps the best of the bunch, although again this is subjective because no formal report survives, was the 2/73rd, which, although not having seen prior service, was reasonably strong with 563 men in the ranks upon landing and, according to Morris, 'as fine a regiment [. . .] as any in the service, consisting chiefly of young men, from eighteen to thirty years of age, fit for any sort of duty'.[28] Even so, most of the men in the ranks had never been in action before, and Lieutenant Colonel Harris, though popular and possessed of considerable experience of colonial service as a junior officer, was untested at this level of command.

Notwithstanding the polyglot nature of his command, once the immediate threat to Stralsund was past and the fortifications restored to some semblance of order, Gibbs began to seek opportunities to employ his troops more actively. He initially dispatched the 54th to reconnoitre the area around Stralsund, but the expedition was not a success and the battalion soon returned, without having made contact with the enemy and apparently in a state of some disorder. On the face of things, the choice of this battalion seems an odd one, for its commander, Major Allan Kelly, was fairly junior in his rank and had no other field officer to second him; in any case, whether through Kelly's inexperience or some other cause, the reconnaissance was ineffective and so Gibbs decided to repeat the process with a different battalion. He selected the 2/73rd for the role, but this time, to make sure of things, he accompanied it himself; by any stretch of the imagination this was a creative interpretation of Bathurst's instructions to devote himself primarily to the defence of Stralsund. Morris, in his memoirs, rather gives the impression that his battalion marched aimlessly around North Germany waiting for something to happen, but of course there was more to it than that and the young private, along with the rest of the 2/73rd, was shortly to find himself going into action for the first time.[29]

If Northern Europe is the forgotten theatre so far as the British Army's operations during the Napoleonic Wars are concerned, the events of autumn 1813 in North Germany surely represent that theatre's forgotten campaign. In no small part, this may reflect the fact that very few of the British troops who took part were British in anything other than organization, for the brunt of these operations – so far as the British Army was concerned – was borne by the men of the King's German Legion (KGL). Nevertheless, the fact that there was an army corps operating in North Germany at all during this period was down largely to British funding; what was more, its commander was a new-minted British lieutenant general and his operations were being conducted with British interests very much at heart.

The corps in question was that commanded by Lieutenant General Ludwig, Graf von Wallmoden-Gimborn, and if this seems an unlikely name for a British general officer then there is no wonder, for Wallmoden was something of an anomaly in the British service. Born in Vienna in 1769, his father Johann was a Hanoverian officer and an illegitimate son of King George II. Whilst his father remained in the Hanoverian Army, serving as its last commander prior to its dissolution following the French occupation of 1803, Ludwig entered the Austrian service and eventually attained the rank of Feldmarschalleutnant after distinguished military and diplomatic service. With the renewal of the fight against Napoleon in 1812, Wallmoden made his way first to Russia and then to Britain, where he was chosen as the ideal candidate to direct military operations in North Germany aimed at recovering George III's Hanoverian territories. To this end, he was commissioned as a lieutenant general in the British Army with seniority backdated to 21 January 1812.[30]

Since 1803, Hanoverian exiles had formed the nucleus of the King's German Legion and had fought alongside British troops in most of the war's subsequent battles; now, with Hanoverian territory about to be freed from French rule, the process could be reversed and the KGL used as a basis for a new national army. However, the bulk of the KGL was serving either in the Peninsula or the Mediterranean, with only the infantry depot and some mounted troops available in Britain. In April 1813, a draft being prepared to reinforce Wellington's five KGL infantry battalions in the Peninsula was reformed into four provisional companies and redirected to Germany under Lieutenant Colonel David Martin, along with men from the depots of the 1st KGL Hussars and of the Legion's artillery. The contingent as a whole was placed under Major General James Frederick Lyon, who had previously commanded the 97th Foot (Queen's Own Germans) under Wellington and so was used to working with foreign troops. Also on the staff, having previously been serving as a volunteer with the Russians, was Major General Wilhelm von Dörnberg, who had famously led an uprising in Westphalia in 1809, subsequently served under the Duke of Brunswick, and eventually been commissioned into the British Army.

The force arrived at Hamburg, which was at this stage in Allied hands, on 29 April, where the artillery, hussars, and some of the infantry were employed as cadres for new Hanoverian troops of those arms. The Allied occupation of Hamburg was short-lived and the city, as we have seen, became the base of Davout's French army as Napoleon's forces tightened their control over Germany during early 1813. Wallmoden's growing corps, including the KGL detachments, was compelled to fall back across the Elbe, where it remained until after the termination of the armistice.[31] There it was joined by another detachment from the depots of the KGL, commanded by Lieutenant Colonel Hugh Halkett, which landed at Wismar on 20 June. Using some of these men, and some from the original draft, a half-battalion of four companies was formed under the command of Captain Philip Holtz-ermann. Finally, on 8 August, another detachment came ashore, also at Wismar, composed of the 3rd KGL Hussars, 1st and 2nd KGL Horse Artillery Troops, and the 2nd Rocket Troop of the Royal Horse Artillery (RHA). With these reinforcements, and having gathered in his other con-tingents, Wallmoden began the autumn campaign with a multi-national force of 24,000 men and the primary mission of covering the rear of the Army of the North against the Franco-Danish forces based on Hamburg.[32]

During August and the first weeks of September, Wallmoden and Davout waged a campaign of manoeuvre, ultimately culminating in a stalemate whereby Davout could not seriously threaten the Baltic ports but, conversely, could not himself be assailed in Hamburg. Elsewhere in North Germany, things were going well for the Allies, with the advance guard of the Army of the North – primarily composed of the Prussian III Corps under Bülow – defeating Marshal Oudinot's Armée de Berlin at Grossbeeren on 23 August and thus thwarting the French drive on the Prussian capital. Further south, Blücher's Russo-Prussian Army of Silesia defeated Marshal Macdonald's Armée du Bobr on the Katzbach three days later and although Napoleon was able to defeat the main Allied Army of Bohemia at Dresden on 26–27 August, the tables were to some extent turned when a reinforced corps under Vandamme, attempting to cut off the Allies' retreat, was itself cut off and forced to surrender at Kulm on the 30th. In an attempt to restore matters in the north, and cover the defeated Macdonald's flanks, Napoleon sent Marshal Ney to replace Oudinot and lead a renewed attack on Berlin whilst ordering Davout to break the northern deadlock and reopen communications with the main French forces. The outcome was further upset for the French, with Ney being defeated at Dennewitz on 6 September: Bülow's Prussians again did most of the fighting, but the Crown Prince arrived with his Swedes just in time to claim the laurels for himself, worsening already soured relations and beginning a grudge that, as we shall see, would seriously mar inter-Allied cooperation through into 1814.[33] Meanwhile, Napoleon's orders for Davout would provide Wallmoden with a chance to catch the French dispersed and at a disadvantage.

The initial intelligence coup came about by chance. A French artillery officer taken prisoner on 12 August was found to be bearing papers outlining Davout's response to his new instructions, which entailed detaching 4,500 men under Général de Division Marc-Nicolas-Louis Pécheux to carry out an anti-partisan sweep through the area between Hamburg and Magdeburg. Electing to take the opportunity to attack Pécheux's detachment, Wallmoden left his Swedes and Mecklenburgers to mask Davout and assembled a 12,000-man strike force at Dömitz on the Elbe; it was to join this contingent that Gibbs led out the 2/73rd. Wallmoden had his main force concentrated by 14 September, comprising an advance guard of light troops and Cossacks under the Russian Major General Tettenborn, two divisions of infantry, and a reserve of cavalry. One infantry division was formed of the Russo-German Legion, under Generalmajor von Arentschildt, and the other of Hanoverians and Anhalters under Lyon. The 2/73rd was also attached to Lyon's division, but the men from Stralsund had had a fatiguing march, made worse by a shortage of supplies that was only partially rectified by an issue of bread and beef upon arrival at Dömitz, and thus were allowed some hours to recuperate before setting off after the rest of the corps. After further delays getting across the river, a few hours' rest were again permitted before pressing on to join the rest of the corps with the closing stages of the march invigorated by the sound of the first shots as the Allied advance guard came up with the enemy.[34]

Wallmoden's intention had been to ambush the French as they advanced, and by late morning on 16 September he had his troops in position in the thick forests surrounding the old Hanoverian royal hunting lodge at Göhrde. However, Pécheux failed to continue his approach as expected, and so Wallmoden decided to take the offensive. Having identified the position occupied by the outnumbered and unsuspecting French, Wallmoden took advantage of his numerical superiority to mount a multi-pronged attack. Lyon and Tettenborn were to attack head-on, whilst Arentschildt's Russo-German

Legion would seek to turn the French left. The bulk of the Allied cavalry, under the command of Dörnberg and supported by the KGL horse artillery and a detachment of the 2nd Rocket Troop, would complete the envelopment by crushing the French right.

The emergence of so large an Allied force proved most disconcerting to Pécheux when they appeared around noon, and he at once rode forwards to identify the threat. By the time he knew what he was facing, though, it was rather too late for him to do anything about it. Opening the assault on the left, Arentschildt's battalions stormed the villages of Oldendorf and Eichdorf whilst, on the right, Dörnberg's cavalry moved to threaten the French flank. It was at this point that the 2/73rd reached the field, with Morris observing the main French line backed with artillery in its centre and with its left-most units forming square to fight off the Allied cavalry. For the time being, the French line was holding, with the infantry squares pouring volleys of musketry into any body of horsemen that dared to come too close, and Wallmoden sought to revitalize the assault by sending Lyon's division forwards in the centre.

Riding up to the 2/73rd to address Lieutenant Colonel Harris, the general presented a comical sight, puffing away on a long pipe as he gave the battalion its orders:

> Addressing our commanding officer, he said, 'Colonel, I am glad you are come: I want that hill taken!' pointing to the one with the two pieces of cannon and about a thousand men on it. 'Will you charge them, Colonel?' 'Yes, sir,' was the answer. 'Well,' said the German, 'I shall send a Hanoverian regiment to assist you.' On which our colonel observed, 'Let us try it ourselves, general, first; and if we fail, then assist us.' Addressing the regiment, he said, 'Now, my lads, you see what we have to do. We are the only regiment of English in the field; don't let us disgrace ourselves!' A hearty cheer from the men was the assurance that they would do their duty. The colonel, calling the quarter-master, told him to endeavour to get us a supply of schnaps by the time we had done the job, and then he led us on to the foot of the hill.[35]

Morris's account may be partisan, but he was justifiably proud of his battalion's conduct, for the untested 2/73rd acquitted themselves most creditably in their baptism of fire, marching forwards in good order against the French centre with colours flying. In Morris's telling of the tale, the French had believed that the red-coated Hanoverian and KGL infantry were British troops but their generals had assured them otherwise. Then, when the 2/73rd unfurled their colours, the French thought themselves deceived and broke. A nice story, and it certainly did morale in the battalion no harm at all to believe that the French would not stand at the sight of the British flag, but the fact remains that the French position was already becoming untenable, thanks to Arentschildt's turning movement on the Allied left, even before Harris led his battalion into the fight. Nor, though it conducted itself well, can the 2/73rd have been very closely engaged, since the battalion recorded not one casualty. Morris mentions only a single ragged volley from the French infantry, and nothing from their artillery, which suggests that Pécheux's centre had already begun to retire when the British advanced.

As the French centre and right began to crumble, the deadlock on their left was broken by the 3rd KGL Hussars under Major Johann Küper. Having first been driven off, the Hussars re-formed, charged again, and were finally able to break the infantry on the French left after Lieutenant Strangways of the RHA brought his rockets into action, landing his first shot amidst one of the squares. Capitalizing on the disarray caused by the rockets, the Hussars spurred back in to renew the fight and avenge the losses they had taken in their earlier repulse. Simultaneously, Lieutenant Colonel Halkett's Hanoverian brigade also went forwards, benefitting from the fact that the French were unable to form line for fear of the Allied cavalry, to complete the destruction of the French left. Broken all along the line, the French force fell apart; amidst the confusion, their second-in-command, Général de Brigade Stanislaw Mielzynski, was taken prisoner by Private Heymann and Sergeant Wedermayer of the Hussars. Pécheux escaped a similar fate only by fleeing through the trees on foot, where the Allied cavalry could not follow, but the bulk of his men were less lucky, with over half the total French force either falling during the battle or being taken prisoner afterwards. When they eventually rallied, it was found that they had lost approximately 400 killed and 1,900 prisoners, along with all six guns and one regimental eagle. The Allies, for their part, lost only 530 killed and wounded, but a great many of these casualties came from the 3rd KGL Hussars. The regiment paid dearly for its gallant charges, suffering the loss of 4 officers and 20 men killed or mortally wounded, and a further 4 officers and 55 men wounded, out of a strength of around 600 all ranks.[36]

In the aftermath of the battle, a fierce rainstorm broke out, drenching the troops on the exposed battlefield. Other than Tettenborn's Cossacks, who were sent in pursuit, Wallmoden's troops remained on the field, with the 2/73rd drawing the task of guarding the French prisoners. These were escorted back to Dannenberg, from which place, once the prisoners had been transferred to other guards, Gibbs led the 2/73rd back north towards the

Baltic. Instead of returning to Stralsund, however, the battalion instead moved to occupy Rostock.[37] In order to have a general officer in command at both places, Lieutenant Colonel Arthur Gore of the 33rd was appointed a brigadier general as of 25 September, initially commanding at Rostock before later moving back to Stralsund.[38] Gibbs could at least now afford to spread his battalions more widely, for the 4/1st – over 900 strong, but woefully inexperienced – had arrived at Stralsund in his absence, and so the reinforced British contingent settled back into garrison life whilst greater events unfolded away to the south in Saxony.

At length, and not without yet further recriminations, the Allied command had managed to concentrate all their major field forces against Napoleon at Leipzig, leading to the epic 'Battle of the Nations'. Amongst the great multitudes of Russian, Austrian, Prussian and Swedish troops, Britain was represented only by its attachés and by a single military unit in the shape of the 2nd Rocket Troop RHA. After Göhrde, Strangways' detachment had re-joined the rest of the Troop, under Captain Richard Bogue, which was attached to the Artillery Reserve of the Swedish Corps, and which came into action as the French fell back on 18 October. The bulk of the Swedes played little part in the Allied victory – souring relations between Bülow and the Crown Prince yet further – but Bogue managed to get his command into action in support of the Prussian attack on the village of Paunsdorf. Alone of the entire British Army, the 2nd Rocket Troop was awarded the battle honour 'Leipsic', which distinction was continued officially until 1833 and unofficially for some years thereafter, but Bogue did not live to see his men honoured, being amongst those killed in a French counter-attack as he moved his command up to join the fighting around Sellerhausen later the same day.[39]

Thus, as autumn 1813 began to turn into winter, British troops had already been blooded in action on the battlefields of Northern Europe. Nevertheless, their actions had largely been peripheral and had made no great contribution to the Allied war effort or to Britain's individual war aims. But after the wholesale collapse of French influence east of the Rhine that followed Napoleon's defeat at Leipzig, things would soon change and dramatic events in Holland would create the opportunity for a major British intervention in direct pursuit of the government's last remaining major strategic goal.

Chapter II

'An Essential Service'

THE RAPIDITY OF EVENTS IN THE AFTERMATH of Leipzig took Europe by surprise, causing major reassessments of priorities as the solid edifice that had been Napoleon's empire began to display terminal cracks. That Holland, seemingly a subservient French client for the best part of two decades, should break out into revolt was therefore just one symptom of the crumbling imperial façade, albeit one that filled Britain's ministers with a particular glee. However, it is impossible to understand the events that swept through the Low Countries during the last months of 1813 without first understanding something of what had passed during the previous quarter-century. What is more, such an understanding not only places the revolt in its own national context, but also helps explain some of the actions and stances taken by the Dutch government and the House of Orange during 1813 and 1814, which might well otherwise appear as puzzling to modern readers as they did to contemporary Britons.[1]

By the mid-eighteenth century, the Dutch Republic was generally perceived to be in a state of decline. The French invasion of 1747 had led to the appointment of Prince William IV of Orange as Stadtholder of all seven of the United Provinces, ending four decades of fragmented rule. In effect, this marked a shift from a federal republic to something more akin to a conventional monarchy, the like of which had not been seen since the death of William III in 1702. What was more, the stadholderate was made hereditary, so that when William IV died unexpectedly after only four years the position passed to his infant son. Assuming personal rule in 1766 after a succession of regencies, the new Stadtholder, William V, soon proved to be a less-than-inspiring leader. His education had been neglected, and he was successively bullied by his mother, his ministers and his wife. By the 1780s, war with Britain had exacerbated financial difficulties, and, since the Stadtholder was, *ex-officio*, Captain-General and Admiral-General, it was William who took the blame for the perceived failings of Dutch arms. As the historian Simon Schama points out, the unfortunate Stadtholder had much in common with his contemporary, Louis XVI of France, and, like

Louis, William would find himself facing a revolution before the decade was out.

Those who found themselves drawn into opposition to the Stadholder, most of them upper- and middle-class liberals inspired by recent events in America, identified themselves as Patriots. In their conception, they were seeking to restore the United Provinces to the pure republican heyday of the seventeenth century, removing the rights of hereditary appointment – from the stadholderate right down to local administration – in order to bring about a revival in national fortunes. Although the House of Orange retained much popular support, William's inability to respond decisively to Patriot demands allowed his opponents to increase their power, backed up with paramilitary force in the shape of the Schutterij – 'shooting companies' of bourgeois militia. Matters eventually came to a head in 1787. William had already lost control of the garrison at The Hague, and now armed opposition became more violent. Shots were exchanged between Patriot and Orangist forces, and Princess Wilhelmina, William's Prussian consort, was taken into custody. Since the Patriots had support from France, Britain naturally sided with the House of Orange, as did the Prussians for whom the insult to their princess was the final straw. On 13 September, a Prussian army of 26,000 crossed the Dutch frontier. Patriot Schutterij were no match for Prussian grenadiers and within a month the revolt was over, the Stadtholder restored to his powers, and the Patriot leaders in exile in France.

The respite for the House of Orange would be short-lived. The initial goals of the French Revolution chimed closely with the ideas of the exiled Patriots, who now hoped, with French aid, to win back the freedoms that had been snatched from them in 1787. Somehow, though, it never quite worked out like that. *Realpolitik* soon replaced Revolutionary idealism as the motor of French policy, and successive Dutch statesmen quickly discovered that, although the French Revolution was indeed a revolution, it was also, crucially, French. Thus, although the French armies that drove into the Netherlands in 1795 evicted the Stadtholder and helped Holland's home-grown revolutionaries replace much of the old order, the leaders of the new Batavian Republic soon found that there was a price tag attached. Not only would the Dutch be compelled to provide troops and warships to support France's continued war, leading to the great naval defeat at Camperdown, but their political development was also forced to take its cue from Paris. With varying degrees of official French encouragement, each major shift in the colour of French politics was reflected by a corresponding shift in that of its new northern client. Twice in 1798, and then again in 1801, the government of the Batavian Republic was replaced after a coup d'état, preventing any constitutional continuity and ruining the chances of establishing what the Patriots – many of them now disgusted by the turn that events had taken – had set out to do. With trade crippled by war, Holland was in a worse state than ever.

Worse, however, was to come, for Napoleon remained convinced, despite increasing evidence to the contrary, that the bankers of Amsterdam had gold reserves aplenty to finance his war effort; frustrated by successive Dutch claims that the country was nearly bankrupt, the new Emperor attempted to impose his will by force and wring out the hard cash needed to finance renewed war. At the same time, as we have seen, Antwerp became the focus of Napoleon's renewed naval ambitions after the disasters of 1805. At the imperial behest, the Batavian Republic became first a Commonwealth with a quasi-monarchical Grand Pensionary, and then, when that did not do the trick, had Napoleon's own brother Louis imposed upon it as king. Remarkably, this went rather well – from the Dutch point of view. 'Koning Lodewijk' soon became a surprisingly popular ruler, showing evidence of a common touch lacking in his siblings, encouraging overseas trade in defiance of the Continental System, and espousing Dutch values even when this meant standing up to his brother. This, naturally, went down extremely badly in Paris. Fraternal entreaties were followed by fraternal threats, but Louis refused to budge. Inevitably, the short imperial patience soon snapped, and the Bonapartist Kingdom of Holland was abolished on 9 July 1810 after an existence of only four years. Thenceforth, the remaining rump of the old Dutch territories – the south bank of the Scheldt had gone in 1795, along with enclaves around Maastricht, whilst much of Zeeland and Brabant had already been pruned off earlier in the year – was incorporated directly into the Empire as *départements* of France. In order to keep Napoleon's new subjects under close scrutiny, French officials were imported in considerable numbers with orders to enforce conscription and eradicate smuggling, over-seen by Charles Lebrun, duc de Plaisance and Arch-Treasurer of the Empire, who was installed in Amsterdam as Governor-General. As trade began to fail under the new regime, and the conscription to bite, seething discontent became increasingly vocal – all the more so as casualty lists from Russia began to appear in the Dutch press. And, to make matters worse for the French, the discontent had a growing unity, for the cry of protest was one increasingly one that came from an older past: '*Oranje Boven!*'[†]

Back in 1795, William V had been allowed to pass peacefully into exile. Although the Dutch revolutionaries shared many of the qualities of their French counterparts, bloodlust was not among them and most were just glad

† 'Up with [the House of] Orange!'

to see the wretched man gone. The last Stadtholder made his way to England with his family, where a court in-exile-was established, first at Kew and later at Hampton Court, subsidized by the British crown. To all intents and purposes, William gave up the active leadership of the House of Orange, although not before imposing a wildly ambitious set of conditions under which he would be prepared to reassume the stadholderate, and it was his sons who pursued active measures intended to regain the family's position. Frederick, the younger son, had some success raising a force of Dutch émigrés in Germany but his early death in 1799 prevented any extension of this army-in-exile, most of whom ended up, like the House they followed, as pensioners of the British. The elder son, another William, preferred diplomatic to military measures, and was quite prepared to court all parties – even the French – if it seemed as if they might have something to offer. With a Prussian princess for a mother, and another – also Wilhelmina – for a wife, it was natural that the younger William sought to base himself there rather than in Britain, the more so since he felt that the British had left his country in the lurch after 1795, although this did not stop him joining the Anglo-Russian expedition of 1799. With the Batavian Republic firmly established under French control, neither father nor son was able to obtain any concessions there during the negotiations leading up to the Peace of Amiens, although Napoleon did agree to the restoration of their ancestral German lands. It was thus in Germany that William V passed the final years before his death in 1806, which left the younger William to inherit the title of Prince of Orange and, so far as the Dutch émigrés were concerned, become Stadtholder as William VI.

The year 1806 brought still further blows to the House of Orange, with Napoleon's creation of the Confederation of the Rhine again stripping them of much of their German territories. Feeling himself to have been duped, William sought a command in the Prussian Army that challenged Napoleon in the autumn of that year, and led a division in the defeat at Auerstadt. Having so obviously thrown his lot in with France's enemies, a subsequent attempt to regain Napoleon's favour was of little avail, and the Prince came to realize that if any power could help him then it was Britain. But accepting the situation did not mean that he had to like it. His son and heir the Hereditary Prince – yet another William – was sent to receive a British education, and touted for a match with the Prince Regent's daughter Princess Charlotte, but the Prince himself remained sulking on the continent: he was not even used as a figurehead in the 1809 expedition to Walcheren, since the British administration had become distrustful of his attempts to be all things to all people. Far better, in the eyes of many British statesmen, including

Bathurst, that an Orange restoration be achieved through the person of the young Hereditary Prince, who, after a spell at Oxford, was commissioned into the British Army and sent out to the Peninsula in 1811 as an ADC to Wellington. But if the son was in vogue in Britain, it was the father – an equally unknown quantity, but the legitimate head of the house – whose return was increasingly hoped for in Holland itself as indications grew that the French dominance could not last.[2]

Taken on its own, this national volte-face seems hard to credit, considering the events of 1787 and 1795. Yet many of the common people, particularly in the maritime provinces, had always remained Orangist at heart, whilst the old nobility, though happy enough to take office when it was offered, had only ever paid lip-service to the Kingdom of Holland and the Empire of France. Even for one-time Patriots, bringing back the old dynasty marked less of a reversion to the old ways than an attempt to maintain some continuity with the best of the new. Of all the unhappy experiments in government that the Dutch had suffered over the course of the past two decades, monarchy, even in the unlikely form of Louis Bonaparte, had proved the best of a bad lot, failing only because Louis was unable to maintain the national identity of his adoptive people against the ambitions of his brother. Say what one might about the House of Orange, there was still no denying their commitment to the independence of the lands that they hoped to rule, and so it seemed to many that becoming subjects of the son of the once-despised Stadtholder was by no means an unreasonable price to pay for a regained national identity. Such a regime might also preserve the emerging unitary state that had begun to evolve out of the chaotic political and administrative mess of the federalized republic. In any case, notwithstanding the long love–hate relationship with the House of Orange over the past two centuries, it had always been to that dynasty that the Dutch had turned in times of national crisis: as in 1672 and 1747, so too in 1813.

Of course, it was one thing for the Dutch to wish the French gone, but quite another for that to come to pass. The events of 1813, however, saw Holland almost completely stripped of French troops to meet the demands of the war in Germany, and under these conditions resistance became increasingly overt to the extent that substantial parts of the annexed *départements* were practically ungovernable. Such of Napoleon's troops as were available in the Low Countries were garrison forces that came under the control of the various military districts – the 17th based on Antwerp, 24th based on Brussels, 25th based on Wesel, and 31st based on Amsterdam – most of which were composed of non-French troops, disciplinary units or depot formations. As early as April, Leiden was briefly occupied by protesting local peasantry: the local Garde Nationale – effectively the old Schutterij given a Napoleonic gloss – did nothing to intervene and it took a French flying column to restore order. The fact that this had been a popular revolt, however, gave those in a higher station pause for thought. They had no wish for chaos that might harm their own property and prestige and, in addition to more general moves to disassociate themselves from French rule, the most active amongst them began to plan for a more orderly transfer of powers. Three men in particular emerged as leaders within this patrician resistance, and would ultimately orchestrate the final revolt against the French: Gijsbert Karel van Hogendorp, Count Leopold van Limburg Stirum and Frans van der Duyn van Maasdam, who would together become known as the *Driemanschap* or triumvirate.

In early November 1813, with the eastern frontier wide open and raiding parties of Cossacks already pushing into Dutch territory, it was time to act. Some French forces still remained, but if a revolt were delayed any longer then there seemed equal chances that the Allies would push on and enter Holland as conquerors, or else uncontrolled popular risings might break out over which the aristocratic plotters would have no control. On 9 November, van Hogendorp – very much first among equals within the *Driemanschap* – called a meeting at his home in The Hague, and definite plans were put in motion. In keeping with the orderly and controlled nature of what was intended, it was crucial to ensure that the commanders of the Garde Nationale were brought onside, and with this achieved there was in fact very little violence. By 16 November, Amsterdam and The Hague were in Dutch hands, Governor-General Lebrun had fled with his last few French troops, and the Garde Nationale had miraculously transformed back into Schutterij and were keeping the peace in the streets on behalf of van Hogendorp's provisional government. A final French attempt to restore the situation on 18 November collapsed when the only available forces, a battalion formed from Prussian deserters, mutinied and went over to the rebels. By this time, van Hogendorp had already issued a proclamation declaring that Holland had been liberated and was now under the authority of the Prince of Orange. All that remained was to send word to the exiled Prince and inform him of what had transpired, to which end two commissioners, James Fagel and Hendrick de Perponcher-Sedlnitsky, set out for England on the evening of 19 November.

In Britain, rumours of what was taking place had already begun to come in, and confirmation reached London by telegraph from Yarmouth on 20 November, with the commissioners themselves arriving in person the following morning. Having thus been called back to his homeland, the

Prince of Orange immediately accepted the invitation but made it clear that he expected to be proclaimed not as Stadtholder but as sovereign, and that accordingly his style ought be William I rather than William VI. Since he had also made no secret of his hopes for an expanded realm covering the whole of the Low Countries, and with discussions already under way for a marriage alliance between the houses of Orange and Hanover, it was clear that the Prince's actions represented a significant power play designed to establish himself as a major figure in the European diplomatic system. With his declaration, the Prince had presented the British with something of a *fait accompli* and quashed any lingering hopes that his son might rule Holland as a British client, but the situation was one to which Castlereagh was by no means adverse, and may even have surreptitiously encouraged.

At the same time, Britain's Foreign Secretary was keen to ensure that Britain had a key place in the councils of the new sovereign, and thus when the Prince embarked on HMS *Warrior* to make the short passage across the North Sea, he was accompanied by Richard Trench, 2nd Earl of Clancarty, who was to become Britain's ambassador to the new regime. On the face of it, Clancarty had little to recommend him for the role beyond a strong friendship with Castlereagh and a loyal record of service to the government, under which he had served as a Commissioner for the Affairs of India, as Master of the Mint, and, since September 1813, as President of the Board of Trade.[3] However, there was more to the task than ordinary ambassadorial duties. Under the circumstances, and bearing in mind Britain's preoccupation with the fate of Holland, Clancarty's planned role followed on from the model of a powerful British representative who would coordinate and influence the actions of a client state, in the style of Sir Charles Stuart in Portugal or Lord William Bentinck in Sicily. Ultimately, the 46-year-old Irish aristocrat would prove himself generally adept as a diplomat, both in this role in Holland and, later, at the Congress of Vienna, but Clancarty's early days undoubtedly saw a steep learning curve. His subservience to instructions from higher authority, and a lack of familiarity with military matters, hindered his ability to cooperate effectively with British generals and he made this situation worse by jealously guarding his status as Britain's voice on matters of strategic importance in the Low Countries. From the outset, though, he was clearly Britain's man on the spot in the new Dutch court, and when the Prince of Orange landed at Scheveningen on the afternoon of 30 November, to huge popular acclaim, it was with Clancarty at his side.[4]

Of course, the diplomatic initiative was only part of Britain's response, and preparations were immediately set in motion for the deployment of British troops to the Netherlands. This, though, was easier said than done, for the manpower situation, which had been stretched six months before when troops were needed for the Baltic, had grown even worse. Every infantry battalion that was fit to go overseas, and several that were not, had already been sent to the Peninsula or to North America, and most of the cavalry remaining at home was required for domestic policing duties. The changed situation in Germany had, it is true, seen Gibbs ordered to bring two-thirds of his command back from the Baltic to Britain, but as yet he had not arrived. The staffs at the War Office and at Horse Guards were thus compelled to search for units that might be fit to go overseas in order to make a respectable showing. Eventually, a force with a theoretical strength of 8,705 men was put together on paper, and orders were sent out to prepare the units in question for active service.[5]

Just under a quarter of the total force was to come from the Baltic, based on an estimate of the strength of the battalions Gibbs was bringing back plus any reinforcements from the respective regimental depots, and a further 1,600 were to come from the London-based depots of the Foot Guards. Being close at hand, the Guards would form the vanguard of the expedition, with Gibbs's contingent following on behind as soon as they arrived. The remaining troops – the 2nd KGL Hussars and a further two brigades of infantry – would take longer to assemble, with some being drawn from as far afield as the Channel Islands, and would form a second wave along with a sizeable contingent of artillery and engineers. With the exception of the single-battalion 55th, the seven regular battalions were all the 2nd or 3rd battalions of their regiments; they were to be joined by a half-battalion of the 3/95th Rifles, the remaining companies of which were with Wellington, and by the 1st Royal Veteran Battalion. The fact that it was necessary to send this last unit on active service, when it existed specifically as a posting for men deemed unfit for such duty, was indicative of the crippling shortage of more effective troops. Indeed, the Duke of York would later admit that, in his opinion, the whole of the initial force was essentially composed of 'everything which we could scrape together on the spur of the moment with the idea of their being placed in garrison, and not to be employed on the field'.[6]

If troops were hard to come by, the selection of a commander for the expedition was rather easier thanks to the presence in Brighton on sick leave of Lieutenant General Sir Thomas Graham, Wellington's erstwhile Peninsular second-in-command. Although there were plenty of more senior officers available, none had seen as much service as Graham and none could match his record of service on diplomatic missions and attachments to foreign armies, which between them gave him a level of experience unmatched in the British Army. He was Bathurst's immediate choice for the command, and the request that he undertake it, couched 'in a way that precluded refusal', was dispatched on the same day that the composition of the force was finalized.[7] Graham's unique level of experience stemmed from an unusual military career, which had not begun until his mid-forties. Prior to 1792, Thomas Graham of Balgowan had lived the life of a Scots country gentleman, his only commitment to public life being the support of Whig politics. In that year, however, his beloved wife Mary, immortalized by Gainsborough as 'the beautiful Mrs Graham', died whilst the couple were holidaying in the Mediterranean. During the return journey overland across France, the casket containing Mary Graham's body was broken open by drunken members of the revolutionary Garde Nationale, who affected to believe that it contained arms being smuggled in as part of a royalist plot. This treatment, on top of what he had already seen of the Revolution's excesses, instilled in Thomas Graham a passionate hatred for France and a determination to participate in the struggle against it. Initially, this took the form of voluntary service as a civilian aide during the siege of Toulon, which in turn convinced him to raise a regiment of his own. This became the 90th Foot (Perthshire Volunteers), which was established in 1794 with Graham as Colonel. However, because the Duke of York had recently changed the way officer promotions worked, his regimental colonelcy did not convert into official rank in the Army, something that Graham would spend the next fifteen years trying to achieve. In the meantime, he served extensively in Italy as an observer with the Austrians, and later around the Mediterranean with his regiment.

With the Peace of Amiens, Graham's active employment with the 90th ceased, although the regiment was not disbanded, as he had feared, and he therefore retained his temporary rank. There was no obvious military role for such an anomaly though, and he remained on the sidelines until 1808 when he became an ADC to Sir John Moore. Graham served with Moore in the Baltic and in Spain, and it was as a result of these further distinguished services that York was finally persuaded to accord him permanent rank in the Army. This was in fact a double boon, since Graham's seniority was taken from his 1794 colonelcy, meaning that he entered the regular service well towards the top of the list of major generals: a rank which, had he obtained a regular colonelcy from the outset, would have been his by seniority in 1803. He served on Walcheren, commanding a brigade and then a division, and in 1810, by now a lieutenant general, was given command of the Anglo-Portuguese contingent at Cadiz. He would lead this for eighteen months, distinguishing himself at the Battle of Barrosa on 5 March 1811, before moving to join the main Peninsular field army under Wellington as commander of its First Division and de facto second-in-command.

By now in his sixties, Graham was beginning to develop problems with his eyesight and he was forced to return home prior to Wellington's victory at Salamanca, only to be prevailed upon to return in May 1813. He remained in post until October, exercising command over the whole right wing of the army during the Vitoria campaign and the capture of San Sebastián, before again requesting sick leave due to a recurrence of his eye trouble. He had been back in Britain for only six weeks when he received Bathurst's summons. Notwithstanding his age, Graham remained active and was known as an excellent horseman, so there was no doubt about his ability to stand up to the rigours of command: the health concerns that had precipitated his return from the Peninsula had been greater in his own mind than in reality, and may in part have been a response to criticism of his operations at San Sebastián. As this would suggest, Graham remained at times touchy and querulous in his dealings with others, notwithstanding his long service in military–diplomatic roles, and could be prickly if he felt himself slighted. That he was generally popular is beyond doubt, and, as the historian Sir Charles Oman pointed out, it is well nigh impossible to find a word said against him in the many Peninsular memoirs.[8] These, however, were written in post-war years when Graham was the grand old man of the British Army and no one would wish to slight the Hero of Barrosa in print; the contemporary picture is more varied, and contains definite criticisms of his qualities as a commander.

In particular, the letters of Lieutenant John Aitchison of the 3rd Foot Guards, who served under Graham in 1812 and 1813, paint the general in a decidedly unfavourable light. Of his conduct of operations at Vitoria, which were, at best, an incomplete achievement, Aitchison considered Graham to have 'shown himself a good deal too old – he is as far as concerns himself extremely active but he harasses the troops beyond conception and in the field he displays little science and still less decision'.[9] This opinion was repeated during the first siege of San Sebastián – 'anything but a General – always galloping – constantly deciding yet ever undecided, he creates confusion and fatigue to all under him'[10] – and in even more vehement terms as operations there reached their conclusion, although by this stage Aitchison was also castigating the 'ignorance and indolence of his Staff'.[11] It is hardly unheard of for a subaltern to know better than his superiors, but Aitchison's letters are generally well informed and seem to reflect wider opinion, at least within the Guards. At the very least, his accusations should be borne in mind in any analysis of Graham's command in Holland, for it is impossible to read either Graham's own correspondence, or many of the eyewitness accounts from his campaign, without picking up hints of the same mixture of indecision on the one hand, and snap judgements on the other, that so infuriated Aitchison. And yet, when Graham did make up his mind he was capable of acting with great resolution – as at the storming of San Sebastián when he ordered his heavy artillery to fire directly over the heads of the stalled attacking troops – and there was certainly no denying his personal courage. It now remained to be seen whether courage and resolution could compensate for failing eyesight and sometimes-failing judgement.

Although Graham would assume overall command of the British forces once they arrived in Holland, receiving the acting rank of full General upon doing so,[12] the initial force would go out under the command of Major General George Cooke. Aged forty-five, Cooke's thirty years of soldiering had been almost entirely spent with the 1st Foot Guards, with which he had served in all three of Britain's previous expeditions to the Netherlands. He had also served under Graham at Cadiz, and subsequently succeeded to the command in that place after Graham left it to join Wellington. Relieved at Cadiz in July 1813 due to the reduced nature of the garrison there, he had been in Britain awaiting an appointment ever since.[13] Cooke's command was composed of the 2nd Battalions of all three regiments of Foot Guards, but, because these battalions were normally configured for a depot role as part of the London-based Third Guards Brigade, they would not be able to deploy at full strength. Bathurst's original plan had called for the 2/1st Foot Guards to furnish 800 men and the other two battalions 400 apiece, with the two smaller contingents being combined into a single provisional battalion. This expedient had been used previously, when the same battalions had been drawn on for active service in Graham's old command at Cadiz. This time, though, it was found that the 1st Foot Guards did not have enough men available, whereas the other two regiments had more than had been asked of them. Accordingly, all three battalions were prepared for service as individual units but with only six companies rather than the usual ten. In the event, the 2/1st Foot Guards were able to add a seventh company before departure, and in the months ahead all three battalions would have additional companies drafted out to Holland as more men became available.[14]

The nature of Cooke's orders emphasized how little the British government actually knew about the state of affairs in Holland, even after Fagel and Perponcher had brought news of the revolt and the establishment of the provisional government. Cooke was therefore required to embark his brigade and make for the Dutch coast, but after that Bathurst made it clear that he was on his own:

If you should have reason to believe from information you may be able to collect on the spot, that the enemy are not able either by their position or their strength to resist your disembarkation at Schevelin [*sic* – Scheveningen], that the Hague, Leyden, and Amsterdam are in possession of those that are attached to the Prince of Orange, and that your communication with those places is not likely to be cut off by the advance of the enemy, you will, if the weather permits, land the troops at Schevelin and march upon Amsterdam.

You will take the earliest opportunity of notifying to Admiral [Sir William] Young your arrival at Amsterdam together with such information as to the state of the Country, and its means of defence as you may be enabled to collect, and having as far as may be in your power put yourself in communication with such corps of the allies as may have entered Holland, you will remain in Amsterdam for the orders of Lieut. General Sir Thomas Graham under whose command you are to be placed.

You will not fail to make every preparation to defend the town of Amsterdam if it shall appear to you that it is likely to be attacked, on no account abandoning it so long as there appears a determined spirit in the inhabitants to resist the common Enemy until retreat shall become absolutely necessary.

If your retreat shall become necessary, and you shall not have received any instructions from Sir Thomas Graham, you will fall back upon the Corps of the allies, which is understood to be advancing from the Yssel [*sic*], making your retreat by the Zuider Zee if that shall be practicable.

If your retreat on the Yssel should be cut off you will attempt to act in whatever manner may appear to you at the time to be the least hazardous, bearing in mind that the Fleet under Admiral Young has been ordered to the Roompot.[15]

Having sent one set of instructions, however, Bathurst had his usual second thoughts and followed them up with a second set in which Cooke was given rather more latitude, taking into account the fact that weather conditions might well prevent the initial landing being carried out as planned. If this did indeed prove the case, Cooke was instructed to take his brigade to the Roompot – the anchorage off the mouth of the East Scheldt – and seek to land on the island of Schouwen. From there, he was to cooperate with Gibbs's forces once that officer arrived, and seek to obtain a base for further operations. Brielle or Helvoetsluys both struck Bathurst as likely

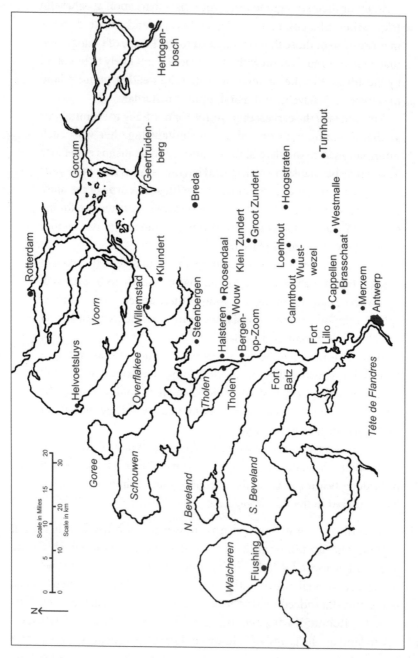

The Central Low Countries in 1813

candidates, assuming Cooke could occupy them, but the general was also given leave to attack the enemy elsewhere if he judged that advantage was likely to follow, 'taking care always not to embark in any attempt which may lead to great length or expose the troops under your command to an unequal contest'. Irrespective of the course of action that he chose, Cooke was further reminded that he should not commit his forces to operations that would prevent him cooperating directly with Graham once the main force arrived, and that he 'take possession of any Town which you may enter, or from which you Expel the Enemy, in the name of his Serene Highness the Prince of Orange'.[16]

As the Guards reorganized themselves for service, news had also been received on the progress of Gibbs. After the 4/1st and 2/91st had been left at Stralsund under Gore, the remainder of the Baltic expedition completed its embarkation by 1 November and set sail for England the following day, only for the transports to be caught in heavy storms and forced to seek shelter at Gothenburg for two weeks.[17] On 26 November, Gibbs, who had gone on ahead by a faster ship, was able to report that his command was expected off Yarmouth on the 30th and that he was on his way overland from Portsmouth to re-join them.[18] This knowledge enabled Bathurst to issue him with orders to complement those already sent to Cooke, but, unlike Cooke, Gibbs was given no flexibility of options but was instructed to proceed to the Roompot and land on Schouwen. If Cooke also elected to land his forces there, Gibbs would come under his orders, but if Cooke did not appear then Gibbs was given the same set of objectives that had been set for Cooke – that is to say, occupying Brielle or Helvoetsluys – in the pursuit of which he might endeavour to cooperate with the detachments of Royal Marines aboard Young's warships.[19]

In effect, then, Cooke and Gibbs were being sent on ahead in order to provide a base of operations to which Graham could bring the remainder of the British force. Whilst preparations to assemble and embark the troops continued, Bathurst could take his time to set out the full objectives of Graham's little army, which he eventually communicated to its commander on 4 December. Bathurst's initial instructions summarized what was known of the situation in Holland – not a lot, beyond the fact of the revolt in favour of the House of Orange – and outlined Graham's initial objectives. Bathurst also emphasized the fact that Graham's force was numerically weak and not what might have been desired, at the same time being all that could be spared, but that the numbers available 'will be sufficient at least to manifest what is the great Object in sending it; the lively interest which His Royal Highness takes in the cause of Holland and his earnest desire of giving to their Exertions while yet in their infancy every possible Countenance & Support'. Notwithstanding these limitations, Graham was to use his troops to aid the Dutch insurgents by 'endeavouring to occupy & maintain those Positions which are calculated either to protect the principal Towns from the Incursions of the Enemy, or to interrupt the arrival of those Reinforcements which the enemy may expect to receive' and thus, in conjunction with other Allied forces – with whom he was enjoined to make early contact – enable the Dutch to complete the organization of their own troops. Even here, however, things were by no means simple, since Bathurst's gesture of sending arms to Holland was now shown to have strings attached. Having informed Graham that 20,000 stands of arms had already been shipped, with more to follow if required, the Secretary of State stressed that Graham must 'give every assistance in your power to the formation of the Regiments which may be raised in Holland, and you will, if applied to, place British Officers in command of such Regiments, taking care however that the Regiments which shall be so officered shall be placed under your Command'. In other words, the Dutch forces should, if at all be possible, become auxiliaries of the British, removing at a stroke the potential for independent Dutch military action and simultaneously increasing British influence in the Allied councils by inflating the numbers of troops under Graham's command.[20]

As was Bathurst's wont, he followed Graham's initial instructions with a further three missives on the same day. The last two of these were short notes dealing with the provisioning of the force and authorizing payments to be made for secret services.[21] The second letter, however, was more explicit about the long-term objective towards which Graham should direct his operations, once he his troops were established ashore and immediate measures for the arming and protection of the Dutch were complete. In contrast to the general and discretionary nature of the initial set of orders, Bathurst's follow-up got straight to the point:

> It is now my Duty to call your attention to another Object in which the British Interests are deeply involved. I mean the destruction of the Naval Armaments at Antwerp. If at any time you should find it possible by marching suddenly on Antwerp to occupy such a position as would enable you to destroy the ships which it is understood are now laid up there, you should perform an essential service to your Country.

Nevertheless, the Secretary of State had sufficient awareness of the military realities to recognize that the limitations of Graham's command rendered successful operations against Antwerp unlikely without additional support:

> A lengthened operation for that purpose is neither compatible with the description of the force under your Command nor with the Service under which you are to be employed under my former instructions: but if in the course of your operations it should be found practicable to bring down to your assistance a considerable force of the allied army much facility might be derived from such assistance. And you will not fail to give me the earliest information of what you may deem necessary for the purpose of undertaking an attack upon the Place: always bearing in mind that it is the destruction of the Naval Armament, not the capture of the Citadel or Town which should be the principal object of your exertions.[22]

Somehow, then, Graham was to try and convince his allies to assist in a plan that quite patently had as its main object the furtherance of Britain's policy of global naval dominance; unsurprisingly, his efforts to do so would lead to considerable friction with the allies on whose support Bathurst was so blithely counting.

Chapter III

'First Blasts of Patriotism'

AS IS EVIDENCED BY THE FACT that Graham did not receive his final instructions until 4 December, there was a substantial lag between Bathurst's orders of 21 November and the actual embarkation of the main British force. Even Cooke's vanguard would take some days to complete its preparations and embark. While these preparations were under way, it was therefore essential to make contact with the Dutch military leaders, ascertain their capabilities, and ensure that their troops were as well equipped as possible in order to take the field alongside the British. The lessons of the Peninsular War showed that it was far easier to work with a subservient ally whose troops could easily be integrated into a British force, as with the Portuguese, than with one who, like the Spanish, insisted on pursuing an inconveniently independent course, so the quicker an element of British military control could be exerted in Holland the better. Transports were already prepared for the 20,000 stands of arms that Bathurst intended for issue to the Dutch, and these were now ordered to Harwich where they were to be convoyed to Holland by the frigate HMS *Jason*. Travelling aboard the *Jason* was Major General Herbert Taylor, an officer who would play a vital role in much of what would follow but who, in this first instance, was assigned to fill a post characterized by the historian G. J. Renier as that of 'Military Agent in Holland'.[1] Taylor's twin tasks were firstly to liaise with, and issue supplies to, any armed forces being raised by the Dutch, and, secondly, to prepare the way for the arrival of a British army in Holland.

Prior to receiving this appointment, Taylor had been serving as Private Secretary to Queen Charlotte, having previously served the King in the same capacity prior to his incapacitation. Indeed, he never relinquished his post, and his foreign service was carried out thanks to the Queen having consented to grant him a temporary leave of absence. On the face of it, the appointment of a courtier to such a role seems an odd choice, but Taylor was no ordinary courtier and his character and experience meant that he was ideally suited to his new job. Furthermore, judging by the frequently enthusiastic and candid tone of his correspondence, he relished the opportunity to get back into the field. Born in 1775, the son of a Kentish clergyman, Taylor was educated on the continent and thus grew up as a gifted linguist. Both he and his younger brother were able to put this education to their advantage in obtaining posts in the diplomatic service, but Herbert soon drifted into the military life, having accompanied the British army to Flanders in 1793 as civilian secretary to Sir James Murray, the Adjutant-General. After serving as a volunteer in several actions and obtaining the interest of the Duke of York, he was awarded a cornet's commission in the 2nd Dragoon Guards, thereafter rapidly rising to obtain his captaincy less than two years later. He continued as Murray's secretary, and then joined the staff of the Duke of York when Murray returned home. When York, in turn, returned to England, Taylor went with him as ADC and Assistant Secretary, before becoming Private Secretary to Lord Cornwallis during the latter's tenure as Lord Lieutenant of Ireland. In February 1799 he returned to York's staff as Private Secretary, serving with him in the Helder campaign of that year, and continued in that post until 1805 when he moved on to be Private Secretary to the King.[2] Although he had not – as he himself readily confessed – seen much at all in the way of regimental soldiering,[3] his combined experiences as staff officer, diplomat and courtier fitted him ideally for the role to which he was assigned, and his performance of it would win him the approbation of those with whom he served.

Taylor's passage was delayed by contrary winds, and he eventually prevailed upon the *Jason*'s Captain James King to push on ahead with the two fastest of the transports carrying the arms shipment and allow the remaining pair to come on later under the escort of the brig HMS *Mercurius*. The delay was not a complete waste of time, however, since Taylor was able to make use of the extended passage to translate his instructions from Bathurst into a series of memoranda outlining his objectives, and upon his arrival he promptly took these with him to present to the Dutch authorities. Having eventually made landfall on 2 December, Taylor set off for The Hague accompanied by three companions who had travelled from England with him: his ADC Colonel Barclay; the Tory politician and royal favourite Lord Yarmouth; and Colonel Robert Fagel, an officer in the service of the Prince of Orange. Yarmouth had no official reason to be in Holland, but seems to have attached himself to Taylor in an unofficial capacity, and would later furnish him with several useful reports. On arrival, they discovered that the Prince and Clancarty were both in Amsterdam, which the Prince had felt it essential to visit in person in order to obtain the allegiance of this politically vital centre.[4] Hogendorp, bed-bound by gout, was also unable to receive them, but Taylor eventually obtained an interview with Count Stirum who provided a lurid and not entirely reassuring account of the events of the past weeks and the current state of the country. Vigorous action by the small number of French troops remaining in Holland, in particular the sack of Woerden, had dampened the ardour of many of those who had supported the initial revolt, whose motives the Count believed in many cases to stem from material rather than patriotic motives. Stirum was also less than positive about the Allied military presence in the Low Countries, which he discounted as being small in numbers and largely composed of cavalry.

With such a discouraging summary from one of the key members of the provisional government, it is hardly surprising that Taylor chose to pose a direct question 'respecting the progress made by the Dutch Nation, in its preparations and arrangements for giving Effect and Consistency to the first Blasts of Patriotism', and equally unsurprisingly the answer failed to satisfy. Stirum, for his part, was careful not to stress that those 'Blasts of Patriotism' had been at least partially kept in check by a regime more concerned with establishing its own legitimacy. Under these circumstances, Taylor was compelled to inform Bathurst, based on the interview with Stirum and on Colonel Fagel's subsequent communications with Hogendorp, that

> the Exertions of the Dutch in this part of the Country have not been such as to afford to them any thing like security in the Event of the Enemy being able to direct their attention to this Quarter, and at this moment their best Protection must be considered the apparent Weakness of the Enemy & that seeming indifference to their proceedings which may possibly be traced to the conviction that before they quitted these parts of Holland, they had completely deprived them of the means of resistance that could render them formidable.[5]

All that the somewhat disillusioned general could offer as a potential consolation was news of a projected Dutch attack on Helvoetsluys, and speculation that Clancarty, having seen more of the country, might be able to offer a better account of the situation elsewhere. If Taylor was disappointed in the reception he had received, however, the courtier in him seems to have prevented his showing it. Reporting to the Duke of York, he was keen to stress that 'I get on very well with the Prussians and Russians, and the Dutch seigneurs',[6] and this would continue to be the case for the remainder of his mission.

Although he evidently devoted much effort to establishing a good working relationship with his allies, Taylor's personal priority seems from the outset to have been to prepare the ground for the British troops, he having been informed before his departure that Cooke's brigade was under orders. The day after his arrival, a false report led him to inform Bathurst that transports with the Guards aboard had arrived off Scheveningen. Until the report was revealed to be erroneous, this was welcome news for Taylor, who had previously entertained doubts about the security of that place and of the store of muskets, half of which remained there although the remainder had been sent on to Delft.[7] In part, Taylor's problem with regards to the distribution of the arms was that, judging by his experiences at The Hague, the Dutch did not particularly seem to want them – at least, not yet – and there appeared to be little in the way of an organized effort to relieve him of their charge. In reality, as Stirum had attempted to emphasize, there was still scarcely anything amounting to an organized Dutch military force yet in existence. Whilst various local irregular and semi-regular forces were beginning to coalesce into the beginnings of a new army, Taylor's instructions did not permit him to issue weapons to these units and Stirum had in any case warned him during their interview that to do so would be 'worse than useless'.[8] Only on 7 December did Bathurst authorize the issue of weapons to irregular units whose zeal was considered by Taylor to be beyond question. 'Serious mischief', warned the Secretary of State, would nevertheless ensue if the arms were not issued via the correct Dutch authorities.[9]

Whilst waiting to clear up the situation regarding the arms shipment, Taylor sought to prepare the way for the British forces, attempting to make sure that they would have a safe beachhead, and logistical support once they were ashore. To ensure the latter, one of Taylor's memoranda, which he had translated into Dutch to enable his wants to be better met, outlined the commissariat requirements of the forces he expected to follow in his wake. To begin with, Taylor noted a necessity, to be filled within fourteen days, for '500 horses for draught for the service of the British artillery as soon as the troops shall be landed'. Taylor wanted 'Geldings or Mares, stout and active, with good bone, and in good order; having been broken to draught. Age from 5 years old to Eight Years and upwards. Size from 15 hands to 15 hands three inches [. . .] perfectly sound in Eye, Wind, and Limb, and free from any Blemish.' Having added a note to acquaint any confused Dutch reader that 'The Hand is four inches English measure', Taylor went on to note that British officers would likely wish to purchase riding horses, and outlined a second, rather more refined, set of requirements, albeit with the proviso that contractors should not expect to receive more than £30 to £40 for these animals should they be able to procure them. Considering that the whole of occupied Europe had been scoured for horses to remount the Grande Armée for the 1813 campaign, these requirements were wildly overoptimistic but no more so than those outlined in the rest of the memorandum, which attempted to impose upon the Dutch the entire responsibility for the commissariat arrangements of the British troops. Taylor emphasized that there would be a sizeable requirement for 'large Supplies of Hay, Oats and Straw [. . .] flour and meat and spirits', and that this would be paid for 'in British Currency by bills in England'. Not only did Taylor want the Dutch to feed the British troops, however, he also expected them to provide transport, concluding his memorandum by emphasizing that:

> It is also earnestly requested that the Dutch Government will make such preliminary arrangements as may be necessary for the supply of Wagons of the Country with Horses and Drivers, for the Conveyance of the stores and baggage of the British Troops. To be collected at such probable points of Landing & of Operations as may be hereafter settled.[10]

These operations, in Bathurst's conception as conveyed by Taylor, would remain entirely the responsibility of the Dutch government.

From the outset, therefore, the British planned and worked on the assumptions that the Dutch were more militarily organized than they actually were, and would function as loyal but subservient allies, furnishing supplies and troops in accordance with Britain's wishes. The failure of the Dutch to live up to this ideal would prove a source of repeated frustration and friction for British officers unaccustomed to fitting their actions around the requirements of foreign powers. In a similar fashion, the Dutch were expected to be able to cooperate in operational matters, at least until British troops could be landed in force, with Taylor being instructed to attempt to ensure that either Helvoetsluys, Goree, or both, could be occupied by friendly forces in order to create a bridgehead for the British. Whilst it was accepted that evicting the French from Helvoetsluys might prove too much to ask, it was felt that

> Goree might be easily carried, and it becomes necessary to ascertain whether the Dutch Government can supply a few hundred men in Schuyts and to proceed under Convoy of His Majesty's Ship Jason to make an attempt on Goree in which they would be assisted by a small Detachment of Seamen and Marines from that ship.[11]

In the continued absence of any great interest in the arms that he had brought, and under the impression that the first British troops could be expected imminently, Taylor began to concentrate his activities towards this objective.

Despite the optimistic assumptions about the level of Dutch support for the operations that Taylor was required to arrange, a British military presence was not completely lacking even at this early date. On 20 November, in parallel with the War Office decision to prepare a land force for service in Holland, the Admiralty had issued instructions for the dispatch of a contingent of Royal Marines. Marines had been formed into provisional battalions to support coastal operations during the Peninsular War and in North America, so the creation of such a detachment to go to the Low Countries was by no means a revolutionary initiative, but the fact that the troops in question were already at Chatham meant that they could proceed on service more rapidly even than Cooke's London-based Guards. The initial contingent comprised a battalion of infantry of 420 all ranks, under the command of Lieutenant Colonel James Campbell, and a 132-strong detachment of Royal Marine Artillery. Three days later, with the force assembling at Deal ready to embark, a further 30 gunners and 135 infantry were added.[12] By no stretch of the imagination was this detachment a substitute for the planned military presence, but the speed with which they could be dispatched ensured that there would be redcoats on Dutch soil sooner rather than later, so as to back up Britain's intended status as the dominant Allied power in the region.

The first of Campbell's marines had been embarked with the flotilla that had conveyed the Prince of Orange and Clancarty to Scheveningen, and had gone on with them as a guard to The Hague, but arrival of the full contingent allowed Taylor to consider using them in a more active role, in order to secure a bridgehead for the rest of the army. First, however, it was necessary to coordinate such operations with the Dutch – whose own solo attempt to seize Helvoetsluys had failed through lack of resources – and with the commanders of the Russian and Prussian forces that were moving into the region. These troops comprised two distinct bodies, although both were ultimately under the orders of the Crown Prince of Sweden as commander of the Army of the North. The Russians were a mobile column, composed largely of Cossacks but backed up by a regular regiment of hussars and three battalions of infantry, under the command of Major General Alexander Benckendorff. Numbering some 3,500 men in total, they were nominally the advanced guard of a larger Russian corps under Lieutenant General Ferdinand von Wintzingerode, but in practice had been operating independently in Holland for some weeks; indeed, it had been the arrival of these troops that had helped encourage the Dutch revolt in the first place. More significant was Bülow's Prussian III Corps, reported to Taylor as being some 15,000 strong. However, Bülow's men were still some distance away, having taken Arnhem but not yet passed the line of the Waal; furthermore, parts of his command had been tied down to mask various enemy garrisons. Although desirous of reassembling his whole command and continuing with a forward movement, Bülow was hampered by the fact that the Crown Prince, his superior, was more concerned with affairs in North Germany and Denmark. Taylor, for his part, found it necessary to emphasize to his allies that,

> there is no reason to expect the <u>immediate</u> arrival of any other part
> of the Corps than the Brigade of Guards, that a large part of the
> infantry ordered to Holland on the spur of the moment, is unfit for
> active operations in the field, and that, at all events the whole Corps
> will require a short time for its Equipment.[13]

In the absence both of Bülow and the expected British contingent, all that could be done for the moment was for Taylor and Benckendorff to coordinate their activities with the Dutch insurgents with a view to obtaining the most advantageous position from which to begin offensive movements once a larger force was available.[14]

To this end, Taylor began to plan for 300 of Campbell's marines to be conveyed by boats to Brielle on the morning of 5 December, that place having been liberated by the Dutch some days previously. From there, Campbell could support the Dutch and observe the French garrison at Helvoetsluys, on the opposite side of the island of Voorn, which was reported to have been reinforced. Meanwhile, a naval movement against Goree, as Taylor had already proposed, would enable small warships to move up as far as Helvoetsluys and 'batter the sea face' in conjunction with land operations. Dutch expectations, notwithstanding their own failure to capture the place, were high, but Taylor could not conceive that 'anything short of a combined naval and land attack will reduce this important point'.[15] Taylor's orders to Campbell therefore stressed that he was to establish himself at Brielle and post strong picquets between there and Helvoetsluys in order to obtain further intelligence of the garrison's strength and movements. Taylor recognized that Campbell would 'probably be pushed by the Dutch troops engaged in operations against Helvoetsluys to move forward & assist them, but he will not consider himself at liberty to comply with such requests'; instead, the Royal Marine officer was to make preparations for the arrival of the expected brigade of Foot Guards, after which he hoped it would be possible to mount more active operations.[16] Having sent Campbell on his way, Taylor remained at The Hague where, after the informal discussions of the past few days, Allied strategy was to be decided in a meeting between the principal representatives of all four powers.

The Prince of Orange hosted the meeting, with Taylor and Clancarty representing Britain, Bülow and his chief-of-staff, Oberst Hermann von Boyen, representing Prussia, and Benckendorff representing Russia along with a German-born staff officer Major General Karl Ludwig von Pfuel. The last was ostensibly in Holland as a mentor to the sixteen-year-old Prince Fredrick of Orange, but was also clearly there as the eyes and ears of the Emperor, who would make him Ambassador to the Netherlands the following year. Notwithstanding his somewhat irregular status within the Allied command, Pfuel came to the meeting with a plan of his own for subsequent Allied moves, but since this dealt primarily with 'general principles' for cooperation it seems to have been quickly glossed over as the delegates got down to the details. Since he commanded the largest number of men, Bülow's was the dominant voice, but, happily, his stated position largely chimed with the hopes that Taylor had entertained prior to the meeting, eliminating concerns as to what might happen if the Prussians elected to retreat. Since leading his corps at Leipzig, Bülow had conducted an aggressive campaign to drive the French out of Westphalia, and was now keen to continue his advance with the ultimate view of linking up with the right wing of Blücher's Army of Silesia in time to join the forthcoming Allied offensive against Paris. By calling in detachments and mobilizing the newly formed Westphalian Landwehr, Bülow expected to have 30,000 men at his disposal for this movement. In part, the Prussian commander was motivated by a desire to detach his corps from the command of the Crown Prince, with whom his relationship had deteriorated even further once it became clear that the latter was now focussing all his attentions on Hamburg and Denmark and showing little apparent inclination to join the attack on France. Bülow was also disgusted by the apathy shown by many of the Dutch during the early stages of his campaign – perhaps not without reason considering the circumstances the last time Prussian troops had crossed the Dutch border back in 1787 – which further reinforced his preference for a rapid advance into Flanders.[17]

Bülow's plans were well received by Benckendorff, who, keen for action and with his forces already assembled, proposed to move on Breda and then threaten Antwerp: this would have the dual effects of tying up the French forces in that area, and of protecting Bülow's flank for his own proposed movement on Heusden and Geertruidenberg, and ultimately onwards to Brussels. In Bülow's conception, Benckendorff would also have a third role, namely that of providing a link between his own forces and those of Graham, once they arrived, which the Prussian commander envisaged as making a forward movement in the direction of Bruges. This was unwelcome news for Taylor, who had expressed concern before the meeting that the Allied commanders would either want to break up the British corps in support of their own movements, or else commit it to rash operations that would be both beyond its capabilities and at odds with the objectives set for it by the British government. Together with Clancarty, he sought to make it plain that, although Graham would eventually have a corps of 10,000 men at his disposal,

> the troops which might be expected within a very short time if the wind favoured would be about 5,500 infantry of which a proportion invalids and Boys not equal to great exertions[,] 500 cavalry and artillery in proportion. But that those actually at hand and therefore probably disposable within a few days (including the Marines) be considered as not exceeding 2,000.[18]

Accordingly, the two men emphasized that the British contingent could only play a more limited role, albeit within the general spirit of Bülow's scheme. Instead of Bruges, Antwerp would be the primary objective, but this could not be attempted until a base had been secured at Helvoetsluys, and, if necessary, the fortresses at Willemstad and Bergen-op-Zoom also reduced. Benckendorff, despite his general optimism, also questioned the wisdom of commencing operations that relied on the arrival of troops that were not yet on hand; in the context of the discussion, this had more to do with the likelihood of Bülow's expectation to be reinforced by the Saxon and Westphalian levies, but it served to reinforce the point that Taylor and Clancarty were trying to make.

Notwithstanding these caveats, Bülow was evidently determined to proceed with his own plans, although he also emphasized that it would prove impossible to begin operations for eight to ten days due to a need to bring in outlying detachments and replace them with second-line troops, and, more importantly, to a want of shoes to the extent of several thousand pairs. Some help with the former problem was offered by the Prince of Orange, who offered 3,000 new levies as potential garrison troops to help hold the posts in Bülow's rear, and the possibility of using Dutch naval gunners to man the fortress guns at Breda and elsewhere was also explored. Before the meeting broke up, news was also received regarding the grand strategy to be adopted by the Allies for the forthcoming invasion of France, by which the Army of Bohemia would move into central France by way of Switzerland whilst the Army of Silesia would cross the upper Rhine between Frankfurt and Metz. This naturally cast further doubts on the likelihood of substantial Allied reinforcements for Holland, but was nevertheless applauded by Bülow, who, despite being personally engaged in just such an undertaking, questioned the very wisdom of any major movement in the north at all. For Taylor and Clancarty, however, the Allied plans – both the general concentration on the upper Rhine, and Bülow's desire to be gone from Holland as soon as possible – were less than ideal since they offered no guarantee of sufficient Allied troops being available to aid the British in the capture of Antwerp. In Taylor's view, this issue was so important as to require diplomatic intervention on the part of Britain, and in reporting back to Bathurst he argued that it was:

> of the utmost Consequence to the eventual success of any operation on their side, in which the interests of England are so materially concerned that more powerful Interference be used than can flow from hence to obtain a considerable accession of force to the Corps directed towards the Meuse and the Scheldt, and although I have no doubt that Lord Clancarty has not failed to press this, I hope your Lordship will forgive me for suggesting it.[19]

Quite apart from the fact that it failed to address Britain's own interests, Taylor in any case was not convinced of the soundness of Bülow's plan, since he believed that the forces committed to it were too weak, the more so since there was no concrete intelligence available as to the nature of the enemy forces that might oppose them. Bülow and Benckendorff believed that they could succeed by 'taking advantage of the Enemy's weakness and the impoverished state of his fortresses', but even if this did prove to be the case, Taylor remained concerned that 'with the means at their disposal, they may obtain [their objectives] for a moment and yet not be able to secure and maintain the objects in view'.[20]

In fact Bülow's hopes were closer to reality than Taylor's fears, for the French forces in the Low Countries were thinly stretched and in a precarious position. Command of the French forces on the lower Rhine had been entrusted to Marshal Macdonald, who on paper had the V and XI Army Corps and II and III Cavalry Corps at his disposal for a total of 28,273 men. Independent of Macdonald's command, Général de Division Nicolas Maison's I Corps was in the process of being formed in Antwerp from conscripts and garrison detachments already in the Low Countries, and there were additional forces assigned to the various military districts. With the Prussians across the Ijssel and now threatening the line of the Waal,

Macdonald was greatly concerned for his northern flank, and in late November moved up elements of XI Corps and II Cavalry Corps to block Bülow's advance. This, however, had been to no avail as these troops had not only failed to prevent the Prussians capturing Arnhem but were themselves badly mauled during the fighting there. With his other forces holding the line further south, covering a front of more than a hundred miles, all Macdonald could do was use XI Corps to establish a new cordon behind the Waal, linked on its left to Général de Division Gabriel Molitor's troops at Utrecht. By early December, though, as the local Allied commanders set out for their strategy meeting at The Hague, it had become clear to Macdonald that even his new position might well be too exposed. Threatened by Bülow from the north-east, he now received intelligence suggesting that more Allied troops were crossing the Rhine further south: if this were true, he risked encirclement and destruction. With his army melting away through sickness and desertion, and many of his generals increasingly despondent, Macdonald's only option was to order a further retreat. Napoleon, though, was having none of it: reinforcements and supplies would be sent, but Macdonald must continue to maintain his position. Meanwhile, forces would be massed at Antwerp ready to mount a counter-offensive and regain the lost territory.[21]

As the third city of his Empire and a vital naval base, Antwerp naturally became a focus for Napoleon's plans for the conduct of the war on his north-eastern frontier. In order to bolster the forces already being assembled there, the Emperor ordered two divisions of the Imperial Guard to join its defence, ordered three more to Belgium in support, and placed Général de Division Charles Decaen in command of all his forces in the Netherlands. Meanwhile, Governor-General Lebrun was given instructions to double the numbers of the Antwerp Garde Nationale. Ultimately, Napoleon expected to assemble an active force of 50,000 men based on the city as the first stage to regaining control of Holland, but, like the Emperor's other increasingly chimerical schemes to restore his fortunes, the plan never stood much chance of becoming reality. What seemed possible from Paris was quite another thing for Lebrun, who, until Decaen arrived, was the man on the spot. Maison's I Corps, in the absence of the Imperial Guard detachments, consisted only of eight battalions of conscripts, several of them not yet complete; Molitor's 17th Military District had some active battalions, but they were all off to the east screening against a further Prussian advance; the available troops from Général de Division Jean-Jacques Ambert's evacuated 31st Military District consisted only of Ambert and his staff. Far from preparing Antwerp as a base for Napoleon's putative offensive, Lebrun was more concerned about preserving it long enough in French hands for Decaen to arrive and relieve him of the responsibility. He could do little to increase troop numbers, but he could at least make better use of what he had, sacrificing outlying detachments in order to concentrate sufficient force to defend the centre. Not only did he authorize the withdrawal from Brielle, thereby allowing Campbell's Royal Marines to gain their foothold on Voorn, but he also ordered the evacuation of Helvoetsluys and Goree as well.

Under cover of darkness, the French pulled out of Helvoetsluys on the night of 5–6 December, retiring in boats to Overflakee. Campbell, reporting back to Taylor, stated the strongly held belief that it was the arrival of his marines that had prompted the French to pull out; Taylor forbore to comment on this, but ordered the colonel to occupy the place with 300 of his men and put it in a state of defence. After the less than perfect outcome of the previous day's meeting, 6 December was rapidly becoming a good day for Herbert Taylor. Not only could he report to Bathurst that Helvoetsluys was in Allied hands, but also that the Dutch had occupied Goree. And, as if to cap this sudden shift in Allied fortunes, news also came in that a flotilla of transports had anchored off Scheveningen. This time it was no rumour – at last, the Guards had arrived.[22]

The arrival of Cooke at the head of his command brought an end to Taylor's time as Britain's senior military man on the spot in Holland – a status that he seems to have enjoyed – and left him 'a little at a loss what to do with myself, not liking to remain idle here, and having no positive business or duty as matters have turned out'.[23] In fact, though, Herbert Taylor would continue to play a vital role in events for some time to come. Cooke in the first instance made his way to The Hague, where Clancarty was able to furnish him with up-to-date intelligence of the Allied dispositions. This knowledge rendered a march on Amsterdam futile, and so Cooke elected to exercise the discretion contained within his orders and land his brigade on Schouwen, which was successfully accomplished although 'rather tedious on account of the heavy surf upon the shore'.[24] Indeed, in doing so he was pre-empting Bathurst, who on 4 December had modified his instructions in light of the Allied advance and instructed him to do just that.[25] With Clancarty's sanction, and the Prince of Orange's active encouragement, Cooke took as his primary objective the reduction of Willemstad so as to provide a secure base for further operations. This, along with the occupation of the islands of Voorn, Stirum and Overflakee, would secure the frontier of Holland along the course of the Maas. To this end, Cooke dispatched Taylor to Helvoetsluys to liaise with the Dutch and with the Royal Navy and, he hoped, obtain additional forces. Clancarty had already requested that 150 of the newly-arrived guardsmen be kept back to garrison Helvoetsluys, and, since Cooke had no accurate intelligence of the garrison at Willemstad, he did not want to take any risk. Taylor was asked to ascertain what help might be obtained in terms of engineer officers, boats, tools and artillerymen, with Cooke speculating that the latter deficiency might be made up by borrowing marines from the fleet 'as they are all used to Great Guns and would be an invaluable addition to the small force to be employed'.[26]

On arriving at Helvoetsluys, Taylor discovered the Dutch Admiral Kikkert in command of the forces there, which included four gunboats and a schooner. Kikkert was able to supply more detailed intelligence of the forces at Willemstad, where the garrison was understood to amount to between two and three thousand men, although this did include the crews of the various armed vessels there. These amounted to one corvette of eighteen guns; ten schooners each mounting five heavy guns and three gunbrigs each mounting four, all with crews of thirty men; six small gunboats each with three guns and twenty men; and a lugger armed with six swivels. Kikkert was unable to furnish any details of the other French garrisons, but did express the view that 'generally speaking the Enemy's disposable means between the Scheldt and the Meuse are at this moment so small that [. . .] a force of 10,000 men might push forwards without risk and gain possession of Antwerp'. At the very least, the behaviour of the garrison at Helvoetsluys suggested to the Admiral that its counterpart at Willemstad would likely abandon the place in the event of an Allied advance. With such an advance in mind, Kikkert proposed seizing the islands along the coast between the Goree passage and the Scheldt, and arming the inhabitants who, unlike the British troops, were immune to the fevers prevalent in the area. In passing this suggestion on, Taylor – perhaps influenced by his earlier meeting with Count Stirum – observed that the 'present spirit of opposition to the French Nation' amongst the Dutch stemmed from the French imposition of heavy customs dues on even the smallest businesses, and that the spirit of insurrection 'may be traced to this Cause rather than any Political feeling'.[27]

Even without Taylor's doubtful opinion of Dutch patriotism, the small size of Kikkert's forces, and the apparently substantial nature of the French garrison, made Cooke abandon any hopes of an immediate movement against Willemstad. Instead, he informed Bathurst that he would shift his whole brigade to Helvoetsluys and Brielle, 'from whence we can be moved to such points as Sir Thomas Graham may order when he reaches Schouwen. The Corps of Marines now at Helvoet[sluys] will then be ready to join Admiral Young, or to be employed as circumstances may require.'[28] In helping to strengthen the Allied hold over the Scheldt islands, Taylor oversaw the provision of 1,000 stands of arms for the Dutch at Helvoetsluys in order to enable the inhabitants of the islands to aid in their defence, and was able to report that the Prince of Orange was sending officers to help organize and train the levies there. Cooke also sent 200 of Campbell's marines to Overflakee, providing a redcoat presence on that island as well as on Voorn and Schouwen.[29]

Having met with the Prince, Taylor was also able to obtain up-to-date intelligence of the moves of the Russians and Prussians, which he passed on to Cooke and Bathurst, but the tidings were mixed. Wintzingerode's Russian corps was believed to be on its way to Holland, but since it was mainly composed of cavalry its utility was questionable. Bülow's advance had been delayed by his unwillingness to leave Gorcum in French hands behind him 'considering its strength[,] the numbers of troops in the place and their being commanded by General Rampon[,] a very determined and intelligent officer[,] he could not attack it with much prospect of success'. Meanwhile, Major Reiche, commanding a Prussian Volunteer Jäger battalion attached to Bülow's command, had incurred the Prince's wrath by issuing a call for a mass popular rising against the French. Taylor considered that 'The proclamation itself is perhaps no otherwise to be regretted than as tending for the moment to lower & call in question a Sovereign Authority which is barely established', but that, of course, was exactly the point so far as Orange and the provisional government were concerned.[30]

Once again, however, Allied pessimism would prove to be unfounded. Upon arriving at Antwerp and assuming command, Decaen quickly realized that Napoleon's planned counter-offensive was utterly impracticable, and would remain so for the foreseeable future. All that could be done was to establish a strong defensive cordon to cover Antwerp and the Belgian provinces, thus preventing any further Allied advance. Rather than seek to hold every post, and thus risk losing the lot, Decaen elected to concentrate his limited forces at a small number of strong posts at Breda, Gorcum, Geertruidenberg, Bergen-op-Zoom and Hertogenbosch. In order to augment his meagre resources, Decaen called upon Vice-Amiral Edouard-Thomas de Missiessy, commanding the Antwerp Fleet, to provide sailors and marines to bolster the forces on land: some of these were assigned to the fortresses, whilst others, along with a battalion of conscripts, were formed into a flying column under Ambert in order to keep communications open between the various posts. Lebrun, meanwhile, was appointed Governor of Antwerp with responsibility for both the city itself and the posts at Breda, Bergen-op-Zoom and the forts at the mouth of the Scheldt. Decaen's plan had merit, but he lacked the time to put it into complete organization before Bülow and Benckendorff began to move forwards as agreed. Macdonald, lacking the forces to oppose the Prussians successfully, fell back steadily, although his presence on Bülow's open southern flank would continue to give that officer repeated cause for concern. As Taylor had learnt from Orange, the Prussian advance was delayed by the need to mask the various fortresses in their rear, but Benckendorff's fast-moving light forces had no need to concern themselves with such matters and were soon pushing deep into French-held territory. Since Decaen lacked much in the way of cavalry, there was little he could do to resist the Russian advance, and he was instead obliged to order Ambert, at Breda with his flying column, as well as Colonel Legrand commanding at Willemstad, to abandon those posts if pressed, rather than risk their commands being cut off.[31]

Although Cooke felt himself too weak to attack Willemstad, Benckendorff had no such reservations about Breda, which he reached on 9 December. Gorcum and Willemstad he bypassed and left to be observed by the Dutch. Presenting himself as the advance guard of a larger force, Benckendorff hoped to persuade the French at Breda to surrender, but Ambert hung on until nightfall before extricating the bulk of his command under the cover of darkness. The following day, he continued his retreat as far as Brasschaat, only six miles from Antwerp, but in the event he was able to escape further pursuit as Benckendorff felt unable to push on any further, even after Bülow reinforced him with the Streifcorps of Major von Colomb.[32]

With Ambert forced back, Willemstad was now left extremely exposed, and it too was evacuated on the 10th. Taylor believed that this was on orders from Antwerp, but it seems that this was true only in the indirect sense of Legrand having acted on his discretionary orders from Decaen once Benckendorff's advance left his position exposed. In any event, Taylor was able to report that,

> The garrison whose numbers are variously stated at from 900 to 1,600 retired in the direction of Bergen-op-Zoom. They left in the place 100,000 barrels of powder, 152 guns mounted and on service-able carriages but spiked, & the supply of Provisions was small [. . .] They carried away with them 4 Field Pieces, and are said to have withdrawn the Irish Battalion as soon as they learned that British troops had landed in Holland.[33]

Furthermore, although an attempt had been made to destroy the war-ships, this had been imperfectly executed and it was anticipated that the corvette and several smaller vessels could likely be recovered. Since

Campbell's marines had not yet embarked for Overflakee, Taylor sent them to Willemstad instead where Cooke joined them with the bulk of his brigade, leaving only 2/Coldstream Guards to garrison Helvoetsluys.[34]

Subsequently, when news was received that the island of Tholen had also been evacuated, Cooke sent his second-in-command, Colonel Lord Proby, to occupy it with the Royal Marines and 2/1st Foot Guards. By now, Cooke was thinking in terms of a further advance. Taylor had been sent off on another round of liaison visits to establish the extent of Allied progress and ascertain the revised intentions of Bülow and Benckendorff in light of the French retreat, whilst Proby was informed 'that Tholen being a point of entry from Brabant into Zeeland, the security of it is the object of his detachment; but that if the French should be induced to evacuate Bergen-op-Zoom as they did other places, he might find it expedient to take immediate advantage of such an event.' Then, on the night of 15 December, Cooke received news that Gibbs's brigade was preparing to land at Helvoetsluys: this enabled him to bring the Coldstreamers up to Willemstad, which, in turn, freed 2/3rd Foot Guards to move to Steenbergen where they could maintain communications with Proby and also participate in any movement that officer might make against Bergen-op-Zoom. With his forces becoming somewhat spread out, Cooke sought to borrow sufficient cavalry from Benckendorff to permit his various posts to communicate with each other, and was also keen to obtain the services of any available artillerymen to help defend them. Bringing Bathurst up to date with these developments in a despatch of the 16th, Cooke bemoaned the fact that he had still had no communication with Graham.[35] In fact, however, George Cooke's period of independent command was about to come to an end, for as he put pen to paper his superior officer was likewise engaged, in his cabin aboard HMS *Ulysses*, reporting the arrival of his troops in the Roompot the previous afternoon.[36]

Chapter IV

'Experienced Troops Are So Much Wanted'

THE PRIMARY REASON FOR THE LATE APPEARANCE of Graham and the remainder of the force had been the weather. Contrary winds had delayed the arrival of the transports at Deal, and when the wind did come it came with such force that it rendered loading the troops and stores more than unusually difficult. Although the last two brigades were ready by 9 December they were not all loaded until the 12th, and it was a further day before they were finally able to set sail.[1] Naturally, considering the rapidity with which the force was assembled, there were other trials to be endured as staff work failed to coincide with reality. Newly promoted Lieutenant Thomas Austin was on leave from the 2/35th, stationed in Guernsey, when the battalion received orders to proceed first to the regimental depot at Chichester and then with all dispatch to join Graham's army. When word reached Austin in Nottingham, he at once returned to the depot, only to find that the battalion had already left. Having ascertained that he was not – as he had feared – under orders to remain with the depot, Austin made all haste to re-join the 2/35th at Margate where he resumed his place as second-in-command of its Light Company. On arrival, he discovered that the battalion 'had been hurried by forced marches from Chichester to the coast of Kent; but [. . .] after hurrying night and day to the point of embarkation, it was found that the [transports] still remained at Portsmouth, only eighteen miles from Chichester, whence the 35th had been sent with such precipitous haste!' Like Thomas Morris, Austin had joined the Army at a young age following the example of an older brother. Unlike Private Morris, though, Austin's family connections were sufficient to secure him an ensigncy in the West Middlesex Militia at the age of fourteen, from which he transferred into the 35th less than a year later. Now a few days shy of his nineteenth birthday, Austin was keen to see active service after spending two years learning his trade amidst the tedium of garrison duty, but this did not seem the most promising beginning.[2]

The circumstances of the embarkation did little to increase Austin's faith in those who directed the Army's operations, although he spoke highly of the ‘great skill and intelligence’ shown by the Deal boatmen as a result of which, despite the heavy seas, only one boat was swamped, and that with no lives lost.[3] Unfortunately, the boat in question was carrying men of the 95th Rifles, and although the men were saved, the reserve rifle ammunition was spoiled. To add insult to injury, the replacement consignment of cartridges would suffer a similar fate on being landed at Scheveningen, so that it would be January before the riflemen were fully supplied.[4] At Yarmouth, meanwhile, embarkation had posed no problems because the men from Gibbs's four battalions had never disembarked. Women and children were sent ashore, since it was anticipated that the brigade might have to make an opposed landing, and the men were sent on to Holland as soon as the wind permitted. After storms in the Baltic and the North Sea, not to mention a fortnight at Gothenburg with limited supplies, sickness was prevalent in all four battalions and particularly in the 2/73rd due to its ‘excessive fatigue, and bad living’ during the Göhrde campaign. Although, as he put it, ‘a few days judicious treatment, with proper diet, and medicines’ upon landing put things to rights, Morris's battalion still had forty men sick out of 450 on 25 December.[5]

By that date, the bulk of Graham's forces were established ashore, wanting only the arrival of the 2nd KGL Hussars and of the artillery horses to complete their organization.[6] The process of landing, however, had been scarcely less eventful than that of embarkation. The transports reached the Dutch coast in the midst of a ‘cold, dense fog’,[7] and it was not until after much groping amongst the sandbanks that a safe anchorage within the Scheldt was reached. Even then, it was not immediately practicable to get the large ships upriver to Willemstad. The morning of 16 December had already seen an abortive move to land forces on Walcheren – greeted with horror by the veterans of the 2/35th, which had taken part in the 1809 expedition and still contained survivors of the island's fevers – but news of the French retreats, and a change in the wind, caused this to be cancelled and the flotilla moved slowly upriver until it anchored again off the island of Tholen. This, now, was to be the point of landing, opposed only by ‘a few straggling shots’ that had little effect beyond spurring the seamen manning the boats to increase their exertions at the oars. The Light Company of the 2/35th was amongst the first ashore, and Austin was sent on with a party of twenty to endeavour to cut off the French outpost, which, however, made good its escape with no casualties on either side.[8] There now followed further confusion as the remaining troops came ashore, as a result of which Austin's vanguard detachment, for want of orders to the contrary, continued well past Sint Maartensdijk, where it was afterwards established that they ought to have stopped, and carried on almost to the town of Tholen itself before having to retrace their steps. In that this detour caused an unnecessary twelve miles of marching, on roads that had degenerated into 'an appalling conglomeration of mud', and that by the time the men of the 2/35th staggered back into Sint Maartensdijk all the best billets had already been taken, it is not to be wondered that the young subaltern continued to be less than impressed with the British Army's ability to organize itself for a campaign.[9]

Austin's misadventures aside, however, the full strength of Graham's infantry was now established on Dutch soil, although they remained dispersed. Cooke's forces were still divided, with Proby's detachment at Tholen and the rest of the Guards at Willemstad and Steenbergen. Gibbs's brigade was also ordered to Steenbergen, but Graham, in directing this, was unaware that Cooke had sent 2/3rd Foot Guards there already: accordingly, Gibbs dropped off the sickly 2/73rd to reinforce the Coldstreamers at Willemstad, giving the battalion the breathing space that Morris found so beneficial, and took his other three battalions on to Steenbergen. The bulk of the reinforcements from England were safely ashore on Tholen, although not initially in contact with Proby at the other end of the island, but some detachments were still not yet landed. The 2/37th and 3/56th had in the first instance gone to Scheveningen and would need to be brought up to join the rest of the force; upon arrival, it was anticipated that they could relieve the troops at Willemstad, allowing the two battalions left there to re-join their respective brigades.[10] It would take several more days to get all the organizational tangles straightened out, but – for all of Austin's criticisms from the sharp end of things – the consolidation of the various commands went relatively smoothly. Having his full force assembled, however, enabled Graham to make a more effective assessment of its qualities, and what he found was not, on the whole, such as might be expected to fill the general with confidence.

To be sure, Graham cannot have been under many illusions from the outset, since Bathurst had been as honest as he could about the limitations of the forces available. Although having features in common with the battalions sent to the Baltic with Gibbs the previous summer, the units that formed the second wave of reinforcements were rather more of a mixed bag. The best of the bunch seems to have been the 2/35th, which was both fairly strong – 461 rank and file on landing – and also reasonably efficient. Although functioning as a feeder unit for the 1/35th in the Mediterranean, the battalion's posting on Guernsey required it to retain enough trained men to remain effective in its own right. Austin was proud of the fact that of the battalions being assembled at Margate, his was one of only three that were able to carry out the drills successfully for forming square to receive cavalry, indicating that they were fully proficient in the manoeuvres required for service in the field.[11] Lest Austin's account be considered unduly partisan, it is only fair to add that Lieutenant General Doyle, their commander on Guernsey, had recently reported them as 'a good body of men very fit for service, with a healthy and cleanly appearance'.[12]

The other two units capable of forming square when required were the expedition's two light infantry battalions, but, unlike the 2/35th, these were both numerically weak. Bathurst's planned order of battle had required the five home-based companies of the 3/95th to provide 250 riflemen, and the 2/52nd a further 300 redcoat light infantry, but the actual numbers available fell far short of that. A decent-sized rifle battalion of four companies was eventually assembled, with 305 men in the ranks upon landing in Holland, but this could only be managed by forming the fit men of the 3/95th into two companies, and then adding a company apiece from the depots of the regiment's other two battalions.[13] In the case of the 3/95th, the problem was quite simply that the men were not available: with the 2/52nd, on the other hand, it was that the available men were not of a sufficient quality. After returning from the Peninsula in February 1812, the 52nd's 2nd Battalion had been reconfigured to function solely as a depot and feeder unit for its 1st, a mainstay of Wellington's Light Division: as soon as recruits were deemed fit for service, they went out as drafts to the Peninsula. Thus, the 369 men on the 2nd Battalion's strength as of 25 October 1813 – this being the date of the last return submitted to Horse Guards prior to its being ordered on service – were almost entirely composed of either untrained recruits not yet ready for service, or else men sent back as unfit by the 1/52nd. Accordingly, Lieutenant Charles Shaw recorded that 'the idea of the battalion being sent on foreign service never entered the mind of anyone'.[14] Another young officer eager to see action for the first time, Shaw, an eighteen-year-old Scot who had only obtained his commission the previous January, was nevertheless overjoyed when such orders were received. Although the battalion had recently reported not a single man 'fit for immediate service', just over half its strength were eventually prepared to embark; they might not have met the regiment's own exacting standards, but, as Austin's account of their proficiency makes clear, they were still amongst the best that Graham had.[15]

Like the 2/52nd, the 2/44th had also served for a time in the Peninsula, having been recalled during the spring of 1813 due to its shrunken numbers. Conceding second place to the regiment's 1st Battalion, serving in eastern Spain, the 2/44th had only limited resources from which to reconstitute itself, and under normal circumstances would likely have remained in a depot role for the foreseeable future. Mustering 422 rank and file upon landing, the battalion was not unduly weak, but the survivors of Badajoz and Salamanca in the ranks were outnumbered by new men, over half of whom had less than a year's service. A recent inspection noted that 'some of the young officers want much instruction', as did several of the battalion's NCOs.[16] A similar level of inexperience was to be found in the ranks of the 2/69th, although the lack of veterans was this time down to the fact that, like the 2/52nd, this unit had been functioning largely as a feeder unit for an active battalion overseas, in this case in India. The 2/69th's rank and file were reported as being 'in general fit for service, but very young'.[17]

Colonial service was also responsible for the weakness of the 55th, this being one of several weak single-battalion regiments – like the 33rd and 54th serving with Gibbs – to have been recalled to Britain after a lengthy spell overseas. Eight companies of the battalion had been brought home from the West Indies during the course of 1810 and 1811, leaving two behind, the remnants of which were still there.[18] Two years at home ought have been enough to put the 55th back in order, but autumn 1813 found it reeling from a scandal that had struck its officers' mess, the repercussions of which would ensure that its time overseas would be short. The root of things was a quarrel between Captain Hamilton Clune and Lieutenant Richard Blake, the origin of which apparently extended back to the battalion's Caribbean service. Clune's absence on staff duties allowed things to calm down, but when he re-joined the battalion at Windsor in the summer of 1813 matters flared up again until Blake resolved to force Clune into a duel. He first insulted the captain whilst on parade on 13 August, insinuating that Clune was no gentleman, and then protested in 'gross and vulgar language' when Clune had him placed in arrest. Three days later Blake broke his arrest, sought out Clune, who was on duty in the town, and 'violently assaulted him [. . .] by silently, and unawares, striking him a most severe blow on the head with a stick, which knocked him down, which blow he repeated several times'. Blake subsequently absconded, but eventually gave himself up after five days and was placed in close arrest, from where he directed further insubordinate letters to his commanding officer, Major Robert Frederick, and to the Adjutant-General at Horse Guards.[19] The wounds from this scandal were still raw when the 55th received its orders for Holland. Blake, without the witnesses necessary to make his defence, remained under close arrest to await their return.

The quarrels of its officers aside, the 55th had at least had time to make some progress towards rendering its new recruits fit for service, which was more than could be said for the 2/37th and 3/56th, whose very existence was measurable only in weeks. Their formation was part of a recent initiative by the Duke of York to form new field units by converting the depots of regiments that had their senior battalion or battalions serving in overseas garrisons. York's logic was sound enough – the 1/37th at Gibraltar had no pressing need for new men, and nor did the two senior battalions of the 56th in India – but the orders for the creation of the new battalions only went out in the early autumn of 1813 and none of them were complete when the call came for service.[20] Neither was at anything like full strength, with the 2/37th having only sufficient men to form six companies, and the 3/56th five.

The latter battalion did, however, have the advantage of a first-rate commanding officer in the shape of Lieutenant Colonel John Brown, who, as a major in the 28th, had distinguished himself leading a flank battalion under Graham's command at Barrosa. Thomas Austin, who knew him on Guernsey and travelled down to Ramsgate with him as both men sought to re-join their battalions, described him as an imposing figure with obvious natural authority, 'of soldierly habits and speech, of great personal courage but a rough exterior. The few short sentences he usually addressed to his men when leading them into action had a wonderful effect in inspiring them with a confidence in themselves and in their leader.'[21] Brown would need every bit of charisma that he could muster in the months ahead.

Although the hastily raised 2/37th and 3/56th were undoubtedly the most lacking in terms of experience, the vast majority of Graham's regular infantry were men who had never undergone the rigours of a campaign, nor heard a shot fired in anger. The men of the 1st Royal Veteran Battalion were of course veterans, two of the unit's corporals having in excess of thirty years' service behind them, but the best that could be said of the bulk of the battalion's 461 rank and file was that although 'not fit for very active service [they] would be able to under go fatigues in our foreign garrisons'.[22] Even amongst Gibbs's four battalions, only the 2/73rd had seen any real active service during their Baltic sojourn.

In the Guards, at least, the picture was rather more promising, with a good leavening of experienced men who had seen service overseas, either with the companies that had served at Cadiz in 1810 and 1811 or else, in the case of the Coldstreamers and 3rd Foot Guards, with the regiments' respective 1st Battalions under Wellington.[23] But even with a higher proportion of experienced men relative to the line battalions, the Guards were not without problems. Most notably, the fact that the men had been distributed in billets around London meant that they had not been issued with camp equipment and when first embarked did not even have blankets, something Cooke sought to address by trying to purchase replacements locally.[24]

Whatever the Secretary of State's reservations about the units assigned to Graham's command, Bathurst had been rather more optimistic about the two additional brigadiers who would command them, writing that, although chosen chiefly because of their availability, both were 'very good'.[25] Not everyone would have agreed with that assessment, as we shall see, but what was beyond doubt was that two men less alike would have been hard to find. The senior of the two was 59-year-old Kenneth Mackenzie, a veteran of over forty years in the Army and an experienced commander of light infantry who had helped Graham instruct the 90th Foot in light infantry drill back in the 1790s. Given command of the 52nd in 1802, he had been instrumental in training Britain's first light infantry regiments and was responsible, at least in a practical sense, for many of the innovations more commonly associated with Sir John Moore. A bad fall from a horse led to his retiring on half-pay, and his subsequent promotion to major general in 1811 was down only to the inexorable progress of seniority.[26] His health had not been good for the past decade, but he was fit enough when the call came in 1813, and Graham would make good use of him as commander of his own limited contingent of light troops. As befitted a disciple of Moore he was a humane commander, with a pronounced concern for the welfare of his troops and an abhorrence of physical punishment.

By contrast, John Byne Skerrett was Mackenzie's junior by a quarter-century in age and two years in seniority as a major general, and a completely different character. Where Mackenzie was humane, Skerrett was choleric and aloof; whilst Mackenzie was a doyen of the light infantry, Skerrett was characterized as a 'gallant Grenadier'.[27] The latter description, however, might not quite be the compliment it appears, for it comes from the pen of Harry Smith of the 95th, Skerrett's brigade major in his brief spell with the Light Division during the Battles of the Pyrenees, and from a Rifleman's perspective 'grenadier' was as good as synonymous with 'blockhead'. Smith, too, even though he composed his memoirs after Skerrett's death, could still not forgive his former commander for the incident that had effectively ended Skerrett's career in the Peninsula.

Posted to take over a brigade in the Light Division after Vitoria, Skerrett quickly demonstrated that he lacked the swiftness of judgement needed for such a command, and his insistence on standing out in the open under fire, which might have been inspiring to most troops, was simply ridiculed by his 'light bobs' who had been trained to make the best use of any cover. Smith and the battalion commanders did their best to carry on despite him, but during the fighting at Vera on 31 August they were unable to prevent Skerrett from leaving an inadequate picquet to cover a vital bridge rather than moving his whole brigade to block it. The result was that the retreating French, who would otherwise have been cut off, crushed the picquet – killing its popular commander, Captain Cadoux of the 95th – and fought their way to safety. Having patently lost the confidence of his brigade, Skerrett reported himself sick and left the Peninsula: Smith rather nastily implied that his real motivation was to enjoy the fortune and estate he had recently inherited on the death of his father.[28] Unfortunately, this was only the last of several instances from his Peninsular service that called Skerrett's judgement into question. Sent to help the Spaniards hold Tarragona in 1811 he had refused to land his troops and the place had ultimately fallen; at Tarifa the following year he had continually counselled evacuation and generally served to hamper what was ultimately, despite him, a successful defence.[29] In these earlier incidents Skerrett had served under first Graham and then Cooke, both of whom seem to have retained confidence in him when he joined them for the Dutch expedition, but he certainly had something of a point to prove in his new posting. Personally brave to a fault, he seems to have lacked the moral courage to match, leaving him incapable of decision in moments of crisis.

With such a mixture of troops and commanders, Graham could at least make the best of what he had by beginning to reorganize his forces. Years of precedent dictated that the Guards must remain brigaded together under an officer who was himself a guardsman, so Cooke's brigade remained intact, but Graham swiftly dispensed with Bathurst's plan that Gibbs should remain in command of the four battalions he had brought from the Baltic whilst Mackenzie and Skerrett commanded those from Britain. Instead, Graham formed a Light Brigade under Mackenzie by adding the 2/35th to the Rifle detachments and 2/52nd. Once the 2/73rd was ready for service, it too was given to Mackenzie and Gibbs received the 3/56th so as to keep his brigade – now designated the Second – at four battalions. Skerrett's First Brigade, meanwhile, contained the remaining four line battalions sent from Britain, and the 1st Royal Veterans.[30]

These reorganizations made the best of what there was, but it was also readily apparent that what there was, especially in terms of troops fit to take the field, was not very much.[31] As a result of Graham's representations, however, Horse Guards was already responding 'to the desire expressed by Earl Bathurst, that a reinforcement of troops should proceed without delay' to reinforce Graham, and orders were given to dispatch a further four battalions, taken from garrisons in Scotland and Jersey, with an assumed strength of a further 1,870 rank and file.[32] It was recognized that there was little point in sending drafts to the line battalions already in Holland, such men as remained at their depots amounting only to 'a few hundred unarmed and unequipped militiamen who will be in a state of drunkenness and confusion until their [enlistment bounty] money is spent', but the depots of the Foot Guards were seen as in a position to provide extra men, and orders were given for them to do so.[33] Prior to his departure, Graham had also discussed with Bathurst the possibility that the KGL troops and the Russo-German Legion serving with Wallmoden might be sent to Holland, where their arrival, as he reminded the Secretary of State, 'would give great consistency to this Corps, where experienced troops are so much wanted',[34] but it would not be until January that reinforcements from this source were confirmed, and even then only the 3rd KGL Hussars and the artillery were to be sent.[35] By then, however, Graham's force was already engaged with the enemy and its commander obliged to make do with what he had.

Graham's first moves, once the new arrivals were ashore, were a continuation of those already set in motion by Taylor and Cooke. His initial plan was to carry on the movement towards Bergen-op-Zoom begun by Cooke – hence the deployments already outlined – but he remained doubtful about the chances of the place being taken, writing to Bathurst that:

> one can scarcely think it possible that the Enemy sh'd be equally ready to evacuate Bergen-op-Zoom, yet after what has happened at Willemstad and Breda, it would be wrong not to make some demonstration with a view of feeling & ascertaining their strength & determination relative to its defence. We are utterly w'out the means to attack, but this movement will not oppose us to any risk if Genl. Benckendorff remains in his forward positions. I should fear, however that he holds Breda by a very precarious tenure should Macdonald have anything to send there.[36]

Other than crediting Macdonald with being a greater threat than was actually the case, this was a fairly prescient analysis of things. Over and above the obvious vulnerability of the Russians at Breda, Graham also bemoaned the fact that Gorcum remained in French hands and thus served as a potential 'tête de pont' via which the French might attempt a counter-offensive, although the Allied occupation of Willemstad did at least secure the lowest reaches of the Maas.

Three days later, after having reconnoitred the place himself, and aware that the French had been able to reinforce the garrison, Graham was even more forthright in his dismissal of Britain's hopes of taking Bergen-op-Zoom, noting that:

> from the great profile of the works, it is scarcely to have been expected that any attempt at escalade would have been successful. We must have broken ground & erected a battery or two to have afforded the Governor a pretence for surrendering. For tho' the place is very extensive we could only have made the attempt on this side where the elevation of the ground prevents the water from flowing into the ditch. The enemy's attention therefore would have been confined to that particular space, which he might have defended with even a small garrison.[37]

Thus, in Graham's opinion, even the original garrison would likely have been sufficient to hold the place, and nothing had been lost – with regards to Bergen-op-Zoom at least – by the delayed arrival of the main British force. Furthermore, he considered the works to be formidable in their own right, such that it would be 'a task of some difficulty to get into the place (supposing the gates shut) even if there were no garrison at all [. . .] there being water in the ditch everywhere, but for a certain space each side of the Steenbergen gate'.[38]

Graham's view was not shared by his chief of engineers, Lieutenant Colonel James Carmichael Smyth, who would continue throughout the campaign to advocate aggressive action and whose reports to his London-based superior, Lieutenant General Gother Mann, Colonel-Commandant of the Royal Engineers and Inspector-General of Fortifications, provide an interesting counterpart to the reports that Graham and Taylor were sending to Bathurst at the War Office and York at Horse Guards. Aged thirty-four, Smyth was an experienced officer whose twenty years in the Royal Engineers had included extensive service at the Cape as well as with Moore's army during the Corunna campaign. Unfortunately, as Carmichael Smyth was quick to point out in one of his first reports, his subordinates were for the most part young and inexperienced, whilst the detachment of Royal Sappers and Miners under his command was badly deficient in NCOs.[39] Typical of the young engineer subalterns was Lieutenant John Sperling, twenty-one years old and on his first active posting after two years' home service: a devout and serious-minded youth, judging by his letters home, Sperling quickly developed a high opinion of Carmichael Smyth's capabilities, and of the care that he took of his young subordinates.[40] This good opinion would come to be shared by their superiors.

After his initial report concerning the inadequacy of the detachment under his command, Carmichael Smyth did not make a full report until the end of December. This enabled him to sum up the first month's operations, but also meant that what he wrote contained more by way of hindsight than the despatches that Graham was sending home almost daily. On the subject of Bergen-op-Zoom, Carmichael Smyth wrote that:

> The French garrison [. . .] was unquestionably contemptible & I am in my own opinion convinced that had the unlucky easterly winds that prevented our departure at an earlier period, not prevailed we should have got into the place without any trouble, & as easily as the Russians entered Breda. At Antwerp the Enemy had concentrated the whole of their disposable force & our little Corps could not yet even attempt to invest Bergen-op-Zoom. The day after our arrival they threw in one new-raised battalion & they have since sent in another. With, however, the addition of these reinforcements I do not believe that the Garrison exceeds 2,500 men from every information I have been able to procure.[41]

Graham's ADC, Major James Stanhope, was also of a similar mind-set and blamed only the delay in the arrival of the main British force for the fact that Bergen-op-Zoom had not fallen: otherwise, he reasoned, the un-reinforced garrison of only a thousand men could not possibly have held such an extensive perimeter.[42] The size, nature and quality of the garrison and fortifications at Bergen-op-Zoom would become a matter of considerable debate over the coming months, with those who favoured an assault generally producing reports that stressed its weakness and disaffected state, whereas those holding less sanguine expectations talked up the strength of the fortifications and elected to believe those reports that spoke of a strong garrison.

Whilst Graham was assessing the situation around Bergen-op-Zoom, Mackenzie's Light Brigade – at this point still lacking the 2/73rd – was thrown forwards to observe the place. This meant another punishing march on muddy roads, with Austin, who had drawn the short straw of commanding the brigade baggage-guard, having a particularly hard time of things and taking the best part of a day to cover four miles. He was nevertheless impressed by the good humour maintained by his men, who cracked 'all kinds of rough jokes, one asking another if he did not find the road exceedingly hard when he got to the bottom of it, and so on'.[43] On arrival, the men of the Light Brigade found that the French had abandoned the extensive outworks around the town, confining themselves to defending the main fortress itself, but that patrols were being sent out to harass the British picquets. Even an innocent – if optimistic – attempt by the Light Company officers of the 2/35th to fish in the ditch of one of the outworks was evidently seen as an affront by the garrison, who responded with a fusillade of shots that dispersed the would-be anglers. Beyond outpost squabbling, however, there was no serious attempt by either side to disturb the other.

This duty did, however, bring Mackenzie's men into contact with their allies for the first time, since Benckendorff had posted a squadron of the Pavlograd Hussars and a hundred Cossacks to observe the place and, in the continued absence of their own cavalry, the British would be forced to rely on these troops for scouting and communications for some time to come.[44] As Graham ruefully explained, their utility was limited by the rather obvious fact that, quite apart from their not being very many of them, 'we do not understand each other well'.[45]

To his troops, however, the Russians were a source of fascination, although initial favourable impressions of martial prowess were soon tempered by more prosaic realities. Austin thought them, 'as a military body, the greatest rabble in Europe' useful only in irregular warfare. His suspicion of their 'predatory habits' was confirmed by one of their own officers, who warned him that the 'wings' or epaulettes worn by light infantry officers such as Austin 'would be too great a temptation for the Cossacks to resist, if they met with an opportunity where they could despoil the wearer of the costly ornaments without fear of detection'.[46] James Stanhope, meanwhile, had to deal with a Cossack officer who arrived at headquarters with a message from Benckendorff. The man had:

> long lank hair and the most brutal manners, understanding no language but his own. I offered him a chair, he threw it over, a cigar, it went on the fire, schnapps (brandy) it went down his throat and he began to talk exceedingly but unfortunately nobody understood his language. I sent for a dried tongue for him & he pared it with his patent attention and I began to hope we had a civilised man to deal with but alas when I saw that he only pared the rind to select it as the best I gave all hope up, which was speedily confirmed by his taking off a bottle of claret, decanting it down his throat without drawing breath.[47]

More to the point so far as military operations were concerned, Stanhope also came to realize that it was impossible to rely on the Russian outposts to give any warning of their own or the French movements, rendering them useless as a screen.

Far more of a threat than the French or the Cossacks, though, was the weather. The winter of 1813–14 would prove to be unusually bitter, and for Graham's inexperienced troops, sent on service in many cases without the full allowance of camp equipment, it proved particularly hard to bear. After only a week in their advanced posts, Graham was obliged to report that:

> the number of sick in the Light Brigade, particularly of the 95th, [has] increased to an alarming degree – this is owing to the extreme youth of a great proportion of these troops. Before we fully take the field, I must have an inspection of every Regt. to draught [sic] from them the unserviceable Boys &c to be left behind – this will rid us of a great encumbrance, & save the lives of many.[48]

It would not have been so bad, Graham went on, if the rejected men were fit even for lighter duties, since garrisons would need to be found for Tholen, Willemstad, and Helvoetsluys, but the condition of these troops was so bad that he did not even consider them fit to be left in this role, which would in turn necessitate the detachment of effective troops for garrison duty and thus further reduce the numbers available to take the field.

Naturally, Graham sought to do all that he could to relieve his men of as much of their hardship as he could manage, sending to Rotterdam for camp kettles and blankets, but he was also obliged to report that the state of the Dutch roads was so bad that many of his men were already in need of replacement shoes. It was therefore all the more galling that supplies in apparent abundance were being shipped across for the use of the Dutch, who seemed to be being given more than they needed. In fact, Bathurst had already been alerted, via Taylor, of the need for shoes, and had authorized the dispatch of 10,000 pairs, along with the same quantity of blankets, but it would take time for the news of this to reach Graham, let alone the articles themselves.[49]

Happy in his own mind that Bergen-op-Zoom was not a practical objective with the means that he had available, and therefore needing to decide on what course of action his forces should take, it was necessary for Graham to obtain information about what his allies were doing, and what they knew or suspected of French forces and intentions. Cooke had already sent Taylor off on just such a mission, and, once ashore, Graham had sent his own military secretary and kinsman, Lieutenant Colonel John Graham of Fintry, to The Hague so as to bring back a report of Taylor's findings and also to obtain Clancarty's views on the progress of events. The colonel met Taylor on 17 December, and returned to Graham's headquarters that same day. He was thus able to acquaint Graham with Taylor's activities over the last few days, a period that had proved frustrating in the extreme and which brought little in the way of positive news.[50] The major negative was that Taylor had been unable to make contact with Wintzingerode, reported to have moved his headquarters to Zutphen preparatory to advancing into Holland, for the very good reason that Wintzingerode had never been there and that no such advance was now intended. Taylor did, however, meet Bülow, who stated himself still keen to participate in a general advance but who was fuming at the fact that the Crown Prince had redirected Wintzingerode's corps elsewhere. Taylor, whilst accepting the basic facts at face value, nevertheless stated:

> [I am] aware however that whatever concerned the Prince Royal should be received with caution from General Bülow who has not concealed from me on a former occasion, as he repeated on this, that he had differed with him severely, that he had no opinion of him as a soldier, and that disputes had run so high that the Prince Royal had twice complained of him to the King of Prussia.[51]

The Crown Prince, of course, was far more interested in attacking Denmark than moving into Holland, and his attempts towards that end led to a redirection of much of the Army of the North. Not only was Wintzingerode's move westward cancelled, but Wallmoden also found himself sucked into these subsidiary operations, fighting a sharp action at Sehested on 10 December against a superior Danish force, in which Captain Holtzermann's KGL half-battalion was badly cut up and its commander captured. In Britain, the Crown Prince's actions were seen as something of a betrayal of the common cause, with suspicions voiced that the erstwhile French marshal wanted no part in the invasion of French territory. However, British negotiators the previous year had offered Denmark to him as part of his price for joining the Allies. His timing and sense of priorities were deplored by Britons and Prussians alike but there was no obvious leverage that could be exerted to make him change his plans, although some did advocate the stripping of non-Swedish troops from his command.[52] Certainly, the Crown Prince remained enough of a Frenchman – and had enough of an eye on his potential future in that country – to want no part in any operations designed to cut France's power back beyond the 'natural frontier' of the Rhine that he himself had helped win for it almost twenty years before.[53]

The Swedes were not the only Allies who did not seem to be doing their bit, since Bülow also bemoaned the fact that the Austrians 'were thinking only of Alsace' and could not be expected to contribute any force to the efforts in the Low Countries. His own monarch and the Emperor of Russia were both in favour of the planned advance, but for all this royal approval, and his own stated keenness, Bülow seemed no closer to moving forwards and had only around 7,000 men immediately disposable. It was not just the apparent stagnation of the Allied plans that had upset Taylor, but the conflicting personal demands that he found himself under. On the one hand, he felt obliged to return to his secretarial duties with Queen Charlotte, his leave from which was fast expiring, but, on the other, both Bathurst and the Prince of Orange were pressing him to stay on in Holland. His personal inclination was also to stay, and if possible do so in an active post under Graham, but he was struggling to make up his mind whether the opportunity to do so was outweighed by his pre-existing duty to the Queen. Of one thing, however, he was entirely certain, and that was his desire to be rid of the thankless task of trying to find horses for Graham's army.[54] The over-optimism of his initial set of requirements had quickly been replaced with a growing awareness of how difficult this task actually was. Such was the short-age of animals that demand had also driven up the prices, with up to £26 being asked, but of 200 horses presented for purchase on 13 December only 52 proved to be of any use.[55] The only positive aspect of his travels was that Taylor had at least been able to satisfy himself that the zeal of the Dutch people for the Allied cause was rather more pronounced than he had initially assumed, or than Stirum had led him to believe.

Whilst Graham continued to grapple with the confusing situation on the ground and tried to formulate a plan of campaign, Bathurst seemed to expect that he would have considerable liberty to consolidate his forces before any moves were made, and was still keen to increase their numbers by increasingly desperate expedients. On 13 December he proposed to Graham and Clancarty that the former seek to enlist up to 100 Dutchmen in each of his infantry battalions, with a sizeable bounty to be offered. A day later, having had second thoughts, he suggested that it would be more appropriate to seek to recruit any 'Flemish Soldiers in Holland, who may be inclined to enlist into the British service [. . .] as the Dutch Government may perhaps be more inclined that the force under your command should be recruited by enlisting them rather than enlisting any of the Dutch inhabitants', and that a lesser bounty should be offered.[56] He had earlier suggested to Taylor that recruits might well be found from amongst the battalion of Prussian deserters in French pay that had gone over to the insurgents at Amsterdam, but Taylor was obliged to report that both the Prince of Orange and the Duke of Brunswick were also seeking to add these men to their own forces, and that if Bathurst wanted them to be used in Holland then the best thing would be to allow the Prince to have them and distribute them by fifties amongst the Dutch battalions then being raised.[57] Neither Graham nor

Clancarty had much faith in Bathurst's latest scheme, the former because he was already finding himself obliged to weed out ineffective men from his battalions and had no wish to replace them with untrained foreign recruits, and the latter because such a move was likely to be received as an affront by the Prince of Orange and to delay the progress of the Dutch levies. In any case, Graham was able to inform Bathurst with a clear conscience on 21 December that changed conditions made it impossible to comply with such instructions.[58]

The problem that had distracted Graham's attention was Breda, or, more specifically, the exposure of its Russian garrison to French counter-attack. Having pushed forwards full of zeal in the aftermath of the 5 December planning conference, Benckendorff now found that support from the Prussians to his left and the British to his right was sadly lacking, and that he was grievously exposed. Stanhope estimated that a minimum of 8,000 men would be needed to hold Breda, and more if the ditch were to freeze.[59] Benckendorff, though, had nothing like that force, with only 1,200 infantry in the form of two battalions of the Tula Infantry Regiment and one of the 2nd Jagers, plus some cavalry who could be dismounted if necessary. For artillery, he possessed only four light pieces.[60] Fully aware that this was insufficient, Benckendorff began to appeal for reinforcements. On 15 December, he wrote to Cooke – not knowing that that officer was about to be superseded – with a request for:

> 39 pieces to arm the 13 bastions of Breda. These guns should be accompanied by 100 to 150 artillery men and at least 50 rounds for each gun. If Genl. Cooke has any infantry disposable Genl. Benckendorff will be glad to be reinforced in Breda & if Genl. Cooke should chuse [sic] to come himself Genl. Benckendorff will be happy to consider himself under Genl. Cooke's orders.[61]

This was accompanied by a report that at least 5,000 French reinforcements were on their way to Antwerp and would thus be in a position to move against him. Cooke, of course, had no means of complying and nor did Graham. His own field artillery had not yet arrived, let alone any heavy guns suitable for fortress use, but as the days went on the demands that he move to the aid of Breda continued to come in, from the Dutch authorities, from Bülow, and most of all from Benckendorff.[62]

There were two major reasons for this clamour. The first was that Benckendorff's report of French reinforcements was entirely accurate. Having learnt with displeasure that, far from leading a counter-attack,

Decaen had continued Lebrun's policy of withdrawal, Napoleon had recalled him to Paris and replaced him with Maison, commander of I Corps. Reinforced by elements of the Young Guard, Maison was to secure Antwerp by means of constructing an extensive entrenched camp to support the fortifications; in this way, Napoleon believed that the 30,000 men that he planned to assemble there would be able to resist twice their number. As a prerequisite, however, Maison was ordered first to recapture Breda and so restore communication with the garrison at Gorcum. Macdonald had also had an eye on Breda, but had not been able to bring together sufficient troops to make any advance towrds it due to the continued threat posed by Bülow, as well as his commitments further south. Now, however, he was instructed to aid the new counter-offensive, not by moving directly on Breda but instead moving to the relief of Hertogenbosch, which was under attack by part of Bülow's corps. Napoleon hoped this would prevent the Prussians coming to Benckendorff's aid. Graham's British, meanwhile, the Emperor dismissed as amounting to no more than 4,000 men, a surprisingly accurate assessment of the effective forces then available.[63]

The second reason that so much was expected of Graham, however, was that whilst Napoleon had recognized that the British had only limited numbers, Graham's own allies had received an entirely erroneous impression as to the strength and capabilities of the British force. This, to a considerable degree, was Bathurst's doing, since the Secretary of State had been keen from the outset to make the British force appear as powerful as possible – as evidenced, amongst other things, in his desire to see Dutch recruits in red coats – and was less than pleased with Taylor's honest reporting to the Dutch of the true nature of Graham's command. As early as 7 December, whilst in the same letter bemoaning the actual weakness of Graham's corps, he told Taylor that he had 'been a little too candid in the description of the troops we are sending out. They are better than any which will appear there, and you must cry them up.'[64] This Taylor had the good sense not to do, but Clancarty had no such misgivings – or grasp of military realities – and was soon touting the figure of 10,000 men to both the Dutch and the Prussians, who in turn passed it on to Benckendorff.[65]

For all his calls for help, however, Benckendorff was for the most part forced to rely on his own resources when the French began their forward movement on 19 December. With 6,000 men of his 6th Young Guard Division, 800 cavalry and 30 guns, Général de Division François Roguet marched out of Antwerp and drove in the Russian advance picket at Wuust-wezel, before appearing before the walls of Breda the following day. During the course of the night of 20–21 December, French guns began to bombard the town, and on the 21st two unsuccessful attacks were launched against the town gates; thankfully, at this date, the ditch remained unfrozen and so Benckendorff could concentrate his defence.

Both Graham and Bülow received renewed calls to come to the aid of the garrison, with the Dutch very keen that the French not recapture the historic fortress. In practical terms, however, neither commander could do a great deal. The British were not yet fully organized, and were too badly dispersed to make any immediate move. Graham was in any case loath to send men to Breda, arguing that 'Nothing would so entirely cripple the exertion of this Corps for ever as having the regiments parcelled out in garrisons without a chance of getting them back.'[66] Rather than move directly to aid Benckendorff and risk having his troops pulled into a siege, he thought that a movement on Roosendaal would relieve Breda just as well, but such an advance would not be possible until a reasonable force could be assembled. This movement would also require cavalry to help screen the advance, which would pass though open country, and Graham was understandably unwilling to rely on the mercurial Cossacks. Bülow, too, could not immediately provide any help and continued to express concern about the potential threat posed by Macdonald against his left flank, although Generalmajor Karl-August von Krafft's brigade was redirected from Hertogenbosch to move via Heusden and attack the French rear. Meanwhile, the night of 21–22 December saw the arrival of 500 Dutch levies and eighteen heavy cannon, which had already been on their way from Geertruidenberg, and by morning on the 22nd the guns were in place on the ramparts and ready to reply to the French bombardment.[67]

Unclear if the French advance on Breda was an end in itself, or whether it formed part of a larger offensive, Graham pulled in his forces to cover Willemstad, to which place he would shift his headquarters on 25 December. From here, he could potentially also move to relieve Breda.[68] Meanwhile, conscious that he must at least do something to aid Benckendorff, he sent a patrol out towards Roosendaal with orders to give out that it represented the vanguard of a 5,000-man relief force.[69] It was a slender effort, but it served to complement Prussian actions since Bülow had already set in motion a similar *ruse de guerre*, allowing a message to fall into French hands that purported to announce his imminent arrival at Breda with 15,000 men. Roguet had meanwhile been reinforced by more cavalry, under Général de Division Charles Lefebvre-Desnouëttes, who was his senior and assumed command. Already disillusioned by the failure of their assaults on the 21st and of the arrival of the Dutch artillery, the French commanders now received intelligence of Krafft's advance and assumed that this was the vanguard of Bülow's whole corps. The Allied bluff was therefore successful and led to a French withdrawal, accelerated by the arrival of Prussian cavalry.[70]

Breda was therefore safe, at least for the moment, but the fact that Graham and his '10,000 men' had been unable to do anything to aid the defence stood as an obvious mark against him so far as his allies were concerned. Clancarty, notwithstanding that it was his exaggeration of Graham's force that had led to so much being expected of it, now helpfully pointed out 'How detrimental it would be to the cause of the Allies in general, but now especially to that part of it, which we are particularly engaged to advance, that any serious check or even impediment, should be suffered to exist between the Commandants of the different bodies of troops of the allies.' Graham should be aware, Clancarty went on, of the boost to French morale, 'and the equal discouragement of the insurrectionary spirit of the [Dutch] people' as a result of Roguet's movement against Breda, and advised Graham to take measures to keep the French more closely pinned in Antwerp.[71] Fully aware that his inability to help would be counted against him, Graham complained to Bathurst that the exaggeration of his forces had 'placed me in a very unfavourable point of view to the allies, which is unlucky as first impressions are not easily removed',[72] but any recriminations were swiftly overtaken by a renewed crisis. Scarcely had the French withdrawn from before its walls than Benckendorff announced that he had received orders to evacuate Breda without further ado and reunite with Wintzingerode's corps at Düsseldorf.[73] Since the French forces were still in the field, this would again expose Breda to attack, and it was clear that a replacement garrison would have to be provided. So far as the Allies were concerned, Graham's troops, since they were apparently not fit to take the field, seemed the obvious choice.

This development placed Graham in a new quandary, for not only did he remain averse to tying any of his meagre forces up in garrisons, but now the weather began to turn even colder and created a new fear that the waterways might freeze and thus open up much of the country to a renewed French advance. Such a freeze would also render the fortress ditches useless, and if that were the case Graham felt that he would have his work cut out just to hold Willemstad. Carmichael Smyth was ordered to lay out fieldworks that would 'keep the enemy at some distance from this town [as] we should be in a bad state indeed if forced back into it for the accommodation for troops is scarcely equal to what an ordinary garrison would consist of', and the ditch would be useless if there was a freeze.[74] All this meant that he did not feel able to send any troops to Breda, and considered in any case that doing so would create far too long a defensive line for so small a force. Taylor, who had at last received his much-desired permission to join Graham's staff, saw it as a straight choice between Breda or Willemstad, and whilst deeming it a 'great evil' if the former fell, considered it impossible to give the latter up. All that could be hoped was that Benckendorff could be persuaded to stay long enough for a garrison to be assembled from somewhere, to which end Graham urged Clancarty and the Prince of Orange to each exert such influence as they possessed to delay the departure of the Russian troops.[75]

In the meantime, in order to have a full appraisal of the situation, and presumably to show willing, Graham sent both Mackenzie and Carmichael Smyth to Breda in order to add their voices to the appeals, but also to make an appraisal of the feasibility of defending the place and assess what forces would be required to do so. Neither officer formed a positive opinion, with Mackenzie reiterating the view that Breda was 'totally untenable by a small garrison in time of frost' and also acquainting Graham with the troubling fact that the fortifications – and particularly the ditch – were far less significant obstacles than had been thought.

Up until this point Graham had assumed that the Breda defences were of a similar nature to those at Bergen-op-Zoom; since this was not the case he now failed to understand why the Dutch wanted to defend it at all.[76] This, of course, missed the historical significance of the town, hard-won from the Spaniards during the Eighty Years War, and so the Dutch continued to send troops there. Carmichael Smyth, after his visit on 27 December, was 'much gratified at seeing three new raised Dutch battalions' serving alongside the Russians, and was more sanguine about the defensibility of the place,[77] but his interview with Benckendorff was less successful. As Graham reported to Clancarty, the Russian general was:

> a lively, clever, active fellow and he knows it & decides for others with all the fatuité of a conceited Frenchman. He told Col. Smyth that he was quite clear that I should give up Tholen & till I was in sufficient force, I should come to Breda and afterwards take up a position at Roosendaal to threaten Bergen-op-Zoom and Antwerp & cover Tholen. This would do very well with a large force but is in no way suitable to mine.[78]

The only way Graham felt that he could aid Breda would be to throw his entire force into the place, which would expose it to utter disaster if the town were to fall. Accordingly, he was only prepared to take such a course on receipt of a direct order from the British government.

In the event, however, things did not come to such a pass. Whilst Wintzingerode's concentration at Düsseldorf would deprive the Allies in Holland of the services of Benckendorff's flying column, it would also occupy the attention of Macdonald's forces and thereby cover Bülow's left. With the Prussians now relieved of the threat from the south, and freshly equipped with shoes and greatcoats from British stocks, there was now nothing to prevent them making a forward movement with a large force, and Bülow announced his intention of doing so in a letter of 25 December.[79] Taylor was sent to Breda in order to emphasize that Graham could not, and would not, move his whole force there, leading to a stormy three-sided interview with Benckendorff and the Dutch Governor, General van der Plaat, but was eventually able to convince them that it made far more sense for the Prussians to occupy the place than the British, since Bülow already intended to make it his depot for future operations.[80] This left only a short window of vulnerability between Benckendorff's departure – which could not be delayed beyond 2 January – and the arrival in force of the Prussians. In order to fill this gap, and as a temporary measure only, Gibbs's Second Brigade, less the 2/25th left at Klundert, was moved down to help hold Breda until Bülow could furnish a Prussian garrison.[81] This still represented a risk for Graham, but, happily, a temporary thaw set in, removing the possibility of an assault across a frozen ditch. By 7 January, Bülow had established his headquarters at Breda and the arrival of significant numbers of Prussians rendered Gibbs's presence superfluous.[82]

On the same day as Bülow reached Breda, the 2nd KGL Hussars finally disembarked, and this, along with the arrival of his field artillery, meant that Graham was at last in a position to participate in active operations alongside the Prussians. Plans were set in motion for a combined advance, but it was abundantly clear that the British were to be the junior partners in the forthcoming operations. In part, this was an inevitable consequence of the limited numbers that Graham could commit to field service, but the inability of the British to come to the aid of Breda, coming immediately after the overstating of the means at Graham's disposal, had also cast doubts on their reliability, albeit to a greater extent with the Dutch than with the Prussians. Undoubtedly, Graham had the truth of it when he cautioned Clancarty that 'it may sometimes be very politick to deceive an enemy but it can never be so to exaggerate one's force to friends'.[83]

Chapter V

'We Drove Them Before Us Like Sheep'

THAT BÜLOW WAS PREPARED to take responsibility for the defence of Breda, even to the extent of establishing his own headquarters there, is understandable enough in light of the strategy agreed upon at the 5 December meeting. The city was at the centre of a good road network, and was an obvious base for a further advance. What does, perhaps, come as a surprise, is the fact that the Prussian commander now declared himself prepared – at least for the moment – to subordinate his own ambitions for a rapid advance into Flanders in favour of cooperation with the British in a movement against Antwerp. There were certainly sound operational reasons for such a movement, for it was now clear to Bülow that Graham's corps was insufficient either to take Antwerp on its own, or even to mask Maison's reinforced garrison satisfactorily. Thus, even if the Prussians were to drive straight on towards Brussels, troops would need to be left to cover their flank against any movement from Antwerp. Since Bülow was still trying to recover the detachments left to besiege Gorcum and Hertogenbosch, the last thing that he needed to do was to shed yet more troops. What was more, although Allied preparations to cross the Rhine by Wintzingerode at Düsseldorf and Blücher around Koblenz seemed likely to draw Macdonald's forces away to the south, this would take some time. All in all, logic dictated that it was far better to accept a temporary delay and join the British in dealing with Maison before moving on into Flanders.

There were other reasons why it was in Bülow's interest to cooperate with Graham, and some of them had a hidden sting to them. Bülow struck up a good personal relationship with Graham when the two men eventually met, and was genuinely grateful that he had detached Gibbs's brigade to help hold Breda until the Prussians could arrive. He was also impressed with Graham's resolve, and by the fact that the British commander was entirely prepared to waive his seniority in rank and to subordinate his forces to the Prussians if necessary. Graham's gesture was no more than a reflection of the relative sizes of the two forces, but it was a very timely one since Bülow was at the time furious that Wintzingerode had just been promoted to full general of cavalry, thus making him Bülow's senior.[1] Wintzingerode's subsequent attempts to pull rank – backed both by the Crown Prince and Emperor Alexander – led to a complete breakdown in relations between the Prussian commander and his nominal seniors within the Army of the North, fuelling his desire to be done with the lot of them and unite his forces with Blücher's at the first opportunity.[2] Whilst this was very much a personal matter, albeit one that would eventually have wider repercussions, Bülow's other motive for cooperation with the British was a matter of state policy, developed with half an eye on the post-war shape of Europe and the relative positions of Prussia and Holland within it. To understand its implications, it is first necessary to see how Britain's own plans for the Low Countries had also developed since Castlereagh's manifesto of the previous July.

By the end of 1813, with Schwarzenberg and Blücher poised to cross the Rhine and Wellington already over the Pyrenees, it was clear that whatever French state emerged from the war – be it a bobtailed empire, a restored Bourbon monarchy, or something else again – was going to have frontiers not too different to those of 1793. In order to establish a sustainable peace it was therefore essential to ensure that France remained within those frontiers and all the more so if a peace was concluded that ensured the survival of the current regime. This in turn required strong states on the French borders and, in the case of the Low Countries, meant one of two alternatives. The first was a return to the situation prior to 1792, whereby the Belgian provinces were ruled by one of Europe's great powers; the second was the absorption of those provinces into an expanded United Netherlands ruled by the House of Orange. In the first instance, the former prospect seemed more appealing to Britain, and Castlereagh advocated it in a memorandum of 5 November 1813. It soon became apparent, though, that Vienna had mixed feelings about resurrecting the Austrian Netherlands, which had been a source of more trouble than pride to the Habsburgs. Thus, the alternative of a strong United Netherlands based on an expanded Holland increasingly began to seem like the best solution and by January 1814, when he travelled to join the Allied headquarters, this was Castlereagh's stated aim, although the precise borders of the new state remained undefined. The Prince of Orange preferred extensive annexations to the south that would link his Dutch and German lands, whilst Castlereagh was still willing to accept that some of the southern provinces might remain French, pass to a third power, or perhaps form a principality for one of the Habsburg archdukes. One thing that the Foreign Secretary was certain of, however, was that the new United Netherlands must contain Antwerp.[3]

Off the back of this growing commonality of war aims, the Prince of Orange's hopes of a match between his heir and Princess Charlotte of Wales, only daughter of the Prince Regent and thus heir presumptive to the British crown, held growing attractions. Politically, the match was advantageous for both parties since such a union would give increased prestige to the Dutch in their relations with the Allies and in any eventual peace settlement, making it easier for shared Anglo-Dutch aims to become reality. For Britain, it also ensured that the Low Countries would be dominated by a client state closely bound to British interests. However, the Prince Regent also had personal motives for wishing to see his daughter married. The Regent had been estranged from his wife, Caroline of Brunswick, since shortly after their own marriage, and the two were now bitter foes. Charlotte, repelled by her father's neglectful and boorish behaviour, was a natural source of support for her mother, and with his daughter safely married off the Regent felt it far more likely that he would be able to get the better of his wife, perhaps even to the extent of being able to obtain a divorce. That the seventeen-year-old Charlotte was as beloved by the crowd as her father was despised may also have helped sway the Regent's decision to favour the Orange match. In any event, the young Hereditary Prince was recalled from the Peninsula, and heavy-handed pressure was placed on Charlotte to accept him as a suitor. Historical opinion of the Hereditary Prince tends to be coloured, in British eyes at least, by his conduct as a corps commander under Wellington in 1815. Yet his undoubted errors in that role stemmed from inexperience rather than any particular character defect, whereas his military role in the Peninsula, as a lieutenant colonel on the staff, gave him the potential to shine in 1813 as the dashing young hero. Unfortunately, however, young William did not have the looks to match, and his character was still that of a youth rather than a mature prince. Charlotte, something of a tomboy, something of an intellectual, and certainly older than her years, was not impressed. Only direct intervention by the Regent forced the matter until the Princess, placed on the spot in public, gave her consent on 12 December 1813.[4]

It may initially seem unusual that the planned marriage, news of which soon began to leak out, should have any impact on the operations of a Prussian army corps. However, so far as Prussia's Chancellor, Karl-August von Hardenberg, and the officers of the Prussian General Staff were concerned, the Hanover–Orange marriage plans created a situation that might well develop to Prussia's long-term advantage. For a start, and irrespective of who the Hereditary Prince might marry, the establishment of the Prince of Orange on the throne of an enlarged United Netherlands would create a vital barrier state between Prussia and France, behind which Prussia could consolidate its intended position of dominance in Germany. The House of Orange was already tied to Prussia's Hohenzollerns through several generations of intermarriage, but now – and here the hopeful Prussians moved into guesswork – there was the potential for an Orange succession to the British throne that might, in the future, facilitate the detachment of Hanover from the British crown and into Prussia's orbit. The last bit was wishful thinking, since neither the British nor the Dutch wished to see a union of the two crowns. The details were still being thrashed out, but the hypothetical first son of Charlotte and William's marriage would inherit in Britain whilst, in different proposals, the Dutch throne would ultimately pass either to their second son, to the Hereditary Prince's younger brother Frederick, or to the German branch of the Orange dynasty.[5] Thus, Prussian long-term hopes were illusory, but the short-term goals were perfectly reasonable as both Britain and Prussia wanted a strong post-war United Netherlands. Prussia was less concerned than Britain as to whether or not the Dutch barrier state included Antwerp, but was prepared to accept that it would, and help bring that situation about, if it ensured a common commitment. The fact that doing so meant that Prussia would be seen to be doing Britain a favour – Castlereagh having made a direct request for Prussian help in taking Antwerp – meant that Prussia might also expect some future quid pro quo in return. This new alignment of interests meant that, with Breda secure, Bülow and Graham could begin planning for a joint attack on Antwerp.

The two generals met at Breda on 8 January, with Graham being accompanied by Taylor, in whom he had detected qualities that would have made him an excellent chief of staff had such a post existed within the British system, writing that 'his judgement & arrangements are so clear & good on all occasions – and he seems to like service as if he had liv'd always in a Camp instead of a Court'.[6] It was the skills of the court that were perhaps most useful on this occasion, although Graham's own tact evidently did wonders, and Taylor remarked on the 'handsome and liberal manner' in which he repeated his resolve to waive his own senior rank and 'conform in all respects to General Bülow's wishes'. In a more worrying development, Taylor also observed that 'the wind has come to the N.E., and the frost has increased. Our ride from Breda yesterday evening, partly in the dark and across such roads, was not a pleasant one.'[7] With the weather continuing to worsen, the coming operations would represent a testing ordeal for the troops taking part in them. Such omens aside, however, the meeting was a success and a clear plan of operations was decided upon. With Macdonald apparently concentrating his forces away to the south, in consequence of Blücher's Army of Silesia having crossed the middle Rhine on 1 January, Maison's forces around Turnhout and Hoogstraten were to be the main target. Bülow's hope 'was, by a major flank movement, to cut them off, if possible, from their retreat to Antwerp'.[8] It is important to note that this point was understood by the British staff from the outset, and that no mention of actually attacking Antwerp – or even reconnoitring the place – was made at this stage. Later, the objectives of the operation, as differently understood by the two allies, would become something of a contentious issue.

Bülow had three of his four brigades available – formations that would, in any other army, have been considered as divisions, each containing three regiments of infantry with supporting cavalry and guns – as well as powerful reserves of cavalry and artillery. Allowing for detachments to mask Gorcum and to hold the towns in his rear, this meant that the Prussians could commit to the operation '19,000 men of which about 14,400 infantry, in 24 Battns. of 600 each upon a general average, beside some Light Corps'.[9] Because Macdonald's exact movements were still unclear, Bülow sent considerable numbers of light troops as far south as Venlo in order to cover his left and obtain early warning in the event of Macdonald attempting to move north-wards. In an ideal world, Wintzingerode's corps would have covered this flank but the Russian had not yet crossed the Rhine in any force, much to Bülow's disgust. The British would play a subsidiary part, covering the right flank of the advance with 5,500 men; Taylor, for one, did not expect them to see much action unless, as he feared, the French were themselves to make an advance of their own, perhaps with a view to relieving Bergen-op-Zoom.[10] In order to control his troops better during the forthcoming operations, Graham decided to implement a temporary divisional system, elevating Cooke and Mackenzie to command the First and Second Divisions respectively. Cooke would control the First and Guards Brigades, Mackenzie the Second and Light, and each division would also have a battery of field artillery attached to it. Lord Proby replaced Cooke in command of the Guards Brigade, whilst Gibbs moved across to command the Light Brigade in lieu of Mackenzie. Taylor, in turn, was earmarked to replace Gibbs, but this appointment would be changed before he could take it up.[11]

As well as being reorganized, Graham's command had been reinforced, with two battalions sent from Leith coming ashore just as the new operation was about to begin. The 2/21st was delayed by bad weather, with two trans-ports only narrowly escaping shipwreck, and on landing was further delayed by the rivers being choked by floating ice which, according to Sperling, who was supervising bridging operations near Oudenbosch, 'came down the river in large sheets with much force'.[12] Until the conditions improved all the 2/21st could do was sit tight at the village of Buytensluys, opposite

Willemstad, where the battalion's officers 'began to practise the Dutch accomplishments of drinking gin and smoking, for which we had a convenient excuse in the humidity and coldness of the climate', or, by way of variety, tried their hands at skating.[13]

On the other hand, the 2/78th, having landed on 10 January, was able to join the advance, being assigned to the Second Brigade. Unlike the 2/73rd, which had lost its Highland status in 1809, the 2/78th remained a kilted battalion and had seen extensive active service in the Mediterranean during the early part of the Napoleonic Wars, fighting at Maida in 1806 and in Egypt in 1807. After returning home in 1808 it had functioned as a feeder unit for the 1/78th in the East Indies, and, to Graham's considerable regret, had sent off a strong reinforcing draft only days before the orders came to prepare for service in Holland.[14] There were few Maida veterans in the ranks eight years on, but the 320 rank and file who arrived in Holland were a valuable reinforcement: a 'stout, healthy body of young men', well led, and commanded by the veteran Colonel John Macleod.[15] Macleod's arrival was particularly timely for Graham, who was now short of a brigade commander after Skerrett had managed to injure himself in a fall from his horse. Macleod's rank and experience made him the obvious replacement, but so as not to take him away from his battalion he was given command of the Second Brigade rather than replacing Skerrett directly. Taylor, instead of receiving the Second Brigade as planned, now replaced Skerrett at the head of the First and was enthused by the chance to enjoy an active command at last.[16]

Those troops intended to participate in the British share of the advance were mostly concentrated at Roosendaal on 11 January, although the 2/78th were still marching up to join, and spent the night of the 10th at Oudenbosch, which was also the location of Graham's headquarters. As well as the 2/21st, ice-bound at Buytensluys, the 2/37th and 1st Royal Veterans did not join the advance.[17] Roosendaal had only been secured on the 9th, when the Light Company of the 2/35th helped evict a French vedette, although Austin thought the operation mismanaged, and believed that the French troopers could have been captured if more care had been taken; as it was the advance was made in plain sight, up the road, and the Frenchmen had saddled up and were away by the time the infantry got close. On the evening of the 10th, Mackenzie took the Light Brigade and two squadrons of Lieutenant Colonel Baron Linsingen's 2nd KGL Hussars on ahead to secure Calmthout, a village only twelve miles from Antwerp and believed to be still held by the French. In fact, the French had already evacuated the place, and the men of the Light

Brigade were able not only to move in but also to push picquets out beyond the village, towards Antwerp.[18]

Private Morris's narrative presents a rather disorientated picture of this phase of operations, with his dates somewhat confused. His account of the freezing night on Brasschaat Heath is nevertheless unmistakable as such, and repeats the belief then prevalent that the French were mounting either a renewed attack against Breda or else were trying to throw additional forces into Bergen-op-Zoom.[19]

> We took up our position on a common, on the line of road which they were expected to traverse, and waited for them some hours, exposed to the drifting snow, and a bitter northeast wind. Some dragoons were dispatched in search of the enemy; and on their return, we learned that the French had been already encountered, and beaten, by some of the Dutch troops, at Westwesel [sic]. After this disappointment, we separated, and sought shelter from the cold. Our commissariat arrangements were as yet tolerably good, the bread and meat being served out with the utmost regularity; but the food, if not eaten directly, became frozen so very hard, as to require great force to break it, and I have seen a piece of meat actually freezing on one side, while it was frying on the other that was when they were cooking their meat at the fire, lit on the ground, in the open air.[20]

In fact, the suffering was for nothing and the French advance a false alarm: far from making an offensive movement, the French were concentrating closer to Antwerp in order to meet the Allied attack.

For the remainder of Graham's troops, 11 January marked the beginning of the operation proper, as they set out to march the twelve miles from Roosendaal to Calmthout. For those involved, the over-riding memory would be of the weather, which had worsened further since Graham and Taylor's uncomfortable ride back from Bülow's headquarters. Morris, who had made the march the day before, described how the flooding of land that was already frozen, followed by further severe frosts, meant that:

> successive layers of ice were formed, of which the top surface not always being sufficiently strong to bear us, we would go down to the next and have to wade through the water: and whenever we came to dry ground, or firm ice, the trowsers would instantly freeze, making them uncomfortable for the rest of the journey. The hardships we suffered in these marches, would be sufficient to kill any

solitary traveller, but there being a large body of us together, we kept each other alive.[21]

Once the ice had been broken, the result was 'a slushy mixture of mud, ice, and water', which made progress extremely hard and uncomfortable.[22] For the troops following, over roads churned up by those who had gone ahead, the conditions must surely have been even worse, and worse again for the men of the 2/78th, toiling up from the rear. The highlanders did not take their place with the rest of their brigade until the evening of the 12th, by which time the Second Division had been pushed onwards to Cappellen, after a forced march estimated by one of those who made it as having totalled thirty miles – in fact, it was more like seventeen, but the exaggeration is surely forgivable under the circumstances.[23] Until Colonel Macleod and his battalion joined, it is not clear who had command of the Second Brigade: quite possibly Gibbs remained with it until Macleod joined and only transferred to the Light Brigade thereafter.

The other feature that was remarked upon, at least by those not entirely preoccupied with the weather and the roads, was the fact that it was becoming increasingly clear that fighting was under way off to the left. Contrary to Morris's belief that this involved Dutch troops, it was of course Bülow's Prussians who were engaged, having moved out of Breda on the 10th in three columns. Of these, the leftmost under Generalmajor Karl von Borstell was to advance directly on Hoogstraten whilst Generalmajor August von Thümen's brigade, forming the centre column, was to move via Zundert on Wuustwezel and Loenhout. Finally, Generalleutnant Adolf von Oppen, with his own reserve cavalry and Generalmajor Karl von Krafft's brigade, was initially to follow Thümen before swinging further to his right so as to cut the French off from Antwerp. From the outset, however, things had not gone to plan. Like the British, the Prussians were hampered by the awful weather and poor roads. Because of these delays, it was not until 11 January that Bülow was in a position to launch a serious attack, and then only with the commands of Borstell and Thümen since Oppen had still not yet come up. Finding it impossible to move his troops by the planned route, Oppen had diverted further to his right, expecting to follow in Graham's tracks, but instead found himself ahead of the British main body. It was the appearance of these unknown troops, taken at first to be French, that had led to the Light Brigade spending the night of the 10th on Brasschaat Heath. Oppen, for his part, likewise began deploying for battle in the assumption that Mackenzie's troops were the enemy. Thankfully, the mistake was realized before any harm was done and Oppen redirected his march back to his left. The confusion was understandable considering that the men of all three armies were wrapped up in their greatcoats: this made it extremely hard for the British to distinguish Prussians from French, whilst 'the Prussians inseparably connected a scarlet uniform with British troops',[24] and assumed that if no red was visible then any unknown troops were French. Under such circumstances, this would not be the last case of mistaken identity.

The main French forces in the field consisted of the same troops who had made the initial movement against Breda. Roguet had half his infantry concentrated at Hoogstraten, with two more battalions at Wuustwezel to cover his left. To the right, the French position extended as far as Turnhout, which was held by a full brigade with cavalry support. The organization of I Corps was still incomplete, and most of its strength was made up of garrison forces, but the equivalent of a weak division was available, under Ambert, as a mobile reserve based on Antwerp. Aware that the Allies were moving, Roguet pushed a brigade forwards from Hoogstraten on the morning of the 11th, which ran into Borstell's advancing Prussians near Minderhout. The Prussians were eventually able to secure that town, and the defeated French fell back on Hoogstraten where Roguet was concentrating his forces. By midday, Borstell was in a position to assault Hoogstraten, but the French made good use of the defensive terrain and it was not until near nightfall, after a heavy artillery bombardment and the commitment of reserves, that the Prussians secured the town. Meanwhile, Thümen had advanced as far as Wuustwezel, from which place his troops had evicted two French battalions. Oppen's wayward column also regained contact with the main Prussian force by late afternoon, whereupon Bülow left Krafft's infantry at Wuustwezel in reserve, but pushed some of Oppen's cavalry up as far as Westmalle. Being thoroughly exhausted, the Prussian dragoons settled down and neglected to post adequate vedettes, with the result that they were surprised and dispersed by a French counter-attack around 21.00 that night.

Having marched hard, suffered substantial casualties, and now been on the receiving end of a dangerous counter-attack, Bülow assumed that the French remained full of fight and that he would be able to continue his offensive on the morning of the 12th. In fact, Maison had ordered a retreat, and his subordinates were able to extricate their forces successfully during the remaining hours of darkness, less 600 casualties sustained during the 11th.

By the morning of the 12th, Roguet had pulled two brigades back to the outskirts of Antwerp, where they were joined by Ambert to prepare a defensive position in advance of the city's own works. The main line stretched from Merxem to Deurne, with outposts thrown out as far as

Schilde to cover the left. Roguet's third brigade, pulled in from Turnhout, had fallen back to Lier along with the bulk of the French cavalry. From here they could cover the Brussels road, and would be joined by Général de Division Pierre Barrois's 4th Young Guard Division which had been ordered up from Brussels in order to block any further Prussian advance in that direction. Maison, indeed, believed that this was just what the Allies intended, and planned in this event to withdraw his active forces from Antwerp in order to prevent them being tied down in a siege and thus become unavailable for the defence of France proper. In fact, Bülow's revised plans for the 12th saw Borstell advancing towards Lier whilst Thümen moved on Brasschaat to link with Graham's advance. Wrong-footed by the French withdrawal, the Prussians were initially somewhat at a loss and it was some time before the changed nature of the situation became apparent.[25]

Because of the unexpected French withdrawal, 12 January was primarily taken up with outpost fighting as the Allies sought to locate the new French defensive line and, once they had done so, to push it further back towards Antwerp. The bulk of the fighting again fell to the Prussians, whose advance – by Thümen on the right and Borstell on the left – eventually shoved the French back across the Klein Schijn brook and inflicted a further 500 casualties on Roguet's guardsmen. Graham, meanwhile, having concentrated his forces at Calmthout and Cappellen in accordance with Bülow's original plan, and having heard nothing since, was eventually compelled to send Stanhope to re-establish contact with the Prussian headquarters and find out just what his allies now intended to do. By the time an answer was received, however, it was too late to do anything but make arrangements for the following day. In accordance with the new Allied plan, Bülow moved to concentrate his forces at Brasschaat, and Graham his at Cappellen. From these points, Krafft, Thümen and Mackenzie, forming the left, centre and right respectively, were to attack the French position between Wijnegem and Merxem on the morning of 13 January. Borstell, whose troops had seen heavy fighting on the 11th and 12th, was to form a reserve whilst Cooke was to cover the Allied right against any potential sortie by the French garrison of Fort Lillo. The objective was to 'complete the reconnaissance by driving the enemy into Antwerp'.[26]

This, then, sets the scene for the fighting on the 13th that would see Graham's troops in serious action for this first time. The question remains, though, as to whether they could, or should, have been able to engage the French at an earlier stage in the operations. The author of *Letters from Germany and Holland* certainly thought that an opportunity had been missed, recording how:

the Prussians, who had advanced at the same time from Breda, came up with the Enemy at Turnhout, a village considerably on our left, when a severe action took place. We heard the firing and saw the smoke, but either from our ignorance of the ground or uncertainty as to the number of the Enemy, we were prevented from giving that assistance which it was afterwards ascertained to have been in our power to give, and that with effect.

He then goes on to record how the army remained stationary in front of Calmthout for the greater part of 12 January, opining that 'had we known how matters stood, we might easily have cut off the Enemy's retreat, as we were considerably in advance, and between him and Antwerp'.[27]

These are major criticisms, but they fall down on several points. In the first instance, relating to a failure to give aid to the Prussians at Turnhout – by which it can only be assumed the author meant the action around Hoogstraten on 11 January – there seems to be little case even to answer. Graham was under instructions from Bülow, to whom he had voluntarily subordinated himself, to move on Calmthout and Cappellen and understood his main purpose to be that of screening the Prussian right flank.[28] To do otherwise would have meant deviating from that agreed plan. We have already seen how mistaken identity had already almost caused a friendly fire incident, and for Graham to have diverted his march towards Hoogstraten could well have led to a similar, or worse, error as his path intersected the Prussian line of advance.

As to the second point, relating to the non-involvement of the British in the fighting on the 12th, it may with hindsight be regretted that Graham did not move until he had received new instructions from Bülow, but his decision to remain stationary until the French and Prussian positions were clarified is entirely understandable considering the limited forces at his disposal. Since Bülow had taken upon himself the conduct of Allied operations, it also behove him to give instructions to Graham as he, Bülow, saw fit, not to wait until the British commander asked for them. Since, as we shall see, the lack of orders for the 12th was not the only such failure, Graham had a fair point when he subsequently complained that 'I cannot say that I am satisfied with the manner in which our communications have been kept up during the whole operation.'[29] Irrespective of apportioning blame for the lack of Allied coordination, it is in any case nonsensical to say that a movement on the 12th could have cut the French off from Antwerp, because they had already established their positions there by the morning of that day.

Certainly, most of his subordinates saw little to fault in Graham's dispositions, with Carmichael Smyth stating that the retreating enemy 'avoided our troops altogether notwithstanding every exertion was made to intercept him'.[30] This perhaps overstates the case a little, since it would have been hard for the British to intercept any French force unless it moved via Cappellen and Brasschaat. Then again, this was the sector that Graham had been assigned to cover and he cannot be faulted for assuming – if this was indeed his logic – that if the French were to retreat by another route then Bülow would have made provision to intercept them with his own forces. Stanhope, indeed, thought that Bülow could have done just that on 11 January, had he been quicker to grasp the nature of the enemy positions and realize that the French concentration was further to his left than he had assumed.[31] Taylor, meanwhile, thought that it was the mismanagement of Bülow's right wing under Oppen that was to blame, and that his slowness on the 10th was the cause of the Allied failure to cut off the French.[32] This in turn links in to the argument put forwards by Fortescue, who suggests that had Bülow ordered a more rapid advance on the 10th and 11th then his right wing – Oppen and Graham combined – could indeed have cut the French off from Antwerp and that 'a promising operation was wrecked by Prussian imbecility'. However, these arguments take no account of the weather and the state of the roads, which together delayed all Allied movements, and Fortescue's is also laced with the heavy anti-German sentiment, which, perhaps inevitably considering its preparation during and after the First World War, biases his account of Anglo-Prussian relations during 1814 and 1815.[33] Collectively, both Allied forces suffered delays that prevented them either destroying Roguet's force or separating it from Antwerp on the 11th; equally, both commanders were taken aback by the speed of the French retreat that night and took some time to appreciate the new situation fully. By the evening of the 12th, though, all that had changed and Graham's troops were 'on the tiptoe of expectation' as they prepared to attack the French on the morrow.[34]

The most obvious and direct route from Cappellen to the British objective at Merxem was by the main Breda–Antwerp *chaussée*. However, this axis of advance was to be used by Thümen's Prussians, advancing from Brasschaat, and the British were therefore obliged to take a more circuitous route, swinging out through Ekeren and then back to the south to attack Merxem from the flank. Meanwhile, Krafft's Prussians would attack Wijnegem at the other extremity of the French position, four miles to the south. Although they were under arms at first light, it would be late morning before

Mackenzie's troops were within reach of their objective. This much, at least, is clear, but thereafter things became confused for the participants and, as a result, confusing for the historian. Matters are not helped by the fact that many of the campaign's more observant and dependable eyewitnesses were not involved in the action, whilst the account left by Austin, who was there, is so confused as to be worse than useless. Whether through mistaken memory by the author, or muddled editing by his great-nephew who 'arranged' his account for publication, much of this passage in his narrative in fact relates to the early stages of the second action fought on the same ground nearly a month later. Graham's own report, too, is surprisingly deficient on details of the early stages of the operation, and only comes into its own when its narrative reaches the successful conclusion of events. Indeed, for the early stages of the action the most helpful account is in fact the report of Général de Division Ambert, commanding the French in Merxem, although the eyewitness accounts reproduced in Davidson's history of the 78th Highlanders give a detailed picture of the activities of both the 2/78th and the units that fought alongside it.

The village that Ambert was tasked with defending was in 1814 a narrow, straggling, collection of houses strung out along the line of the *chaussée*, which terminated a short distance beyond it and split into several lesser roads. The British were approaching the long, north-west, side of the village. To their right, on an axis a little to the south of due east, the embankment of the Sint Ferdinandsdijk cut across the lower lying ground towards the Scheldt. Less than a mile separated Merxem from the main defences of Antwerp, the outworks of which were closer still. The British advance was made with its weight on the left, this column taking as its axis a minor road that intersected with the *chaussée* towards the head of the village. The riflemen of the 95th went on ahead as a skirmish line, supported by the 2/35th, 2/52nd, and 2/78th, with the last-named battalion advancing immediately to the right of the road. The open left flank was covered by the highlanders' Light Company and by Captain James Fullerton's company of the 3/95th, deployed on the opposite side of the road. Further to the rear, also to the left of the road, were the 2/25th and 33rd. The 54th, 3/56th, and 2/73rd did not form part of this advance, and, indeed, are ignored in most relations of the battle. Private Morris's brief account of the action strongly suggests that the 2/73rd was one of the two battalions that Ambert recorded moving to cross the Sint Ferdinandsdijk to threaten the French rear later in the day. Whether the other of these was the 3/56th, is less clear: Richard Cannon's history of the regiment initially positions the battalion in support of the 2/78th, which would logically place it with the 2/25th and 33rd, but

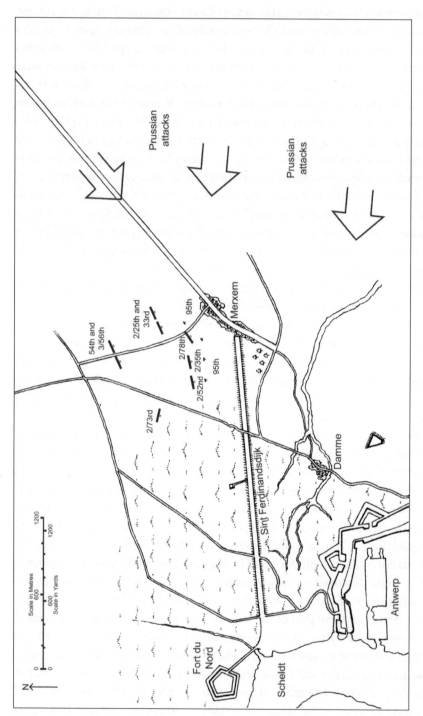

British Positions in the First Battle of Merxem

also asserts that they 'were engaged in a sharp skirmish, and had four men killed and fourteen wounded', something that could only have occurred if they were detached to the right with the 2/73rd.[35] However, neither Graham's report of the action, nor the battalion's own monthly strength returns, indicate that the 3/56th lost any men on the 13th. Furthermore, Austin's account of the fighting, which seems to have straightened its chronology out by this juncture, suggests that the 2/35th was the other battalion that crossed the dyke.[36] It seems most likely that the 54th and 3/56th were kept right back in reserve behind the 2/25th and 33rd, leaving only the 2/73rd to cover the right of the British attack.

This emphasis on the main push on the left is reinforced by the fact that both Graham and Mackenzie stationed themselves there. It was at this point that things began to get confusing for the British commanders, as a Prussian officer rode up with news that Thümen had already taken Merxem. Prior to this point, Graham had had no communication with his allies since he had set his troops in motion that morning, as he noted at the time:

> Having appraised the troops at Calmthout on the mor'g of the 13th inst & not hav'g heard any thing more from Gl. Bülow, I mov'd the Brigades as mentioned in my Despatch & at once hav'g met a staff officer of Gl. Bülow's I requested him to let the Genl. know that I had the troops ready & in their proper places to cooperate in the attack by mov'g on Mercxem [sic] by roads to the right of the Chaussée & that I sh'd be regulated as to the time by what I heard further from him or by the firing.[37]

Whether the new courier was prompted by this request for information or not, his news seemed to indicate that Graham need only close up with the Prussians in the village to consolidate what had already been won. Nevertheless, something must have appeared not to be quite right, for the Rifles continued to advance in skirmish order and soon found themselves coming under fire from the village. Evidently, something had gone horribly wrong, but previous cases of mistaken identity rendered it unclear whether the troops in the village were Frenchmen, who knew that the new arrivals were British, or Prussians who thought that the new arrivals were French. Until the matter could be cleared up, Graham ordered the Rifles to cease fire – they, not unnaturally, having responded in kind when the shooting began – but when the firing from the village increased rather than slackened in response it became clear that Merxem was in French hands.

To understand fully the reasons for this confusion, it is necessary to review the Prussian operations during the morning. Bülow was accompanying his left column, attacking towards Wijnegem. Moving forwards at 08.00, the Prussians drove the French back into the village and became engaged in close-quarters street fighting during the course of which the village changed hands several times. The French on this flank were mostly fighting in small detachments of battalion size or smaller, Maison having withdrawn another thousand infantry during the night to reinforce the position at Lier, where he had also shifted his own headquarters. Because these small bodies of French were handled aggressively under the direction of Roguet and Général de Brigade Jean-Francois Flamand, who had come up from Damme with two battalions, they delayed the Prussian advance and caused considerable confusion as to the strength and location of the enemy forces. This added to Bülow's caution, fuelling his fears for his open left flank, and as the Prussian advance slowed down the French were able to regroup at Deurne. The disruption caused by the localized French counter-attacks was considerable, with Oppen at one point having to lead his own staff, as the only mounted force available, against a party of French lancers. Under the circumstances it is not entirely surprising that Bülow was not in a position to keep track of events on his right, or to communicate with Graham.

Meanwhile, Thümen's brigade had moved forwards on the direct route from Brasschaat to Merxem, only to find its advance checked short of the village by a French battalion holding a fortified château and an abatis blocking the *chaussée*, backed by cannon in Merxem. These positions were held against the Prussians for some time by the under-strength 3/25ème Ligne, which was eventually driven back into the village. This enabled Thümen to push into the eastern extremity of Merxem. Crucially, however, he was unable to secure the whole village and Ambert and his second-in-command, Général de Brigade Antoine-Sylvain Avy, brought up the 3/58ème Ligne to evict the Prussians. Thümen nevertheless reported that he had taken Merxem, and this in turn explains why this false intelligence was passed on to Graham even though, by the time it reached him, Ambert's successful counter-attack meant that it was out of date. Prussian accounts gloss over this aspect of events, whereas pretty much every British telling of the story emphasizes it, some adding detail alleging that it was the appearance of Graham's column – mistaken for French reinforcements – that precipitated Thümen's withdrawal. In fact, the Prussians simply regrouped, brought up their artillery, and prepared to continue the fight, but it was whilst they were doing so that Graham and Mackenzie approached the village.[38]

With the advancing British now dangerously close to the French position, quick and decisive action was called for, and, after the fact, there were no shortage of accounts that claimed or bestowed the praise for it. In a sense, though, it is of no great importance whether the response came from Graham, Mackenzie or Macleod, or, indeed, whether – as seems likely – the three men were close enough together to agree quickly on the best course. Presumably having benefited from the better terrain along the road, the 2/78th was the most advanced of Graham's line battalions, and the order was rapidly given for the highlanders to charge straight ahead into the village. Retreat was not an option, Stanhope asserting that it 'would not have looked well to retire, being so near',[39] whilst to stand still and return fire would commit them to an unequal struggle against an enemy firing from cover and supported by artillery. Only shock action might restore the situation, and, to the three Scotsmen directing the British advance, the battalion best fitted to deliver it was perfectly on hand. Since Macleod was now acting as a brigadier it was Lieutenant Colonel Martin Lindsay who received the order for the 2/78th to advance, but Macleod was not prepared to let his battalion go into action without him and also made ready to join the charge, accompanied by his devoted setter, Buff. Colonel and dog took their place immediately behind the centre of the line, ranks were quickly dressed, and the battalion advanced across the snow-covered ground to the skirl of pipes.

Even before the highlanders reached Merxem, they found themselves engaged, first by skirmishers in the rough ground to the left of the road, and then by a larger body of the enemy who had pushed forwards from the shelter of the houses: this was the 3/25ème, which Ambert had thrown out to cover his threatened left flank. To the fire of the skirmishers no reply had been made save by the Light Company and Fullerton's riflemen, but the appearance of a French battalion, albeit a weak one with a bare 200 men in the ranks, required an appropriate response. The 2/78th had begun the advance in oblique echelon, but now they formed line on the leading division, halted, and opened fire. Having been heavily engaged for some time with the Prussians, and now hurried across to face a new enemy, the conscripts of the 3/25ème did not stand, and the highlanders were able to follow up their volley with a charge that carried them into the village itself. Meanwhile, the Light Company and riflemen continued to conform to the advance, but rather than entering the village detoured to their left, crossed the *chaussée*, and then swung back to re-join the main body from the Antwerp side of the village.

Although the rapidity of their advance preserved the highlanders from heavy casualties, it was by no means accomplished without loss. Macleod was badly wounded, and there were several casualties within the 2/78th, as one of its officers related in a letter written the following day:

Colonel Lindsay had his horse shot under him, and himself and the horse fell into a deep ditch, where the Colonel was obliged to leave the animal. Lieutenant W. M'Kenzie was mortally wounded in the body while gallantly cheering the 2nd Company into the village, and I am very sorry to say that he died last night, to the great regret of his brother officers. Lieutenant W. Bath was severely wounded in the left arm, just below the elbow, as he was bravely leading the 6th Company into the same village; I am happy to say that he is doing well and out of danger. Lieutenant Chisholm was slightly wounded in the left breast, but not so much as to prevent him performing his duty. Ensign Ormsby, who carried the regimental colour, was killed in the field; Sergeant Finlay took up the colours and retained them during the remaining part of the day. Captain Callie received four different balls through his greatcoat without the smallest injury to himself. Captain Sime was likewise struck by a spent ball, but not materially hurt. None of the Sergeants were hurt.[40]

In addition to the officer casualties already detailed, the 2/78th lost 9 rank and file killed, 29 wounded, and 1 missing during the operation as a whole, although only four of these are mentioned by name in the account cited above: Privates Macdonald, Simpson, McLean and Chambers.[41]

The death of Alex Macdonald was witnessed by another member of the battalion whose eyewitness account has survived, this being in the form of a letter by an anonymous sergeant of Number Three Company, whose account is clear testimony to the heavy fire taken by the highlanders as they closed with the enemy:

I had two balls through my bonnet, a third ball passed through the bottom of my halbert [*sic*], and a fourth, having struck the blade of it, bounded against my head and grazed my right cheek. The severe stroke it gave me so stupefied me and made my head so dizzy that I fell flat on my back. Every person about me thought I was killed, but I rose in a moment with renewed vigour, and thanked God for the narrow escape I had made. Just as I fell into the ranks again my next man, a fine lad Macdonald, was shot through the head. By this time our Highland blood got warm, and though infinitely inferior in number we attacked the whole 3,000 opposed to us, and drove them before us like sheep.[42]

The '3,000' is an obvious exaggeration: Ambert had perhaps half that number in Merxem, and not all of them were engaged against the British.

Nevertheless, most British accounts inflate both the number and quality of the French defenders, with Stanhope asserting that the attack had afforded the opportunity 'for some of our young troops licking the old ones of the enemy, those indeed who next to the Imperial Guard are counted their best troops'.[43] In fact, Ambert's garrison consisted of three battalions of conscripts, backed up with one of Ouvriers de la Marine.

Colonel Macleod's wound was by a musket shot in the arm, received early in the advance, perhaps from one of the French sharpshooters, who seem to have concentrated their fire on the mounted officers. Nevertheless, as Graham reported, he continued to follow the advance and 'did not quit the command of the Brigade, till he became faint from loss of blood'.[44] Less fortunate was the Colonel's dog: the officer's letter cited above goes on to relate how the setter Buff, 'notwithstanding the very warm fire from the enemy, could not be restrained, & was soon wounded by a shot, but continued to run along the line, barking and keeping an eye on his master, until another shot laid the faithful animal dead on the spot'.[45] As well as praising Macleod, Graham was also able to report that 'We have another Vimiera [sic] piper with the 78th. Gen'l McKenzie ordered him to begin to play when the Reg't advanced – a moment after he was struck and fell but continued his time – I was glad to find that he only got a severe contusion.'[46] The allusion was to Piper Clarke of the 71st, shot through the ankles at Vimeiro, who continued to play as his battalion advanced; his counterpart in the 2/78th was Piper A. Munro, 'who was wounded and unable to stand, sat where he fell & played "Johnie Cope" and "Highland Laddie" with the spirit of a true Caledonian'.[47]

Such was the extent of Graham's praise for the 2/78th that he felt obliged to stress to Bathurst that 'I have not exaggerated their merit in the smallest degree (from partiality to my countrymen)' and he hoped also that their performance might also induce the Duke of York to order the draft that had been sent off to the regiment's 1st Battalion to be redirected to the 2nd in the event that it had not already sailed for the Indies.[48] Nevertheless, it is important to place the battalion's charge – gallant though it undoubtedly was – in its wider perspective. For a start, 300-odd men of the 2/78th and 3/95th did not defeat five times their number of Frenchmen completely unaided. Graham's despatch records the efforts of Major Peter Fyers, commanding the battery attached to the Second Division, to support the attack with his guns, two of which were brought into action with good effect.[49] Moreover, the advance of the 2/25th and 33rd provided moral, if not actual, support for the charge, and the former was closely enough engaged to lose one man killed and three wounded whilst the latter had one missing. The advance of the Light Brigade on the left of the attack also provided vital support, although its only casualties were one man dead and one wounded in the 3/95th, presumably from Fullerton's company.[50] Furthermore, as Ambert makes clear, the French had been put into some confusion simply by the appearance of Graham's troops on their flank, and he had already given orders to evacuate the position and fall back to Damme.

Ambert relates how the collapse of the 3/25ème spread to the troops in the village, who had already begun to retreat from the barricade at its head:

> Our young soldiers [. . .] thought they were outflanked and retreated in disorder. Ouvriers Militaires stationed at the head of the village with artillery behind the abatis, rushed pell-mell into the village street and it was impossible to stop. I immediately removed the artillery which was found abandoned by most of the gunners and drivers.
>
> At the same time, a battalion of Scots debouched at the head of the village where I was with General Avy and fifty men who also retreated in disorder into the village despite all our efforts. All exits onto the high road were found lined with enemy skirmishers. I then begged General Avy to stand at the entrance of the village to stop and reform the column, saying he would find the detachment of Lancers of the Guard. At that moment he was struck by a bullet to the head and fell dead at my side. I moved to the Ferdinand Dam after rallying two infantry platoons to stop the enemy who could not see that this disorder of our troops continued a while behind Merksem.[51]

This French collapse created an obvious opportunity for the Allies to exploit. Most of Graham's troops were still fresh, and Thümen was moving forwards to join them. Instead an order came from Bülow for the advance to halt and for the Allied troops to prepare to withdraw.

The order to suspend operations in fact reached Graham just as the 2/78th began their advance but, being so close to the enemy position, he did not feel himself able to obey what seemed so patently nonsensical an order. Bülow's note blamed the suspension of operations on the poor state of the weather, which necessitated the Allies returning to their cantonments, but it is evident that its true cause was his growing concern for his left. The withdrawal was to begin during the late afternoon, and was to be covered by Borstell's fresh brigade, reinforced with additional Prussian cavalry and artillery.[52] Realizing that an immediate withdrawal would leave the troops in Merxem horribly exposed, Graham at once rode in search of Bülow, but by the time he had located the Prussian commander it was 16.00, the light was fading, and the Prussians had already begun to withdraw. Bülow explained his concern that his left was in danger from attack by Macdonald's corps and that 20,000 more men were needed to cover this flank; with the Prussian commander so despondent, all that Graham was able to achieve was permission for two of Thümen's battalions to re-enter Merxem and help cover the withdrawal of the forces there.[53]

Meanwhile, the British attack petered out and the French were able to withdraw, aided by the arrival of a battalion sent forwards from the Antwerp defences on the orders of Lebrun, who had been left in command there after Maison's departure. Any chance of mounting a counter-attack had, however, been lost when Roguet had moved Flamand's two Young Guard battalions from Damme earlier in the day, depriving Ambert of his only real reserve. Quite possibly, a determined advance by the British right could have cut off at least some of the French troops withdrawing from Merxem. Ambert's report notes that two British battalions, supported by cavalry and guns, did move forwards on his flank, but claims that these units halted at the Sint Ferdinandsdijk, sending forwards only skirmishers who continued to engage the French rearguard until around 15.00. Morris, on the other hand, suggests that there was more of a fight here, recalling that an initial push forwards was checked, but that 'on our again advancing the enemy immediately fled, and we pursued them even to the gates of Antwerp; but, as they opened upon us from the batteries, we, in our turn, were forced to retire'.[54] Once the French were secure in the main fortifications there was little point in a further advance, which would only have served to expose the attackers to artillery fire from the city's bastions. Some Prussian artillery was brought forwards, but fired only briefly before being withdrawn.

For the disgruntled and frustrated Graham, it now remained only to oversee the safe withdrawal of his troops, but even this – which, with the French driven back into Antwerp, should have been a straightforward affair – descended into farce and almost into tragedy. As the Allies began to pull back, the Second Brigade was withdrawn and the Light Brigade deployed to cover the withdrawal with the 2/52nd under Lieutenant Colonel Edward Gibbs, the one-eyed younger brother of the general, sent into Merxem to relieve the highlanders. However, as Shaw related, the battalion entered wearing their greatcoats and, with the Prussians clad likewise, another case of mistaken identity ensued. 'Each took the other for an enemy; but Colonel Gibbs, who was an excellent German Scholar, prevented a collision which might otherwise have taken place.'[55] Taylor also alludes to an earlier friendly fire incident, in which the Prussians on returning to Merxem fired on the

2/78th, although he must have had this story second-hand, and both he and Graham reported upon a final instance as the British were pulling back, in which, as Graham later complained, 'some Prussian cavalry actually attacked and overturn'd one of our Sprung wagons carrying wounded men' – in Taylor's understanding, this wagon was conveying the wounded Colonel Macleod.[56] All in all, it was a sad end to what had, for a moment, seemed a promising day for British arms. To be compelled to retreat when the army was so close to its greatest objective was a bitter pill to swallow, and the more so since it seemed as though the campaign had failed through the fault of others. As Graham was finding out the hard way, to be the junior partner in an alliance where the goals of the two parties did not coincide was not a situation to be envied. Nor, if he could help it, was it one to be repeated.

Chapter VI

'A Want of Bon Foi'

NOTWITHSTANDING THAT THE OPERATIONS towards Antwerp had ended in retreat, Graham and his senior officers remained in good spirits as the British troops began their withdrawal. The general feeling was that the troops had performed well – better, certainly, than had been expected – and that the fault for the unsatisfactory outcome of the operation lay firmly with the Prussians. Whilst Graham accepted that Bülow had been less enthusiastic about the operation, and had entered it with limited goals in mind, he nevertheless remained bitter about the events of 13 January, telling Bathurst that:

> there was either a want of *bon foi* [good faith] in the communications of the plan or honest cooperation in the execution – for it appears perfectly evident that [Bülow] never meant to go the length of forcing the enemy's post at Merxem or that the General employed held back when it was most important for success to push on vigorously by the Chaussée.

In retrospect, Prussian half-heartedness made Graham wonder whether or not the operation had truly been worthwhile, and he continued his letter with an assessment of its failings, merits and potential consequences:

> We have certainly got great information about the place: – & fortunately without costing us many men, & the impression of the superiority of ours, I trust, will be confirmed, for tho' there were conscripts amongst the troops at Merxem yet there were many old soldiers by the account of the prisoners, & the appearance of some K[illed] & W[ounded] lying in the street, amongst them was a Fr. officer of rank said to be a General. On the other hand, the Enemy, tho' not supposed to be ignorant of the weak points must be still more aware of those w'ch require immediate attention.[1]

The last point was a prescient one, and the French would indeed have made considerable improvements to their defences before the Allies again presented themselves before Antwerp.

Whilst Graham saw potential problems, others were still glorying in what had been achieved, and the men of the 2/78th came away from Antwerp with a very high opinion of their merits. After his recovery, Colonel Macleod, who would be made a CB for his actions on the 13th, added a note to the battalion's records to assert that:

> There were upwards of 3,000 men (the French admit of four battalions) put to the most shameful flight by the 78th, not quite 300 men, and about forty riflemen; and it may be assumed the panic struck that day into the garrison of Antwerp, prevented any subsequent sortie from the garrison till the day it was given up.[2]

The remainder of the force were scarcely less proud of what they had achieved, but this then made the retreat all the more inexplicable, leading to 'the wildest conjectures' as to its cause. By the time the news of Bülow's fear of a French movement against his left had filtered its way through the rumour mill and into the ranks of the retreating British battalions, it had taken on a rather more concrete form to the effect that 'Marshal Macdonald is on our track with eighty thousand men' and produced speculation that the army was heading for the coast in order to be whisked to safety by the Royal Navy.[3] In fact, however, Maison remained largely quiescent – much to the disgust of Napoleon, who berated him for inactivity and defeatism – and it was not until 22 January that he felt able to concentrate the divisions of Roguet and Barrois at Antwerp, with his cavalry under Général de Division Bertrand Castex thrown out to cover his front and screen his right flank. In addition, far from marching against Bülow's left, let alone moving to pursue the British, Macdonald was in fact preparing for a retreat, first to Liége and then to Namur, in consequence of the belated movements of Wintzingerode and news of the more significant advance by Blücher's Army of Silesia further to the south. Upon receipt of instructions from his Emperor, Macdonald fell back to join the forces assembling to defend France itself, leaving operations in the Low Countries to Maison's lone corps.[4]

The Allied retreat was therefore unmolested, but it was by no means easy. The weather remained as hard as it had been throughout the operation, and the cold imposed a severe toll on the exhausted troops, many of them completely new to campaigning of any sort let alone operations in conditions such as these. The result was that organization began to falter, with Shaw recording how bonds of unit cohesion began to break down:

> All the troops were overpowered with fatigue. The night was intensely cold, and before morning each man was marching as

suited his own convenience. There was but a brigade of our men in the road, but this sample of service gave me some idea of what Napoleon's army must have suffered in its retreat from Russia.[5]

On the face of it, the parallel with the retreat from Moscow seems ludicrous, but it is easy to see why those who took part in the Antwerp operations might have thought the simile entirely fitting. The winter of 1813–14 was one of the harshest on record, with frost fairs on the Thames and temperatures across Europe falling far lower than the norm, and, as we have already seen, not all of Graham's troops had received their full allowance of field equipment. Austin recorded the measures that his men were forced to resort to in order to keep warm:

> The cold was so severe that at every temporary halt the men threw themselves down on the road in heaps, with the idea that the united warmth of the mass would impart fresh vigour to their stiffened and almost frozen limbs. How those underneath, who formed the substratum of each heap upon which the incumbent group rested, escaped suffocation, it is difficult to imagine; for thirty or forty men would sometimes huddle together and form one heap [. . .] Every individual soldier in that army was as thickly covered with hoar-frost as the trees which studded the adjacent country; and the moustaches of those who wisely cultivated the hirsute appendage, as a protection against the cold, soon found their breath freeze on the hair after every expiration until the moustache became converted to a solid cake of ice. Those who shaved the upper lip had the skin scarified in a remarkable manner by the action of the frost.[6]

Even mounted officers did not escape the effects of the weather, with Stanhope recording three severe falls from his horse during the course of the operations against Antwerp, as a result of the animal losing its footing on the ice, although he escaped with nothing worse than an injured knee.[7] Major General Gibbs, indeed, eschewed riding completely and marched throughout the 15th on foot at the head of his brigade, chatting to its officers. No doubt his primary concern, in which he was successful, was to show all ranks that their general shared their hardships, but such a mode of transport was likely altogether safer than riding.[8]

Even if the conditions on the retreat were truly as bad as those suffered by the Grande Armée just over a year previously, they were of nothing like the duration and by 16 January the army was back in its cantonments. Graham had now had rather more time to think over the lessons of the operation, and although he remained positive, it was now clear to him, particularly after the retreat, that serious shortcomings had been exposed within his command, which he was obliged to report to Bathurst:

> This little march, tho' it will probably increase the sick list, will do us all good in future, as it show'd everybody the necessity of attending strictly to all the established rules of the service, which, in such weak Battn's, as are supposed to be scarcely applicable to service, are oft to be neglected. From which a confusion about returns has arisen, that I could not have believed possible amongst British troops. There is a total want of system in the conduct of many of the battn's & the number of officers is quite a nuisance. For the less officers have to do the more difficult it is to make them do that little. But now that the troops are more collected, a few days will do a great deal to get the better of the bad habits that have occasioned so much trouble. We should go on much better too if all the boys were to be sent home to the depots of their Regt's.
>
> There is nothing worse than being encumbered with useless mouths on a service requiring the power of bearing fatigue. It is a sacrifice of the health of fine lads who ought soon grow up to be soldiers & it gives a nominal strength on paper to the different Corps when it in fact diminishes the number of effectives as good N.C. Officers must be left in charge of the helpless.[9]

This was a fairly damning indictment of Bathurst's policy of concentrating on numbers alone, but worse still was the fact that Graham's criticism extended beyond those corps that were newly raised, or pulled from depot duties. Even the Guards were not exempt, with many of the older men in the ranks, though experienced, so worn down as to be useless for anything other than the easiest garrison duty. Indeed, so unfit were those guardsmen left in garrison at Tholen that the 2/44th had to be temporarily detached from Taylor's brigade to supplement them. Graham addressed other concerns to Colonel Bunbury, who found himself receiving complaints that the army lacked both medical staff and sufficient engineers; the latter problem was also vexing Carmichael Smyth, whose own superiors were getting similar complaints. Graham also informed Bunbury that pack saddles for horses were needed, 'so as to enable us to carry in that manner the Camp Kettles, Blankets, and tents. Carriage of these articles in wagons increases the length of the line of march exceptionally & besides, carriages never can be close up when these things are most wanted.'[10] On the other hand, Graham was pleased with the result of his decision to organize his forces into two divisions for the Antwerp operations, finding this organization 'so much more convenient than any other' and resolving to retain it 'in hopes of the numbers increasing so as to bear the appellation without being ridiculous'.[11]

One last advantage also needed to be taken into account, which, if it did not lead to any great increment of Graham's forces, at least added to what he knew of the enemy's. When Louis Bonaparte's Kingdom of Holland had been absorbed into France, so had the Dutch Army been incorporated into the French. There were thus a not insignificant number of Dutch officers, some fairly senior, still in the French service; some of them remained loyal to the oath they had taken to Napoleon, but others sought to return to their national allegiance. Amongst those who fell into the latter camp were two engineer officers from the Antwerp garrison, Chef de Battalion Willem van Ingen and Capitaine Jan van Gorkum. During the fighting on the 13th, the two men contrived to slip out of the fortress and make their way into the Allied lines. Van Ingen was newly arrived at Antwerp, having been stationed at Willemstad until it was evacuated, but van Gorkum had been there for two years and was able to furnish the Allies with useful information about its defences and garrison. Interviewed by Bülow and Carmichael Smyth at the former's headquarters, van Gorkum strongly argued that it was entirely possible for the Allies to seize the remaining French-held fortresses in Holland by 'vive force' due to the poor state of the garrisons. This prompted Carmichael Smyth to enquire whether this held true for Bergen-op-Zoom, harking back to his own view that the place could be taken by storm, but van Gorkum stated that he was unable to give an opinion on the matter, being unacquainted with the current state of its defences and garrison.[12] The idea had been planted, however, and Bergen-op-Zoom became a renewed focus of interest amongst the British staff, with Taylor relating how Carmichael Smyth reconnoitred the place in company of another Dutch officer, Captain de Bère, who believed that the fortress could be taken by surprise but lacked the knowledge of fortifications to come up with a detailed plan.[13] Van Gorkum, too, having been commissioned into the new Dutch Army, also reconnoitred the place at Graham's behest and reported back with his thoughts as to how best to proceed with an attack.[14]

Although every effort was made to gain more intelligence about it, Bergen-op-Zoom was not placed under close observation after the return from Antwerp. Instead, the Guards Brigade was posted at Steenbergen, the 55th and 2/69th from the First Brigade at Wouw, and the Second and Light Brigades around Roosendaal. The 1st Royal Veteran Battalion had been taken out of the brigade structure upon the arrival of the 2/21st, which had nominally replaced it in the First Brigade, and was now in garrison at Willemstad along with the 2/37th. However, the 2/21st was not yet deemed fit for field service, and, rather than joining its brigade at Wouw, was put into garrison at Tholen.[15] Thus, the two main fortified points in Graham's rear were each held by two battalions supported by artillery, that at Tholen being the two companies of Royal Marine Artillery under Major William Minto. Lieutenant Colonel Campbell's Royal Marine infantry, meanwhile, had been shifted across to South Beveland to cooperate with a naval detachment, under Captain Edward Owen of HMS *Cornwall*, which had landed the previous month to support the Dutch insurgents there.[16] The primary task of this force was to mask the French strongpoint of Fort Batz, which, situated on the south-east tip of the island, dominated the passage of the Scheldt; as yet, sufficient forces could not be spared to attempt an attack on this post.

At Tholen, the weather had caused the defensive ditch to freeze over, causing the garrison some concern due to the proximity of the French at Bergen-op-Zoom and keeping them hard at work to ensure at least a modicum of security was retained. Lieutenant Dunbar Moodie of the 2/21st related how:

> a great part of the inhabitants, as well as garrison, were every day employed in breaking the ice in the ditches of the fortifications. The frost, however, was so intense that, before the circuit was completed, which was towards evening, we were often skaiting [sic] on the places which had been broken in the morning; we could not, with all our exertions, break more than nine feet in width, which was but an ineffectual protection against the enemy, had they felt any inclination to attack us in this half-dilapidated fortress, with our small garrison.[17]

Of course, such fears of a French counter-offensive were groundless in reality, although Taylor, feeling somewhat exposed with his two battalions at Wouw, continued to send out aggressive patrols to ascertain the extent of any French movement out of Antwerp, and to harass their picquets and patrols.[18] For the rest, though, Graham's troops were free to do their best to make themselves as comfortable as they could in their billets.

Scarcely were the troops back in their quarters before Graham began seeking Prussian cooperation for renewed offensive operations leading towards a direct attack on Antwerp and the French fleet. Nevertheless, it was evident that it would be some time before any such movement could take place, and this time could therefore be put to use in attempting to rectify some of the problems that had beset the army since its landing, and which had hampered its ability to make an effective contribution to the previous advance on Antwerp. Nothing more could be done about reinforcing the corps, although some comfort could at least be taken from the fact that additional troops were on the way from Jersey and from North Germany, but measures were certainly needed to improve its efficiency. In particular, Graham was finding that his staff organization was severely at fault, and that two of his three department heads were simply not up to their jobs. Lieutenant Colonel Arthur Macdonald, the Deputy Adjutant-General, fully met Graham's approbation, but both the Commissary-General, George Spiller, and Deputy Quartermaster-General, Lieutenant Colonel Frederick Trench, had been found wanting. Since the former post entailed responsibility for keeping the troops supplied and fed, and the latter for organizing their marches and billets, the effective prosecution of a winter campaign made it imperative that capable men filled both positions. As there was no point in dispensing with the present incumbent if no one better was available, Graham wrote to Wellington to enquire if suitably experienced officers might be spared to join him in Holland.

On the face of it, checking with Wellington before asking Horse Guards and the War Office to approve the changes to his staff seemed a logical step to take, particularly since Graham's strong loyalty to his old Peninsular chief meant that he had no wish to prioritize his own requirements over Welling-ton's. Unfortunately, Graham had not reckoned with the fact that Wellington, at this stage in his career, felt himself of sufficient consequence to be able to take matters into his own hands and sent two of his best men back to England forthwith. These were Lieutenant Colonel the Hon. Charles Cathcart, to replace Trench, and Thomas Dunmore to replace Spiller. It should be noted that Wellington first offered Colonel William de Lancey and Lieutenant Colonel Richard Jackson the chance to become Graham's Deputy Quarter-master-General, but both officers preferred their current posts whereas Cathcart, who was then filling a more junior position, and who had served previously with Graham at Cadiz, was happy to take the promotion.[19]

This high-handed action on Wellington's part served to place Graham in something of a quandary when news of it reached him in February; by this time Graham had made another lengthy operation in the field with his original inadequate staff, but it is as well to follow matters to their conclusion now. Graham laid out the problem, as he saw it, in a letter to the Quartermaster-General at Horse Guards, Major General James Willoughby Gordon, explaining both his reasons for wishing Trench replaced and the awkwardness of his position thanks to Wellington's well-intentioned meddling.

> My dear General, I am sure you will excuse me for troubling you with a few lines confidentially on a subject of great delicacy relative to your Department with this Corps.
>
> I was very early of the opinion that Lieutenant Colonel Trench with the greatest activity & most indefatigable zeal, making him a most useful officer in a Department, was not, at present, at least, qualified to be at the Head of it. I wrote confidentially to Colonel Torrens, & soon after (& long before I received his answer) I wrote to Lord Wellington on the same subject <u>merely to consult him</u>, as it were, & to <u>find out whether he could spare any officer from the Department fit to direct it & likewise one for the Commissariat Department</u>. I did this with a view to smoothing the way, & being able to say afterwards, that I had authority from Lord Wellington himself to state to His Royal Highness that he would not object to an Officer being withdrawn from his Army.
>
> I had not the most distant idea that his Lordship would immediately have <u>acted</u> upon my letter, & I am anxious that his having done so may naturally expose my proceeding to be mis-construed into a dissatisfaction & improper interference amounting to an unauthorised substitution of one officer for another, in so important a situation. I give you my honor [*sic*] no such idea ever entered my head; & I never was more surprised, & I may say annoyed, than when I found out Lord Wellington had gone so far beyond what I wished, or expected him to do. It is chiefly to clear myself from this suspicion that I look to you now; but at the same time I wish to state to you, that, things having gone this length, & Lieutenant Colonel Cathcart having actually resigned the very eligible situation he held in that Army, & having been sent home by Lord Wellington, who first made the offer to Colonel de Lancey, & I believe to Lt. Col Jackson, I feel most deeply interested in his appointment being carried thro' & I have therefore written a long confidential letter to Colonel Torrens, to put him in possession of such facts as would justify me, in bringing a direct charge of un-fitness for filling the chief situation against Lieut. Col. Trench. I should be very sorry to be forced to do so. I trust the arrangement may be made without any such necessity. Lieut. Col. Trench has had the benefit of Promotion by the appointment, & he cannot himself,

nor can any one in the Army, be surprised, that I sh'd prefer having an officer of great experience from Lord Wellington's Army, & one who served with me in the same situation at Cadiz, & who was long personally attached to me with the Army in the Peninsula, to him.

I do not at all mean by this to set up any claim of right to choose any officer I might fancy for filling this important office. But circumstances having brought the matter to this crisis most unexpectedly, & knowing that the one is fit, & the other is not, to conduct the Department satisfactorily, I trust as a matter of courtesy, that His Royal Highness will not deny my anxious request, that in some way or other an arrangement may be made to put Lieut. Col. Cathcart at the head of the Department.[20]

At the same time, Graham wrote in rather stronger terms to Bathurst, making his anger clear that Horse Guards had filled the post improperly in the first place, and that the fault for the problem lay there and not with him. He went on to observe that, in all the expeditions with which he had served, under Stuart, Abercrombie, Cathcart and Moore, he did not know one occasion where the commander had not been permitted to choose his own staff officers, and that he was 'quite sure that w'thout such an indulgence they would not have accepted the command'. He also reminded Bathurst that he, Graham, had accepted his current command under duress and that denying him such a choice was even less acceptable:

> Your L'd ship knows that I did not court this service & that I most reluctantly undertook it as a public duty; & tho' under such circumstances I might have tried to stipulate for the nomination of staff appointments I never open'd my lips on the subject having no personal object in view by accepting the Command. If the thing can be quietly arang'd now I shall be extremely glad, but I will not submit to have Lieutenant Col. Trench impos'd on me longer & Lieutenant Col. Cathcart so disappointed, as would be the case were a refusal to be the result of all this discussion.[21]

Having already incurred the wrath of Horse Guards by obtaining Bathurst's assistance in getting the services of Dr Sir James Grant to head his medical staff, Graham begged the Secretary of State not to involve himself in the matter unless pressed, or unless, as Graham feared, 'it ever come to the question which of us, Lt Col. Trench or me, should quit our situations'. Thankfully, matters never came to such a pass, and both Cathcart and Dunmore would eventually join the army in Holland. Returning to matters as they stood in January, however, Graham was obliged to continue to do himself much of the work that should have fallen to Trench – who may, by the by, have owed his appointment to being a distant relative of Clancarty's – and to rely on Spiller's assistants, who were thankfully more active than their chief, to organize his commissariat.

The problems of supply were not made any easier by continued friction with the Dutch, with whom effective liaison was still problematic. Graham was obliged to write to Clancarty complaining of the 'impertinence of the subaltern Dutch authorities extending their requisitions for Breda into all our cantonments', but when Clancarty tried to do something about it this led to a counter-complaint that the British were interfering with the arrangement of requisitions for the Prussian III Corps at Breda. With more important things on his mind, Graham decided that this was one argument that was best left to Clancarty.[22] Clancarty, for his part, was keen that the British continue to work with the Dutch and supply their demands for arms. Graham remained happy to comply, but Bathurst had begun to worry about the lack of correlation between the arms and equipment being sent and the numbers of Dutch troops actually in the field. Therefore, whilst acquainting Graham that the *Atalanta* transport, with 5,000 stands of arms embarked, was under orders for Helvoetsluys and that this would place 10,000 stands at Graham's disposal, the Secretary of State recommended 'as a general Rule, that you should not give more arms for the use of the Dutch Levies, until you are satisfied that the quantities already issued have been distributed, and will be employed usefully'. Graham was, in any event, to keep back a portion of these muskets to arm the people of Flanders and Brabant should they rise against the French.[23]

At the same time, Bathurst was still of the opinion that the Dutch should be pressed to provide assistance for the British in return, and, in response to Graham's shortage of both men and horses to equip his artillery for field service, proposed a solution that made it clear that he had still not grasped the extent to which military resources in continental Europe had been diminished by two decades of war:

> In regard to Artillery Drivers I am sorry to say that there is little or no probability that the Master General of the Ordnance will be able to spare you a Reinforcement and as I understand you have procured a considerable number of Dutch Horses, I recommend strongly that you should endeavour to engage Brabançons for this service and that you should also try to obtain some Drivers by application to the Duke of Cambridge, and to General Bülow.

The Duke of Cambridge, seventh son of George III, had been sent to Hanover as Military Governor with the primary task of overseeing the re-raising of the Hanoverian Army, but, as he told Taylor, he had insufficient resources for his own purposes, let alone to spare for service elsewhere.[24] So far as horses were concerned, Taylor's earlier efforts had demonstrated the impracticability of obtaining animals in any quantity from Dutch sources, but towards the end of January Graham was able to report that, 'we have got a few Dutch drivers hired for the artillery & in order to induce others, I have directed [Colonel] Sir G. Wood to provide them with [. . .] Slop Clothing which indeed is necessary for distinguishing them'.[25] By this stage, the issue of requisitions had also been addressed, and daily issues of food for the men and fodder for the horses could be made out of local resources rather than the army's own reserve stocks.[26]

But if the military authorities were struggling to obtain horses, it was harder still for the army's junior officers. Few, perhaps, could have in any case afforded the riding horses that Taylor's memorandum had suggested would be required, but baggage animals were most certainly in demand, particularly after an order forbade the use of Dutch country wagons to haul regimental baggage. Since pay was at this point two months in arrears, and since, according to Austin, the officers of the staff and the Foot Guards had contrived to obtain advance warning of the new edict and had already cornered the market, obtaining animals was difficult in the extreme. A large black mare was eventually obtained by Austin and his fellow officers of the 2/35th's Light Company, but the farmer from whom it was purchased was 'as knowing as a Yorkshire horse-dealer' and it was only after lengthy negotiations that he could be persuaded to accept a price that the officers, by pooling their resources, could afford. Thus reimbursed, 'he then made a virtue of letting us have, on the plea of patriotism for his country, and love of the House of Nassau, a mare, harness and light cart for about double their true value'.[27] Perhaps benefiting from the advance warning that infuriated Austin, Sperling on the other hand recorded no difficulty in purchasing 'a horse and light cart' for his baggage.[28]

Whilst impecunious officers were wrestling with the problems of horse-flesh, those lower down the military hierarchy soon found that years of blockade, French requisitions and the economic stagnation brought on by failure of the Continental System had all contributed to an enforced frugality amongst the rural populace that, in turn, reflected itself in the provision that could be made for the soldiers who were now imposed upon them. Morris observed that,

The cottagers whom we were billeted on, were so very poor, that very few indeed had the second bed; and all we could expect from them was potatoes and tobacco, both grown by themselves, and for which, they generally received from us an equivalent in meat, which was to them a great luxury. Their dinner generally consisted of a large bowl of potatoes, they always selecting the smallest for their own use, and giving the large ones to the cows or pigs. Over the potatoes, when boiled, they poured some sweet oil and vinegar, and this, with some very brown bread, was their usual fare. There was a fork laid for each person, and they used their own clasp knives. When the oil used, was really sweet, I was rather fond of their mess. On Sundays they generally had a piece of bacon with their potatoes. Such of them as indulged in the use of coffee, had a very small cup, something like what the children in England play with. Sugar was a prohibited article, and as a substitute for it, they would put a piece of sugar candy in the mouth, to sweeten the coffee in its passage. After each meal, the whole of the family produce their pipes, and taking from the pouch which they invariably carry with them a portion of their home-grown tobacco, after cutting it in small pieces, and rolling it in their hands, they would fill their pipes, and indulge in the luxury of smoking: in which habit even the children indulge.[29]

Officers' billets, naturally, tended to be in the better sort of house if such was available, and the author of *Letters from Germany and Holland* described a rather more substantial meal served to him at a farmhouse on Schouwen, with a roasted fowl to accompany bread, butter, cheese and beer, enjoyed in the midst of what was evidently a devoted and devout family.[30] It was, nevertheless, still basic enough fare, and Austin, whose memoir becomes increasingly disgruntled as its narrative progresses, complained that the local bread, issued to the troops as well as consumed by the locals, was 'a nauseous compound of black saw-dust like rye', and failed to understand why this was so, when wheat was apparently available: Shaw also noted that available bread was typically 'the blackest rye'.[31]

The Dutch character also came in for assessment, with the old complaint that there was no enthusiasm for the war continuing to make itself apparent. Stanhope, who took the opportunity to travel to The Hague in the aftermath of the retreat from Antwerp, drew on his return an unflattering comparison between the Dutch and the other nations of Europe, noting that where the Prussians, Russians, Spaniards, and even Austrians were motivated by patriotic zeal and a desire for revenge, 'the Dutch complain bitterly of the douaniers, the suppression of commerce & the diminished goodness & increased prices of sugar, coffee & tobacco', and that such complaints took apparent priority over any efforts to assist in the war that was being enthusiastically promoted by the Prince of Orange and his sons.[32] Indeed, there was even the beginning of a backlash against the presence of the British and other Allied troops in the country. Finding that Dutch shopkeepers were taking the same cue as the farmer from whom his fellows had purchased their mare, Austin discovered that prices had increased several-fold since the arrival of the first British troops, who, to be fair, had queered the market for themselves by initially exclaiming how cheap things were:

> At one shop, a shrewd pretty Dutch girl had contrived to pick up a smattering of English; and when an old campaigner ventured to remark that prices had been greatly enhanced since our arrival in the town, the *vrow*, affecting surprise at such an idea being entertained, replied in a curious mixture of Dutch and broken English, 'Drinky de schnapps, smoky de pipe and kissen de vrow, and all vor nix; dat is goot vor de Englishman.' Even those who could not 'Hollands spraken' understood this remark was meant to imply the English wanted their goods for nothing.[33]

Sperling, who may have been amongst those guilty of exacerbating the situation, since he initially commented favourably on the cheapness of many items, was another whose good first impressions of Dutch generosity were later soured by attempts to cash in on the British presence, although he did not let this colour his collective view of the Dutch, whom he generally continued to admire for their simple and devout lifestyles.[34]

Yet, when one considers the unthinking arrogance of the official British stance towards Holland, and the unrealistic expectations of the military and other aid that might be afforded by its people, it is hardly to be wondered that a similar attitude was at times taken by some of those in subordinate positions, nor that offence was taken as a result. Indeed, perhaps the only benefit of so few of Graham's officers being Peninsular veterans was that it prevented more of them taking their cue from the Quartermaster of the 2/52nd, who Shaw encountered 'haranguing a burgomaster of one of the villages in very villainous Portuguese, of which the said burgomaster understood not one word. My friend, however, was evidently impressed with the idea, that if he spoke Portuguese to any foreigner he must of course be understood.'[35]

On the other hand, others amongst the British contingent were able to enjoy rather more success in making themselves understood and getting their feet under the table, perhaps no more so than Dunbar Moodie. The Fusilier subaltern had already benefited, whilst at Buytensluys, from particular kindness due to his being Scots, which apparently obtained for him a greater sympathy – due to a perceived similarity of national character-istics – and led him to conclude, unlike many of his fellows, that the Dutch possessed 'in a high degree, the kindly, charitable feelings of human nature, which show themselves to the greater advantage, from the native simplicity of their manners'. This feeling was emphasized by the fact that his host, a miller, refused any payment for the services that he had rendered, leaving Moodie to reassess his perception of the Dutch as avaricious.[36]

Having done well at Buytensluys, Moodie determined to secure himself an equally good billet when his battalion was shifted across to Tholen and accordingly enlisted the services of a German-born corporal who had volunteered into the 2/21st from the 6th Royal Veteran Battalion, pre-sumably in order to get back to the Continent. His interpreter found Moodie accommodation in the home of a retired sea captain, but Moodie found its greatest attraction to be the skipper's widowed daughter-in-law, Johanna, with whom he quickly struck up a romance. Attracted by her 'innocence and simplicity' and 'soft, dark and liquid' eyes, the young officer proposed that he instruct Johanna in English and she him in Dutch, thus obtaining an excuse to spend hours in her company. His methods of instruction, however, were unorthodox:

> She would frequently come into my room to ask the pronunciation of some word, for she was particularly scrupulous on this head. On these occasions, I would make her sit down beside me, and endeavour to make her perfect in each word in succession; but she found such difficulty in bringing her pretty lips into the proper form, that I was under the necessity of enforcing my instructions, by punishing her with a kiss for every failure. But so far from quickening her apprehension, that the difficulties seemed to increase at every step. Poor Johanna, notwithstanding this little innocent occupation, could not, however, be weaned from her affection for the memory of her departed husband, for her grief would often break out in torrents of tears; when this was the case, we had no lessons for that day.[37]

Moodie's attentions were seemingly welcomed as much by the family as by Johanna, and the subaltern would remain a popular member of the house-hold for some time to come. The poor condition of the 2/21st meant that only the flank companies were prepared for field service, leaving the rest of the battalion confined to garrison duty and allowing Moodie's romance to continue, but plans were now afoot that would set much of the rest of the army in motion again.

Although it had proved impossible during the first advance on Antwerp to achieve anything against the city itself, the course of these operations had clearly demonstrated both that Graham and Bülow between them had sufficient forces to drive the French back within their fortifications, and that this in turn rendered the French warships extremely vulnerable. When Carmichael Smyth composed his report on the first advance, he was in no doubt whatsoever that if the Allies were able to remain for a few days before Antwerp then the fleet could be destroyed:

> Our Advance upon Antwerp has afforded me an opportunity of seeing the Works of the Place, and I have no hesitation in giving it as my decided opinion that whenever circumstances will allow us to advance in front of Antwerp for 48 hours we can burn the Naval Arsenal and the fifteen sail of the line now moor'd within the Docks or great basins lately excavated. The Ships lay with their broadsides touching each other, or nearly so. There are several most advantageous positions for Mortars & Howitzers within so short a range as 1500 and even 1000 yards. Great works have been projected by the French, and in particular one or two detached forts with a view of occupying some commanding ground & of keeping an Enemy at a distance from the shipping, but none of them have been executed. They have merely added redoubts to the former fortifications of Antwerp on the face looking down the Scheldt & these are not in a finished state.[38]

In this opinion, Carmichael Smyth had the support of Lieutenant Colonel Sir George Wood, commanding Graham's artillery and therefore the man who would have to organize any bombardment, and of van Gorkum with his inside knowledge of the Antwerp defences. So far as Carmichael Smyth was concerned, the aborted operations of the 13th were also useful in that they had showed up the inadequate nature of the siege equipment then available. A small train had been assembled, composed of five 24-pounders, six howitzers, four mortars, and four 68-pounder carronades, and another day would have enabled this to be brought forwards, but a deficiency of hammers and augers with the beds for these pieces would have delayed their being emplaced. This, and a shortage of experienced NCOs to back up his willing but inexperienced junior engineer officers, Carmichael Smyth hoped to be able to rectify before any further operations were embarked upon.

It was all very well, though, for Carmichael Smyth to plan for a second operation, but, as even the sanguine engineer was forced to accept, such an operation would only be possible with Prussian support. Graham was of a like mind, but his first few days after the return to cantonments were spent sorting out administrative matters before he was in a position to open negotiations with Bülow for a resumption of operations. When the Prussian requested a meeting on 19 January, however, Graham was obliged to send Taylor in his stead, since he himself had to play host to a surprise visitor to Holland in the shape of HRH the Duke of Clarence. Third son of George III, the Duke as a young man had served as a naval officer, but, despite repeatedly badgering the Admiralty for an active command, had not been employed in the current war. His presence on the Continent was therefore purely in a private capacity, and may be attributed in part to the somewhat parlous state of his finances. That he should go to Holland to escape his creditors is less surprising than it might seem: after all, we have already seen how Lord Yarmouth, also in poor financial straits, had earlier attached himself to Taylor's mission, and British tourists had started to visit the Continent in some numbers ever since the events of the previous year had opened up the ports to them. Judging by subsequent events, it may well also be that the Duke was also on the lookout for a bride: having separated from his long-term mistress Mrs Jordan two years previously, marriage to one of Europe's newly accessible and eligible princesses would help him solve his financial worries. In all events, he clearly could not resist the lure of a chance for action by joining Graham's headquarters, and since a royal duke trumped a Prussian general, on social grounds if not military ones, Graham's initial gambit in respect of Bülow was carried out by proxy.

Judging by what followed, though, this was likely no bad thing since Taylor's lively account of the meeting, which took place at Breda, suggests that he needed every inch of his skills as a courtier to cajole and flatter Bülow into falling in line with the British plans. As Taylor discovered, although the Prussian commander had plans of his own, their initial focus was the completion of his various siege operations, in order to render his whole force disposable for a renewed advance. His priority was to capture Gorcum, where Rampon's 3,500-strong garrison was still holding out and tying up Generalmajor Karl von Zielinsky's 5,000 Prussians. Rather than allow this to continue, Bülow informed Taylor that he was making preparations to bombard the place; although this was contrary to the Prince of Orange's wishes, Bülow felt that he could no longer allow this concern to 'paralyse his operations'. In any case, he continued, if the Dutch wished to be respected in such matters they ought put some troops in the field themselves; he had even threatened to withdraw his corps from Holland, to see if that would spur them into activity, but this had failed to have any effect. Once Gorcum had fallen, Bülow planned also to secure Hertogenbosch, which would then leave his corps free to begin an advance on Malines and Brussels. Although Wintzingerode had not yet advanced far enough to cooperate with this movement, it might be hoped that he would do so now that Macdonald had retreated, and, in any case, a Saxon corps was also believed to be moving into the Low Countries and could reinforce Bülow if needed. In support of this offensive, he hoped that Graham might serve to mask Antwerp, and also enquired whether the British 'could not make some early attempt on Bergen-op-Zoom, in which all his reports stated that there were not more than 700 men, not sufficient to secure the gates'. Taylor, in response, pointed out that no appreciable reinforcement had yet arrived and asked Bülow to consider whether 6,000 British could really be expected to contain the Antwerp garrison and act against Bergen-op-Zoom, where, in any case, Graham's intelligence reported that the garrison stood at between two and three thousand men.[39]

In allowing himself to be drawn into a discussion of Bülow's own plans, Taylor realized that he was being side-tracked from his own purpose, as instructed by Graham, 'viz the early renewal of the Attempt on Antwerp'. Taylor told Bülow that the British government had ordered this to be pursued, as a result of which Graham had assembled 'at Oudenbosch 16 Mortars and heavy howitzers and six 24-pounders which could follow the movement'. Bülow stated his opinion that, with these means, 'the destruction of the French Fleet would be no difficult matter, [and] that after Gorcum had surrendered, the other Corps were come up & Macdonald was quite removed it might be attempted'. This was not enough for Taylor, who countered with the argument that if the operation could be pushed now that this would make it clear that the first attempt had only been a recon-naissance, and the Allied retreat thus painted in a better light; furthermore, the greater honours for a successful attack would naturally go to the larger corps, that is to say Bülow and his Prussians. In any case, Taylor went on, the advantages inherent in a successful attack on the fleet would benefit the Allies as well as the British, although he felt obliged to add that Britain certainly did have 'a leading interest in it'. To Bülow this was all very well, but he remained unconvinced, remaining preoccupied with 'Gorcum & his left flank &c.'

Taylor seemed to be losing his case, but now fate intervened in a timely manner to sway the argument back in his favour. This took the form of the arrival of a report by the Crown Prince of Sweden, which had been printed in the London *Times* of 1 January. Described by Bülow as 'a tissue of false-hoods, coming from a source equally deceitful, and with which you will be better acquainted in time', and confirming the Prussian's view that 'the Prince Royal is playing his own Game and will sacrifice our cause whenever it suits him', the report took for the Prince full credit for the operations in Holland and referred to Bülow's corps as a subordinate part of Wintzin-gerode's command. Bülow was clearly furious, and Taylor immediately sought to capitalize on this, telling Graham that:

> This was most fortunate, and it was impossible not to endeavour to turn the Temper he was in to our advantage, which I had the less hesitation in doing, as what I might say, from myself, and not as arising from Your Instructions could not commit you or His Majesty's Government. I said warmly that nothing could be more infamous than [. . .] such false paragraphs, & that I rejoiced he had taken measures to contradict them, but that they did not surprize [*sic*] me, after all I had learnt from him of the Prince Royal's conduct, and which had been confirmed by his more ostensible proceedings. That I had reason to believe from his last letter received, from Kiel, that he talked of coming to Holland 'pour faire aller les Chocs' as if nothing had been done and that of course his object was to reap the reward and credit of General Bülow and the Energy and talent he had shown.

Bülow replied that 'Why, he is always writing to me to urge me to caution, but I shall know what is about I have a person about him who will keep me au fait,' to which Taylor 'observed that all this might be very well, but that if we delayed the attempt on Antwerp, and the forward movement on Brussels; if we did not risk something with our present means, the Prince Royal would come up, the *Coup d'Eclat* would be his.'

Bülow countered that the Crown Prince could not arrive in Holland before February, but, as Taylor quickly pointed out, this would not prevent him appointing Wintzingerode to direct operations in his stead thus placing Bülow – 'The Conqueror of Dennewitz, The Saviour of Holland' – in a sub-ordinate post. This suggestion had the desired effect, and Bülow, with some vigour and not without wit, cried that,

> That shall not be. Ce Jean Charles, ce Jean Charlatan, shall not have the credit – we will burn the Antwerp fleet, we will be at Brussels and [across] the old French frontier before he comes up, and my good friend (clapping me on the shoulder) I am delighted to have

to do with such comrades as the British Soldier, with so excellent an officer, and so witty a man as General Graham; he and his troops have fulfilled the utmost of my Expectation and I am certain that the Harmony will be as permanent as it is sincere. I only wish he had 20,000 men, we should want no Wintzingerode, he might remain in Düsseldorf as long as he pleased. I will set about Gorcum immediately, and in the Course of a Week I trust we may begin our movement on Antwerp; even if Gorcum should not fall, we may possibly attempt something; I can draw troops from Bommel &c, & perhaps Bois le Duc [i.e. Hertogenbosch] may fall.

Having obtained Bülow's cooperation, Taylor wasted no time in moving on to the details, passing on Graham's proposal that the British siege train be moved to Breda, so that it could then be advanced along the *chaussée* in case the smaller roads became impracticable. If the Prussians agreed, the British would provide horses, and, rather than alerting the French that another move was planned against Antwerp, it might be let out that the guns were for the defence of Breda. Bülow agreed that this was an excellent idea and that the guns could move with his own reserve artillery, before calling in a Prussian colonel of artillery whom he quizzed over the course of operations against Gorcum. The gunner reported that the Dutch could provide no artillerymen, and no guns could be spared from Breda either, but Bülow was able to tell him that this was no longer an issue now that the British siege train was to be moved there. The un-named officer – most likely Oberst Karl-Friedrich von Holtzendorff, III Corps' chief of artillery – was accordingly instructed to expedite matters so that an advance could begin, with Bülow telling him that 'Gorcum must be on fire the day after tomorrow.'

Before the meeting broke up, however, Bülow raised the delicate point of ensuring better cooperation between the troops of the two nations. Both officers agreed that each party was in part responsible for the past cases of mistaken identity and consequent friendly fire incidents, and that measures needed to be taken to prevent their recurrence. Bülow therefore proposed to attach two squadrons of cavalry to Graham to provide a communications link between the Allies, whilst in order to prevent against recurrences of friendly fire he asked Taylor to stress to his colleagues the different distinguishing features of French and Prussian headgear. Bülow also proposed that it would be better for the British officers to wear their sashes over their greatcoats so that even if some of them were in blue this should not be an issue.

With Taylor's persuasive talents having seemingly done the trick, all that remained was for Bülow and Graham to agree formally upon a plan of operations, which was done the following day when the Prussian commander travelled to Graham's headquarters at Oudenbosch. Bülow had had time to finalize his plans for the bombardment of Gorcum, which was now to begin on 22 January, but the two commanders agreed that the offensive against Antwerp would proceed irrespective of whether or not Rampon could be induced to surrender. Thus, the British siege train was to move to Breda during the course of the 22nd and 23rd, so as to be able to use the *chaussée* for its advance. The remaining British forces would again form the right wing of the advance, and move forward by Calmthout on 25 January. On the same day, Bülow would advance in two columns: one under his own direct command along the *chaussée*, and the other, under Borstell, towards Malines to act as a flank guard. Additional flank protection would be furnished by a detachment of light troops thrown out further to the south, which would, it was hoped, be able to link up with the advance guard of Wintzingerode's corps. By Bülow's calculations, even allowing for the fact that there was to be no marching by night, the Allies should be before Antwerp on 26 January, and be able to commence their bombardment the following day.[40]

This was all well and good, suggesting a clear commitment to the bombardment, a simple and effective plan, and an appreciation of the measures needed to implement it without undue confusion. But whilst this suggested that there was unlikely to be a repeat of the failures of the first operation, Bülow's announcement of his subsequent intentions were more worrying, as the British account of the conference makes clear:

> His further intention is to move on Brussels, Valencienes, &c and he seemed to wish that Sir Thos. Graham should take Charge of the Blockade of Antwerp & thence cover the Right, but it was agreed that this should be determined by the Information received of the Force & Disposition of the Enemy & by general Circumstances, after the fleet had been destroyed until which period the Corps of Bülow & that of Sir Thos. Graham should remain united whilst Borstell's should begin a forward Movement as Circumstances might direct.[41]

Evidently, then, Taylor had not entirely swung Bülow away from his own initial scheme of a rapid advance into Brabant and Flanders, and the Prussian commander clearly did not see himself as having made any commitment towards joining the British in a formal siege of Antwerp. In order to ensure British cooperation he was prepared to go along with the bombardment plan, but that was all. Otherwise, as he reminded Graham, the rest of the Allied armies were advancing; he himself had already had a letter from

Emperor Alexander urging him to conform with this movement, and he had no intention of remaining in Holland where he might find himself again under the command of the Crown Prince of Sweden. Bülow therefore 'trusted that all would be successfully executed before the Great Man from Holstein made his appearance'. This, at least, suggested that there would be no more delay in moving forward to begin the bombardment, and if this could be carried out successfully, even without Antwerp being captured, then that was a great deal better than nothing. The coming days, however, would demonstrate that these hopes were too optimistic and that relations between the British and their allies remained as strained as ever.

Chapter VII

'A Fair Trial Against Antwerp'

DESPITE THE APPARENT ACCORD reached after the meetings of 19 and 20 January, the old problems quickly began to reappear, and Bülow felt himself obliged to delay the planned advance until the 27th. The cause remained his ongoing concern for his left flank, which he now perceived to be threatened by a concentration of 10,000 French troops around Malines and Louvain. This he interpreted as being the advance guard of Macdonald's corps, prefiguring a full-scale counter-attack, and leaving him with no choice but to postpone the movement on Antwerp. In fact, although the intelligence of a French concentration was correct, these troops were not Macdonald's but Maison's, and were concentrating prior to a withdrawal. Seeing Antwerp as a trap, Maison was pulling back most of his mobile forces in order to retain enough troops to cover the French frontier. Only Roguet's Young Guard infantry would remain at Antwerp to support the garrison forces, and Maison himself intended to leave the place as soon as possible. In the British camp, opinions were divided as to what to do: Taylor felt strongly that it would be best to deal with the French field army first, after which Antwerp could be attacked at leisure, but Graham remained committed to the original scheme. Bülow insisted on another postponement, this time because the garrison of Hertogenbosch had unexpectedly capitulated on the 26th after a rising by the civil populace, whereupon Graham wrote to him to press him not to delay the movement on Antwerp any further.[1]

Matters were further complicated, however, by the arrival of a new senior officer in the area in the shape of General der Kavallerie Karl-August, Herzog von Saxe-Weimar-Eisenach. Saxe-Weimar was the commander of the III Corps of the German Confederation, on paper composed of 14,000 Saxon troops, which had been placed under the orders of the Crown Prince of Sweden and directed to join the Allies in the Low Countries. This was one of several contingents raised for Allied service from the forces of Napoleon's erstwhile German allies, and like the others of its kind, it was earmarked for second-line duties in order to release more effective formations for active operations. Thus, when the Saxons arrived, Bülow would be free to take his

Prussians southwards to join Blücher, but, for the moment, the Saxons were still moving up through Germany and it would be February before they could be expected in Holland. It is not immediately obvious why Saxe-Weimar travelled so far in advance of his corps: Graham came to the conclusion that, since he was a full general of several years' seniority, the Tsar had sent him to coordinate the movements of Bülow, Wintzingerode and Graham himself. This does not seem to have been the case, although Saxe-Weimar would certainly have the senior position, both by virtue of rank and of numbers of troops under command, once his corps replaced Bülow's, and it seems entirely reasonable for him to familiarize himself with the area in which he would be operating. More prosaically, as became evident when Graham met with him on 27 January, Saxe-Weimar was also seeking to secure supplies and equipment for his corps, which was particularly deficient in ammunition since the Saxons were using French muskets. However, Graham could only offer powder and lead rather than made-up cartridges, which would have been of the wrong calibre. Saxe-Weimar also reported that, due to the retention of part of his corps in Saxony, and the non-arrival of other elements, he would initially be able to bring into Holland between seven and nine thousand troops.[2]

Although the Saxons would be some time coming, the surrender of Hertogenbosch did release more Prussian troops to join Bülow's advance. When Graham sent Carmichael Smyth to Bülow's headquarters on 27 January to ascertain Prussian intentions, the report that came back was accordingly positive, although it also emphasized Bülow's on-going preoccupation with clearing his left flank and his desire to advance in that direction at the earliest opportunity:

> Lieut. General Bülow said that he still considered Antwerp as the immediate object of the proposed forward movement; & that in advancing upon Louvain or Malines (should it be necessary) his plan was to throw back the Enemy in order that his left Flank might be secure and that we might not be interrupted in our operations before the place.
>
> He said that the time when he would be able to advance would depend upon the movement of those Battalions lately employed at Bois le Duc [i.e. Hertogenbosch] who were ordered to march upon Tilburg, that the moment they arrived at Tilburg the whole would advance together, that he did not intend to wait for the Saxons as their arrival was very uncertain in consequence of the difficulty in passing the Waal, but that they would follow his movements & support him where necessary.

He added that in every respect the spirit of the arrangement as provisionally drawn up the day before yesterday would be adhered to, that his Head Quarters would be the first day's march at Wuustwezel & that if Sir Thomas Graham would place his at Calmthout on the same day; he would communicate with him that evening & either proceed towards Antwerp as agreed upon or move towards Lier & Malines according to the information he expected to receive from General Borstell who had sent a strong reconnaissance of cavalry towards Lier which he was ordered if possible to occupy.

With respect to the Mortars & heavy stores at Breda he still wishes them to move one day's march in his rear upon the great causeway – as they will consequently not have left Breda on the Evening of the first day's march when he will communicate with Sir Thomas Graham, orders can be sent to delay them should he leave the Antwerp road and move towards Malines; or they can be suffered to advance to Wuustwezel if it should be prudent to allow this.

In answer to the observation I made respecting our situation at Calmthout should the Prussians march towards their left; Genl. Bülow said that he could leave two or three battalions to reinforce us; & that as the Saxons were not to move with him he would direct them to join us. He also said that if he moved towards Malines he should at any rate go through Brasschaat & that he would there leave a post of observation.

In going over both to General Bülow & to General Boyen the probable details of the operations before Antwerp, I pointed out in consequence of recent information, Sir Thomas Graham might perhaps judge it right to make some alterations in the first plan & that it might be advisable to occupy the remains of the Fort Pimentel on the banks of the Scheldt; which would thus be the *point d'appui* upon our right. Genl. Bülow stated that it would make no difference – and both he and Genl. Boyen afterwards stated (in another room) that we ought not to embrace a greater front than our means would allow and that wherever we placed the left they would place their right & General Boyen assured me that if requisite they would cordially cooperate in the attack upon Merxem; the possession of which appears so indispensable to our success.[3]

This, then, indicated that things were back on track, even if a date still needed to be set for the advance to begin, but the fact that Bülow no longer intended to allow his movements to be dictated by the arrival, or otherwise, of Saxe-Weimar's corps was a worrying development. It is interesting too that Bülow seems to have assumed that he could direct Saxe-Weimar's movements when that officer outranked him. Still, however unwelcome the news that he did not plan to linger in Holland, Bülow had made his intention to move southwards as soon as possible clear enough and subsequent accusations of Prussian ill faith on this front are groundless.

Graham was therefore not entirely happy with the situation as it now stood. Whilst believing that he had done all that he could to secure Prussian cooperation against Antwerp, he was deeply concerned about what might happen when the Prussians moved on, telling Bathurst that:

> unless both Antwerp & Bergen-op-Zoom were to fall I do not well see how I could pass on into Flanders, at least till I am joined by all the reinforcements coming for w'th so small a force I could not separate myself from Bülow without great risk, & there are many fortified places on the left bank of the Scheldt that my situation would be quite precarious in all respects till I could get possession of some sea port of which I believe there is none good before Ostend a place of very considerable strength & too near France.[4]

The implication seems to be that Bathurst had hinted at such a movement in a previous letter, although if this was indeed the case then it was privately rather than in an official despatch. Bathurst also hinted – apparently in a private letter of 17 January, judging by Graham's reference – that it might prove necessary to withdraw the British corps in order to furnish a reinforcement for Wellington, prompting Graham to state that 'however anxious I should be, while I remain, to command a good Corps, capable of exertion & likely to have success, I shall be most ready to relinquish the situation I am placed in whenever the troops can be better employed'. For the moment though, as he informed the Secretary of State, he was committed to the Antwerp operation and although the delays were unfortunate the only risk was that a thaw might set in that would hamper the advance; in all other respects 'a few days can make little difference one way or the other'.[5]

In any case, Graham did not have much longer to wait. With the Prussian troops from Hertogenbosch moving up, it was agreed that the advance would begin on 30 January. Accordingly, orders were given for the British troops to be ready to march at 04.00 that morning. Bad weather subsequently caused this to be set back several hours but the Second Division had reached its objective at Calmthout by early afternoon, with the First Division moving up in its rear. It was another horrific march, with Austin describing how:

Rain, snow, hail and large pieces of jagged pointed ice mingled in one incessant shower, and these on falling to the ground became frozen into slippery sheets of ice; while the wind blew furiously from the north-east, and it seemed as though the elements had conspired to prevent our moving.[6]

So bad were conditions that Shaw was 'convinced the troops could not have withstood it, if they had not been convinced they were marching to France'.[7]

Although there had been no reinforcement of Graham's little army, a limited reorganization had taken place, with the 2/35th and some of the riflemen moving from the Light Brigade to the Second in exchange for the 2/25th and 54th. Skerrett, recovered from his fall, resumed command of the First Brigade, which was re-joined by the detached 2/44th, and by the flank companies of the 2/21st and 2/37th. Skerrett's return to duty in turn released Taylor to command the Second Brigade as originally planned. Since Macleod's wounding, this formation had been under Lieutenant Colonel Browne of the 3/56th and Taylor felt some disquiet at replacing this veteran, but the two men quickly struck up a rapport.[8] By stripping the garrisons to the bare minimum, it was possible to put around 6,000 men into the field but continued bad weather had prevented the arrival of supplies from Britain. This meant a continued shortage of campaign equipment, and a lack of heavy guns that had to be compensated for by the employment of a mixed bag of Dutch pieces.

Such as it was, the siege train was now assembled at Breda ready to join in Bülow's advance, but to move the twelve British and thirteen Dutch pieces and their ammunition, and to convey the engineering stores necessary to emplace them, a large array of wagons was needed. Sperling was in charge of receiving the stores as they arrived and organizing the wagons so that they would be ready to move as soon as the orders were given, and this kept him busy throughout the last week of January. As he explained,

> The stores consist of a quantity of timber adapted for the laying of platforms for artillery, making magazines, and whatever may be required for the construction of field batteries, a quantity of sandbags, entrenching tools, and so forth. These are all packed in the country wagons, most unfit for their present object, and especially for the Artillery stores. Not half the number of such wagons as ours would be required. The wagons and horses are levied upon the farmers, who receive a very adequate remuneration.[9]

By the end of the month, Sperling's charge had grown to a hundred wagons each with two horses and it was necessary to billet them in the surrounding villages so as to obtain adequate shelter for men and beasts: something that would prove a problem when the time came for them to join the advance.

The orders for the siege train came on 29 January, so as to conform with the Prussian advance the following morning. Bülow's movements on the 30th were as per the plan agreed ten days before but both he and Saxe-Weimar, who accompanied the Prussian headquarters, continued to entertain reservations about the project and told Graham so when the commanders met that evening at Wuustwezel. Despite his earlier concerns for his own right, Graham proposed that, if Bülow could not be dissuaded from shifting more troops towards the Allied left, the British would conform with the Prussian movements and shift their axis of advance southwards to the Breda–Antwerp *chaussée*. Accordingly, the Second Division moved from Calmthout to Brecht on 31 January, with an outpost pushed forwards to Brasschaat, whilst the First Division was shifted to Wuustwezel and Loenhout. The movement of both divisions was by side roads rendered 'nearly impracticable from the quantity of water which covered the old ice', although it was again completed by early afternoon giving the troops time to find shelter and begin to dry themselves out before the night-time cold set in with a vengeance. The rain on the 30th had precipitated a partial thaw, causing the flooding that hampered the next day's movements, and Graham remained concerned about its continued impact on operations, although he was able to take some comfort in the fact that there was a frost again on the night of 30–31 January, meaning that it was 'not now a decided thaw'.[10]

Even with the two armies realigned, Graham remained unclear as to whether or not Bülow would conform with the advance on Antwerp or would simply swing southwards and bypass the place. As during the first advance, Bülow was being remarkably close-mouthed about his intentions, and had revealed nothing of his plans for 1 February, nor of what was required from the British on that day. To clear matters up, Graham sent Taylor and Carmichael Smyth to the Prussian headquarters, now at Westmalle, to press for a definite answer and encourage conformity to the original plan; only after they returned could he at last be assured that the Prussian commander was not going to move south, leaving Graham 'happy to think that we should at last have an opportunity of making a fair trial against Antwerp'.[11]

However, although Taylor and Carmichael Smyth were able to return from their meeting with good news, this did not indicate a change of heart by the Prussian commander, nor a shift in his long-term objectives. Arriving at the Prussian headquarters just after midday on 31 January, Taylor and Carmichael Smyth were surprised to find out that, far from needing to be persuaded of the need to move on Antwerp, Bülow had his maps of the city spread out before him and was apparently fully committed to the advance and bombardment. Having ascertained the location of Graham's troops – although it seems odd that he needed to, unless Graham on the previous day had agreed only to a shift to the left rather than providing details – Bülow said that 'this would do & we might proceed in the Movement Tomorrow'. He himself planned to have his main force at Wijnegem, with his advance guard at Schoten and a flank guard under Borstell at Malines. He further recommended that Graham concentrate at Brasschaat with advanced posts at Donk and Ekeren. This deployment would then permit the British to attack Merxem on 2 February whilst the Prussians tackled the French outpost at Deurne along with the 'other posts of which the Possession would be required to establish Mortar Batteries for bombarding the Fleet'. Bülow also expressed the hope 'that the Mortars and Howitzers, Entrenching Tools & Sand Bags could be brought up at once', and Carmichael Smyth was able to assure him that six 24-pounders and the necessary tools to emplace them would be at Brasschaat by nightfall on 1 February, with the remainder of the siege train close behind.

In order to prevent any friendly fire incidents, a clear line of demarcation was agreed between the two corps, with the British having responsibility for Merxem and all points to the north, and the offer of Prussian cavalry to assist in maintaining communications was accepted. Taylor, gratified that all was going well, rather heavy-handedly added a further incentive for Prussian cooperation, telling Bülow:

> that I had forgotten on a former occasion to mention as instructed by [Graham] that, in the event of the Capture of the French ships, the Prize Money to be distributed to the troops concerned British & Prussian would be very considerable, & that even if we should only succeed in burning them a very handsome gratuity would be made to the Troops. He appeared to receive this information with Pleasure.[12]

As the meeting prepared to break up, however, Bülow 'partly let the cat out of the bag by lamenting that the Saxon troops were not come up', revealing that neither second thoughts nor the lure of prize money had swayed his decision to continue with the Antwerp operation, but rather that he remained bound by his instructions not to advance until Saxe-Weimar's troops had come up. Otherwise, he left Taylor in little doubt that he would have pursued his 'grand operation against Valenciennes', and his haste to get the heavy guns up is therefore best understood not as zeal for the cause but rather to a desire to get the bombardment, for which he evidently had little enthusiasm, over and done with so that he would be free to march as soon as his troops were relieved by the Saxons.[13]

In accordance with this scheme, the Second Division moved forward on 1 February, with the Light Brigade under Gibbs moving out to cover the right flank at Donk whilst Taylor's Second Brigade advanced directly along the *chaussée* from Brasschaat to within a mile of the French outer defences. These had been little modified since the previous attack, with the *chaussée* blocked by a well-manned abatis a mile outside Merxem. This therefore places the main body of Taylor's brigade some two miles short of Merxem when it halted. The First Division remained in reserve, but several companies from Proby's Guards Brigade were thrown out to cover the British left and reinforce the patrols that Taylor had sent to make contact with the Prussians.

Little word reached Graham of what his allies were doing, but one message had come through that had a wider import, since it yet again called into doubt the continuance of the whole operation. As Bülow now reported, he had received orders from Schwarzenberg to move on Mons in support of Wintzingerode. Since these instructions made no mention of waiting until Saxe-Weimar's troops came up, there was nothing to stop the Prussian commander using them as an excuse to abandon his cooperation with Graham, but, for the moment, with his troops already moving forwards, Bülow elected to continue operations against Antwerp. Whilst Krafft's brigade occupied Schotten, Thümen's pushed up towards Wijnegem, which was defended by part of Roguet's division under Général de Brigade Antoine Aymard. Aymard initially fell back before counter-attacking, leading to a running battle in which the Prussians were drawn forwards until they were contesting control of the outermost houses of Deurne, which the French had fortified.

Finding himself more heavily engaged than he had envisaged, Bülow sent a request to Graham that the British make an attack on Merxem in order to relieve the pressure on the Prussians. By the time this message was received, it was getting dark and too late for a serious attack to be mounted, particularly since Taylor had scouted the ground to his front and found it 'very much intersected and covered with brushwood', and there was a strong feeling amongst the British staff that it was hardly their fault if the Prussians had attacked early and got themselves into trouble. Nevertheless, Graham agreed to a reconnaissance in force along the *chaussée*, which perforce fell to Taylor since his brigade was best placed to do so.[14]

Making the best of this assignment, Taylor elected to attempt to drive in the French picquet manning the abatis, which would not only provide the necessary diversion but would also make the main attack on the following morning more straightforward. Taylor's account of the brief operation, written three days later, is a model of concision that cannot be bettered, but makes clear, in emphasizing the confusion of the near darkness, that any attempt to mount a larger attack would have descended into farce, if not tragedy:

> I moved with half the pickets, two companies 35th and about 30 of the 95th, and I detached Major Macalister with the [flank] companies 35th and 20 riflemen to turn the picket by its left, while we made a show along the road. It was getting dusk and was quite dark before Major M. could get round, while we moved very slowly and cautiously to be at hand to support him. He came upon their flank and rear, and had nearly surprised them, but the advanced sentry got off, was fired at, and a very smart fire of musketry was engaged on both sides. I kept moving on very quietly without firing until close up to the French picket. We were challenged by Major Macalister's party, and I ordered them into the road to cease firing; and finding all present I was preparing to move off when one of our Hussars having gone close up to the abatis drew upon us a heavy volley, but fired so high that it only wounded one man and hit some others in their caps, etc. I ordered the rear companies immediately to face about and retire slowly, and the riflemen and light company of the 35th to keep up a heavy fire to cover us – constantly retiring.[15]

Austin was with the Light Company of the 2/35th, and also commented on the confusion that ensued with even a few score men deployed in darkness and broken terrain, noting how an attempt by his company commander, Captain Alexander Shaw, to overpower a French sentry was thwarted when a rifleman, against orders, took a shot at the Frenchman, missing his target but nearly hitting Shaw. He also corroborates Taylor's assertion that the French for the most part fired high, although evidently not on every occasion since Austin himself was wounded in the left elbow by a musket ball during the final push to drive the French from the abatis, prior to the British withdrawal. Not wishing to miss the promised battle on the morrow, Austin concealed the severity of his injury so as to remain with his company.[16]

With the diversion carried out, Taylor invited Macalister and the other officers who had taken part in the attack to join him for a late dinner to show his appreciation for their services. Austin for one was extremely grateful for what was, by his standards, 'a sumptuous feast', although by the time he sat down to eat shock was evidently beginning to set in after his wound, and he found that he had little appetite. As the party broke up, Taylor bid his guests farewell with a reminder that there would be work to be done on the morrow, and the officers attempted to get some sleep in a bivouac surrounded by deep snow. At length, after straw had been secured to cover the ground, and a rudimentary shelter erected, the officers settled down in a circle with their feet close to a large fire, and attempted to pass what remained of the night in as little discomfort as possible. Even without Taylor's admonition, however, it was impossible for Austin and his comrades to forget their situation, for 'as we thus reclined we could plainly hear the "Wer da?" challenge of the Prussian sentries on our left, and the "Qui vive?" of the French to our front'.[17]

By this time Graham, still not having had any communication from Bülow with respect to the arrangements for the following day, had given up waiting and begun to issue his own orders to implement the planned attack. His conception called for the main thrust to be made by the Second Division, both brigades attacking along the line of the *chaussée*, supported on its left by Skerrett and with the Guards Brigade forming a reserve behind the centre. In communicating these dispositions to Cooke at 20.30 on 1 February, Graham was obliged to emphasize that he could not give a time for the attack to begin until he had received some communication from Bülow: nevertheless, Cooke was informed that Mackenzie had been directed to be in position by dawn. With the lack of communication from the Prussians suggesting the renewed possibility of mistaken identity, Cooke was also informed that Graham desired 'all the men to be without having their greatcoats over their red coats, to prevent mistakes'.[18] With this message sent, as much had been done as could be done to prepare the First Division for its supporting role. For the Second Division, however, which was tasked with leading the attack, a last-minute change of command threatened to throw the plans into turmoil. As he was riding back to Graham's headquarters after supervising Taylor's diversionary attack on the evening of 1 February, Mackenzie's horse fell on the ice and threw him from the saddle. The general suffered a severe blow to the head, and was then further injured by his horse crashing down on top of him. Knocked unconscious, he was not found until some time after the fall, and was evidently in no fit state to continue in command of his division: indeed, unsurprisingly for a man of his age, it would be some weeks before he was well enough to return to his post.[19] In the interim, Gibbs, as the senior brigade commander, took over the Second

Division whilst Lieutenant Colonel Harris of the 2/73rd handed his battalion over to Major Dawson Kelly and assumed command of the Light Brigade.

In contrast to the rather scrambling nature of the first capture of Merxem, four weeks previously, the second attack was carefully organized, as laid down by Trench in a Disposition that elaborated upon Graham's intentions as related to Cooke the previous evening:

> The attack on Merxem will be made this morning by the Second Division, having a brigade of Guards and the first division in reserve on the great Chaussée. Major-General Skerrett's brigade with the three flank companies of the picket at Denhoorst [*sic* Denhorst, near Schoten – these were the Guards companies thrown out on that flank the previous evening] will move from that place by the most direct paths leading on Antwerp to the left of Merxem, but as nearly parallel to the great Road as possible.
>
> As far as circumstances will permit, light troops will be detached on each side of the Chaussée from the head of the second division, so as to endeavour to get in by the flanks of the village; care will be taken, however, that the troops so employed shall always have supports in reserve; and frequent reports will be sent in by the officers to the head of the column. Sir George Wood will take care that the heavy artillery shall be ready to be brought up in case it shall be found necessary to employ it against the village of Merxem.
>
> As soon as the enemy is driven out of the village, the avenues leading to Antwerp will be strongly occupied; and Lieut. Colonel Carmichael Smyth, commanding the Engineers, will lose no time in forming barricades and such other works as he may think necessary to defend it against any attempts of the enemy.
>
> As it may be expected that the Enemy will throw shells from the Ramparts of Antwerp, the Village will at first be occupied with all attention to find shelter for the troops from the effect of such Bombardment, no more being allowed to remain in the Village and within range of the Artillery of the place than what are necessary for its defence and for carrying on the works already mentioned.
>
> Lieut. Colonel Smyth will likewise mark out such mortar batteries as he may think necessary, and will send in to the Adjutant-General a detail of such working parties as he may require.[20]

Other than some confused wording that manages to imply that the Guards were somehow not part of the First Division – which, with Skerrett detached, would have left Cooke with no command – the plan is set out clearly enough, and the need to render Merxem secure and defensible once in British hands displays clear forward thinking. Either Trench's staff work was improving, or else there is the hand of another in the detail of these arrangements.

However, the improved preparations were at least to some degree offset by the fact that, as Graham had feared, the French had taken advantage of the lessons learnt in their defeat of 13 January to improve the fortifications before Merxem. Thinking ahead, when the operation was still in the planning stages, Taylor had noted how the trees along the *chaussée* had been felled to obstruct the road, and how two additional batteries had been established – one at the rear of Merxem to command the exits from the place, and the other, by a windmill, to enfilade the Sint Ferdinandsdijk. Furthermore, the French had increased the extent of the inundations, further reducing the potential angles of attack for the British. Based on these reports, Taylor speculated 'that our attacks by infantry must now be carried to the right and left of Merxem, and directed upon the further extremity so as to threaten to cut off the retreat of the French while we amuse them with a 24-pound shot and shells from the front' regretting that this would risk the lives of any inhabitants remaining in Merxem but seeing no alternative.[21] These ideas correspond very closely to the attack plan that Graham produced, although this did differ from Taylor's scheme in that, although it called for a wide outflanking manoeuvre by Skerrett's brigade, the main attack was to go in along the *chaussée* with only light infantry being employed to work around the flanks of the village. In the event, however, the original plan would not long survive first contact with the enemy and, for a variety of reasons, the eventual battle would take on a different form.

Once contact had been made with the Prussians in order to ensure a co-ordination of effort, the attack was set to begin at 08.00.[22] However, 2 February dawned bleak and snowy, and when the attacking troops went forwards it was into the teeth of a blizzard. As befitted the set-piece attack outlined in Trench's disposition, the Second Division was deployed with Harris's brigade leading and Taylor's echeloned back to the right, with the Rifles and 2/52nd pushed out in front of everyone. Although Brevet Lieutenant Colonel Alexander Cameron of the 1/95th had come out in mid-January, and the Monthly Returns continue to aggregate the various Rifle companies together as a single battalion, it seems only to have been at this point that all four companies were brought together under Cameron's command, having been divided between the two brigades of the Second Division since the reorganization following the first attack on Antwerp.[23]

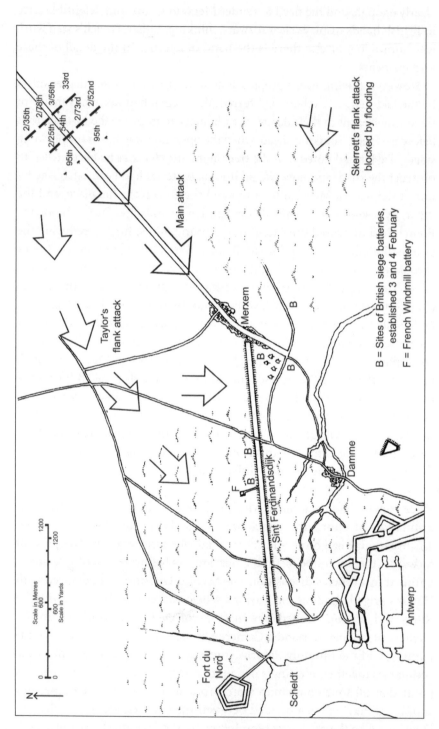

British Positions in the Second Battle of Merxem

Austin's account places the Light Company of the 2/35th in this skirmish line as well, most likely to cover its extreme right.

Contact was soon made with the French outposts, who had resumed their old positions after the British had withdrawn the previous evening. With the falling snow dampening the powder in the musket pans, it proved difficult to sustain a firefight, and it took a bayonet charge to clear the French from the abatis. During this first rush, the dénouement was played out of one of those coincidences often remarked upon in memoirs, whereby one who has had a premonition of death is unfortunate enough to have it proven accurate. The victim was a private of the 2/73rd, who, on the order being given to advance,

> made rather an extraordinary request to the officer, viz., that he might be placed on the baggage guard, as he had received an intimation, by a dream, that if he went on, he would be the first man killed. Of course, his request was not complied with; and we endeavoured to laugh him out of his fears, but in vain. We were soon discovered by the enemy; who, in the first instance, opened on us some of their light artillery. The first shot that took effect, was a six-pounder, which struck poor Francis, whose dream was thus unhappily realized – he was the first man killed.[24]

A second defensive position, some distance to the rear of the abatis, was also cleared in this way; at this, the French retired towards Merxem itself and left only skirmishers to impede the continued British advance. Even so, and despite the fact that the weather had now eased up, movement across ploughed fields bordered by hedges, and through the last of the brushwood, meant that progress remained slow.

If the main attack was moving slowly, however, Skerrett's flank attack was making even less progress. Since the French had opened the sluices, much of the land to the south of the *chaussée* was flooded to a depth of several feet, making movement impossible. By the time his brigade had retraced its steps and followed the advance along the *chaussée*, Skerrett was too late to play any part in the action. The original plan of attack, for a major turning movement by the left, was now impossible to implement, whilst a head-on attack also seemed a daunting prospect. Graham therefore elected to shift the weight of his attack to his right, extending his line in that direction so as to swing round and attack Merxem from the north. Taylor recalled how Graham:

> ordered me to turn off to the right with the 52nd, 35th, and 78th, and four guns, with orders to endeavour to find a route that should carry me sufficiently to the right to come in upon the left of the

enemy's post, and thence join in the attack, but with strict injunctions not to commit myself until I saw the centre attack well advanced.

After proceeding a little way while the attack was carrying on very briskly in the centre (close upon our left), I found a very intelligent and willing guide who took us by a road which brought us across the Polder, and in face of a battery of two guns near a windmill on the left, and rear of Merxem with S. Ferdinand's Dyke nearly parallel to our front – a thick fall of snow concealing our approach.[25]

It is evident that Graham, in his haste, simply gave Taylor command of the units most readily available for this movement, plucking the 2/52nd out of the skirmish line even though they did not belong to Taylor's own brigade, whilst at the same time leaving two of Taylor's own battalions behind with the main body. The fact that it was the 2/35th and 2/78th that were detached also suggests that the Second Brigade was deployed in inverted order, with its most senior unit on the left and the next senior, the 2/35th, on the right, something that does actually make sense when one applies the Army's doctrines of unit seniority to the situation, and which in turn makes it easier to place the remaining battalions in the division.[26] It was typical of Graham to make a snap decision like this, and the redeployment was certainly effective in resurrecting a stalled advance, but it did mean that, as during the first action on this same ground and, indeed, as during Graham's first independent fight at Barrosa three years before, command structures were broken up at an early stage and subordinate commanders left in charge of unfamiliar troops. Indeed, so rapid was the movement to the right that the 2/35th marched off without its Light Company, which, as is evident from Austin's account, continued to advance with the main body along the *chaussée*.

As Taylor moved out to the right, Graham continued to feed units into the gap between his detachment and the main advance, sending Lieutenant Colonel Brown's 3/56th to follow Taylor, along with at least a company's worth of riflemen. At the same time he shifted the Light Brigade to its right so that the 2/73rd was advancing directly down the *chaussée*, flanked to the right by the 54th and 2/25th, and with the whole brigade screened by the remaining riflemen. Alone of the Second Brigade, the 33rd did not follow Taylor and therefore presumably continued in support of Harris's advance: the battalion had only three men wounded, and none killed, suggesting that they were only lightly engaged.[27] On the other hand, the 2/73rd were in the thick of it as they approached Merxem, with Morris describing how the head of the village was covered by two cannon whose close-range fire of grape and canister swept the *chaussée* and forced the attackers to take cover to either side of the road, behind the first houses of the village:

> Upon this, Lieutenant [John] Acres, of our Grenadiers more familiarly known as 'Bob Acres,' a man of gigantic stature, as brave as a lion, and almost as strong as one rushing into the middle of the street, called on us to follow him; nor did he call in vain. In a moment, every man was after him. We drove the enemy from the main street, took the two pieces of cannon, and pursued the foe up one of the side streets.[28]

The cannon were 8-pounders mounted on iron garrison carriages rather than the usual field mountings, and this may explain why it did not prove possible for the French to get them away. However, there is also no denying that the French in the village, again under the direction of Ambert, put up far less of a fight than during the previous action. A counter-attack of sorts was mounted, but was quickly broken and then, 'amidst the thunder of artillery, the rattle of musketry, the loud hurrahs, and the defiant shouts of "Vive l'Empereur," Merxem was a second time in our possession'.[29]

Without taking any credit away from those who made the attack down the *chaussée*, the unwillingness of the French to defend the village also owed much to the fact that the position was already outflanked as Taylor's command threatened to cut the defenders off from Antwerp. They in turn, however, now found their advance checked by the fire of the French battery at the Sint Ferdinandsdijk windmill, which would clearly need to be silenced or captured if the enemy were to be driven back into their fortifications. Taylor's advance, as we have seen, had taken him to a road cutting across the polder towards the dyke – presumably the same one by which the 2/73rd had advanced during the first action – and this now became the axis of his advance. To the right of the road, the 2/52nd were pushed forwards as a screen, behind which the four cannon that Graham had attached to Taylor's command unlimbered to answer the fire of the two French pieces. On the left of the road, the 2/35th and 2/78th worked their way forwards using the cover of the tree-lined ditches to screen their movements, and were thereby able to push close up to the dyke without being fired upon. The 3/56th, which had come up to extend the left of Taylor's line, were less circumspect, as might well be imagined for a battalion under the command of an officer like John Brown. According to Austin, Brown 'thus addressed his men: "do you see those two guns and the rascals firing them at us?" The men all looked in the direction indicated. "Let us take a run at them." And away went John

Brown and his Pompadours, and carried the battery in an instant.'[30] Austin may have the language right, but Taylor makes it clear that it was the combined advance of the British right wing and the superior fire of the British guns that silenced the French battery, rather than the rush of a single battalion. Furthermore enough time had elapsed for the French to see that the fall of Merxem had left their flank and rear exposed, since, as Austin's own narrative makes clear, the skirmishers who had covered the attack on Merxem also had time to shift to the right and take part in this movement.

Indeed, it seems that the Light Company of the 2/35th was able to re-join its parent battalion before Taylor made his final advance against the French battery; although Austin's narrative does not make this explicit, his description of events tallies too closely with Taylor's account of what the 2/35th were doing for this not to have been the case. And whilst Austin's narrative is sometimes not entirely reliable with its timings and sequence of events, the attack on the windmill battery was not something that the young officer was likely to forget in a hurry for it was there that he received the wound that crippled him. As he relates, the problem was not the fire from the battery itself, which was soon evacuated, but that of the heavier pieces firing from the city ramparts. These had been increased in number in this sector since the last British attack, and caused heavy casualties amongst the leading British troops seeking to drive the French back from the dyke and capture the loop-holed windmill. Austin was in the act of trying to break down the defensive palisades on the crest of the dyke, and cursing the fact that the pioneers with their billhooks and hatchets were back with the main body of the battalion, when the French found the range. The first shot took off the arm of a private of the 2/25th, spraying Austin with blood, but before he could react a second ball crashed through the palisades and smashed his left leg just below the knee.

Austin experienced no immediate pain or faintness, instead feeling 'excessively hot, thirsty and savage', which spurred him to urge the men of his company forwards to avenge his wounding. Once the first rage had passed, Austin was able to sit up and examine his wound:

> I found that the bones were laid bare for some distance up the limb, and appeared white as the finest ivory, the tendons dangling and quivering like so many pieces of thread; while the haemorrhage was much less than might have been expected. This latter circumstance was probably due, in some measure, to the severe cold which retarded in a small degree the circulation, and made the blood less active.

Soon after receiving my wound, however, there came on a burning sensation in the injured part which gradually spread over my whole frame, and I felt a parching thirst which seemed to have constricted my tongue into a fire-brand, and my constricted throat into a heated furnace; but there was no water at hand to allay the heat which seemed as though it would consume me.[31]

At length, Austin was able to receive some medical attention, but with the position still under heavy fire it was impossible to move the causalities and he spent over an hour on the road as French shot continued to fall around him before his soldier-servant, assisted by two bandsmen of the 2/52nd, carried him back to safety.

For a time, the fight was sustained such that the French on the one side of the dyke, and the British on the other, were hotly engaged at very close range with musket fire. Eventually, though, the French fell back under the cover of the city's heavy guns, whose fire prevented Taylor from pushing beyond the Sint Ferdinandsdijk. Unable to achieve anything more in this sector, he sent most of the troops who had accompanied him back to re-join the main body of the Second Division in Merxem, retaining only a small force to cover this flank until finally relieved by Proby with the Guards during the afternoon. Meanwhile, Merxem itself had been secured and Graham and his staff were able to enter the place, from where the British commander sought to get a view of the augmented defences of Antwerp.

Accompanying the headquarters was the Duke of Clarence, who had followed the troops in his carriage at Graham's invitation. The popular conception of events has the Duke ambling amongst the advanced skirmishers during the attack, with several accounts suggesting that he came so close to the enemy as to have musket balls through his coat. That the Duke was physically brave there is no doubt, but these stories date for the most part from well after the fact, when the Duke had followed his brother onto the throne as William IV and there were officers aplenty who saw the advantage of stretching the truth if it flattered their monarch. Austin inserts an entirely fictitious meeting into his narrative of the first action at Merxem, which is impossible since the Duke had not even joined Graham by this point, whilst others credited him with additional heroics. The only story that seems plausible, since its circumstances fit the official reports and its teller is usually an honest reporter, is that told by Charles Shaw although he, like Austin, confuses matters by his belief that it took place in the January action. There is certainly an element of exaggeration, but enough circumstantial evidence to suggest the bare bones, shifted to the events of 2 February, are true:

The regiment had removed to the left, and I was with the rear company, when a gentleman dressed in a blue coat with white lining came up. From his dress I thought he was one of the Commissariat; but remarking two musket-shots through his coat, I thought him a rather rash commissary. I felt inclined to be offended, when, addressing me in a loud commanding tone, he asked, 'What regiment is that. Who commands it?'

'That gentleman', said I, pointing to Captain Diggle.

'Is he the commanding officer?'

'No; Colonel Gibbs commands.'

It was odd that the men should have had the same idea of the mysterious stranger as I had myself. They, too, supposed he must be a Commissary, and began muttering something about 'Bread Bags better in the rear,' when my friend Captain Anderson of the Artillery suddenly rode up. What was my astonishment on seeing him salute the supposed Mr. Commissary Bread Bags in the most respectful fashion, uttering at the same time the following words: 'If your Royal Highness moves a little more to the left you can have a little better view of the enemy. Sir Thomas Graham is in the steeple of the Church.' [. . .] The Duke's courage continued to be the talk of the army for some days; but I said little, thinking I had gotten into a scrape for having mistaken his Royal Highness for a Commissary.[32]

If the Duke was truly mistaken for a commissary, he seems to have taken it all in good part and there was no punishment for Shaw or his men. Indeed, unless later writers were cribbing from a single original source, it seems to have been a common mistake, being also mentioned in the account of 'P. W.', officer of an unspecified regiment, published in the *United Service Magazine* in the same year that the Duke ascended to the throne.[33]

Merxem was certainly under artillery fire when Graham's staff entered the village, but it is rather less likely that the Duke was permitted to get so close to the action as to have his coat pierced by one musket ball, never mind several: he himself made no mention of this, and, as Austin pointed out, 'bullets are not such respecters of persons as to perforate coats of royal personages without touching bone or muscle'.[34] Furthermore, although Graham and the Duke did indeed ascend the bell-tower it was not until the afternoon, well after the village was cleared, although admittedly whilst it was still under French artillery fire.[35]

Possible royal heroics aside, however, the morning had undoubtedly gone well for Graham. After two hours of fighting Merxem was secure, albeit under continued French bombardment, whilst Taylor's advance along the Sint Ferdinandsdijk had secured an advantageous forward post that ideally lent itself to the establishment of battery positions close to the docks and arsenal. To the other flank, no such approach was possible due to the inundations caused by the French, but these had proved to be a double-edged sword since a part of the retreating garrison of Merxem, evicted from the village, had become encumbered as they struggled through the ice and water to the south of the *chaussée* and a substantial – though no doubt exaggerated – number were killed there before the rest surrendered to be included amongst the 180 prisoners taken in the action. Further south, Thümen's Prussians had taken Deurne after a hard fight, being repulsed on the first occasion but renewing their attack and carrying the place by a frontal assault: Prussian casualties amounted to some 650 over the two days, whilst Graham had lost only 151 killed or wounded. Despite their losses, the Prussians were now closing in on Antwerp from the south and the time was seemingly at hand to establish the battery positions and bring up the mortars and guns that would destroy the French fleet. The reality, though, would prove far less straightforward.

Chapter VIII

'Want of Means and of Time'

THERE WERE SEVERAL REASONS why Antwerp and the fleet would prove a far tougher nut to crack than had been hoped. One major factor would prove to be the direction of the French defence, which, as had already been demonstrated by the fierce counter-bombardment that had checked the British advance, was far more inspired than hitherto. This, in turn, was due to the fact that the garrison had a new commander in the shape of Général de Division Lazare Carnot, replacing Maison who had departed with the last of his field forces on 29 January. The French Revolution's 'Organizer of Victories' had come out of retirement at the age of sixty in order to help defend his country and, after a hasty promotion when it was belatedly realized that his last military rank had been that of chef de battalion of engineers a quarter-century before, been posted as Governor of Antwerp where his energy and engineering skills were felt to be ideally suited to thwarting any Allied attack. Although he had only arrived on 30 January, it was on Carnot's orders that additional artillery had been shifted to oppose the sector attacked by the British, and he was also responsible for drafting thousands of the townspeople to make sandbags with which the gun emplacements could be strengthened to withstand the inevitable bombardment. According to one of his officers, 'Carnot's presence alone was equal to a reinforcement of troops; it both encouraged the soldiery and imposed on the immense population, which could not with safety be entrusted at this critical moment' and the new Governor 'seemed quite in his element having so important a place to defend, and he gained new vigour according as the danger increased'.[1] In all, Carnot had a garrison composed of around 10,000 men, not including the crews of Missiessy's warships, was well supplied with artillery, and had food for a six-month siege; nevertheless, many of his troops were conscripts or foreigners whose reliability could not entirely be counted on.

Graham, on the outside, had as much energy as his fellow veteran within but lacked the material resources that Carnot could draw on. Whereas Carnot could shift heavy 36-pounder cannon to bolster his defences,

Graham was forced to make his attack with a decidedly inferior siege train. This was not from want of preparation, for guns and rockets had been sent from England, but most of these pieces remained aboard their transports, ice-bound off the Scheldt, and Graham had to make do with what was available. Sadly, what was available was not very much. Only twelve heavy pieces had been successfully shipped across from England: four 10-inch mortars, two 8-inch howitzers, and six long 24-pounders. To supplement these, Graham had been obliged to take guns from the defences of Willem-stad. He thereby obtained a further thirteen mortars varying in calibre between 12 and 7½ inches, but of these only the three largest were modern pieces incorporating the modifications devised by the Chevalier de Gomer in the 1790s.[2]

As soon as he had completed his reconnaissance from the belfry of Merxem's church, Graham set things in motion to establish battery positions so that the guns and mortars could be emplaced and the bombardment commenced. The most important thing was to take advantage of the forward position that Taylor had occupied on the right, and Graham first made his way there to assess the situation:

> He agreed that the right was the weakest point, as the continuation of the dyke up to the works exposed it to sorties and to being enfiladed by cannon which they could bring forward. He desired Colonel Cameron of the 95th and me to go to the right and see how it could be covered.
>
> We found the means of making an abatis across the dyke, and agreed that this, with a good epaulment and traverses, should be commenced at dusk, and a gun if possible placed behind this cover; also a picket in a house behind the dyke.[3]

Taylor himself had neither the time nor the resources to begin to execute this work, which became Proby's responsibility once the Guards relieved Taylor's detachment during the afternoon and was begun that night under the direction of John Sperling. Carmichael Smyth had ensured that a convoy of wagons carrying entrenching tools and other equipment had been brought up close behind the infantry, arriving in Merxem by 19.00, and this allowed construction of the batteries to begin once suitable sites had been selected and secured. As well as the Sint Ferdinandsdijk position, three more batteries were constructed around Merxem itself.[4]

In order to get the positions complete as soon as possible, many of the troops continued to work through the night under the direction of the Royal Engineer officers. The task itself, as described by Morris, was simple enough:

> Such a number of men, as may be deemed sufficient, are provided
> each with a canvas bag, which is to be filled with sand and secured
> at the mouth by a string. These are then deposited in rows, under
> the superintendence of the artillery-men, and in an hour or two a
> battery may be so formed, which will bear a great deal of battering.[5]

However, the workers were the subject of concentrated French fire designed
to prevent the batteries being established. Eventually, once the main works
had been completed, 'splinter-proofs' were constructed 'by throwing up
earth against the walls of outbuildings on the side towards the town, and
laying sloping beams of timber against the other side', and by this means,
and the reinforcements of the parapets, greater protection was afforded to
the gunners.[6] For the moment, however, the working parties were left somewhat exposed and the work hindered, so that it was not until late on 3
February that the positions were complete, the guns emplaced, and the
batteries ready to open fire.[7] By this time, however, the continuance of the
operations had yet again been called into question.

The news reached Graham early on the morning of 3 February, in the
form of a letter sent by Bülow the previous night from his headquarters at
Schilde, which reported that he had now received positive orders to march
his corps southwards in order that he might join with Wintzingerode in
reinforcing the right wing of Blücher's advance on Paris. The letter was, as
Taylor observed on being shown it, 'friendly and cordial', but unless something could be done to change Bülow's mind it would be the death knell of
the whole operation. Whilst ordering Wood and Carmichael Smyth to
expedite the completion of the batteries, Graham sent Taylor to Bülow in a
last-ditch attempt to convince the Prussian commander to remain before
Antwerp long enough for the bombardment to take place. Accompanied by
Lieutenant Colonel Graham of Fintry, Graham's ADC, Taylor set off for
Deurne, where he believed Bülow had relocated his headquarters, but found
on arrival that he had not yet appeared. After being conducted by Thümen
over the ground where the Prussians had fought the previous day, Taylor
was informed that Bülow now intended to remain at Schilde and so carried
on to that place and finally obtained his audience. On the way, he met one
of Bülow's staff officers, 'who told me that the arrangements were made for
moving the troops from the stations then occupied on the 6th'.[8] Armed with
this knowledge, Taylor was unsurprised when Bülow, in a meeting also
attended by Saxe-Weimar, 'without difficulty agreed to stay upon our left
until the 6th, and, in short, until our business was done and everything
brought off down to the last platform'.[9] Stanhope may well have the truth of

it when he notes that the orders to move would have been drafted in the expectation that Bülow was at Breda, rather than outside Antwerp: this meant that he was three days' march ahead of where he needed to be, and that waiting until the 6th to oblige the British would simply put him back on schedule.[10] That aside, it must have been obvious to Bülow that abandoning an operation so important to Britain, just as it reached so critical a point, would have severe political repercussions that would severely hamper the various diplomatic initiatives that had caused the Prussians to cooperate against Antwerp in the first place.

Graham had thus obtained three days' grace in which to complete the bombardment, but, when the British guns opened fire at 15.30 that afternoon, it soon became clear that this would be no easy task. Only a short time remained before nightfall for the gunners to begin their practice, but even during the course of this limited window 'the defective state of the Willemstad mortars and ammunition was too visible'.[11] Some damage was nevertheless done, with a large fire being kindled around the arsenal, but by the time the firing ended the French had begun to get this under control. The problem, as Stanhope pointed out, was that it was impossible, due to the small number of pieces available, to keep up a sufficient volume of shells not only to set fires within Antwerp but also to keep down the heads of the firefighters: thus, a good hit might well start a blaze, but it would be extinguished before it could spread. Nor did it help that many of the Dutch mortars were as good as useless: several of them would burst during the course of the operations, and, other than the three big 12-inch Gomers, they lacked the range to carry the distance required.[12] Because of these failures, it was decided to shift some of the guns to the right, establishing a second battery position behind the Sint Ferdinandsdijk from where fire could be kept up from a closer range.[13] The delays in effecting this move, however, meant that it would not be until noon on 4 February that the bombardment could recommence, and when it did so only five of the Dutch mortars – the three 12-inch and two of the 7½-inch – were in a fit state to be employed.[14]

Throughout the bombardment on the 3rd, and again when it recommenced on the 4th, French counter-battery fire continued to be heavy and left the British infantry, pushed forwards to cover their artillerymen, feeling very exposed. Merxem came in for a very heavy pounding, but all along the line the infantry had to dig in, as Morris related:

Fortunately for us, there happened to be a mound of earth which screened us from their shot, while we lay down; we had to remain on this spot, not only through the day but during the following night; and, as the evening drew in, we began to dig caves to keep off a portion of the cold air, as well as a shelter from the shot. The ground being chiefly sand, we were enabled to do this with the aid of some pickaxes and shovels, the loan of which we obtained from the sappers and miners.[15]

Morris established just such a cave to shelter himself and his friend Sergeant Burton, a fellow Londoner in his fifties who had volunteered into the 73rd from the Tower Hamlets Militia. Having shivered through the first night of the bombardment, the two men hoped that, by spreading straw inside their shelter, they might spend a comfortable night, and Burton left Morris to make the finishing touches whilst he returned the borrowed tools to their owners. Unfortunately, whilst the Sergeant was so engaged,

> one of the largest sized shells, from the enemy's battery, burst in the air, immediately over us, and literally descended among us as a shower of iron. A large portion of the shell fell directly on the top of our cave, and destroyed in one moment the work of an hour. On Burton's return, he swore bitterly at the destruction of our work, and said to me, with the utmost seriousness, 'D—n it, Tom, how came you to let them do that!' As we could not again obtain the loan of the tools, we were obliged to walk or run about the whole night to keep the blood in circulation.[16]

Later, after Morris's company had been pulled back beyond Merxem to cook their rations, the French added insult to injury by dropping a long-range shot right into the fire on which the meat ration was being boiled, shattering the cauldron and injuring several men.

Under these conditions, the work of the Royal Artillery, Royal Engineers, and Royal Sappers and Miners in constructing, manning, and repairing the gun positions under French fire was an ordeal to say the least. Sperling described the situation around the 24-pounder battery, which was the most exposed post and under heavy French counter-bombardment, as:

> not a little appalling; the whiz of the shells carrying death and desolation; the crash upon the houses; the branches of the trees split and falling about. Considering our position very few suffered. One man's escape seemed remarkable; himself thrown down, his hat knocked off by a shell, falling close and apparently touching him, who, getting up, resumed his work as if nothing had happened. Another, however, was killed, though the shot did not seem to touch him.[17]

Despite the risks the work was undertaken with a calm professionalism that won the praise of those who saw it, with Carmichael Smyth writing afterwards in order to recommend one particularly distinguished subordinate for a suitable reward. As he explained to Lieutenant General Mann,

> Serjt. [William] Stevens of the Company of Sappers and Miners is the only Serjeant [sic] present with the Company. He is a remarkably good Man, and having superintended the laying of Platforms and made a Splinter Proof Magazine under a heavy fire with Coolness and Courage I am fully justified in recommending him to your Notice to be made Colour Sergeant to the Company & which appointment (I believe) is extended to the Companies of Sappers and Miners by His Royal Highness the Prince Regent's last Regulations on the subject.[18]

Carmichael Smyth's belief in the regulations allowing for Stevens's promotion was correct and his colour-sergeantcy confirmed, and in due course he was further rewarded with a commission as sub-lieutenant in November 1815.[19]

The French infantry remained as active as their gunners, mounting raids and sorties which were largely countered by the activities of the four Rifle companies under Lieutenant Colonel Cameron, whom Graham praised for the effective screening service carried out by the troops under his command. Taylor's brigade was held at readiness to deal with any major sorties, but in the event their services were not required and such fighting as there was did not escalate beyond the level of outpost skirmishing. To the south, the Prussians were also engaged as the French attempted to mount diversionary attacks in that direction as well, but the main threat continued to be from the French artillery. The danger was particularly apparent on the far right of the British position – where the French could take the British line in enfilade with the guns of the Fort du Nord, backed up by lighter pieces on the lower extremities of the Sint Ferdinandsdijk – and in Merxem itself which presented a large and obvious target, and which was still packed with troops. Stanhope related how one French shell, falling in a crowded house, killed or wounded seventeen men, and recounted a bizarre incident whereby another shot 'took off the legs of two officers who were walking together, a third one who was walking between them escaping unhurt'.[20] One might set this last aside as a tall story, were it not for the fact that it is corroborated by the account of 'P. W.', who states that all three officers belonged to the 2/37th, and by Austin who confirms this and explains that the ball was a spent one, rolling along the roadway, 'and as the two young officers were keeping step, it carried away the advanced foot of one, and the next moment the rear foot of the other; so that the one lost his right foot and the other one his left'.[21] Sure enough, the return of casualties for this phase of the operation records that Lieutenant Robert Stowers and Ensign George Chapman of the 2/37th both lost a leg as a result of this freakish occurrence; the identity of their lucky companion is not recorded.[22]

In this fashion the British bombardment continued, against the city and the fleet, but with increasingly diminishing returns. This was not helped by the fact that the firing on the 4th saw the disabling of five of the 24-pounders, which up to this point had been doing good work with heated shot against the French warships. Two of the disabled guns were repaired in time to fire on the 5th, as were the four damaged Dutch 7½-inch mortars, but this was still a marked decrease in the volume of fire that could be maintained and so the problems that had been experienced on the evening of the 3rd continued to thwart the efforts to start a serious fire either amongst the shipping or within the arsenal.[23] Nevertheless, the bombardment was quite enough of an ordeal for those on the receiving end, and much work was entailed in preventing the fires from spreading. Particular precautions were taken to preserve the warships in the basin, with the crews working to break the ice around the ships so as to ensure a supply of water, and covering the decks in a thick layer of dung and clay to render them as fireproof as possible.[24] Adrian Hayes, a Dutch conscript in the French artillery, had been wounded in the hand during the fight for the windmill on 2 February and spent the bombardment in hospital, where, as he reported when he deserted to the British a week later, the medical staff were swamped by over 400 casualties. His report also suggests that the relocation of the British batteries on the morning of the 4th may well have been counter-productive. As his interrogator, Captain Charles Hamilton Smith of Graham's staff, recorded, 'the shells did the greatest mischief the first day; and one ship was on fire – the two following days they fell almost all in a street to the left of the basin. He believes that six or seven shells only fell amongst the ships – 5 inhabitants & 2 galley slaves were killed – no soldiers lost their lives.'[25]

It was in all events clear by the end of 5 February that both time and ammunition were running out, and that nothing more could be done before the deadline for the Prussian withdrawal. Accordingly, preparations were made to dismantle the batteries during the night, remove the remaining ordnance, and prepare for retreat. The failing, quite simply, was down to a lack of material resources fit to do the job. As Taylor summed it up,

Want of means and of time, with the precautions which the enemy probably had taken to secure their ships from fire, have disappointed our hopes of a flaming result, but everything has been done to deserve success, and too much credit cannot be given to the artillery and engineers, whose exertions exceed all description.[26]

Carmichael Smyth, as befitted an engineer, was more thorough in his assessment but ultimately came to the same conclusion, writing that:

It was impossible to sustain the most sanguine hopes of a favourable result, notwithstanding however the utmost exertions of every officer and man in the Army and the very excellent practice made by the artillery who threw more than 2,000 shells & a continued fire of three days we have not obtained the objective in view. The ships were repeatedly on fire, several fires kindled in buildings round them, and a large Store Room containing the biscuit and provisions for the fleet being destroyed by being put on fire. The vessels themselves, however, have not been burnt and I am afraid it is not possible to destroy them without much larger means than we at present possess. The Enemy kept a number of people on board of these provided with Buckets and Fire Engines, and as fast as a fire was kindled it was extinguished. It appears therefore absolutely necessary to ensure success that we should not only have Mortars enough to set fire to the shipping but to enable us to throw such an overwhelming quantity of shells as to render it totally impossible for any men to work whilst exposed to it. Congreave Rockets have been requested as peculiarly adapted for this sort of service but as I have never seen them used I cannot give an opinion. We have none with this Army, or they would unquestionably have been made use of, and had a fair trial.[27]

Of course, rockets had been sent, along with more siege guns, but these remained ice-bound and out of reach. Under those circumstances, it might be argued that Graham would have done better to wait, but doing so would almost certainly have deprived him of Prussian support without which it would have been impossible for his force of no more than 6,000 effective infantry to have kept a garrison of nearly twice that number pinned within the Antwerp fortifications. It is true that he might ultimately have gained the support of Saxon and Dutch troops, but this was by no means a certainty and so the choice effectively came down to attempting an early operation with inadequate means but with Prussian support, or waiting in the hope of better means and Allied support, neither of which could be guaranteed. Under the circumstances it is therefore hard to criticize Graham's decision to make the best of things and try for an early bombardment. Now that he had tried and failed, though, he had no choice but to order another ignominious retreat.

Even before the withdrawal of the main British force began, steps had been taken to remove the wounded from the scene of the fighting. Those who had been hit on 2 February had been carried into Merxem itself, but with the village crowded with troops and under French bombardment it had been impossible to establish safely even a basic field hospital. Austin, when it was finally safe for him to be moved away from the fighting, was initially carried into the village but it quickly became apparent that there was no way that the inevitable amputation that had to follow so severe a leg wound could be carried out in such makeshift surroundings. Accordingly, those casualties most immediately in need of medical aid were loaded into hospital wagons, each capable of bearing four casualties, and these wagons were then convoyed back to Brasschaat. By this stage, Austin's shattered leg, around which a tourniquet had been fastened to prevent the loss of any more blood, 'had assumed a deep purple hue, and was thickly frosted up to the knee with shining particles of hoar frost. The pressure of the field tourniquet produced a numbing but painful sensation, which caused a most uneasy sickly feeling.'[28] Under such circumstances, in a wagon with three other men as badly wounded as himself, Austin's journey back to Brasschaat was not a pleasant one but at length it was over and the wounded were deposited in a château that had been requisitioned as a temporary hospital. Notwithstanding this appellation, it was completely devoid of facilities when the first wounded arrived, with no beds or blankets, and the best that could be provided by way of comfort was a little straw for the wounded to lie on.

Austin did his best to keep up his own spirits, and those of the men around him, whilst nerving himself for the agony of amputation, eventually receiving word that the surgeons were ready for him:

> I was then carried to the kitchen and placed upon a heap of bricks, which had been hastily piled together for the purpose of an operating table. Spread out on the dresser, the highly-polished surgical instruments glittered; while a sergeant of Rifles, who had just died of his wounds, occupied the farthest end of the said dresser. Several buckets were disposed in convenient places around the brick platform on which I reclined. A bevy of soldiers, mostly skulkers

'Soldiers of the 1st Regt. of Foot Guards in Marching Order.' This winter dress typifies the appearance of British infantry during the operations against Antwerp. Pen and ink and wash drawing by Charles Hamilton Smith.

Sir James Carmichael Smyth, 1st Bt. Mezzotint by Thomas Hodgett, after Eugenio H. Latilla.

James Hamilton Stanhope. Stipple engraving by Edward Scrivern, after Samuel John Stump.

'Engelsche Soldaat en Eene Eyer Verkoopster' (English Soldier and an Egg-seller). Hand-coloured engraving by Johannes-Adriaansz Bemme, after Jan Anthonie Langendijk.

'Stadhuis en Markt te Bergen op Zoom' (Town Hall and Market in Bergen-op-Zoom). Pen and ink with watercolour by Abraham de Haen.

The 'De Zoom' Ravelin, which is now all that remains of Bergen-op-Zoom's once extensive defences. Out of picture immediately to the left was the site of the ill-fated Centre Attack across the ice. That part of the ditch is now filled in, however.

The formidable medieval Gevangenpoort, viewed from the harbour area.

The harbour at Bergen-op-Zoom, now somewhat truncated and with the innermost basin, once behind this viewpoint, now filled in. Survivors of Skerrett's party, including Moodie, were trapped on the right-hand quay and had to swim across under fire.

Looking out of the town to the Gevangenpoort; a view which emphasises the narrow, hemmed-in streets of Bergen-op-Zoom.

and scamps who had contrived to get employed as hospital orderlies, by pretending to have received wounds or contusions any old woman would have cured in a couple of days, were marshalled in readiness to support and hold me.

Once Austin was on the table, four of the orderlies stepped up to hold him in position: brandy was offered but Austin refused it and, after accepting a draught of water, braced himself for the ordeal:

> When everything was prepared, one of the operators, with knife in hand, inquired if I was ready: and the reply 'Yes' was scarcely uttered when the keen, well-tempered blade had completed the first part of the operation. Next in order came the saw; and although I had frequently heard that the pain caused by separating the bone and marrow was dreadful, I found it in reality not more painful than other parts of the operation. Sawing through the bone produced no particular pain beyond a jarring kind of feeling that extended up the whole limb. Taking up the arteries caused a much more sickening sensation than either the cutting or sawing.
>
> In about ten minutes' time from the commencement of the operation, the stump was strapped up with adhesive plaster and bandaged, and the whole affair completed. During the operation I was painfully alive to everything that passed; and if my nerves did quiver when the knife divided the living flesh, I was too proud, holding the position of an officer who was bound by duty to set an example to the wounded soldiers, to allow a groan or sigh to escape me.[29]

The leg was afterwards buried in the garden of the château, whilst its former owner was carried to an adjacent room and placed before a roaring fire where he was tended to by two Irish women, wives of soldiers. After an hour in which he continued to experience phantom pains in the leg that was no longer there, Austin was taken out and loaded onto another wagon to be transported further to the rear; during this time, either the orderlies or the women had contrived to steal most of the small possessions from his person.

Austin was amongst the first of the wounded to be sent back over the four days that Graham's army remained before Antwerp, and it was doubtless the recognition that there would be more to follow that speeded the evacuation of the first wave, notwithstanding that this condemned them to a journey through the freezing night on extremely bad roads, with accommodation during the day in a series of temporary hospitals. In total, the journey took five days, during which those who had been hit in the action on 2 February were joined by those wounded during the bombardment. Graham's medical staff were initially overwhelmed by the numbers of wounded, and it took some while for matters to be fully arranged for the wounded officers, although Austin at least had the aid of his servant, which is more than any of the wounded rank and file could expect. On the other hand, he rightly complained of the heavy-handed attentions of a drunken surgeon, and of the unnecessary suffering of Lieutenant Samuel Brown of the 2/25th who underwent repeated probings of his wounded shoulder to establish the reason for his poor condition before it was finally realized that part of his collarbone had been shot away, leaving his arm without support and its owner in great pain.[30] These unfortunate experiences did not detract from Austin's obvious admiration for the medical staff who had treated him in the field, whilst the difficulties in the base hospital – not that this would have been much comfort – were the product of a system adjusting to a sudden influx of patients rather than any real inadequacy.

The problem was that not only were there the wounded to be cared for but also a growing number of sick 'as might be expected from the great severity of the weather & the youth of a great proportion of the soldiers'. Despite these difficulties, Graham was able to report that the bulk of the sick and wounded were doing well, and that although greatcoats continued to be in short supply the shortage of 'trowsers' and shoes had been at least partially made up by the requisitioning of some of those originally consigned for use by the Dutch, whilst the enterprising Storekeeper-General, John Trotter, had been able to compensate for a continued lack of flannel waistcoats by obtaining a supply of 'knit Guernsey worsted shirts' from Rotterdam.[31]

Considering the increased responsibility placed on his command by the departure of Bülow's corps, it was perhaps no bad thing that the British continued to maintain a reasonably healthy force, with only 10 per cent of Graham's men on the sick list as of 25 February.[32] Nevertheless, his troops remained thinly stretched and this was made worse by the fact that Bülow had asked that Graham occupy Brecht in order to maintain communication with the Prussian right wing at Westmalle. Graham unwisely agreed to this 'without having had an opportunity of examining the country or of ascertaining the accommodation for troops which the villages on or near the Great Breda Road offered' and, on discovering the inadequate state of the accommodation in the area, was obliged to cancel his initial scheme to post a whole brigade at Brecht and instead leave only a cavalry outpost to watch the place and keep up communication with his allies.[33] This was necessary because, notwithstanding his orders to join Blücher, Bülow had been obliged to leave Borstell's brigade behind as a reinforcement for Saxe-Weimar's corps, which was otherwise inadequate for its assigned task of occupying Brabant and supporting the apparently strong anti-French sentiment in that province. On the other hand, Gorcum had finally surrendered on 6 February, releasing the Prussian siege forces to march into France with Bülow.[34]

Although limited British reinforcements were on the way, Graham knew that any remaining hopes of achieving anything against Antwerp depended on maintaining a good relationship with Saxe-Weimar and so some means of keeping communications open was imperative. Otherwise, though, British dispositions were for the moment focussed largely on keeping the available forces sheltered until operations might begin again. Although the Antwerp garrison had reoccupied its advanced posts around Merxem after the British pulled back, Graham felt confident that the poor quality of Carnot's troops would prevent any aggressive French moves from that direction and therefore relied on a light screen to give early warning of a French advance whilst dispersing the bulk of his forces into billets. As he reported to Bathurst, headquarters were at Groot Zundert along with the bulk of the Second Division, which also had two battalions and two guns detached to Loenhout and Wuustwezel, whilst the First Division was posted at Roosendaal with outposts in the surrounding villages. Two squadrons of the 2nd KGL Hussars were with the outposts of the Second Division, 'observing the great road & patrolling to the front', and the third at Wouw covering communications. Two companies of artillery were with the heavy guns at Breda, one at Tholen in garrison, and one with each of the divisions.[35]

In reporting his dispositions to Bathurst on the 10th, Graham felt obliged to express his surprise that there was still no sign of transports in the Scheldt bringing either his heavy guns or the expected infantry reinforcements; nor was there any word of the progress of the expected reinforcements from Germany.[36] In fact, although Graham did not yet know it, the reinforcements were not far off whilst despatches from Bathurst received on the 14th – their arrival in itself indicating that the sea passage was open again – did serve to remind him that preparations were already under way to ship additional heavy guns and that his request that another siege train be prepared was unnecessary. Graham put this oversight down to his 'Not having the lists of transports by me when I wrote to Yr L'dship on the 11th inst.', but a siege train is rather a large thing to forget and the fact that Graham managed to let its existence slip his mind is indicative both of the pressure he was working under and the lack of support he was getting from his staff. Nevertheless, it remained a concern that Bathurst reported that some of the heavy guns had still not sailed as of 7 February, and Graham rightly observed that it would 'be very unlucky should another considerable delay take place, for except in some operations of siege I do not see how we can be usefully employed'.[37]

The same change in the weather that brought Graham his despatches from Bathurst also brought him the first of his reinforcements in the shape of the two battalions from Jersey, which came ashore at Helvoetsluys on 10 February after an epic voyage of more than a month's duration. Having received their orders in the dying days of 1813, the 2/30th and 2/81st boarded their transports on 2 January and set sail the following day. Immediately, however, a heavy gale blew in off the Atlantic and it was impossible to make any progress for the best part of a week, during which time the *Saragossa* transport, with half of the 2/30th embarked, became detached from the rest of the convoy. When the storm finally abated the remaining transports made an easy passage to Spithead but the wind then shifted to an easterly, making progress up the Channel difficult, and it soon became apparent that the master of the *Union* transport, carrying the other half of the 2/30th, was not up to his job. After he missed an opportunity to get into the Downs along with the rest of the convoy when the wind finally turned favourable, the night of 28 January found the *Union* off the South Foreland where a strong south-westerly gale blew up and threatened to drive the ship aground. The battalion's Surgeon, James Elkington, a Peninsular veteran who had been promoted into the 30th the previous year, recalled how all those on board were kept up all night by the danger, knowing that only the ship's two anchors prevented them from being driven ashore:

> The Master drunk and many of the crew. Having some deserters from the Navy among our men they were useful in lashing old jackets around the [anchor] cables to prevent them chafing. No Pilot could leave Dover to our aid. A regiment from the garrison was sent on the beach, waiting with assistance in case we should part from our anchors, that was expected every moment. It was a Sunday, and we afterwards heard that the prayers of the church were offered up for a transport full of troops in distress.[38]

Thankfully, the anchors held until the wind died down, but the *Union* was too battered to continue the voyage and the men were obliged to transfer to another ship, the *Sophia*, at Ramsgate in which they completed their voyage. Four days later, on 14 February, the missing *Saragossa* with the rest of the battalion on board also arrived off Helvoetsluys and, thus reunited, the 2/30th was able to join the 2/81st and march overland to join Graham.[39]

In many respects, the two new battalions were similar units: both had served abroad earlier in the war before returning home to serve in garrison and act as feeder units for their respective 1st Battalions overseas. Of the two, the 2/30th was the more experienced, having gone out to the Peninsula in 1809, served with Graham at Cadiz and then with Wellington during the 1811 and 1812 campaigns before returning home, much reduced in numbers, in early 1813. It was well-led, with many veteran officers and a first-class commanding officer in the shape of Lieutenant Colonel Alexander Hamilton, but the 464 rank and file were a mixed bag of Peninsular veterans and new recruits, and the manpower situation was not helped by the fact that a draft had been sent off to the 1/30th in India on 1 January.[40] The 2/81st was a little weaker, with only 376 rank and file on strength, and although it had seen previous active service this had been in the twin debacles of Corunna and Walcheren since when most of the regiment's effective manpower had gone to the 1st Battalion in the Mediterranean. Nevertheless, there were enough veterans left for Major General John Hatton, when inspecting the battalion three months previously, to note that 'the privates, with the exception of a hundred and fifty much too young for service, are a good body of men' and that there was a good cadre of experienced NCOs. This was not exactly unreserved praise, but considerably better than the state of most of the first batch of regiments sent to Holland the previous December.[41] Both of these newly arrived battalions were assigned to the Second Division.

If the 2/81st was a decent enough unit, though, there is no denying that Graham quite evidently thought the 2/30th the better bargain. He demonstrated this preference when he chose the 2/30th as the new home for one Edward Nevil McCready, a volunteer who had arrived in Holland with a letter of introduction asking Graham to post its young bearer to one of his battalions, where he would serve in the ranks in the hope of distinguishing himself sufficiently to obtain an ensign's commission. This way into the Army was not unusual for someone like McCready, who had the social standing expected of a potential officer but lacked the money to buy his first step, but it is certainly telling that although he had connections with Captain John Lewis Watson of the 2/69th, and sought to join that unit, Graham dismissed this and sent McCready to the 2/30th, where he assured him that Hamilton would take care of him. The colonel did just as Graham had expected, making McCready at once at home and introducing him to the battalion's officers, whose society as fellow gentlemen he could share in his off-duty hours. However, for McCready to gain a commission and become a full member of their mess he would need to learn his trade and prove himself in action and for instruction in this he relied on his new comrades in the ranks of the battalion's Light Company, whom he found to be 'fine young fellows'. McCready also realized 'from their swarthy cheeks and frequent expressions of "Jesu Maria" and "Malvito Carrhaco" that many of them had shared in the Spanish campaigns', and also noted 'their uncommon cleanliness' – another sign of a well-run battalion. In their company, McCready quickly learnt the rudiments of his chosen profession, as well as 'the accomplishments of smoking and gin drinking', whilst spending the next few weeks on outpost duty near Brasschaat.[42]

As McCready noted when he listed the troops present under Graham's command, the two battalions that had been left behind in the Baltic also now joined the army in Holland, having marched down through Germany. After some delays, they reached Breda by 28 February with a paper strength of 955 all ranks in the 4/1st and 498 in the 2/91st: of these, however, 157 had been left behind sick, mostly at Bremen. A small detachment was also left behind at Stralsund as a baggage guard, but several men who had been left behind from Gibbs's other battalions did re-join with this column along with '100 Foreign Recruits for the 33rd Regiment'.[43] These latter seem to have been hardly worth the bother, since there was trouble equipping them and they proved to be 'generally discontented & unhappy': by April many of them had deserted and Lieutenant Colonel William Elphinstone, commanding the 33rd, was looking to get rid of those who remained.[44] The two battalions remained as a brigade under Gore, attached to the First Division.

In terms of British troops, Graham now had at hand nearly the full force that he could expect to command. In addition, further foreign troops had become available to work directly with the British in the unlikely form of a detachment of Russian seamen sent to do garrison duty on the Scheldt islands and thus release the British forces there, freeing the Royal Marines for other duties and enabling the detachments from Graham's line battalions to return to their units. This reinforcement had been planned as early as January, but had been delayed by the same bad weather that had also deprived Graham of his siege train, and it was not until February that the Russians were able to land. Although often referred to in contemporary accounts as marines, due to their having been drilled and uniformed as infantry, the sailors came from the crews of Russian warships then laid up in British ports. As with the army's earlier encounters with Benckendorff's Cossacks, meeting these Russians led to inevitable comparisons with the British service, with Shaw shocked 'to see the brutal and unfeeling manner in which they were treated by their officers'.[45] Moodie, meanwhile, though pleased to note that despite their differences the British and Russian troops got on surprisingly well, was amused by the quarrelsome antics of the Russian officers, whom he described as having 'a snappish petulant manner, like enraged pug-dogs', and appalled by their extraction without payment of lavish meals, and the liquor to wash them down, from the Dutch on whom they were billeted. He too, though, was shocked by the treatment of the Russian rank and file, contrasting the harsh but fair discipline of the British service with the arbitrary and degrading beatings handed out by Russian officers.[46] Admiral Young, commanding the British warships and having overall responsibility for the Allied marine forces, was also less than impressed with the Russians, and Graham groused about having to feed them, but they did free the bulk of the Royal Marines for service elsewhere; that service, however, transpired to be away from the Low Countries, leaving the Allies there not much better off.[47]

With his regular reinforcements alone, however, Graham's force was now well in excess of the original strength that Bathurst had envisaged back in November, with 8,597 effective rank and file out of a total strength of 11,812,[48] but, even with the limited Dutch help that was available, there still seemed little that could be done with the force at hand. Heavy guns, if and when they arrived, might permit a movement against one or another of the Dutch fortresses remaining in French hands, but these had still not materialized and even when they arrived they would be insufficient for an attack on Antwerp. At home the utility of maintaining a force in the Low Countries at all was being questioned, whilst in Holland Graham sought either allies to help him against Antwerp, or, failing that, for a new role that would enable him to at least do something to aid the Allied war effort. In this atmosphere of uncertainty, the very future of the British army in Holland seemed in doubt.

Chapter IX

'We Might Get Hold of Bergen-op-Zoom'

GRAHAM'S EFFORTS TO FIND SUPPORT for continued operations had begun almost as soon as the army was back in cantonments. Even once the reinforcements from Jersey and Germany joined, he still lacked the means for a renewed movement on Antwerp and could do no more than place the city and its garrison under observation. On the other hand, once the heavy guns and rockets could be landed, it might be possible to attempt something against one of the smaller fortresses still remaining in French hands. This would not only be a worthwhile objective in its own right but would also make any future operations against Antwerp easier by removing any French presence in the Allied rear that would divert troops from the main effort.

The two obvious targets for such an attack were Bergen-op-Zoom and Fort Batz, the latter being situated on the island of South Beveland. The Royal Navy was particularly keen that Fort Batz be taken at the earliest opportunity, but Graham felt that this would be difficult unless Bergen-op-Zoom were in Allied hands since the former could be reinforced from the latter: on the other hand, if Bergen-op-Zoom were to fall it would likely render Fort Batz untenable, or, at the least, make it easier to take. Possession of these places would enable Graham to isolate Antwerp, cut French access to the Scheldt, and open up better communications with Saxe-Weimar and Borstell in Brabant: it would also situate him ideally for a renewed attack on Antwerp if the means permitted it.[1]

The question, then, became one of whether or not an attack on Bergen-op-Zoom was feasible, and if so, how best it might be carried out. Throughout the rest of February, Graham continued to vacillate as to the best way to proceed, sanguine about his chances the one day then despondent the next as new intelligence came in. His first report to Bathurst, written in the immediate aftermath of the return from Antwerp, and seeking to ascertain the Secretary of State's views as to how the army should now be employed, was largely positive, opining that:

I am inclined to think that if the reinforcements were arrived & the weather tolerably steady we might get hold of Bergen-op-Zoom, the garrison of which is certainly of a bad description. I have desired Lt. Col. C. Smythe to make out an estimate of the means that he thinks this siege w'd require. We have 14 24pdrs [. . .] at Willemstad & also 6 large howitzers & 4 Carronades and we have 4 of our own mortars brought back from Antwerp for w'ch there are shells enough but we cannot count on the Dutch mortars tho' the Gomers are very fine pieces of ordnance, as it is doubtful whether any more 12" shells can be procur'd.[2]

It would nevertheless be impossible to mount a formal siege operation without the aid of the Dutch, if only to provide detachments to labour in the trenches. Graham requested that 3,000 Dutch troops be made available for the prospective operation, but had no doubts that 'the Dutch Govt. w'd give all their disposable troops, after Gorcum falls, for an object of such vast assistance to Holland'.[3] In this expectation, however, he was to discover that matters were not as straightforward as he had hoped.

The root of the problem was that the Prince of Orange was thinking increasingly of his role in a post-war Europe, and of the ways in which his ambitions for an expanded United Netherlands might be furthered. In order to forward these ambitions, it was necessary for him to demonstrate the military strength at his disposal and if possible to do so within the southern provinces that he hoped would form part of his expanded realm; these objectives did not readily permit the detachment of troops to the pursuit of a secondary objective that would see them placed under British command. At this stage, however, the Prince's resolve was not so solid as to be closed to persuasion, and Clancarty promised to add his voice to Graham's military opinion in altering the Dutch plans:

I shall in the strictest confidence confide your ideas on future operations to HRH the P. of Orange. 1st because without his direct orders nothing can be done, & 2ndly because from several circumstances which have drop'd from HRH in conversation with me I am led to conclude, that upon the release of his blockading force before Gorcum, his object is to collect all the Dutch force both regular & Militia in his power, for the purpose of operation upon the side of Venloo, & Maestricht, & consequently I should despair of being able to draw from the Dutch Govt. any expression which might be construed into a wish on their part that the operation against B. op Zoom should be preferred, & their troops employed therein, which

I am disposed to admit would under other circumstances have been the most politic course:– whereas a plan of future military proceeding contemplated by you, may have the effect of influencing them to cooperate with you, & wean them from their own project, which if adopted would probably render both so weak in support as to leave little hope for the success of either. With this view I shall take the earliest favourable opportunity of conversing most confidentially with the Prince of Orange upon the possibility of your taking the project of an attack on Bergen into your contemplation, under instructions from England for this purpose; & tho' I can by no means, under the impressions on his mind in favor [*sic*] of an operation on the side of Venloo &c, promise success in obtaining the cooperation for you of the Dutch troops I believe you will give me credit for the assurance that nothing shall be spared on my part to procure it.[4]

In this resolve, Clancarty and Graham were successful, and after a meeting on 19 February Orange agreed to place 'a strong Dutch Brigade' at Graham's disposal.[5]

Taken from the garrison at Breda, and placed under the command of Perponcher-Sedlnitsky, the Dutch reinforcements proved to be an uncertain blessing. Graham was again left grousing over the fact that, as with the Russian seamen, he had to step in to supplement their inadequate commissariat, and was less than impressed with their quality. He deemed one of the four battalions so poor as to request via Clancarty that it be withdrawn and a replacement provided, and he further complained:

that the other three Battn's are not immediately fit for active service not having yet got their clothing, & that until they are put in a proper state I cannot agree to feed them. I made the same observations ab't the Horses & drivers of a fine Brigade of artillery attached to it. It is quite out of the question for use in action – the drivers being peasants, each man rid'g his own horse w'thout saddle or bridle. I sent them back to Breda at once.[6]

These comments suggest a belief that there was something tokenistic in the assignment of this brigade to Graham, and Clancarty was obliged to complain to the Prince of Orange that the Dutch were prioritizing their other forces, including local militias, over the troops serving with the British when it came to the issue of supplies and equipment.[7] In order to provide these new levies with some regular stiffening, and raise the strength of the total force, it was hoped to reinforce Perponcher with the men of the 2nd Nassau

Regiment, which, along with a battalion from Frankfurt, had gone over to the Allies in the south of France where it had been part of Soult's army facing Wellington.[8] Unfortunately, the on-going bad weather in the North Sea led to the tragic loss of many of the Nassauers by shipwreck off the Texel on the night of 8–9 February. This left only around 400 men, consolidated into a single battalion, who were posted to garrison Breda. The 200-strong remnant of the Frankfurt battalion, which disembarked safely at Helvoetsluys, were ordered home by their government.[9]

The Dutch reinforcements joined Gore's brigade in the concentration of troops around Bergen-op-Zoom. This redistribution of forces indicated Graham's shifting priorities, with the Second Division assuming the role of a screening force, masking the French in Antwerp and the Scheldt forts, and leaving the reinforced First Division, which had previously seen little action, to take on the main role. The Second Division was also down to a single effective general officer since not only was Mackenzie still incapacitated but, in addition, Taylor's royal duties finally forced that talented and promising officer to return to Britain; he left the army on 22 February.[10] In both his military and diplomatic capacities, Taylor had greatly distinguished himself during his three months in Holland, and Graham spoke of 'his merit & most valuable services' and the respect in which he was held by all who had served with him.[11] Gibbs had the division whilst Mackenzie remained unfit, leaving the two brigades under Lieutenant Colonels Harris and Browne with Gibbs replacing the latter once Mackenzie resumed command in early March.[12]

Exactly what the reinforced First Division might be required to do, however, remained unclear. A close reconnaissance of Bergen-op-Zoom, carried out, amongst others, by Jan van Gorkum, who had re-joined Graham's headquarters on 19 February after spending some time detached at The Hague,[13] confirmed that the fortifications remained formidable even though the garrison was by all accounts weak. Accordingly, Graham did 'not think there is any chance of taking B. op Zoom by a *Coup de Main*, unless I succeed in establishing a good understanding within, which I am trying to do', although he was more hopeful about the prospects for a conventional siege, assuming the resources could be assembled to mount one.[14] This, indeed, was the root of the problem because Graham still did not have the heavy guns that he needed. A sizeable contingent of artillery – the bulk of them captured Danish guns, intended for use in the Dutch fortresses but obviously adaptable to siege work as well – had been shipped across when the wind shifted, only to be caught in the same series of gales that had shipwrecked the unfortunate Nassauers. It took some time to ascertain the fate of all the transports, so dispersed were they by the storms, but by 28 February it was established that three ships, between them carrying twenty 24-pounders, ten 18-pounders, and 1,585 barrels of gunpowder, were aground off Goree – two of them swamped and full of water. A fourth transport – the *Albion* with a further ten 24-pounders on board – was still missing, believed to have gone ashore off the Hinder.[15] Those guns that did arrive safely – twenty 24-pounders and ten 18-pounders, all Danish, and twenty British 12-pounders – could not be brought up to Willemstad because of the volume of ice still choking the river.[16] Deprived of these means to aid in the mounting of a formal siege, Graham was obliged to cast around for an alternative.

Some thought was given to the use of gold rather than arms to win Britain's goals. Bathurst's original instructions to Graham had authorized the expenditure of funds for secret services, but this was meant only to cover the everyday business of intelligence gathering, such as payment of £150 to an un-named foreigner to make a trip to Paris and report back. Now a more extensive use of bribery was proposed, aimed at buying Britain's way into Antwerp. The idea was not Graham's – indeed, the general thought it a waste of time – but came from Clancarty who sought to offer Maison, and then Carnot, a sum of one million francs to deliver up Antwerp. The man chosen to carry out the scheme was John Mordaunt Johnson, a veteran of several secret assignments of this nature, who, despite having recruited an agent prepared to deliver the offer, nevertheless delayed his plan after receiving a report that Carnot was about to open negotiations with Graham. As the general was obliged to inform the spy, however, 'all that has been reported, and what you have heard of <u>a desire to enter into a *pour parler*</u>, has been exaggerated'. Furthermore, Graham confessed that he was:

> not sanguine in my expectations of any proposal being listened to and I am quite clear that none such as was formerly made would be worth trying; and if done at all it should be done in such a manner as to hold out a <u>real temptation</u> & if the value of the object in question be taken into consideration, with the very uncertain chance of its ever being attained by any other means, & more especially of its effect at this particular period, I should certainly think it a very cheap purchase at <u>three times the sum you mention in your letter</u>, & I have no scruple to give sanction that my name and responsibility from situation here will afford, to authorize the offer being made to that extent.[17]

Even the enlarged offer, to an old patriot such as Carnot, was unlikely to receive the reception that its instigators desired, and Graham was no doubt aware of this.

On the other hand, it was unlikely that all those resisting the Allies were possessed of such sound virtues, and Graham had been receiving repeated intelligence about the alleged incapacity and disaffection, not to mention fondness for the bottle, of the commandant at Bergen-op-Zoom, Général de Brigade Guilin-Laurent Bizanet. Such an officer might well succumb to temptation and it was surely with this in mind that Graham told Johnson that, for all his doubts about Antwerp, 'there is another object of the same kind that I am anxious to pay for in the same way & which by all accounts there might be reason to hope might be obtained by an offer of half what you mention'. In the event, nothing came of this scheme, further details of which are not available because Graham entrusted them to a messenger rather than paper, and Johnson, in any case, had other, more fruitful projects to attend to from his headquarters in Brussels, where he would eventually become Britain's chargé d'affaires after the peace. Van Gorkum, still engaged in reconnoitring the fortress and obtaining intelligence from the inside, was also authorized to put feelers out as to the possibility of Graham buying his way in.[18] It was doubtless with such a course of action in mind that Graham suggested to Bunbury that it might be possible to get into Bergen-op-Zoom by obtaining an 'understanding' on the inside, although Fortescue mis-construes it as implying that Graham was expecting the assistance of the civil population.[19]

As things stood, though, Graham could neither batter nor buy his way into Bergen-op-Zoom, at least not as yet, and so the only other option was to return to the idea of an escalade, a prospect which had been under sporadic discussion ever since the first troops had landed back in December. The general consensus amongst the engineering staff – British and Dutch – was that it would be perfectly viable to seize the place, inadequately gar-risoned as it was, by this means. Carmichael Smyth, indeed, had never wavered from his belief that this was the best course of action, and van Gorkum seems to have joined him in this opinion once he had acquainted himself with the nature of the place. Graham, however, was not yet fully committed to the prospect, and as late as 7 March was continuing to think primarily in terms of a siege operation, and fretting to Bathurst that not only were his available means inadequate but that they were likely to be reduced further if, as he feared, resources were drawn off to aid an attempt against Maastricht.[20] Nor was this the only potential draw on Graham's resources, for a warning was also sent from Bathurst that,

> the circumstances of the war make it appear probable that His Majesty's Government will find it advisable, within a short time, to

break up the army which is employed at present under your command, and to direct that a large proportion of the troops should proceed direct from Holland to North America.[21]

If it did prove necessary to implement this plan – and, as Bathurst made clear, it was by no means definite – Graham was also to send the Foot Guards to join Wellington and retain only a small force in Holland. In the opinion of Graham's biographers, this news served to precipitate the attack on Bergen-op-Zoom, with Delavoye asserting that 'it made General Graham more than ever desirous of getting possession of one, at least, of the many strongholds held by the enemy before the means of so doing were taken from him',[22] but this seems to stem largely from an after-the-fact assertion in Stanhope's memoirs, taken partially out of context, and is not supported by Graham's own correspondence.[23] We shall return to the role of Bathurst's letter later, but, as we have seen, the fortress had been a British objective since the very beginning of the campaign, with serious planning for the eventuality of either a siege or storm already under way when Bathurst's new instructions arrived. It should also be remembered that Graham had received a hint some time previously, prior to the second advance on Antwerp, that some or all of his troops might be removed for service elsewhere: the news that this withdrawal was imminent could therefore be no surprise. Instead, to understand fully the imperatives that finally caused Graham to make up his mind and authorize an attack, we need to look – as Graham himself was anxiously doing in the first days of March 1814 – at the strategic situation in northern Europe as a whole.

During January 1814, the Allies had rolled forwards across the middle and upper Rhine on a broad front. In the south, the Army of Bohemia, 201,000 Austrians, Russians, Bavarians and Württembergers under Schwarzenberg, advanced through Switzerland to seize the Langres Plateau and thereby turn the successive north–south river lines that would otherwise offer Napoleon a series of excellent defensive positions between the Rhine and Paris. Meanwhile, further north, Blücher's Army of Silesia, with an initial strength of 98,000 Prussians and Russians, began a more direct advance designed to pin down the French forces and prevent them moving against Schwarzenberg.[24] Napoleon, for his part, had deployed the bulk of his 67,000 available troops in a cordon covering the full extent of the frontier. This was further divided into three distinct commands under Marshal Macdonald in the north, Marshal Marmont in the centre, and Marshal Victor in the south. We have already seen how badly Macdonald fared against the Allies in the north, and Marmont and Victor, outnumbered to an even greater extent, managed worse still. By the last week of January the cordon had collapsed and the Allies were moving forward in earnest, but Napoleon was nevertheless able to assemble a central reserve some 41,000 strong, with the rebuilt Imperial Guard as its core, in order to strike back. The French were initially successful at Brienne on 29 January, defeating Blücher's advance guard, but were then narrowly beaten at La Rothière three days later when elements of the Army of Bohemia arrived to bolster the Allied forces. In the aftermath of this victory, however, Schwarzenberg inexplicably allowed a gap to redevelop between the two armies, allowing Napoleon to launch a whirlwind campaign against Blücher and inflict several stinging blows between 10 and 14 February. The Army of Silesia was forced to retreat, allowing Napoleon to turn on Schwarzenberg – who believed himself to be facing superior numbers – forcing him to withdraw as well. Whilst this was going on, Allied ministers – including Castlereagh, who had joined Allied headquarters – sought to broker a peace deal, but Napoleon, inspired by his recent successes, turned down the Allied proposals, leading to a hardening of attitudes and a growing preference for a settlement that would remove the Bonaparte dynasty from the French throne; in Britain, where the thought of the Crown Prince of Sweden ruling France as a Russian puppet was met with horror, this led to growing support for a Bourbon restoration.[25]

The news that reached Holland of the progress of these and subsequent battles was fragmentary, confused, and frequently out of date by the time that it arrived, but it was clear that the shift of the Allies' main focus to eastern France left something of a vacuum further north, leaving Graham unsure what – if anything – Allied headquarters expected to happen there. The remainder of the Army of the North – less Bülow and Wintzingerode detached to reinforce Blücher – was still largely unengaged and might yet provide additional forces that would enable the British to operate more effectively in Holland. Since the Army of the North had been left out of the plans for the Allied advance largely because of the self-willed actions of its commander, Graham rightly reasoned that it would be necessary to liaise directly with the Crown Prince rather than via Schwarzenberg whose command-in-chief, so far as the Crown Prince was concerned, was nominal in the extreme.

Since he had lost the services of Taylor, his expert at such missions, the task of obtaining support for Graham's operations fell to Stanhope. The mission was precipitated by the fact that Stanhope, who was in Brussels on private business, there received word from Saxe-Weimar that the latter's corps was to follow Bülow's movement southwards as 'a reserve for the Prussians', keeping only scattered light forces around Antwerp. This would have the effect of completely separating the forces of Saxe-Weimar and Graham, with the Antwerp garrison unmolested between the two, and would leave the British with only the newly raised Dutch forces to support them. Under these circumstances, Saxe-Weimar advised Stanhope that he believed that Graham's best option would be to have Wallmoden's corps placed under his orders or else obtain another reinforcement from the Crown Prince. These reinforcements could move on Lier to press Antwerp more closely from 'the other bank of the Scheldt'. As Stanhope explained to Graham,

> The Duke then said that were he to write to the Crown Prince, his representations would probably be entirely disregarded, but that considering the Corps of Wallmoden to be directly in the pay of England, and that the Crown Prince both by subsidy and interests must be disposed to acquiesce with his wishes, he hinted that a representation from you explaining the great Importance of putting your own Corps and his (The Duke) in a state of activity would have the desired effect.[26]

On receiving this intelligence, Graham took Saxe-Weimar's advice and tasked Stanhope with making his way to the Crown Prince's headquarters at Cologne with a letter from Graham 'referring HRH to me for information about the situation of the corps and expressing a wish to be reinforced'.[27]

Graham told Bathurst that he had instructed Stanhope to stress 'the great advantage it would be to gain possession of Bergen op Zoom', although he accepted that this objective, and all other local concerns, were 'of minor importance compar'd to the object of reinforcing adequately the Grand Army – of which our latest accounts come down only to what was known in England on the 15th'.[28] Stanhope had two meetings with the Crown Prince on 22 and 23 February and seems to have been rather impressed by him, describing him as 'penetrating and impenetrable' and defending his decision – extremely unpopular in Britain – not to have cooperated with Schwarzenberg and Blücher in what, at that time, seemed to be a flawed campaign in France.[29] On the other hand, he recognized that he was dealing with 'a good actor who will act well whatever part may be allotted to him and who will leave an advantageous or unfavourable impression on the mind according to the intrinsic merits or faults of the part which ambition or interests causes him to perform', and also commented on the Prince's overweening vanity, which caused him to claim credit – 'good news indeed, just what I told him to do' – for Wintzingerode's capture of Soissons on 14 February.

Stanhope opened the first meeting by asking if the Crown Prince was aware of 'the intended advance of the Duke of Saxe-Weimar', which immediately gave the game away insofar as his intention to ask for reinforcements was concerned. Nevertheless, the Crown Prince stated that he would be happy to order Wallmoden's corps to Holland since it was already in British pay, enabling Graham to restore a reputation that, to his mind, was being lost because he lacked the troops to sustain it; nevertheless, the Crown Prince also made it clear that his own priorities now lay further south and that – like Orange – he was primarily concerned with gaining possession of Maastricht. Having secured the promise of reinforcements, Stanhope reported to Graham that,

> [I] then stated that there was one point which you had not communicated to the Duke of Saxe-Weimar or any one but that you had desired me to communicate to HRH the probability of your Corps being withdrawn. I mentioned to him the number of men you had been promised on accepting the command, the failure of the militia bill, the reduced numbers now sent in consequence of being obliged to reinforce Lord Wellington and the insufficiency of those reinforcements.[30]

This is a key point, since it reiterates the fact that Graham was fully aware of the likelihood of his forces being withdrawn prior to receiving Bathurst's letter of 28 February, and Stanhope's account of what passed next is also revealing since it sheds further light on Graham's plans with regards to Bergen-op-Zoom.[31] Stanhope having detailed Graham's strength, dispositions, and his reasons for wishing to possess the fortress, the Crown Prince not unreasonably asked, 'How do you hope to take it, you cannot escalade it?' to which Stanhope replied 'that from the small number and bad quality of the garrison, one might hope they might surrender after some days of open trenches'. In other words, Graham was hoping that by mounting a formal siege, even a weak one, he would be able to bluff – or, bearing in mind the exchanges with Johnson, perhaps bribe – Bizanet into surrender by giving him grounds for doing so with honour.

The remainder of the meeting was largely taken up by flattery of Graham on the Crown Prince's part, and a discussion of the Allied prospects in France. The latter, however, was based on out-of-date information since on the following day an ADC of Sir Charles Stewart arrived from Allied headquarters bringing news of the reverses suffered by Blücher, and this prompted a second meeting that was also attended by Edward Thornton, Britain's Minister-Plenipotentiary to the Swedish court. This was largely taken up by a general discussion of events and more boasting by the Crown Prince, but the three men met again after dinner and Stanhope was assured that orders would be given for Wallmoden to move on Breda or Malines, which Stanhope believed would be advantageous since from Breda Wallmoden could cover the siege of Bergen-op-Zoom. The Crown Prince did however express some concern that relative rank would be an issue, but this stemmed from an erroneous belief that Wallmoden was now a full general and, as Stanhope pointed out, this was irrelevant since Graham also held that rank for the duration of his service in Holland and was in any case 'appointed Com'r of the Forces which I supposed would remove all difficulty'. Furthermore, the two men were already acquainted, but, even so, the Crown Prince insisted that Thornton write to notify the British court formally that he was placing Wallmoden under Graham's orders. The Britons were informed that Wallmoden would be able to join Graham in less than a fortnight: Thornton subsequently clarified this by giving a date of 15 March at the latest and stating that the reinforcement would total 8,000 men. The Crown Prince stated his hope that Graham 'would be pleased with what he had done and would not find it necessary to ask for more troops but that he would always listen with pleasure to all your demands'. In response to concerns that he would receive timely warning if the British did get orders to embark, Stanhope made it clear 'that the measure was not yet decided upon and might perhaps never be put into execution, but that if it was I was convinced the Gov't at home would communicate with HRH', on which point Thornton wholeheartedly agreed with him.[32]

Perhaps inevitably, bearing in mind the Crown Prince's character, the promised aid was by no means as timely or sizeable as Stanhope and Thornton were led to believe. In the meantime, although pleased to know that reinforcements were on their way, Graham had other things on his mind. Napoleon, having discovered that Schwarzenberg was already withdrawing, and having given him further incentive to retreat by defeating the Württemberg contingent at Montereau on 18 February, switched his attentions back northwards and moved to complete his defeat of Blücher. Blücher, for his part, had cancelled his withdrawal once Napoleon moved against Schwarzenberg, and planned to join with Bülow and Wintzingerode for a renewed drive on Paris; in order to facilitate a union of Allied forces, Blücher moved northwards and drew Napoleon after him.[33] By the time that news of this reached the Low Countries, at the same time as Maison's hitherto quiescent command began to show renewed activity, the impression began to develop that a full-blown French offensive in the north was on the cards, potentially aiming to retake Holland. Saxe-Weimar, whose overstretched corps was still incomplete, began to grow nervous.[34]

It had been hoped that the provinces of the former Austrian Netherlands would prove to be a fruitful recruiting ground for the Allied cause, and several thousand of the muskets that had been shipped across to arm the Dutch were now redirected there. Captain Charles Hamilton Smith of Graham's staff was posted there as Britain's man-on-the-spot, but reported that things were taking longer to develop than had been hoped. Described by Graham as an 'extremely active & intelligent officer',[35] and possessed of a fine reputation as an artist to boot, the 38-year-old Smith had been born in Flanders of British parents and had previously worked under Trench as Headquarters Commandant, before being sent, in mid-February, 'to Ghent, where he has many friends, to get at the most accurate state of that part of Brabant & most particularly of the possibility of getting hold of Newport [*sic*] or Ostend so as to have a sea port for communication with England on the south side of the Scheldt'.[36] This last objective is an interesting one, suggesting that Graham was considering shifting his operations to the other bank of the Scheldt, but Smith was soon reporting that the situation was less promising and that despite the 'favourable disposition of the Brabanters' they were disinclined to enlist in the British service due to a fear of being sent to the West Indies.[37]

This led to a new scheme for raising a small unit of Belgian volunteers under their own officers, to be called Tirailleurs Belges, who would be in British pay until a general peace and then pass into the service of the sovereign to whom the Low Countries would be ceded. NCOs would be provided by detaching foreign veterans from Chelsea Hospital or the Veteran Battalions, and the men would be guaranteed that they would not be deployed outside Europe. There would be two companies, each of four officers and 120 rank-and-file, wearing the same uniform as the 95th Rifles. The men would be armed with muskets, bar twenty men per company with rifles.[38] This would hardly have been a huge increase to Allied arms, but was more realistic than plans being developed by Saxe-Weimar and the Military Governor of Brussels, Count Lottum, for the raising of multiple regiments of nearly 3,000 men apiece by local 'men of fortune who would only be influenced by patriotic motives': neither Smith nor Graham thought much of this scheme, which unsurprisingly produced nothing like the numbers hoped for.[39]

In any event, all these schemes to enlist Belgians would take time to reach fruition, and Saxe-Weimar was left with only scant resources. He sought to take Maubeuge, but to do that he was obliged to ask Graham for the loan of heavy guns. All that was available was the remains of the siege train that had been used in the bombardment of Antwerp, which Graham dutifully sent off to help his ally, although with Maison seemingly moving to raise the siege he felt that this would be an empty gesture that would likely result in the loss of the guns.[40] Certainly, with little by the way of local reinforcements to assist him, Saxe-Weimar would have found himself hard pressed to resist an offensive movement by Maison, let alone by Napoleon in full force if the rumours to that effect were true. Graham's gesture, furthermore, meant that he now had no heavy guns whatsoever at his own immediate disposal, since the shipment from Britain could still not be landed, and he grew increasingly concerned that, at the very least, the increased French strength in the north would enable them to throw a reinforcement into Antwerp. This last concern prompted him to move, and on 4 March he wrote to Bathurst to report,

> that in consequence of the Enemy having repossessed themselves of Courtray [sic] & of the Duke of Saxe-Weimar's having expressed his apprehension that a Corps of 3,000 infantry & a body of Cavalry from there was directing its march on Ghent w'th a view of reinforcing the garrison of Antwerp, I mov'd forward the right of my Corps from its cantonments in Roosendaal to Stabroek & Putten so as to interrupt the communication between Antwerp & B. op Zoom to prevent the latter garrison receiving reinforcements from Antwerp.[41]

This movement was carried out by the Second Division but, with Mackenzie still not having re-joined, Graham shifted his own headquarters to Calmthout in order to supervise the operation in person.

The march got off to a bad start, with Graham obliged to ask for advice following a disastrous fire that destroyed the billets occupied by the 2/25th. As he told Bathurst in a private letter:

> For want of sufficient accommodation for the troops, a Battalion was quartered in a Gentleman's Chateau near Groot Zundert & just as the 25th 2d Bn. was marching off a fire broke out in the upper part of the House & it was not possible by any exertion to save it.
>
> The owner, a baron, formerly in the Austrian Service, came from Brussells [sic] where he generally resides & I told him that if he would state what he had to say in writing that I would transmit the paper home as I could not take it upon me to promise him a satisfactory indemnification for this unlucky accident.
>
> The Regiment is certainly much to blame, as it was the business of the officers to have seen that the fires were all extinguished as the floors of the rooms were covered w'th straw. But it would be a

hopeless case for the sufferer to throw him back on the Regiment.
Indeed the officers have laid in Claims for the loss of baggage some
of w'ch could not be remov'd in time the progress of the flames was
so rapid.

As Graham went on to explain, it was one thing for him to make small
payments 'in cases of losses to individuals of the Country by unavoidable
circumstances' but even at a conservative estimate the cost of the damage
done amounted to £1,500 and this he felt unable to authorize. No formal
action seems to have been taken against the officers of the 2/25th, but the
battalion 'was not in great repute' as a result and became the butt of jokes
for some time to come, most notably – if a little feebly – the repeated
defacing of the regimental title of 'King's Own Borderers', chalked on to the
battalion's billets, by men of the 2/52nd who replaced the 'rd' of Borderers
with 'th'. Consequently, 'there were many squabbles, and much rivalry'
between the two battalions.[42]

As is evidenced by the fact that the men of the Second Division had time
for such japes, the expected French movement did not materialize but the
bulk of its battalions remained in these advanced positions whilst the First
Division continued to observe Bergen-op-Zoom.

This, then, largely completes the strategic picture as it appeared in the first
week of March 1814, and before looking at the decision, made at the end of
that week, to attack Bergen-op-Zoom, it is worth reviewing the extent of
Graham's knowledge of what the French were doing, what the Allies were
doing, and what resources he himself had at hand.

Insofar as the French were concerned, there were two distinct factors:
what Maison might be doing, and what Napoleon might be doing. In respect
of Maison alone, Graham does not seem to have seen him as a major threat.
Saxe-Weimar reported that it was believed 'that 2,000 men have got into
Antwerp', but reports by French deserters stated otherwise and Graham
chose to accept them, believing that 'all these demonstrations [. . .] are meant
to draw the attention of the allies from Mauberge [sic]'.[43] In any case, his
own operations were intended in no small part to free as many troops as
possible for field service so that he could press the Antwerp garrison more
closely. As Carmichael Smyth recorded, the right of the Second Division:

was placed at Fort Frederick close to Lillo upon the Scheldt and [its]
left at the village of Braschaet [sic]. At Fort Frederick a battery
secured by strong palisades, trous de loup &c has been constructed
to cut off all communication by water from Antwerp to Bergen op

Zoom and Batz; and the village of Braschaet upon our left has been strengthened by field works. It is also in contemplation to secure Eckeren and Donk by strong works so as to enable us by a chain of posts to prevent the Garrison of Antwerp deriving any succours from the Country on this side of the Scheldt. By means also of these posts a larger proportion of our force is rendered disposable and a greater assemblage of course may be made upon any one front.[44]

This was all well and good, but the Second Division contained only two-fifths of Graham's infantry, the remainder of which was tied up observing Bergen-op-Zoom and would only become available if that place fell.

This was not the only reason why the attack was ordered, however, since Graham remained concerned about the potential threat posed by a more aggressive French strategy in the north. Such an outcome was only likely to materialize in the event of a major retreat by the main Allied armies in France, but if this did come to pass then Graham knew he would have limited resources with which to resist it. He knew that Saxe-Weimar's incomplete corps was weak and scattered, and had 'no great faith in the Saxon troops' believing them to be 'individually brave & high spirited' but comparing their discipline unfavourably to that of the Prussians.[45] Further-more, a major French advance in the north seemed all too likely based on the most recent news that Graham had of the progress of the fighting in France; although he was painfully aware that he was being forced to operate without up-to-date intelligence, there was no denying that the most recent reliable news, received on the morning of 7 March from Thornton at the Crown Prince's headquarters, indicated 'that there is a very unfavorable [*sic*] turn of the War in France'. The only solid information in the report was 'the fact of the Grand Hd Qtrs being at Chaumont on the 26th', but the inference was that retreat was likely and that 'the allies[,] not possessing any of the strong places on the frontiers[,] may be great sufferers if oblig'd to retreat further'.[46] Under these circumstances, and without giving up his own plans for more active operations if the situation permitted, it was entirely reasonable for Graham to make plans for the defence of Holland in the event of a French offensive in the north.

In preparing for such an eventuality, Graham could take little account of the potential contribution of Saxe-Weimar's corps, or of the Dutch them-selves, whose exertions Graham could only wish were 'more commensurate with the risk that a change of fortune may expose Holland to'.[47] The attention of the Prince of Orange, and of the Crown Prince for that matter, was focussed primarily on getting hold of Maastricht, and so Graham could expect little in the way of Allied help in his own area of operations, beyond the local Dutch garrison forces and Perponcher's single brigade. Wallmoden's corps, he now learnt, was further away than he had been led to believe and would not be with him for some time. Under these circumstances, it would be necessary to secure the best possible defensive line, and the possession of Bergen-op-Zoom became a vital adjunct to this. As Stanhope explained it, by 'gaining Bergen-op-Zoom the line of hostile fortifications from Antwerp to Flushing is broken, our naval cooperation brought into the scale & in short on the occupation *depended the existence of Holland*'.[48] This may be over-stating the case a little, but there is no denying that its possession would have been extremely useful for the Allies, along with Breda, Willemstad, Gorcum and Hertogenbosch, in delaying a French advance into Holland. Conversely, leaving Bergen-op-Zoom in enemy hands would have enabled the French to start any operations with a foothold on the north bank of the Scheldt that would facilitate any movement against the Allied right. At the very least, even if the best the French could achieve in the north was to recover the Belgian provinces and throw a reinforcement into Antwerp, there would be little – save Bergen-op-Zoom if the British could get hold of it first – to prevent the reinforced Antwerp garrison taking to the offensive and driving the British back on Willemstad where, with the rivers still iced up, evacuation would have been difficult if not impossible. In order to prevent the likelihood of such a disaster, 'possession of Bergen-op-Zoom in these urgent circumstances was deemed indispensable by Sir Thomas Graham'.[49]

Van Gorkum and Carmichael Smyth between them seem to have the truth of the matter, that events had reached a point where Bergen-op-Zoom in French hands was simply too much trouble, irrespective of whether the British assumed an offensive or defensive stance. Nevertheless, the role of the potential recall of forces in Graham's thinking needs to be given due consideration, if only to dismiss the inflated prominence that many accounts – largely taking their cue from Stanhope – allow it. Since he was able to discuss its implications in a letter of 7 March, Graham had evidently received Bathurst's letter of 28 February, warning that troops were likely to be withdrawn, and had made such preparations as he could pending definite knowledge that the troops were to go.[50] No record survives that Bathurst ever took the proposed withdrawal any further, and no transports were sent to embark Graham's troops; indeed, the last instructions sent prior to London receiving the news of the failed attack relate to the shipments of arms and supplies, and the retention in Holland of the Russian contingent garrisoning the Scheldt islands, with no mention of withdrawal.[51] In any case, with the rivers frozen it would have made no odds whether transports were sent or not: whatever Bathurst may have planned, Graham could not have evacuated his troops even if he had wanted to, and whilst a strict interpretation of Bathurst's instructions of the 28th would have entailed having the troops who were to go shifted down to Willemstad in readiness, the practicalities of the situation meant that this would have served no purpose. If the weather had begun to improve, and the rivers become navigable again, Graham would have had time enough then to pull back to the ports and await the Secretary of State's instructions, but in the meantime his troops were doing more good in the field.

If the proposed withdrawal had any part in Graham's decision to attack Bergen-op-Zoom, it was not through some desire to strike a blow while he still could, but, rather, because it served only to strengthen the arguments in favour of taking the fortress to serve as a barrier against renewed French aggression in Holland.[52] To weigh against the troops under orders to leave – say 6,000, to include the Guards as well as the 4,000 line infantry slated to go – Graham knew that he could expect to receive 8,000 reinforcements once Wallmoden finally arrived, leaving the Allies marginally stronger than before. There would, however, likely be a window between the British leaving and Wallmoden arriving, and possession of Bergen-op-Zoom would undoubtedly render it easier for the handful of remaining British troops, along with whatever forces the Dutch could spare, to defend Holland during that interim. Bathurst's letter did not, therefore, directly precipitate Graham's decision to attack Bergen-op-Zoom, but it did serve to render yet more pressing the existing imperative – stemming from the fears of a French counter-attack – acting in favour of attempting to gain possession of the place.

Even had time permitted a formal siege – which, judging by his earlier views as represented by Stanhope to the Crown Prince, was Graham's original preference – he did not possess the resources needed to mount one. His original siege train, used at Antwerp, had been sent off to Saxe-Weimar outside Maubeuge, and the replacement guns were still ice-bound aboard ship. On the other hand, planning and reconnaissance had been under way for several weeks with a view to mounting a surprise attack and Graham's engineers – British and Dutch – pronounced themselves in favour of such an operation. Just before noon on 7 March, after the receipt of Thornton's dire reports of the Allied setbacks in France, Graham sent Carmichael Smyth to discuss with van Gorkum the progress of the latter's plan for an attack, and was told that it was ready for his inspection. Having gone over it, the British engineer agreed with his Dutch colleague that the scheme was a sound one, and when van Gorkum informed him that the night of 8–9 March, when there would be a low tide, would be the ideal time to implement it, Carmichael Smyth's 'enthusiasm grew even more, because the commanding general wanted to possess the fortress as soon as possible'.[53] If the attack were to be launched on such a tight schedule, this meant only thirty-six hours before the attempt would be made. With no time to lose, a planning meeting was set for 14.00 that afternoon, in order to finalize the details.

All this emphasizes the role of the potential French threat to Holland as the key factor in Graham's thinking, and it should also be noted that Graham's own account of events makes no mention of the possibility of his troops being withdrawn having any influence on his decision to mount the attack. Writing privately to Bathurst, he asserted that:

> My chief inducement to undertake at last what I had all along resisted the temptation of, arose from three points of attack being satisfactorily explained by Dutch engineers well acquainted with the place, instead of one, and by the consideration of the increased importance of getting hold of such a barrier, should the events of the war in France bring the enemy back in force to this frontier.[54]

Thus, the coincidence of the completion of van Gorkum's planning for the attack and the increase in the imperative for such an attack to be launched led to Graham's decision to go ahead. Once an attack had been decided upon, 'it was necessary to carry into execution the plan almost as soon as it was determined on, to prevent the enemy from receiving information of the movements of the troops', to which must be added the fact that, as van Gorkum had noted, the state of the tides on the night of 8–9 March made this the ideal date to make the attempt.

The irony, of course, is that none of this haste was in fact necessary. Not only had Bathurst's scheme to withdraw part of Graham's force apparently succumbed to the Secretary of State's usual round of second thoughts, but the French threat – beyond that posed by Carnot's command in Antwerp – had, if Graham had only known it, already evaporated. On 27 February, only one day after the date of Graham's most recent intelligence of his doings, Schwarzenberg had realized that Napoleon had moved against Blücher, turned his own forces around, and defeated Marshal Oudinot at Bar-sur-Aube. Meanwhile, although Napoleon was able to win a narrow and bloody victory over Blücher at Craonne on 7 March, he was unable to continue his advance to the north and the Army of Silesia, joined by Bülow's corps, was able to regroup in preparation for the decisive clash three days later at Laon.[55]

That battle would prove to be an Allied victory that would end for good the threat of a French counter-offensive into the Low Countries, but by then Graham's gamble at Bergen-op-Zoom had already been made.

Chapter X

'I Am in First'

PERHAPS UNSURPRISINGLY, since they were its architects, Jan van Gorkum and James Carmichael Smyth both believed that there was nothing whatsoever wrong with the plan that they presented to Graham and his staff at Wouw on the afternoon of 7 March 1814. Things only went amiss, both subsequently asserted, after the troops were inside and, crucially, after their responsibility as engineers had ended. It is a convincing enough *prima facie* argument, albeit rather glib, but on deeper analysis it does not entirely hold water. To appreciate the plan's undoubted merits, though, as well as its potential pitfalls, it is necessary to detail just what the proposal entailed. In turn, in order to understand the nature of the proposal, it is first necessary to understand the nature and layout of the defences of Bergen-op-Zoom.

The fortress had long been one of the strongest places in Brabant, withstanding two sieges by the Spanish during the Eighty Years War. As a result, the fortress became known as 'The Virgin', but although its defences had never been penetrated they had nevertheless grown outdated by the end of the seventeenth century and were therefore scheduled for rebuilding by the great engineer Menno van Coehoorn as part of the Dutch Republic's defensive barrier against the ambitions of Louis XIV. Specifically, the fortress served to anchor the right flank of the Lines of Steenbergen which stretched away northwards to the town of that name and whose dykes and sluices – used with effect against Habsburgs and Bourbons alike – were part of the defensive scheme by which large tracts of land could be flooded to impede the invader.[1] Coehoorn's remodelled defences were, in essence, those that formed the target of Graham's attack but by 1814 the fortress was virgin no longer, having fallen for the first time in 1747 to a French army under the Danish-born Comte de Lowendal, right-hand man of the great Maurice de Saxe. The French had sacked the place after they captured it, but it was returned to Dutch control as part of the Peace of Aix-la-Chapelle the following year and the defences restored.[2]

Although the Lines of Steenbergen in theory provided cover for the northern sector of the main defences, in practice the lack of troops prevented their use and the British had been able to operate with relative impunity on both sides of the Lines ever since December. Similarly, the large entrenched camp on the southern side of the fortress known as the 'Kijk in dem Pot', a relic of the 1747 siege, could also not be held. Other than patrols and gate guards, the entire garrison, such as it was, was pulled back within the main fortifications and, even then, was hard-pressed to cover their full extent. This enabled van Gorkum to carry out extensive communications with the inhabitants as he gathered intelligence during the days before the attack.[3] As the engineer and historian Major General Sir John Jones – who knew the place at first hand – explained, the fortifications had been designed to hold the supplies for an army, and since they were configured to enable the garrison to be resupplied by sea, had been built on an extremely extensive scale that now rendered them vulnerable and enabled Graham, having only a fraction of the resources with which Lowendal had deflowered the virgin fortress, to consider an attack. As the Allies had discovered at Breda and Tholen, ditches were far less of an obstacle when they were iced over – a matter of no concern when the fortresses were laid out, since winter almost inevitably saw eighteenth-century armies retire into quarters until the weather improved – and gave the attackers a further advantage.[4] Yet, even discounting the unmanned outworks and the dubious ditches, the inner works within which Bizanet had concentrated the bulk of his garrison were by no means negligible.

As befitted its name, the fortress straddled the river Zoom, an insignificant stream that flowed into the Scheldt and which, suitably canalized, served to drain the area north of the Lines of Steenbergen. Much of the water that flowed towards the town was diverted to flood the ditches on the north-eastern face, and to inundate further the country on this front so as to limit any siege operations. The stream proper continued along the north front, where it furnished water for the ditches, before flowing into the fortified harbour on the town's western face. Linked to the Scheldt by a canal that enabled access even at low tide, when the fortress was separated from the river by sandbanks and marsh, the harbour extended some distance into Bergen-op-Zoom itself, within the lines of Coehoorn's fortifications. This outer harbour area was, however, partially separated from the original fortress with the primary link being a mediaeval fortified gate called the Gevangenpoort. Covering the outer end of the canal, at its junction with the Scheldt, was a sizeable detached Water Fort. The main fortifications consisted of sixteen bastions, supplemented by a large detached 'De Zoom' Ravelin on the north-east angle as well as smaller lunettes, and the walls were pierced by only three major gates where the Steenbergen, Breda, and

Antwerp roads entered the fortress: the Breda Gate is in some accounts called the Wouw Gate, Wouw being the first place of note on that road after leaving Bergen-op-Zoom. The Scheldt face was protected largely by the waters of the river, kept from freezing around the Water Fort by the efforts of the garrison, whilst the landward sectors were covered to the north and east by flooded ditches and to the south by the extensive entrenched camp. The northern sector was less strong than the others, and the value of the water obstacles had been reduced by the construction of the Tholendijk in the late eighteenth century as part of a land reclamation scheme: cutting across the marshland to the north-west of the fortress, the dyke both limited the extent of the Scheldt inundations and provided a potential line of approach.[5]

Even allowing for its weaknesses, there was no denying that this was a formidable array of defences if fully manned, but this, of course, Bizanet was unable to do. Nevertheless, given adequate warning, the French might still defeat an attack if they could concentrate their strength against it. Thus, the attackers' job was to ensure that the French would be unable to mass sufficient troops against those portions of the defences that were to be assaulted, and this is what the plan developed by the two engineers sought to achieve. In order to prevent the French concentrating their forces, van Gorkum conceived of the attack being made by two distinct forces: the Right Attack would advance along the Tholendijk before fording the Zoom to gain access to the north side of the harbour where the main arsenal was situated, whilst the Left Attack would move through the entrenched camp to escalade the Bastion 'Oranje' and gain control of the ramparts on that side of the town. In order to distract the enemy further, a third, diversionary, attack was to be made as a demonstration shortly prior to the main attacks going in: this would lose an element of surprise, but would hopefully draw off a good part of the garrison. The location for the False Attack was to be the Steenbergen Gate, on the north front of the fortress.

On the whole the plan was well received by Graham and his council of war, but, perhaps inevitably, the desire to tinker with it and suggest improvements was too great. Van Gorkum's fellow engineer, Captain de Bère, who had been brought to the meeting to contribute the findings of his own reconnaissance work, proposed the most significant change in the shape of a third full-scale attack, coming in from the east and endeavouring to get across the wet ditch behind the 'De Zoom' Ravelin. De Bère reported that the ditch here was frozen, and that 'he knew this part of the terrain very well and he believed it would be very easy to reach the main wall by using this route'.[6] Van Gorkum protested that his own reports indicated that there was a strong French presence in this area, along with the guard of the nearby

Breda Gate, and that adding an extra attack was unwise because it would spread the troops too thinly, but in this he states that he was overruled by Graham himself who stated a preference for several distinct points of attack, presumably so as to increase the chance of at least one being successful. This new assault would be designated the Centre Attack, and upon gaining the ramparts was to work its way along them to its left to link up with Cooke. Similarly, the Right Attack was also to link up with the Guards, by moving to its right across the harbour area. There were risks in this, so 'in order to avoid any mistake that might arise from not being able to distinguish our own troops the instant any men are perceived the watch word Orange Boven will be called out which will be answered by God Save the King'.[7] If one column was to gain entry ahead of the others, it was to move such as to aid the entry of those still on the outside but, crucially, once the attackers had gained possession of the ramparts no mention was made of pushing onwards into the town.

If van Gorkum was perturbed by this change to his plan, however, he was considerably more concerned when Graham announced that, leaving aside the feint, the attack proper would be made by a force of fewer than 3,000 men. This, in van Gorkum's opinion, was nowhere near enough, and he went as far as to argue that if this was all the force that Graham could muster then he would be unwise to proceed with the attack, giving his reasons as follows:

> Because if one would be able to penetrate into the fortress, of which I had no doubt, still one had to calculate that losses, perhaps heavy, would be sustained while approaching or climbing the walls, as one could assume that the enemy inside the fortress would be alert, and strong resistance would be encountered at more than one point.
>
> That in all cases, even if the whole force marked out for the attack made it over the walls unharmed, it would only be a third of the force needed to occupy the walls alone.
>
> And that in this case the garrison, being stronger then the attackers, would be forced to go over to the offensive, becoming attacker instead of defender, and that fighting would break out inside the fortress, where the terrain was more favourable for the garrison than for the British troops fighting on unknown terrain.
>
> And as the general had the intention not to venture into the city but only to occupy the walls, not less then 6,000 men would be necessary.
>
> And that by occupying the main walls only, the enemy would stay in possessions of the *place des armes*, market place, and other

concentration points, being able to wait until daylight to see how
the situation was, and to attack the forces on the walls one by one.[8]

These are all valid criticisms, although it does need to be remembered that
van Gorkum's is the only detailed account of this meeting and that it was
written some time after the fact. Nevertheless, he was apparently not alone
in his concerns since he relates that when Graham sent him to wait in
another room whilst a decision was made, Major General Skerrett joined
him there and expressed emphatic agreement with van Gorkum's reservations. On the other hand, the ever-sanguine Carmichael Smyth also
followed van Gorkum out and sought to disabuse him of his concerns, telling
him that a British guardsman was worth three French soldiers in a fight; this
was all very well, retorted the Dutchman, but what was needed here was not
individual valour but sufficient manpower to enable the attackers to seize
and hold an extensive stretch of ramparts.

Upon being called back to the meeting, van Gorkum discovered that he
had been at least partially successful in that Graham had decided to add two
more battalions to the attacking force, giving a total strength of 3,300 men,
and that the units engaged in carrying out the false attack would also become
available as a reserve once they had carried out their diversion. It was
nevertheless made clear that this was all the augmentation that Graham was
prepared to authorize, and that van Gorkum was now to concern himself
only with the implementation of those parts of the scheme that fell to his
direct supervision, primarily the provision of guides to lead the attackers in.

A series of memoranda issued on the morning of 8 March laid out the
exact composition of the attacking forces, which were to form three main
attacking columns and a fourth, diversionary, force intended to act as a
decoy. The composition of these forces is detailed overleaf. Other than the
33rd, called in from Calmthout, all the attacking troops came from the First
Division. Each of the three main attacks was divided into a storming party,
who were to make the initial attack, and supports who were to move up as
required. In that he received Graham's instructions for both the Right and
False Attacks, Skerrett seems to have had general responsibility for the action
on the north side of the fortress; he chose to accompany the Right Attack,
as did Brigadier General Gore, whilst Cooke, who would be the senior officer
of the attacking forces, accompanied Proby on the south side.[9]

Each attack was to be accompanied by a guide and by an officer or officers
of the Royal Engineers. The task of finding the guides fell to van Gorkum,
who had initially intended that each would be a Dutch officer of engineers:
himself with the Left Attack, Captain F. van der Wijck with the Right, and

Forces in the Attack on Bergen-op-Zoom

Left Attack	*Colonel Lord Proby*[†]
Foot Guards	*(600 men, storming party)*
Foot Guards	*(400 men, supports)*
Centre Attack	*Lt Col Charles Morrice (2/69th)*
55th	*(250 men, storming party)*
2/69th	*(350 men, storming party)*
33rd	*(600 men, supports)*
Right Attack	*Lt Col Hon. George Carleton (2/44th)*
2/44th	*(300 men, storming party)*
Flank companies	
2/21st & 2/37th	*(200 men, storming party)*
4/1st	*(600 men, supports)*
False Attack	*Lt Col Benjamin Ottley (2/91st)*
2/21st	*(100 men)*
2/37th	*(150 men)*
2/91st	*(400 men)*

† Proby's command consisted of the flank companies of all three Guards battalions, plus detachments from their centre companies.

Captain de Bère with the False Attack. This scheme quickly collapsed, however, since de Bère was now needed to guide his proposed Centre Attack, whilst on the morning of the 8th van der Wijck was nowhere to be found. Thankfully, van Gorkum had several contacts from within the fortress who were prepared to volunteer for this dangerous task, and had already arranged for two of them to assist the original guides: 'a trader, named Zegers, who knew the harbour-canal in great detail, and a paperhanger, named Hooibroek, who offered help to Captain de Bère'. Later, another of van Gorkum's contacts, a sailmaker called Gerrit Visser, came out of the fortress with a detailed report in which 'the state of the harbour with the defensive works and batteries were so precisely and clearly described by him, that I felt the need to ask and persuade him to guide the column that was intended to attack the harbour'. Visser agreed to help, but only on the promise of compensation for his family if anything happened to him. This gave the Left Attack two guides, and van Gorkum decided to extend this precaution to the Right as well, recruiting 'the skipper Jilles de Haas, who offered his help several times and had already proven himself to be useful'. With de Bère reassigned, the paperhanger Hooibroek was now left in sole charge of guiding the False Attack whilst de Bère himself recruited a youth called Hooidonk to assist him in guiding the Centre Attack.[10]

Carmichael Smyth, meanwhile, was responsible for allocating Royal Engineer officers to each attacking column. As he reported to Mann after the action, he conceived of the Left Attack as the most important and assigned Captain Sir George Hoste and Lieutenant Charles Abbey to assist Proby, along with a detachment of the Royal Sappers and Miners under Sub-Lieutenant Thomas Adamson. Since he also accompanied this attack himself, this left only one other Royal Engineer officer available in the shape of John Sperling, who was attached to the Right Attack along with a second detachment of the Royal Sappers and Miners. This meant that there was no engineer officer to attach to Morrice's Centre Attack, but, as Carmichael Smyth reported, 'Capt. [Edward] Mitchell of the Artillery volunteered and requested of me to be employed as such', which offer the engineer was happy to accept.[11]

It was one thing to guide the columns to their destinations, however, but the responsibility of the engineers also extended to getting the attackers through the defences and this, even if unopposed by the enemy, was no easy task. Indeed, it will be recalled that, on first seeing the place back in December, Graham had questioned the practicality of getting anyone across the ditches, unopposed or not. Of course, the ice – coupled with the fact that the attack was scheduled to coincide with low tide – meant that the ditches might seem more practicable now than they had then, but, their contents aside, they were still significant obstacles in their own right. On the eastern face, where the defences were the most formidable, any attacker who managed to get across the ditch would have found himself facing a masonry counterscarp sixteen feet high topped with a parapet, and the defences on the south face were scarcely less forbidding. To the north, there was no masonry but the ditch was formed by the course of the Zoom and was thus itself a more formidable obstacle, and the re-entrants – the lesser defensive positions between the main bastions – had been built up with palisades.[12] Evidently, scaling ladders would be required in order for the attackers to get across the ditches and on to the ramparts and the task of procuring these fell to van Gorkum, who in turn engaged the mayor of Steenbergen to procure forty wooden ladders of between twenty-five and twenty-eight Dutch feet in length and with rungs spaced a foot apart to enable a speedy climb. In order to prevent any word getting out, only reliable workmen were chosen and the task was carried out within the church at Steenbergen.[13]

*

Although the security precautions may well have delayed French knowledge of the impending attack, it was impossible for those in the British camp not to be aware that something was afoot. John Sperling received orders on the 7th to make his way to the village of Halsteren, and arrived there to find eight sappers and two wagons of tools but no place, due to the numbers of infantrymen filling the houses, for him to sleep. Accordingly, he returned to his old billet in Tholen for the night, riding back to Halsteren the next morning where he was eventually able to obtain basic accommodation in a labourer's cottage. With himself, his servant, and two Dutch wagoners all sharing a single room with the host family, Sperling's initial worry was where everyone was going to sleep, but 'from the number of soldiers collected together in the village, as the day advanced, it became apparent that something was in view, though the particular object remained concealed, and became a subject of discussion and conjecture among the various assembled groups'.[14] It was not until after six that night, however, that Sperling was instructed to report to Skerrett's headquarters where Sir George Hoste had just brought Graham's orders for the attack on Bergen-op-Zoom.

Amongst the troops congregating in Halsteren were the men of the centre companies of the 2/21st, which up until this point had remained in garrison at Tholen and seen no action. With them was Dunbar Moodie, whose main concern as the battalion marched out was that he was being parted from the fair Johanna, 'who had somehow taken a hold of my affections that I was hardly aware of till this moment'. After the Fusilier detachment received its orders on the evening of the 7th, 'she did not even seek the pretext of her English grammar to remain in my room for the few hours we could yet enjoy together'.[15] Because of the secrecy surrounding the planned operation, the belief within the 2/21st was that they were about to join in a renewed attack on Antwerp, and it was not until they reached Halsteren as light was failing on the afternoon of the 8th that they learnt, from officers of the 4/1st, what their true objective was.

Having already elected to spend the hours prior to marching with his lady-love rather than his men, Moodie on arriving at Halsteren continued to maintain a cavalier attitude to his military responsibilities, demonstrating that Graham's earlier expressions of despair at the conduct of many of his inexperienced and under-occupied young subalterns was by no means unfounded. Moodie discovered that an old friend, Lieutenant Allan Robertson, was commanding the Grenadier Company of the 4/1st, only a mile or so away, and decided, since it was some years since he had seen him, to pay a visit. Moodie blithely assumed that 'I should have time to see him and join my regiment before they marched', but things did not work out that way.

The party of the Royals [1st Foot] whom I accompanied lost their way, from their ignorance of the road, and we in consequence made a long circuit, during which I heard from an aid-de-camp [*sic*] who passed us, that the 21st were on the march to attack the place on another quarter from us. In these circumstances I was extremely puzzled what course to take; if I went in search of my regiment, I had every chance of missing them in the night, being quite ignorant of the roads. Knowing that the Royals would be likely to head one of the columns from the number of the regiment, I took what I thought was the surest plan, by attaching myself to the grenadier company under my gallant friend.[16]

Having managed to get himself lost, there was not a lot else Moodie could have done at this stage, but his subsequent conduct is less explicable. Having encountered the flank companies of his own battalion, also forming part of the Right Attack, and being ordered by Captain Nicholas Darrah, commanding the detachment, to remain with him until the rest of the battalion passed by on its way to join the False Attack, Moodie 'waited some time, but hearing nothing of the regiment, and losing patience [. . .] gave him the slip in the dark, and ran on until I regained my place with the grenadier company of the Royals'. Remarkably, Moodie was afterwards able to justify this conduct successfully to his commanding officer, but it meant that, for good or for ill, he was to participate not in the False Attack with his own company but instead would fight that night as part of the Right Attack against the north side of the harbour.[17]

The main body of the 2/21st, minus its flank companies and the errant Moodie, had meanwhile formed up as part of the False Attack. There is some discrepancy in accounts of the action as to who had charge of this attack, with the majority taking their cue from Graham's despatch and listing Brevet Lieutenant Colonel Robert Henry of the 2/21st. However, it seems that Graham was in error and that the man who led the False Attack was in fact Lieutenant Colonel Benjamin Ottley of the 2/91st, who was several years senior both to Henry and to Lieutenant Colonel Simon Hart of the 2/37th. On the face of it, this seems a rather odd mistake for Graham to have made, but the account given in *Letters from Germany and Holland*, being one of the few to have been written before Graham's post-battle despatch was published, helps shed light on the situation. Confirming that Ottley did lead the attack, this account also notes that he had time to receive only the most cursory of briefings from Skerrett, to the effect that he was 'to take possession of an outwork, which he would find near the Steenbergen gate; and by keeping up a heavy fire endeavour to draw the attention of the Enemy to that point'. Earlier in this same account, mention is made of the attachment of the flank companies of the 2/91st to the Right Attack, a measure that was not, in the event, followed through but which suggests that the commitment of the centre companies of the battalion, and, by default, its commanding officer, had not yet been decided upon.[18] Cannon's history of the 1st Foot tells us that the flank companies of this battalion were also initially to be employed separately, further supporting the assumption that the centre companies of the 4/1st and 2/91st were originally to have formed a general reserve, but were later incorporated into the attacks. Presumably these were the two battalions that van Gorkum mentions being added to the attacking force in response to his comments about the low numbers of troops involved. If Gore's brigade was initially not to participate, this may also explain why he was not allocated a command in the attacking force.[19]

Although it is impossible to be certain, it would therefore seem that the decision to assign the 2/91st to the False Attack was taken fairly late in the day and that it was only at this point that Ottley, as the senior of the three battalion commanders, found himself in charge of the whole column. The same written orders that place the whole of the 2/91st in the False Attack delegate the actual arrangements for its execution to Skerrett, who, as we have seen, had little time to attend to them, and less still to report back to Graham that the column had a new senior officer. Thus, Graham was most likely never notified before the attack that Ottley had assumed command, and by the time the fighting was over neither Skerrett, Ottley nor Henry was in any position to make him aware of the fact. No eyewitness accounts survive from those who took part in the False Attack, whilst those written by witnesses who were elsewhere can be forgiven for placing Henry in charge of it because, after all, they had Graham's own despatch to tell them that it was so. Thus the mistake has been perpetuated in successive histories.

Unfortunately, the question of who had the command is of no small significance, for the False Attack did not develop as planned and some accounts – Stanhope's in particular – cite this as one of the main causes for the failure of the operation as a whole. Stanhope's version of events does have something of the character of an apologia about it, shifting the blame for failure away from Graham and his staff and onto the commanders of the attacking troops, but although the assertion that the False Attack went in ahead of schedule is questionable, at least by the margin that Stanhope implies, there is no doubt that it was pressed far more vigorously than had been envisaged.[20] Even if Stanhope's line is taken, and the commander of the False Attack blamed for its failure, it is still important to recognize that

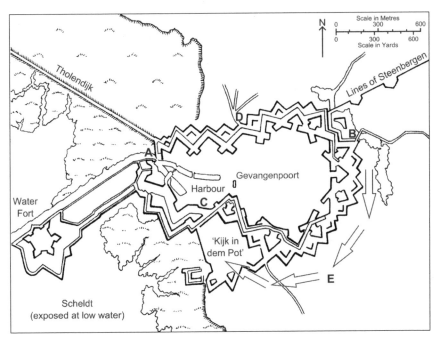

Bergen-op-Zoom, the Initial Attacks

A Right Attack (500 stormers and 600 supports, under Lt. Colonel Carleton) to attack from Tholendijk across the harbour mouth.

B Centre Attack (600 stormers and 600 supports, under Lt. Colonel Morrice) to attack across the frozen ditch between the 'De Zoom' Ravelin and the Breda Gate.

C Left Attack (600 stormers and 600 supports, under Colonel Lord Proby) to atack Bastion 'Oranje'.

D False Attack (650 men under Lt. Colonel Ottley) to demonstrate against the Steenbergen Gate.

E Subsequent movement of Centre Attack survivors to join the Left Attack at Bastion 'Oranje'.

the officer in question was Ottley, not Henry, although it seems rather unfair to blame anything on a man who was apparently pitched into a job at such short notice. Indeed, the last-minute appointment of an officer who, though not without combat experience, had never commanded as much as a battalion in action and who, furthermore, 'had not been above a week in the country' and 'was quite ignorant of the situation or works of the place' is indicative as much as anything of bad staff work.[21]

Then again, had Ottley not been put in over his head, and the False Attack been mounted by the 2/21st and 2/37th alone, Henry would have kept the command just as Graham seems to have assumed. However, Robert Henry was only a major in his regiment, had no more command experience than Ottley and, indeed, had spent the campaign thus far as

Commandant at Tholen. He was therefore an equally poor choice for such a responsible role, which then raises the question of why a more experienced officer was not appointed from the outset. Skerrett had been tasked with the direction of both the False and Right Attacks, and whilst it is perhaps understandable that he himself chose to accompany the larger and more important column, he should nevertheless carry some share of responsibility for the fact that the False Attack was entrusted to a newly arrived officer with limited command experience, particularly when the more experienced Arthur Gore – who also accompanied the over-officered Right Attack – was available. Had Gore been given command of the False Attack from the outset, the relative seniority of the commanders of its component battalions would have made no odds since as a Brigadier General he comfortably outranked all of them. Yet to be fair to Skerrett, he in turn was only left with this decision because Graham had omitted in his written orders to name a commander for the False Attack, or, indeed, to assign Gore to any formal role at all.[22] Following the story back up the chain of command, it seems clear that the real responsibility for the confusion surrounding the False Attack comes from the top, and is symptomatic of the rushed preparations and inadequate staff work surrounding the whole operation.

Although no mention is made in the written instructions, it was agreed that all the attacking troops were to be ready to move forwards by 21.00, that the false attack would reveal itself at 22.15, and that the attack main would begin at 22.30.[23] This aspect is not included in the written orders, which – along with the fact that local time was half an hour behind the time used by the army – may explain why some of the eyewitness accounts are rather confused on the point, and was therefore presumably part of the briefing given by Graham in which he reported that 'these orders were fully explained to Gls. Cooke & Skerrett & Ld. Proby w'th a plan of the town before them'.[24]

According to the plan of attack, Skerrett had been instructed that 'the object of this demonstration is merely to draw off the Enemy's attention from the real point of attack',[25] but it remained for him to pass these orders on to Ottley, and likewise to brief him on the timings of the operation and what he was to do after he had succeeded in drawing the attention of the garrison upon himself. This latter point is a key one, since Stanhope asserts that it was inherent in the plan that 'the false attack having succeeded in drawing off the enemy's attention[,] which was to be done without risking many men[,] was to *reform* and wait for further orders', so that Ottley's troops could subsequently function as a reserve for the genuine attacks.[26]

Unfortunately, as we have seen, circumstances prevented Skerrett briefing Ottley to any greater effect than that he was to furnish a diversion and that the outwork covering the Steenbergen Gate was his initial objective.

In all events, the False Attack began the assault ahead of time when the lead troops opened fire early. Exactly how far before schedule is unclear, with Stanhope asserting that it was as early as 21.30 and van Gorkum 21.45, whereas Sperling says that when the first shots were heard it was 'barely ten'. Sperling's account seems the most believable, since the Right Attack was formed up ready to go in by the time he heard any firing and it is inconceivable that this could have been the case much before 22.00. In *Letters from Germany and Holland* it is stated that the firing began only a few minutes before 22.30 implying that, far from being ahead of time, Ottley was actually slightly late![27] As Ottley's troops approached the outwork that had been assigned as their objective, they were sighted by the defenders and received by cannon and musket fire. The French quickly rushed to reinforce this sector, but not before the thinly manned outer defences had been cleared in the first rush. However, it quickly became apparent that, by assigning the French outwork as the objective for the False Attack, Skerrett had placed these troops in a dangerous position since they were now exposed to the fire of two bastions flanking the Steenbergen Gate. Once these positions were manned a heavy fire was quickly brought down on the attackers and Lieutenant Colonels Ottley and Henry were both hit – each being recorded in the subsequent return of casualties as 'seriously but not dangerously' wounded.[28] This rendered any question of command moot since, with both men down, Hart of the 2/37th took command of the survivors. As well as Ottley himself there were extensive casualties amongst the officers of the 2/91st, although when one of the colour-bearing ensigns was shot down Sergeant Major Patrick Cahill stepped forwards to raise the flag in his place: for this action, and continued gallant conduct throughout the remainder of the fighting, he would subsequently receive an ensigncy of his own.[29]

Despite the confusion, Hart retained direction of at least part of the rapidly fragmenting attack force and, assisted by Lieutenant George Scott, Adjutant of the 2/91st, was able to secure a crossing of the defensive moat by using scaling ladders to connect with the raised drawbridge in front of the Steenbergen Gate. That Hart elected to go forward and push the attack, rather than remain outside of the walls under heavy fire to no obvious end, is understandable; van Gorkum, in his post-mortem of the operation, agreed that it was the wisest course of action even though it was a deviation from his own plan. Furthermore, with Ottley down it must also be questioned how aware his surviving subordinates were of the column's planned

diversionary role, and of the need to retain enough troops to form a worthwhile reserve for the other three attacks.

Once inside, some of the attackers followed Hart and Scott in engaging
the French defenders of the 'Hoogmogende' bastion, whilst others sought
to break down the drawbridge. This was eventually achieved, but by that
time most of the survivors of the False Attack were already inside the
defences and any advantage that was gained by lowering the bridge was in
any case lost since it remained swept by the fire of the French cannon in the
bastions. Split up, under heavy fire, and with two of the three battalion
commanders wounded, this further division of efforts seems to have
completed the fragmentation of the False Attack column which, to all intents
and purposes, was finished as a fighting entity. Pinned down by superior
numbers and firepower, the survivors could neither go forwards nor fall back
and would remain in this unenviable position for some hours to come.[30]

The outbreak of firing around the Steenbergen Gate, as the False Attack
made its presence known, caused a particular problem for the troops of the
Right Attack who were closest to the action and whose likelihood of being
discovered, or of finding the defences ahead of them manned if they delayed
their own attack any further, was now greatly increased. Since Skerrett and
Gore had both accompanied this column, its nominal commander
Lieutenant Colonel the Hon. George Carleton had been relegated to leading
an advance party or Forlorn Hope, composed of picked men from all the
battalions in the column and accompanied by Sperling and his party of
seventeen sappers. Ahead of everyone, and with two men assigned to keep
constant watch on him – as much to prevent confusion in the dark as
through any doubt of his loyalty – was the guide Gerrit Visser, who safely
led the column across the fields from Halsteren and then along the dyke.
Following close behind Carleton's command were Skerrett and Gore with
the 2/44th and the flank companies of the 4/1st, 2/21st, and 2/37th, whilst
the remainder of the 4/1st under Lieutenant Colonel Frederick Muller
brought up the rear with orders to 'avail itself of any opportunity of profiting
by the impression made by the attacking party'.[31] The approach march along
the Tholendijk, heading directly towards one of the French defensive
batteries, had been nerve-wracking thanks to a fresh fall of snow during that
afternoon serving to place the attackers in stark relief against a white landscape, and to the accidental discharge of a musket which, thankfully, went
unnoticed. Nevertheless, the men of the Right Attack remained
undiscovered and when the sound of firing broke out, off to their left,
Carleton's Forlorn Hope was already in position.[32]

Lieutenant Colonel George Carleton was the second surviving son of General Guy Carleton, 1st Baron Dorchester, who had defended Quebec in 1775 and commanded British forces in North America at the very end of the American War of Independence, and who, as a young man, had fought in the defence of Bergen-op-Zoom back in 1747. Born in 1781, Carleton junior followed his father and elder brother into the Army, and took command of the 2/44th in December 1811 when the battalion was still serving under Wellington. Five months later, the 2/44th was part of the Fifth Division attacking Badajoz on the night of 6 April 1812 in the culmination of Britain's greatest Peninsular siege. Whilst the Fourth and Light Divisions fought and died in the breaches, and the Third Division struggled with their scaling ladders against the walls of the castle, the men of the Fifth Division managed to escalade a lightly held stretch of the walls and thus obtain what was arguably the decisive lodgement that brought about the fall of the fortress. Carleton and the 2/44th were conspicuous in the van of this attack, and the battalion's colours were reputedly the first to be raised within the French defences. With this experience behind him Carleton was, as Sperling saw it, the obvious choice to lead this, the most dangerous of the attacks on Bergen-op-Zoom.[33] Certainly, the decision to entrust the responsibility of leading the Forlorn Hope to this 33-year-old veteran would seem to have been justified by his retention of his composure when the outbreak of firing around the Steenbergen Gate necessitated an early move forwards, and the attack continued as planned with the leading troops crossing the dyke marking the outer edge of the defences and descending into the riverbed opposite the Water Gate, their initial objective.

There is certainly no doubt that the task facing Carleton, Sperling and their men was a daunting one. The river, at low tide, was estimated to be only twelve to eighteen inches deep, but this was only part of the problem since, as Carmichael Smyth explained in his report, there was 'an armed vessel with a guard on board at the harbour mouth[,] the Ford of the river was moreover covered with harrows', and additional palisades had been constructed extending across the path of the planned assault from the bastion immediately to the right of the attackers' route. Nevertheless, the report continued, 'these Harrows were removed, and the palisades cut down by a detachment of sappers under Lieutenant Sperling Royal Engineers, who was the Engineer attached to this Column and who conducted himself in a most manly and gallant manner'.[34] Sperling's own account is, as one might expect, rather more modest about his own doings, but it captures the breathless rush of the first attack with great vividness. Once the alarm was given by the discovery of the False Attack, Sperling wrote, it became imperative for the Forlorn Hope to break into the defences as quickly as possible:

> There was no time to be lost. We scrambled up as well as we could the slippery sides of the dyke. The battery opened its fire, accompanied by one of small arms. Our safety consisted in rushing forward. As we jumped into the river, the guard, panic-struck, and ignorant of the extent of danger, hurried out of the vessel, and we, getting through the spikes and water, followed its defenders up the river. I was a little in advance of the Colonel, who, turning suddenly to the right, got up its bank, crying out 'I am in first'. We hastened to the guard-house, which was almost deserted, the men being occupied upon the ramparts firing at our people who were crossing the dyke. They made little defence, and gave up their arms, bewildered by the suddenness and boldness of the attack. The officer of the guard surrendered his sword to me.[35]

The palisades, meanwhile, proved to be no obstacle at all since, in the confusion, the French had omitted to close the gate that had been made in them to allow the defenders to pass to and fro. The drawbridge across the harbour had also been left down, allowing the attackers access to the ramparts on the south side. Almost without a fight, the first British troops had penetrated the main defences of Bergen-op-Zoom.

While Sperling was too concerned about staying alive to bother about the conditions underfoot, those coming after the Forlorn Hope had rather less to distract them and, as Moodie related, the conditions in the riverbed were not only unpleasant but caused severe disruption to the cohesion of the attack:

> On approaching the place of attack, we crossed the Tholen-dike, and immediately entered the bed of the Zoom, through which we had to push our way before we entered the wet ditch. It is not easy to convey an idea of the toil we experienced in getting through the deep mud of the river; we immediately sank nearly to our middles, and when, with great difficulty, we succeeded in freeing one leg from the mire, we sank nearly to the shoulder on the other side before we could get one pace forward. As might be expected, we got into some confusion in labouring through this horrible slough, which was like bird-lime about our legs; regiments got intermixed in the darkness, while some stuck fast, and some unlucky wretches got trodden down and smothered in the mud. Notwithstanding this obstruction, a

considerable portion of the column had got through, when those behind us, discouraged by this unexpected difficulty, raised a shout to encourage themselves. Gen. Skerret [*sic*], who was at the head of the column, was furious with rage, but the mischief was already done. The sluices were opened, and a torrent of water poured down on us through the channel of the river, by which the progress of those behind was effectually stopped for some time.[36]

The French now threw up some form of illumination, and opened fire from the ramparts against the men struggling in the river: the result was that whilst the leading part of the attacking force was already established on the ramparts, their supports were in no position to come to their aid. The best remedy for this situation would, with hindsight, have been if those troops who were already inside the defences had turned to their left to clear the French from the ramparts commanding the river approaches, allowing the whole of the troops forming the Right Attack to regroup inside the defensive perimeter. However, Carleton and his men – following his orders – had already pushed on across the harbour, and when it became clear that something had gone amiss behind them both he and Gore, who had also successfully crossed the river before the French checked the passage of the attackers, agreed that they would be best advised to continue in that direction so as to link up with the expected advance of the Guards.[37]

Whilst Gore and Carleton made their choice, Skerrett and Muller were trying to re-establish some order and get the rest of the attacking force across the river. Moodie had just about made it across the channel when the French opened the sluices, and was able to grab hold of the edge of the ice extending from the far bank. Thus supported, he was able to hang on to this 'till the strength of the torrent had passed, after which I soon gained the firm land, and pushed on with the others to the ditch'. As he then explained,

> The point at which we entered was a bastion to the right of the harbour, from one of the angles of which a row of high palisades was carried through the ditch. To enable us to pass the water, some scaling-ladders had been sunk to support us in proceeding along the palisade, over which we had first to climb with each other's assistance, our soldiers performing the office of ladders to those who preceded them. So great were the obstacles we met with, that had not the attention of the enemy fortunately (or rather most judiciously), been distracted by the false attack [that] it appeared quite impossible for us to have affected an entrance at this point.[38]

By this stage either the whole of the 4/1st had moved up to join the rest of the attack, or else Lieutenant Colonel Muller had made his way forwards and joined the advance party. At all events, having managed to get across the river, he assumed direction of the mixed bag of troops milling around on the far bank and began to organize them with a view to gaining possession of the Water Gate and opening it, and its drawbridge, so as to allow easy access to the remainder of the troops. Moodie volunteered himself for the task, and assembled a mixed party of around twenty men to assist him; the defenders had mostly fled, so the primary problem was the gate itself:

> It was constructed of thin paling, with an iron bar across it about three inches in breadth. Being without tools of any kind, we made several ineffectual attempts to open it. At last, retiring a few paces, we made a rush at it in a body, when the iron bar snapped in the middle like a bit of glass. Some of my people got killed and wounded during this part of the work, but when we got to the drawbridge, we were a little more sheltered from the firing. The bridge was up, and secured by a lock in the hand post of the two which supported it. I was simple enough to attempt to pick the lock with a soldier's bayonet, but after breaking two or three, we at last had an axe brought us from the bastion where the troops were entering. With the assistance of this instrument we soon succeeded in cutting the lock out of the post, and taking hold of the chain, I had the satisfaction to pull down the drawbridge with my own hands.[39]

As Moodie's account emphasizes, this process would have been rather more easily achieved by sappers equipped with the necessary tools, which again suggests, with all the benefits of hindsight, that Carleton and Gore would have done better to have waited to get the gate opened – as, indeed, the guide Visser offered to assist them in doing – rather than taking their whole force, including Sperling's sappers, straight off across the harbour.[40]

The fact remains, however, that the initial wave of attackers did press on – albeit with the most laudable of motives – rather than awaiting the arrival of the rest of the column, and this now brings us to another point in the narrative that would be picked up on after the fact as one of the decisive moments in the progress of the fighting, because once divided the Right Attack did not reunite and ceased from this point to function as a single entity. In effect, the attacking troops ended up split three ways. Carleton and Gore carried on to the right, moving anti-clockwise along the ramparts, but Skerrett, having made his way across the Zoom as well, elected not to follow, nor to join with Muller in securing the Water Gate, but instead gathered a party of men around him and led them off to his left, onto the ramparts, so as to move clockwise in the direction of the Steenbergen Gate. Just what Skerrett was trying to achieve by this was unclear, since, as he must have known, it was quite the opposite of what his orders required. Indeed, Stanhope, admittedly not an eyewitness, records that up until this point Skerrett 'had kept crying out to the troops "Mind men you are to get out of the ditch to the right."'[41] Skerrett is quite the scapegoat so far as Stanhope is concerned, and since he failed to survive the attack he makes rather a convenient one. Certainly his direction of the False and Right Attacks was not all that it could have been, and he must bear a proportion of the responsibility – due to inadequate arrangements before the attack and this apparently bizarre diversion once it was under way – for their rapid loss of cohesion, but, at the same time, it is too simple to write him off as a buffoon who got it wrong.

To try and understand Skerrett's actions, it helps to try and get some sense of what his motivations were. This, of course, takes us into the realms of speculation but one key point that must be stressed is the fact that John Skerrett seems to have gone into action with the state of his reputation very much on his mind. Quite apart from his perceived failings in the Peninsula, he had also missed out on all the action in the current campaign thanks to his fall prior to the first advance on Antwerp and then to the fact, during the second advance, that his brigade had been delayed by the French inundations and had thus failed to carry out its part in the planned attack of 2 February. That he was determined not to miss out on this chance to regain his credit is emphasized by the fact that he participated in the attack although he had evidently not fully recovered from his fall, to the extent that he entered the fortress only with the aid of a crutch.[42] Evidently, this was a chance that he was not prepared to miss, and his personal conduct under fire was as brave as it had been on previous occasions. He also seems to have taken particular pains to acquaint himself with the nature of the fortress and with van Gorkum's plan for its capture, and, as we have seen, agreed with the Dutch engineer about the flaws inherent in Graham's adaptation of that plan. This, in turn, suggests one possible reason for Skerrett's decision to swing to his left, since he was aware that the arsenal and a major powder magazine both lay along this sector of the defences and that van Gorkum believed that their capture was essential for the success of the attack. Since the remainder of his troops seemed to have attained their other objectives, with Carleton and Gore already on their way to link up with the Left Attack, it is quite possible that Skerrett felt that he had the scope to deviate from his orders and make an attempt to seize these other vital objectives.

Furthermore, it was clear that the troops of the False Attack were heavily engaged in this sector and, since these troops remained to an extent his responsibility, he may have felt obliged to try to come to their aid. Ultimately, this has to remain a matter for speculation, but what is certain is that Skerrett, for whatever reason, set off at the head of around 200 men, drawn primarily from the flank companies of the 4/1st, 2/21st and 2/37th.[43]

The French had, of course, not been idle while all this was going on, and the bulk of the garrison – consisting of a battalion apiece from the 12ème, 17ème, 21ème and 51ème Régiments de Ligne, a further battalion of naval troops, and several companies of veterans, gendarmes, engineers and gunners for a total of 2,700 men – had rapidly concentrated against the False Attack around the Steenbergen Gate. This, in turn, caused some dismay when it became apparent that a second attack was developing around the harbour, and additional reserves, held in readiness in the town's sizeable market square, were rushed to meet the new threat.[44] This meant that Skerrett's party was heading straight into the thickest concentration of French troops within the fortress, and although they were able to occupy the arsenal, which lay immediately to the north of the harbour area, and to clear the French out of the 'Dun' and 'Gadelière' Bastions, they soon found themselves in trouble. A strong French force of around 300 men had been detached to protect the powder magazine, and Skerrett led his party straight into them. It was clearly impossible to press on any further, and the British fell back a short distance and took up a strong position based on a windmill situated a little to the west of the magazine, where some of the survivors of the False Attack were also able to filter through and join them.

Thus, the fighting in the northern half of the fortress reached a lull, with the British in control of the Water Gate and harbour area, as well as the first two bastions to the north. On the other hand, the French, by committing the bulk of their reserves, had gained the upper hand in the fighting around the Steenbergen Gate, to the extent that the three battalions forming the False Attack were dispersed and broken. Of course, the objective of the False Attack had been to distract the French, and in this at least it had been successful. That sacrifice would only be rendered worthwhile, however, if the distraction enabled the other columns to get in without opposition. The Right Attack had been able to do just that, but, as yet, nothing seemed to have developed in the southern and eastern sectors of the fortress where, if all was running to plan, the Centre and Left Attacks should have already made their lodgements. We now therefore need to leave events in the northern sector for a moment, to review what progress was being made elsewhere.

Chapter XI

'Filled with Melancholy Forebodings'

THE FIRST BRITISH TROOPS TO PENETRATE into the southern half of Bergen-op-Zoom belonged not to the Centre or Left Attacks, but to that portion of the Right Attack that had followed Gore and Carleton across the harbour during the initial rush, and who now elected to carry on along the ramparts. This body consisted of around a hundred men from the 2/44th, including the battalion's Grenadier Company, along with Sperling and his sappers. Although hindsight suggests that they would have done better to wait for their comrades to catch up with them, the orders for the Right Attack placed considerable store on the need to link up with the Guards contingent forming the Left Attack, and, if possible, aid their entry. Furthermore, the ramparts were all but deserted, guarded only by a few sentries who offered little resistance, and it made sense to occupy them before the French could send any reinforcements. Thus, both senior officers had little trouble in deciding to press onwards, with Carleton leading the advance and Gore supporting at the head of a second group. Since no men could be spared to guard the prisoners they were hustled along with the attackers, making the British numbers seem larger.

Unfortunately, no intelligence had been provided as to exactly where the Left Attack could be expected to enter, but after occupying four successive bastions without resistance it became apparent that they were somewhere near the right spot. Accordingly, a bugle was sounded so as to indicate that the ramparts were already in friendly hands and in the hope of obtaining some response that would reveal the location of the Guards. No answer being obtained, the party pressed on and continued to disperse such resistance as was encountered. As Sperling related,

> It was found that it did not answer to stand and fire, as our adversaries did the same; but when we ran upon them they either surrendered or made their escape down the slopes. Our men, however, could not be kept from firing, which in the darkness was dangerous to ourselves. The Colonel complained of being separated

from his own men, and placed over others who neither knew him nor his voice.[1]

Despite this increasing disorder the party pressed on, reasoning that if the Left Attack had gone astray they might still link up with the Centre Attack. After having made a half-circuit of the ramparts, passing the Antwerp Gate and progressing almost as far as the Breda Gate, it became clear that the Centre Attack, too, was nowhere to be seen. Where were the missing troops, and what had gone wrong?

The Centre Attack, against the Breda Gate and led by Lieutenant Colonel Morrice of the 2/69th, had in fact stepped out largely as planned. Of all the attacking columns, it had the easiest approach march and was guided in by Captain de Bère so it could benefit from his local knowledge. Unfortunately, this knowledge did not stretch to include an awareness of the extent of the French defensive forces in the area and, as van Gorkum had feared, Morrice's troops received a hot reception. Upon hearing firing commence as the False Attack was discovered, Morrice led his men forwards and they were able to reach the ditch in front of the 'Noyelles' Bastion, descend the counterscarp, and get their scaling ladders into place, but by the time they had done so they had already begun to incur casualties. These were not too serious in number – perhaps thirty men – but amongst those thirty were Morrice himself; Lieutenant Colonel Elphinstone, commanding the 33rd; Captain Mitchell of the Royal Artillery, acting as engineer officer for the attack; and Captain de Bère, the column's guide, whose injuries would prove mortal.[2] The fact that Elphinstone was hit suggests that in the Centre Attack – as in the Right, where Muller seems to have brought the 4/1st forwards at an early stage – the distinction between those battalions designated as the storming party and those designated as the supports quickly broke down.

Deprived of leadership, and coming under increasing fire, the attack quickly faltered and then fell back in some disorder. Stanhope nevertheless goes too far in asserting that they were 'seized by a fear of cavalry or by one of those unaccountable panics which have been known at night among the bravest of troops, without the slightest cause or a shot being fired',[3] which is a clear nonsense and an inexcusable one at that since he was on the spot along with the rest of Graham's staff and took part in the subsequent rallying of the repulsed troops. Once order had been restored, the survivors were reorganized under the senior unwounded officer, Major George Muttlebury of the 2/69th, but it was quite apparent that there could be no second attempt in the region of the Breda Gate, where the French were clearly now fully alert. Graham therefore ordered Muttlebury with the bulk of the troops, less the left wing of the 55th left behind to recover the wounded from the glacis, to make their way around the outer perimeter of the defences and link up with Cooke and the Left Attack.[4]

Thus, by the time Carleton led his party round the ramparts towards the Breda Gate, the Left Attack had already left the area. Had they remained, it is possible that Carleton could have assisted the entry of a second attack against this sector but of course Graham had no reason to expect troops from the Right Attack to have penetrated so far around the ramparts and Carleton, for his part, had no means of alerting those on the outside to his progress. Unfortunately, the attention drawn to this sector by Morrice's abortive attack – which was presumably maintained by the continued presence of a hundred or so of the 55th on the glacis – caused the French to send reinforcements to the threatened sector, and this would prove disastrous for Carleton and his party. Sperling explained what happened as they approached the 'Noyelles' Bastion:

> Our progress was arrested by a more numerous body than we had hitherto encountered, who seemed determined to contest our further advance. This bastion was planted with trees, from behind which they fired upon us. Our party returned their fire. Their ardour being damped, were reluctant to come to the charge.
>
> We had, however, become mixed with them in hand to hand fight around the trees, and were making prisoners, when the slow beat of a drum attracted our attention. As this ominous sound grew nearer, our opponents took fresh courage, while it filled us with anxiety. We soon discerned a large body of men advancing with measured step along the curtain [wall] leading toward the bastion in which we were engaged. Our contest was renewed with fresh energy. A ball felled General Gore, which I noted to Colonel Carleton. The column still gradually and cautiously approached, with the same ominous beat of drum, when they came to a halt, as if to discern between friends and foes. This gave our brave Colonel an opportunity of rallying his little band, and the prisoners in our rear concealed in some measure the insignificance of our numbers. Observing their hesitation (for a sort of solemn pause had taken place), our gallant Colonel put on a bold face, and, stepping in advance, said, 'Messieurs, mettez bas vos armes. [Gentlemen, lay down your arms.]'. The answer was a volley of musketry, and this distinguished officer fell to the ground.[5]

Killed instantly by a musket ball through the neck, Carleton left a widow and four children who would later receive a government pension of £200 a year in recognition of his services.

This body of troops was the 3/12ème Ligne under Chef de Battalion Baron, some 600 strong, which had been dispatched too late to take a part in repulsing Morrice but which now enabled the French to bring an over-whelming force against the new arrivals. Nevertheless, the French seemed unwilling to push their advantage – possibly, as Sperling suggests, because they assumed the small force to be the vanguard of a larger body – and the British survivors were able to begin a slow and steady withdrawal back the way they had come, in the hope of being able to link up with friendly troops.[6] All seemed to be going well, Sperling reported, until they reached 'the place where the advance had been sounded during our previous progress'. There the survivors of Carleton's party 'discerned a large body of men in front of us [and] anxiously hailed them'. For a moment, both parties prepared to open fire until the belated realization dawned on Sperling and his comrades that the troops were guardsmen from the Left Attack, who had finally made their way up onto the ramparts. They, for their part, 'knowing that no column had entered from the direction in which we came, had so entirely concluded us enemies', and an exchange of friendly fire was only narrowly averted.[7] Once mutual identities had been re-established, however, it can hardly be wondered if the men who had pushed on so far from the Right Attack came to ask their colleagues of the Left what had taken them so long.

This question, indeed, is one that just as much needs answering today as it did then, for the late arrival of the Left Attack marks another significant failing in the conduct of the assault and another major contributor to its eventual failure. To an extent, the delay could be excused by the fact that the Guards, despite having moved up from Hoogstraten to their staging area around the village of Hoogerheide, had further to go than any of the other attackers. It was thought to compensate for this by setting off at 20.30, but even this did not prevent the column falling behind time due to the fresh snow. All in all, it was a pretty miserable march, having 'more the appearance of a funeral than anything else',[8] and it took the troop the best part of two hours to reach their objective. Thus delayed, the main body of the Guards were still short of the 'Kijk in dem Pot' entrenched camp when the sound of firing broke out, and further still from the walls of the fortress itself. It was here that Cooke received more bad news from his guides, who reported that the ice in the outer ditches was not strong enough to allow the troops to cross, due to the rise and fall of the tides having prevented the formation of a single solid layer. This necessitated a change of plan, but as the senior officers conferred with the guides it was clear to all that their comrades were already engaged inside the fortress: 'The French drums were heard beating to arms in every direction. The horizon seemed a blaze; and from the loud cheering of our fellows it was evident that some of them had penetrated the place'.[9]

After some investigation, it proved possible to gain access through the western extremity of the entrenched camp and up to the line of palisades covering the main defences by the Bastion 'Oranje'. Here, a bâtardeau or sluice-dam prevented the water in the ditch being affected by any tidal action and thus allowed the formation of ice sufficiently solid as to be able to support the weight of ladders and enabled them to be placed close enough to the walls to give access. As Cooke and Proby sought to get the troops moving again, the engineer detachment went on ahead to clear the way. Jan van Gorkum was with this party, and described their advance as they hurried to make up lost time:

> I positioned myself at the head of this column, together with lieutenant-adjutant of engineers Abbey and the commanding officer of the small vanguard of the Guards. The guides de Haas and van den Enden followed between two NCOs, after these the commander of the sappers, with fifty men, bearing ladders and on top of that axes and other tools. Even with this load the march was fast, the ladders were carried over the palisades of the covered way with great speed, and the officers and soldiers jumped across.[10]

The sappers were under Sub-Lieutenant Thomas Adamson, and were accompanied by a ladder party of guardsmen under Captain the Hon. James Berkeley Rodney of 2/3rd Foot Guards, assisted by Ensigns Henry Gooch of 2/Coldstream and Edward Pardoe of 2/1st Foot Guards. Adamson's detachment, once they had completed their primary task of cutting down the palisades of the covered way, were also to assist with the ladders which here were needed both to gain access to the ditch and then to ascend from its bed to the ramparts.

Initially, the advance was unopposed but before it could be completed the party was detected and a heavy fire was opened from Bastion 'Oranje' and the 'Stoelemat' Ravelin. Adamson – a veteran ex-ranker whose experience was greatly valued by the young engineer officers – was killed instantly by a cannonball as he ascended the glacis, and the attacking party partially dispersed so that only van Gorkum, Abbey, Rodney, the guide de Haas, and about thirty men made it to the ditch with just eight ladders between them. Van Gorkum and Abbey managed to get down into the ditch and confirm that the ladders could be emplaced. A further delay ensued whilst axes were brought forwards to clear away obstructions in the ditch, during which time heavy casualties were inflicted on the engineers and sappers by fire from the flanking bastions. Abbey was hit twice, in the arm and leg – wounds that would sadly prove mortal – and several others were brought down. Eventually, though, the advance party, now down to only twenty men, made it over the wall and were quickly able to clear the bastion, taking several prisoners including three officers. Their position remained precarious, but they were quickly joined by some men of the 2/44th who had been left behind by Carleton's party as it pushed onwards. With these reinforcements, Rodney and van Gorkum were able to secure the area around the ladders and allow the remainder of the Left Attack to enter.[11]

Although there were some delays getting everyone up the ladders, the guardsmen began to establish themselves on the walls, fanning out to clear the French from the adjacent bastions and sending detachments forwards into the houses immediately to their front. The Left Attack had thus secured its designated objective, but the time was now 23.30 and the Guards thus gained access to the fortress over an hour after the first British lodgement had been made. By this time, the False and Right Attacks had dispersed into several uncoordinated bodies, whilst the Centre Attack had been repulsed. With a thousand fresh troops, Cooke certainly had the potential to restore the momentum of the attack, but much depended on what orders he now elected to give. The progress of the fighting remained in the balance, and much could yet have been achieved, had Cooke realized it, by the prompt and vigorous action of a concentrated force. But Cooke, knowing little of the progress of the other attacks, elected to divide his troops in the hope of making contact with friendly forces. This was by no means a bad idea, but once patrols had been detailed to this task the main party was left weakened and compelled to remain in place until these parties reported back.

As Sir John Jones observed, it would have been prudent, bearing in mind the division of the attack into four distinct columns, to have provided each detachment 'with its peculiar signal, either blue-lights, rockets, or parachutes, as a means to communicate its success, or failure, to the other columns'.[12] No such precaution having been taken, there was little option but to send out scouting detachments to ascertain the outcome of the fighting that had been heard by all members of the Left Attack on their way in. Accordingly, as Cooke later reported, he 'sent a strong Patrol towards the Point at which M. Genl. Skerrett and Lt. Col. Carleton had entered, [and] detached Lt. Col. [George] Clifton with part of the 1st Guards to secure the Antwerp Gate and see if he could get any Information of the Column under Lt. Col. Morrice'.[13]

As Cooke's report then makes clear, however, he subsequently received only limited intelligence from these patrols, recording of Clifton's command only that he had reached the Antwerp Gate but 'found that it could not be opened by his men, the enemy throwing a very heavy fire up a street leading to it. It was found also that they held an outwork commanding the bridge which would effectively render that outwork useless'. After this initial report, Cooke 'heard nothing more of this detachment, but considered it as lost, the communication having been interrupted by the enemy'.[14]

In fact, the enemy had done far more than interrupt Clifton's communications as is made clear by the narrative of van Gorkum, who accompanied this column. Initially, all went well, to the pleasant surprise of van Gorkum who had previously protested that Clifton's fifty-man force was insufficient for the task, and the Antwerp Gate was carried at the rush. From there, van Gorkum and Lieutenant Colonel the Hon. James MacDonald of 2/1st Foot Guards were sent to reconnoitre the streets leading into the main part of the town. Pushing along the Roskamstraatje, they were able to take a handful of French prisoners, including an NCO of Flemish extraction who told van Gorkum that if the British could push on to the Market Place in the centre of the town they would be able to capture four pieces of French artillery parked there. Before anything else could be done, however, the party came under fire from further up the street, and MacDonald was mortally wounded. Van Gorkum therefore returned to the Antwerp Gate, reporting this intelligence to Clifton and asking permission for an advance in force towards the Market Place.[15]

By this stage, Clifton had a larger force under his command, having been joined by some survivors from Carleton's party. Nevertheless, the Guards officer remained unwilling either to push into the town or to force open the Antwerp Gate, explaining to van Gorkum that his orders did not permit him to do either. Van Gorkum then attempted to open the Antwerp gate himself, with an NCO and a few men, but was unable to lower the drawbridge. He sent the NCO back to Carmichael Smyth with a request for the necessary engineer tools, but on discovering the presence of the French troops in the outwork he gave up the attempt. It was presumably around this point, shortly after midnight, that Clifton's last message was sent back to Cooke, since the latter makes no mention of ever getting van Gorkum's subsequent report that the French in the outwork seemed willing to surrender.

In any case, if the French outside the gate were of a mind to give up on the fight, those inside the fortress certainly were not, and Clifton's party now found itself under pressure both from French troops advancing through the streets from the Market Place, and by the force that had defeated Carleton and was now advancing along the ramparts. Since the former party was the smaller – around fifty men, although accompanied by one of the cannon – Clifton elected to attack them, and led his men in a bayonet charge, capturing the cannon and chasing the defeated Frenchmen along the Hoogstraat almost all the way to the Market Place. For a moment, it seemed as if the centre of the town might fall into British hands, but as Clifton's troops approached the Market Place they were met by a concentrated volley from a second body of French concealed in a side-street. Clifton was killed, along with several of those around him, and the survivors fell back towards the Antwerp Gate. Lieutenant Colonel Leslie Jones of 2/1st Foot Guards took command of the remaining British troops, and for a time was able to continue the fight, but his men were soon split up as the struggle spread into the surrounding streets. Jones and those with him eventually found themselves cut off in the Beulstraat and were forced to surrender.

Things now looked very black indeed for the last mixed group of survivors. Van Gorkum led them back towards the Antwerp Gate but to attempt to hold this position was too much to ask, since the French had re-manned their cannon and turned it on the British. Already lightly wounded, van Gorkum now found himself literally with his back to the wall as the French surged forwards, fighting with musket butts and bayonets to regain the gate. The only way to retreat was to try and get out of the gate. Van Gorkum was amongst those who made it, eventually tumbling into the ditch as he endeavoured to get across the drawbridge outside the walls. In the company of a single NCO, he floundered for some time in the water, having broken the ice in his fall, but the noise inevitably attracted French attention and brought down a renewed fusillade. Wounded in the head by this fire, and having lost touch with his companion, van Gorkum eventually managed to work his way back along the defences, deep in the water for much of the way, until able to regain contact with Cooke's party at the 'Oranje' Bastion. Here he remained for some time before eventually, once it was clear that there would be no further advance, leaving to have his wound attended to.[16]

Meanwhile, having heard no further report of Clifton's progress, Cooke elected to send off another detachment, this time under Lieutenant Colonel Henry Rooke of 2/3rd Foot Guards. The French had reoccupied part of the ramparts and Rooke was obliged to fight his way through to regain control of the Antwerp Gate. Upon reaching that point, Rooke, having 'found it useless to attempt any thing and ascertained that the outwork was still occupied',[17] withdrew his detachment and re-joined the main body under Cooke and Proby. Sir John Jones is rightly critical of this lack of initiative with respect to the Antwerp Gate, which was twice in British hands but which was not forced on either occasion. As he points out, outworks are 'invariably so constructed as to afford no cover against the fire of the place' and had the Guards managed to get the gate open 'the French guard in the lunette would have been completely at their mercy'.[18] Clifton, at least, may be forgiven for turning his attentions elsewhere, but Rooke had rather less to distract him and might at least have made the attempt. In the event, however, there was nothing lost by the failure to take possession of the Antwerp Gate, beyond the potential psychological advantage, since Major Muttlebury had managed to bring the survivors of the stalled Centre Attack around the perimeter of the fortress and onto the ramparts via the same ladders that the Guards had used to enter. This added two-and-a-half battalions, just over a thousand men, to Cooke's command and further increased his potential to act decisively and restore the fortunes of the attack.

Instead, however, Cooke remained stationary. He had pushed patrols out through the streets as far as the quayside on the southern side of the harbour, and was in contact with the troops under Muller that were still holding on around the Water Gate. Cooke's intention was now to hang on where he was until morning, rather than risk further confusion, and potential defeat, by attempting to achieve more during the hours of darkness. It is evident in particular that the disappearance of Clifton's detachment had filled him with a horror of pushing further into the streets of the town itself – as distinct from the area around the harbour – since he would later report to Graham that 'the state of Uncertainty as to what had passed at other Points determined me not to weaken the force now collected, by attempting to carry Points which we could not maintain or penetrate through the streets with the certain loss of a great number of men'.[19] His only concession, based on his knowledge that 'that the troops at the Water Port Gate under Lieutenant Col. Muller were very seriously opposed' was to detach the 33rd, now under Major Edward Parkinson, to reinforce the 4/1st.[20]

Amongst the other senior officers, the perception of events was apparently largely in line with Cooke's: essentially to the effect that the British lodgement was now secure and that it would be best left until daylight to finish off such resistance as remained, rather than risk what had already been achieved by trying to do more in the dark. Indeed, Carmichael Smyth expressed his pleasure, even after the subsequent disaster, that at this point:

> We had tranquil possession of the Rampart as far as we extended.
> The firing was apparently completely at an end. About 4 o'clock
> in the morning I went out of the town to report to Sir Thomas
> Graham the state of things and at the same time authorized [sic] by

M. General Cooke to say that his intentions were to keep his people
well together and as little exposed as possible until day light when
he would be enabled to see what the enemy were about and he would
then act accordingly.[21]

Sir George Hoste accompanied his chief on this mission, the two men
apparently believing that the task of the engineers was over now that the
infantry were inside and leaving Sperling – who after his various scrapes had
developed a rather less optimistic view of British chances – as the only Royal
Engineer officer inside the fortress. Sperling had every right to feel unhappy,
however, since with these dispositions Cooke had effectively surrendered all
initiative to the French.

Even as Cooke was trying and failing to expand his control of the southern
sector of the town, the French had already begun to go back onto the
offensive along the northern walls. Here, Skerrett's detachment remained
pinned down near the windmill, coming under increasing pressure as more
French troops became available following the dispersal of the False Attack.
After Skerrett made his move to the left, he seems to have lost contact with
the main body of the Right Attack remaining around the Water Gate.
Indeed, when Muller's troops heard firing off to the east – probably the
fighting around the Breda Gate – there was some speculation that this in
fact represented rapid progress by Skerrett. Accordingly young Moodie,
still seeking distinction, elected to try and join up with him. With two
soldiers, he managed to get up the length of the harbour unopposed but
was stopped near the Gevangenpoort, which was held by the French, and
forced to return. Reporting the situation to Muller, Moodie was ordered to
return as a guide to a detachment of the 4/1st, who pushed the French back.
This done, Moodie made a renewed attempt to link up with Skerrett's party,
but after eventually making his way through the streets to join them he
found the survivors in a bad way, driven back from the windmill and
endeavouring to hang on to the 'Gadelière' Bastion. With them he found
his friend Robertson of the 4/1st, who was able to fill him in on what had
happened. As Robertson explained, 'the party, which was now commanded
by Capt. [James] Guthrie of the 33d regiment, had been compelled by
numbers to retire from the bastion which the enemy now occupied, and
should endeavour to maintain the one which they now possessed, until they
could procure a reinforcement'. The reason that Guthrie was in command,
Robertson went on, was because Skerrett had been amongst those who fell
when the British were driven from their position around the windmill,

which was 'an irreparable loss to our party, as Capt. Guthrie was ignorant of the General's intentions'.[22]

The French counter-attack had been made in overwhelming force, with 300 naval troops under Lieutenant de Vaisseau Alexandre Codercq supported by 810 infantrymen of the 3/17ème and 4/51ème Ligne under Chef de Battalion Sombart. There was little hope of holding off this force, which quickly recaptured the windmill and took around seventy-five of its defenders prisoners. Skerrett had already been wounded twice at this point, in the hand and in the thigh, but remained with his troops until finally brought down by a shot to the head. Mortally wounded, he died the following day whilst still in captivity. Controversial to the last, there is no denying his courage but his military judgement remains questionable. Whatever his motives in going off as he did, in doing so he abdicated all control of the remaining troops under his direction and thus added yet more confusion to the already fast-fragmenting situation in the northern sector of the fighting. Codercq, leading his sailors with a cry of 'À l'abordage! [Boarders away!]', was also killed.[23]

The situation for the survivors of Skerrett's party was now precarious, for the rise of the tide meant that their route into the fortress, across the Zoom canal, was now under water. Their only connection with the remaining British forces was via the foot bridge across the harbour, which would allow communication with Muller at the Water Gate, but it was not clear whether this remained in friendly control so the handful of troops remaining with Guthrie barricaded themselves in where they were. Moodie described their unenviable situation:

> In the mean time the enemy continued a sharp firing on us, which we returned as fast as our men could load their firelocks. Several of the enemy who had fallen, as well as of our own men, were lying on the ramparts; one of our officers, who had been wounded in the arm, was walking about, saying occasionally, in rather a discontented manner, 'This is what is called honour'; though I could readily sympathise with him in the pain he suffered, I could not exactly understand how, if there is any honour in getting wounded, any bodily suffering can detract from it.
>
> We found a large pile of logs of wood on the rampart; these we immediately disposed across the gorge of the bastion, so as to form a kind of parapet, over which our people could fire, leaving, however, about half the distance open towards the parapet of the rampart. On the opposite side of the bastion were two twenty-four-

pounders of the enemy's, which being raised on high platforms, we turned upon them, firing along the ramparts over the heads of our own party. However valuable this resource might be to us, we were still far from being on equal terms with the French, who besides greatly exceeding us in numbers, had also brought up two or three fieldpieces, which annoyed us much during the night.[24]

The French also made good use of the windmill now that they had recaptured it, posting men atop it to fire down on the British. Several direct attempts were also made to evict the defenders at bayonet point, but the captured 24-pounders were employed to good effect in breaking up these efforts.

Fighting of this nature continued until around 02.00, after which the intensity of the struggle died down somewhat, allowing the defenders to snatch some sleep during the lulls. Moodie was one of several officers who, by huddling together for warmth, managed to doze for a while, but their rest was short-lived and suddenly Moodie 'felt the ground shake under me, and heard at the same time a crash as if the whole town had been overwhelmed by an earthquake; a bright glare of light burst on my eyes at the same instant and almost blinded me'. A French shell had detonated the magazine from which the captured guns were being supplied, depriving the British of their use and placing the defenders in an even worse situation than before, which the French were quick to exploit:

> Immediately after this disaster, raising a tremendous shout or rather yell, the enemy again attempted to come to close quarters with us, in hopes of our being utterly disheartened; but our charging party, which we had always in readiness, made them wheel round as usual. In the course of the night, we had sent several small parties of men to represent the state of our detachment, and endeavour to procure assistance, but none of them returned, having, we supposed, been intercepted by the enemy. Discouraged as we were by this circumstance, we still continued to hold our ground until break of day.[25]

Having nothing to do but hold on in hope of relief, Guthrie's little party were now in a very precarious position from which the only respite could come in the increasingly unlikely arrival of British reinforcements.

The vulnerability of this small detachment was not lost on the French, and, since the bulk of Bizanet's forces were already concentrated in this sector of the defences it made sense for them to begin here in their attempt to drive the remaining British from the fortress. Other than Guthrie's party clinging on to their bolt-hole on the northern ramparts, the British position extended anti-clockwise from the Water Gate up to a point somewhere short of the Antwerp Gate, which was now securely in French hands. The streets around the harbour remained something of a contested area, but the main part of the town was now fairly secure and the only means left to the British of getting troops into, or out of, the fortress was via the ladders at the Bastion 'Oranje' by which the Centre and Left Attacks had entered. The initial British attack had quite clearly come as a great shock to the defenders of Bergen-op-Zoom, and there had been considerable confusion in the initial stages of the French response, but the successes against Carleton and Clifton had done much to restore morale, and this was further enhanced by the inaction of the British and Cooke's unwillingness to press matters to a conclusion until daylight. As Sperling put it, 'our passiveness was misconstrued, and invited attack'.[26]

The early hours of 9 March thus found the French feeling increasingly confident and the British becoming more and more uneasy. As late as 04.00, when Carmichael Smyth left the fortress to report to Graham, Cooke remained confident that matters could be brought to a successful conclusion when it became light, but the next few hours brought about a definite change. In this, he was influenced by two key factors. The first of these was that the French, growing in confidence, became increasingly aggressive in their harassing of the British on the ramparts. Initially, this consisted of sniping from the houses adjacent to the British positions, but this soon developed into small-scale attacks. These were not pressed, and the French 'retired immediately on our men showing themselves, but these not following up their assailants, it only encouraged a repetition of them'.[27] The French in this sector had by now been reinforced by the 274-strong detachment of the 21ème Ligne, which had been previously held in reserve at the Steenbergen Gate.[28] As their numbers increased, Cooke reported that the French became more aggressive and began to press the British harder:

> The Enemy continued a galling fire upon us, and at one time held the adjoining Bastion, from the angle of which they completely commanded our communication with the exterior, and brought their guns at that angle to bear against us. They were charged and driven away by Majors Muttlebury and Hog [sic: Alexander Hogg] with the 69th and 55th in a very gallant style.[29]

A handful of men from the 2/44th also took part in these charges, which, by their bold front, masked the increasing vulnerability of the British position.

The second factor acting on Cooke was the influence of Lord Proby, who seems early on to have decided that the operation was not going to end in success. Whilst it may well be the case that his Lordship was more prescient than many of his colleagues, his prophecy became self-fulfilling thanks to his interventions with Cooke.

Endeavouring to obtain orders for the remaining engineers and sappers, Sperling made repeated visits during the night to Cooke's command post, established in a small look-out built into the ramparts, and was witness to the exchanges between the two officers:

> Lord Proby, who commanded the Guards, was filled with melan-
> choly forebodings. He had taken up his post with the General, and
> seemed occupied in instilling the diffidence with which his own
> mind was filled. He characterized our situation as desperate
> (although exactly the reverse, as any decisive measure must,
> humanly speaking, have ensured success) and the importance of the
> safety of the Guards.[30]

This defeatism from his principal subordinate, and the increasing difficulty in maintaining the ramparts against the French probes, together meant that by the time that dawn came, and with it the French counter-attack, Cooke was in no position to respond decisively. No doubt somewhat confused by matters, he took refuge from any decision-making by responding to any suggestion of a further advance with the retort, 'Sir, we have our orders.'[31]

It was not, however, on the defenders of the Bastion 'Oranje' that the French blow first fell, but on Guthrie's survivors on the other side of the town. Bizanet had completed the concentration of his troops, bringing the 3/12ème back from the eastern walls to strengthen his attack. As Moodie related, 'the enemy now brought an overwhelming force against us', pinning the defenders against their log barricade whilst sending a second party onto the ramparts to cut their retreat:

> Keeping up an incessant fire to divert our attention, the French (who
> now outnumbered us, at least three to one) detached a part of their
> force, which skirting the outside of the ramparts, and ascending the
> face of the bastion we occupied, suddenly opened a most destructive
> fire on our flank and rear. From this latter party we were totally
> unprotected, while they were sheltered by the top of the rampart:
> we were thus left to defend ourselves from both at once as we best
> could. But still they would not venture to charge us, and it would
> have been of little use for us to charge them, for the moment we
> quitted the parapet, we would have been exposed to a cross fire from
> the other bastion.

The slaughter was now dreadful, and our poor fellows, who had done all that soldiers could in our trying situation, now fell thick and fast. Just at this moment, my friend Robertson, under whose command I had put myself at the beginning of the attack, fell. I had just time to run up to him, and found him stunned from a wound in the head; when our gallant commander, seeing the inutility of continuing the unequal contest, gave the order to retreat. We had retired in good order about three hundred yards, when poor Guthrie received a wound in the head, which I have since been informed deprived him of his sight. The enemy, when they saw us retreating, hung upon our rear, keeping up a sharp fire all the time, but they still seemed to have some respect for us from the trouble we had already given them.[32]

The survivors, although unsure of the strength and location of the remaining British troops within the fortress, attempted to make their way to the Water Gate but found that their retreat had already been cut off. With the French in control of the bridge, the only way to get across the harbour was to swim for it, and this several men – including Moodie – tried to do. Some made it, only to be forced to surrender by the French, who were already waiting for them on the other side, whilst others, succumbing to panic, drowned in the icy waters.

With the French still shooting at the floundering redcoats, it seemed as if all hope had gone. One possible salvation, however, presented itself in the shape of the guard-boat that had been anchored in the harbour mouth and abandoned by its crew during the first British rush the evening before. By the time that Moodie reached the quayside, several men were already making for the boat, and, having fought his way through floating ice and struggling soldiers, he too struck out for this refuge:

All this time some of the enemy continued firing at us, and I saw one or two shot in the water near me. So intent was every one on effecting his escape, that though they sometimes cast a look of commiseration at their drowning comrades, no one thought for a moment of giving us any assistance. The very hope of it had at length so completely faded in our minds, that we had ceased to ask the aid of those that passed us on the fragments of ice. But Providence had reserved one individual who possessed a heart to feel for the distress of his fellow-creatures more than for his own personal safety.[33]

This was Lieutenant John MacDougall of the 2/91st, who first tried to throw Moodie a rope and then, realizing that the latter was too weak with cold to hold it, dragged him bodily over the rail with the assistance of a wounded private who was already in the boat. Once safely inboard, Moodie began to assist MacDougall in hauling others aboard but at this point his luck ran out and he was hit by a musket ball in the wrist. In the casualty returns the wound is listed as only slight, but it was enough to finish off the already exhausted subaltern for the moment. Although MacDougall and some others managed to get off the boat and onto the far quay, Moodie was in no fit state to go any further. Going below to the vessel's cabin, he found Lieutenant James Briggs of the 2/91st, who had been shot through the shoulder, and the two officers attempted to bind their wounds whilst, at the same time, growing increasingly conscious that the boat was filling with water. Thankfully, the waterlogged craft drifted aground before it could sink, although not before Moodie was in water up to his waist. Under such circumstances, escape was no longer an option, and, the two officers 'were glad on the whole to be relieved from our present disagreeable situation by surrendering ourselves prisoners'.[34]

The rest of the British forces did not remain completely idle whilst all this was going on, with Cooke personally bringing up the 33rd to endeavour to give some support from the other side of the harbour. There was a limit to what they could achieve from across the water, and, with their fire now endangering their fleeing compatriots on the north quay, Major Parkinson elected to withdraw his men. By this time – around 09.00 – the last survivors of Guthrie's detachment had been killed or captured, and the French were already pushing into the harbour area and moving against Muller's command around the Water Gate. The 4/1st was somewhat scattered, having been without its flank companies from the outset and then detached more troops to try to secure the harbour. The detached companies of the 4/1st, backed up by the 33rd around the harbour, were initially successful in preventing any French advance from the town into the harbour area, but had lost control of the Gevangenpoort. At the same time, the main thrust of the French counter-attack was swinging round along the ramparts to cut them off from Muller's main body around the Water Gate. Spearheaded by the 3/12ème, this movement also facilitated the French recapture of the arsenal and enabled them to pass troops across the harbour drawbridge. The only way out now was across the mudflats separating the fortress from the main channel of the Scheldt, but these were commanded by the guns of the Water Fort and, what was more, the tide was still high and the avenue of escape accordingly limited. As if this were not bad enough, there had not been the time to spike any of the guns in the bastions to the north of the harbour and these were now re-manned by the French and turned against the troops around the Water Gate.

Graham made it clear in his official report – and clearer still in his private correspondence – that he placed the blame for the British failure directly on the 4/1st, and their commanding officer in particular, writing that 'had the Royals maintained the Water-port gate, General Cooke would have held his ground, and the place must have fallen'.[35] It is hard, however, to understand just how Muller was expected to achieve this when he was under attack from several sides and under close-range fire from heavy guns firing grapeshot. True, he might have ordered those cannon spiked whilst they were still in his possession, and he has been criticized for not doing so,[36] but it is hard to fault a man for failing to take defensive precautions when he was expected to begin the new day by taking the offensive: in any case, under other circumstances, the guns might have been put to good use against the French. Frederick Muller may not have been a first-rate commanding officer – Stanhope thought him 'not qualified to take either any judicious or dashing line of conduct on himself'[37] – but he had been effectively abandoned by his superiors within the Right Attack and left with no real guidance from Cooke either. Up until this point, he had performed adequately enough, and the picture painted by Moodie of an active, if unimaginative, officer is probably fairer than history's scapegoating of him as an incompetent.

What destroyed Muller's reputation, in truth, was likely not his conduct up to this juncture, but what happened after the French attacked. Under heavy fire, the inexperienced 4/1st broke and fell back, many of the men heading for the Water Fort in the apparent belief that this was in British hands. This, of course, was not the case and those who made it down onto the mudflats soon found themselves caught between two fires. Escape was now impossible, and Muller ordered what was left of his battalion to lay down its arms. Before he did so, however, he instructed the battalion's Adjutant, Lieutenant George Galbraith, to conceal the colours. According to regimental tradition, Galbraith attempted to do this by sinking them into the waters of the Zoom, only for the standards to be recovered once the tide was fully out and so fall into French hands. Exactly how, and how well, the colours were concealed is uncertain, but it was certainly not the case, as at least one contemporary account had it, that there was no dishonour in their capture since 'they were only lost when their gallant defenders ceased to breathe'.[38] On the contrary, considerable stigma was attached to both the battalion and its commander, which would greatly hamper any objective assessment of their role in the action as a whole. Taken so late in the war, the flags did not reach Paris in time to be burned with most other such trophies, and so remain today in Les Invalides.[39]

As the pressure increased, the men of the 33rd also began to waver and Parkinson tried to fall back to re-join Muller, only to find that the 4/1st had already abandoned the Water Gate. This placed him in a decidedly awkward position, from which the only way out seemed to be for the 33rd to fight their way through to join Cooke. According to popular report, Parkinson placed himself at the head of his men, informing them that 'if they retreated they would be cut to pieces with the character of cowards, but if they would follow him and charge the enemy, their safety would be ensured, or they would die as heroes'.[40] His own description of events makes no mention of this rousing address, but demonstrates the clear resolve that enabled him to extricate what was left of his battalion from the disaster:

> My next object was to effect a junction with the Guards if possible; and with this view I retired to the ramparts where I could see what I considered to be their posts; but as there was no appearance what-ever of our troops towards that point, and the enemy had collected a considerable force on our right, there was no doubt left in my mind that they had also retired. Thus situated, with the regiment reduced to little more than 200 men, and attacked by a very superior force, with cannon and musketry in front and on flanks; deprived of any point of communication or support and without orders, I considered that it was my duty to make every possible effort in order to save the remnant of the regiment and colours from falling into the hands of the enemy; and I immediately took the resolution of retiring over the works and ditches of the place to the river and inundation, trusting to the ice for a passage along the face of the works towards the point where we first entered. This was fortunately accomplished, not without loss, but without suffering a single prisoner to be taken that was not previously wounded.[41]

With the escape of these survivors, and the surrender of the 4/1st, only the troops under Cooke's direct command remained within Bergen-op-Zoom.

Still, at this point, an aggressive response might yet have restored the situation and Sperling was surprised that Cooke did not make any effort to regain control of the streets on the southern side of the harbour before the French were able to get across the drawbridge in force. All expectation, Sperling asserted, was 'of some decisive movement, to take possession of the place', and it was therefore a matter of considerable surprise to the young

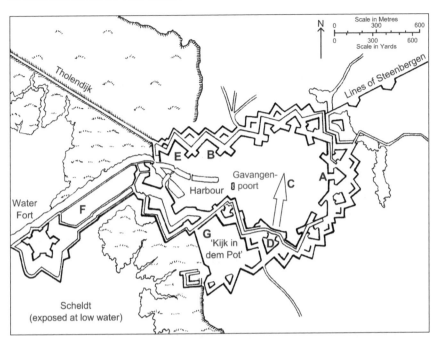

Bergen-op-Zoom – British Confusion and French Counter-Attacks

A Carleton's party dispersed around here, after making an anti-clockwise circuit from the harbour.

B Skerrett's advance clockwise from the harbour checked.

C Clifton secures the Antwerp Gate and advances into the town, but is killed and his party defeated.

D Survivors of Clifton's party try to hold the Antwerp Gate but are driven off.

E French counter-attack the survivors of Skerrett's party and regain control of the harbour.

F 4/1st are pinned under the guns of the Water Fort and are forced to surrender.

G Some survivors escape back down ladders from Bastion 'Oranje', where Cooke and remainder surrender.

engineer to see the Guards begin to file back towards the ladders preparatory to evacuating the ramparts.[42] As Cooke afterwards explained,

> finding that matters were becoming more serious and being still without any information from other Points excepting that of the failure of Lieutenant Col. Morrice's Column near the Wouw Gate, I determined at the suggestion of Col. Lord Proby to let part of the troops withdraw, which was done at the ladders where they entered.[43]

Proby, therefore, had managed to disilluson Cooke sufficiently for the senior officer now to acquiesce in the abandoning of the operation, but his Lordship remained in a minority so far as his troops were concerned.

Sperling saw that 'the Guards were reluctant to abandon their comrades, and many of them gave expression to their feelings in thus retiring before the French and deserting their companions'. With morale in the ranks still high, Sperling was convinced that all that was needed was some direction from above, but with none to be found he too accepted that it was time to get out:

> Those that remained were quite equal to taking the place, had there been a leader. Seeing, however, the turn things were taking, and that a capitulation was purposed, I went to the General to ask him whether, if the Sappers could be of no further service, I might withdraw them.[44]

Cooke agreed, and the sappers followed the guardsmen down the ladders. What is particularly distasteful about all this is Proby's apparent willingness to sacrifice troops of the line so long as the seemingly more valuable guardsmen got off. From the outset his motive seems to have been to preserve the Guards from the dishonour inherent in failure and potential surrender, yet it is hard to argue other than that the greater honour ultimately lay with the men of the 55th and 2/69th who, along with a portion of 2/1st Foot Guards, remained on the ramparts with Cooke to cover the retreat.

As the British began to fall back, the French who had been pressuring them – a mixed bag of troops under Chef de Battalion Lespez, built around the detachment of the 21ème Ligne – began to grow increasingly aggressive and pushed along the wall until they had occupied the bastion immediately adjacent to 'Oranje' on which the British defence was centred. Cooke was accordingly obliged to order the 55th and 2/69th, weak though they were, to clear this position whilst Proby led his portion of the Guards to safety. This they achieved in fine style, driving the French back almost as far as the Antwerp Gate, a circumstance that suggests that Cooke might well have fought his way to that gate with his whole force, and thus enabled them to escape the fortress intact, rather than remaining around the 'Oranje' Bastion. Cooke, however, had no such ideas and began to feed more men off the ramparts by way of the ladders, a movement that was still in progress when 'Lt. Col. Jones who had been taken Prisoner in the night came to me (accompanied by a French officer who summoned me to surrender) and informed me that Lt. Col. Muller and the Corps at the Water Port Gate had been obliged to surrender and were marched Prisoners into the town'. Jones also informed Cooke of the fate of the other columns, and this convinced the general that, 'a longer continuance of the Contest would be a useless loss of lives, and without a Prospect of Relief as we were situated – I therefore consented to adopt the mortifying alternative of laying down our arms'.[45] According to van Gorkum, who, by this stage, had left the fortress, Jones had already caused some of the Guards to surrender even whilst Cooke was still fighting.[46] Since no other accounts mention this, and Jones continued his military career with no stain on his reputation, this would seem to represent confusion on van Gorkum's part, possibly stemming from the fact that, as Cooke himself reported, it was Jones who was able to tell him the fate of those other units that had already surrendered of their own volition.

Again, Cooke's action here is hard to understand. It might well have been clear that the attack had failed, but it was surely better to at least allow the troops the chance to escape than to surrender the whole force *en masse*. Then again, the French had begun to re-man the guns on the walls, and fire was also opened from the lunette outside the Antwerp Gate against the retreating troops. Undoubtedly, had formed bodies of men tried to fight their way out then casualties would have been heavy, but, on the other hand, substantial numbers of troops did manage to make their escape from the two line battalions, despite their distance from the ladders, as well as from the Guards. The 2/69th even managed to bring off their King's Colour, only to lose it a year later at Quatre Bras, and the colours of the 2/44th were also safely carried off. The Regimental Colour of the 2/69th was lost on this occasion however, and those of the 55th could also not be brought to safety. Whilst the former fell into French hands, Ensigns King and Goodall tore the colours of the 55th from their staffs and concealed them within their coats, preserving the precious squares of silk throughout their captivity and subsequently returning them to the regiment.

As well as the Regimental Colour of the 2/69th, and the full stand belonging to the 4/1st recovered from the Zoom, a fourth colour was also reported as captured, apparently belonging to the Guards. The exact identity of this flag is unclear. Although all four captured colours are preserved the descriptions do not entirely fit with the expected appearance of the flags. If that described as 'a blue silk flag with the Union Jack in the top corner [. . .] a large hole in the centre and [. . .] no distinguishing marks' is assumed to be the Regimental Colour of the 2/69th, which is quite an assumption in itself since that colour should have had a green ground, then the unknown 'colour' is in fact an unmarked Union flag, and its origin inexplicable.[47]

Whilst some officers sought to preserve the honour of their regiments by getting the colours to safety, others of all ranks attempted to maintain their credit even as the attack fell apart. One such was Sergeant Townsend of 2/1st Foot Guards, who, according to Austin, when ordered to surrender, stepped out of the ranks, saying to the soldiers around him that 'he'd be d——d if he would lay down his arms' and asking, 'Are there any men here who will follow me'.

Thirteen men stepped forth from the ranks and placed themselves under his direction; and with this little band of brave fellows he crossed the square upon which the enemy had established a cross-fire. After expending all their ammunition in clearing a way, he and his gallant comrades escaped unscathed from the town.[48]

Having survived Waterloo as well, Townsend was ultimately rewarded by being made a steward and porter at Walmer Castle, the Duke of Wellington's residence as Lord Warden of the Cinque Ports, and ended his days as a Yeoman of the Guard at the Tower of London.[49] Although such conduct, and the preservation of most of the colours, allowed the retention of some degree of honour there was no denying that Cooke's surrender marked the conclusion of one of the most embarrassing disasters to attend the course of British arms during the whole of the Napoleonic Wars. More to the point, it left Sir Thomas Graham, his gamble quite clearly having failed, facing a decidedly uncertain future with almost 3,000 of his troops dead, wounded, or prisoners in the hands of the enemy.

Chapter XII

'Out-Generalled and Disgracefully Beaten'

ALTHOUGH THE UTTER FAILURE OF THE ASSAULT did not become apparent to Graham until it was too late to intervene, it was nevertheless clear from an early stage that the plan had not functioned as had been intended, and that reinforcements would likely be required to make good the initial gains. Thus, whilst leaving direction of events within the walls to Cooke, Graham set about ordering up additional troops during the course of the night. Because the bulk of the Second Division was employed in holding the outpost line facing Antwerp, only limited forces were available. However, the 33rd, 2/35th and 54th had been kept further back, allowing the first-named battalion to take part in the initial assault and rendering the latter two available as reinforcements.[1] Additionally, not all of the Guards Brigade had been committed to the attacking force, and Graham was able to call up 400 guardsmen from Putte and a further 200, as well as the whole of the 2/35th, from Wouw.

Graham, who had stationed himself outside the ramparts near the 'Kijk in dem Pot' entrenched camp, intended to use these troops to reinforce Cooke in the 'Oranje' Bastion, in order to enable him to make a strong attack on the morning of the 9th. Artillery was also brought up to support such a move, and the reinforcements were to be guided into the fortress, by way of the ladders, by Carmichael Smyth who was also instructed to convey 'a message to M. General Cooke to recommend that he should send in to the Governor some person to point out the folly of any further resistance which would only irritate our Soldiers to give no quarter'.[2]

Even after it became apparent to those on the outside that things had not gone well in the fighting around the harbour, Graham still hoped to reinforce Cooke; indeed, van Gorkum – who, despite his wound, had remained with Graham and his staff – was convinced that the Antwerp Gate would shortly be opened in order to facilitate the entry of fresh troops.[3] As we have seen, however, that post was by this stage securely in French hands, and by the time the reinforcements finally arrived the Guards were already falling back down the ladders and it was clear that the moment had passed.

Having initially been held at readiness, the troops at Wouw received word around midnight that the attack had succeeded and that they might stand down, before being awoken in the early hours by an urgent summons. By the time they reached the fortress, however, it was already too late and Major MacAlister, commanding the 2/35th, was stopped by a staff officer who told him that 'things are going badly' and that Graham wished to speak with him:

> I then followed my leader, and in a small field touching the glacis of Bergen op Zoom, beheld the gallant Graham, steadily gazing upon the walls of the fortress, occasionally stamping his foot with violence upon the ground; whilst tears, I afterwards perceived, had been stealing down his furrowed cheeks, denoting the conflicting nature of his feelings. He did not notice my approach until I said to him, 'General, shall I enter the town?'
>
> 'It is too late, sir,' he replied, 'Look there!' Turning my eyes in the direction to which he pointed, I observed a stream of men rushing out of one of the gates at no great distance from the spot where we stood; and others scrambling down, and even throwing themselves from the walls on each side of it, seemingly without cause, as no cannon or musketry immediately followed them.
>
> 'Form across the road,' continued the general. 'Remember there are no other troops at hand. If the enemy follows, you must defend yourself HERE to the last man.'[4]

In the event there was no French attempt to carry their advantage outside the fortress – small wonder, when there were now more British prisoners inside than there were fit French troops to guard them – and at length the 2/35th were able to stand down.

With the position outside the fortress secure, and measures set in motion to rally the surviving forces, it now became Graham's priority to gain contact with those on the inside and find out what had happened to the missing troops. The bulk of the day was spent restoring order and bringing up additional forces to join the survivors of the attack, but that evening Lieutenant Colonel Jones was sent out under a flag of truce with a proposal from Bizanet that negotiations be opened relative to the exchange of prisoners. Because the losses he had suffered had effectively crippled half the battalions under his command, Graham was only too glad to accept the offer since if a full exchange could be obtained then much of the damage done to Britain's cause in the Low Countries might be undone.

It might then be questioned, why Bizanet was so keen to open up negotiations, but the French governor was hard-pressed to house, feed, and, above all, guard so many prisoners and was as keen to be rid of them as Graham was to have them back. Dunbar Moodie received better treatment than most, by virtue of his rank and his wound, which together secured him a place in the town's hospital. Nevertheless, his clothes were stolen from him when he – perhaps unwisely – sent them to be dried, and the rations issued were sadly lacking:

> Twice a-day two of the attendants of the hospital went about with buckets in their hands, one containing small pieces of boiled meat, which was discovered to be horseflesh by the medical people, while another contained a miserable kind of stuff, which they called soup, and a third contained bits of bread. One of the pieces of meat was tossed on each bed with a fork in passing; but the patient had always to make his choice between flesh and bread, and soup and bread, it being thought too much to allow them soup and meat at the same time. I was never so much puzzled in my life as by this alternative. Constantly tormented with thirst, I usually asked for soup, but my hunger, with which I was no less tormented, made me as often repent my choice.[5]

Considering that the fortress had been under blockade for some time, and looked to remain so for the foreseeable future, it is perhaps hardly surprising that Bizanet did not issue more substantial rations. In other respects, however, his treatment of the prisoners was as good as could be expected, permitting the British wounded to be attended by their own surgeons, and allowing Cooke to send a report out to Graham giving details of the fighting. As he explained to Stanhope, Bizanet had for a time been a prisoner of the British and was so appreciative of his treatment on that occasion as to deem it a matter of honour to offer the same in return now the roles were reversed.[6]

Stanhope was able to obtain Bizanet's views on the matter since it was he whom Graham sent into the fortress on the morning of 10 March to open negotiations. Graham had begun matters the previous evening, sending Jones back with a note thanking Bizanet for his 'humane and generous conduct to the Prisoners' and making his own opening gambit in the talks:

> Should your Excellency agree to my sending all of them to England on the Condition of not serving again during the war unless regularly exchanged I engage my word of Honor [sic] for the strict execution of this agreement, and that I will do my utmost to procure an immediate release of an equal number of French Officers of corresponding rank and an equal number of non-commissioned

officers and Soldiers, which I have no doubt of my Government
consenting to immediately.

I would propose to your Excellency to send all the Prisoners into
the Island of Tholen in order to be ready for embarkation and that
a French officer as Commissary to see that strict execution of the
agreement should accompany them.[7]

Graham further proposed an immediate exchange of the three French
officers and 119 rank and file prisoners taken by the British during the early
stages of the fighting for an equal quantity of British troops. Following this
up, Stanhope was sent in the following morning bearing a second note
empowering him to make an agreement on Graham's behalf with any officer
that Bizanet cared to nominate, and asking for a suspension of hostilities 'till
any articles which may be agreed on relative to the removal of the Prisoners
in Bergen-op-Zoom can be carried into execution'.[8]

When Stanhope arrived inside the fortress, he discovered that Bizanet had
appointed not one officer to represent him but two: Major Hulot de Neufville
and Chef de Battalion Leclerc. Accordingly, Jones was co-opted as a second
British plenipotentiary and the four men sat down to work matters out.
Stanhope, as a member of Graham's staff, was aware of the fact that the
British government was mooting the idea of transferring a part of Graham's
troops to North America, and therefore sought – successfully – to ensure
that, per the wording of the second of the fifteen articles making up the
convention, the British prisoners would be released on parole of honour not
to serve against 'S.M. l'Empereur des Français et ses allies, en Europe'. In
other words, there was nothing whatsoever to impede their being shipped
straight off to Canada even before the formalities of exchange had been
completed. The only British proposal that was not accepted was the request
that a British officer should remain as commissioner in Bergen-op-Zoom to
ensure that the French stuck to the letter of the convention, but it was agreed
that such an officer might enter on stated days between 10.00 and 14.00.
Otherwise, the terms were mundane and covered such matters as the
continued care in French hospitals of wounded who were unable to be
moved, the granting of safe-conduct to a French officer to go to Antwerp
with news of the agreement, and the guarantee that the British officer
prisoners would be allowed to retain their swords. In order to permit all this
to take place, and the arrangements be put in place to move the paroled
prisoners, a three-day suspension of hostilities was agreed to.[9]

With the details arranged, the prisoners began to be brought out,
beginning with the wounded. Moodie had managed to beg and borrow a

basic wardrobe to replace that which had been stolen from him, including a French hospital shirt which he stubbornly hung on to with the not-unreasonable logic that it represented partial compensation for his stolen uniform. The journey, however, was not pleasant, with echoes of Austin's debilitating carriage back from Antwerp:

> We were marched out of the town by the Breda-gate to Rozendaal [sic], a distance of about fifteen miles, where we arrived the same night. The French soldiers who had fallen in the conflict had all been removed by this time, but as we proceeded, escorted by the victors, many a ghastly corpse of our countrymen met our half-averted eyes. They had all been more or less stripped of their clothing, and some had only their shirts left for a covering, and were turned on their faces. My heart rose at this humiliating spectacle, nor could I breathe freely until we reached the open fields beyond the fortifications. All who were unable to march were crowded into the waggons which had been prepared for them, while those who were less disabled straggled along the road the best way they could. As may be supposed, there were no needless competitors for the waggon conveyance, for the roads were rough, and every jolt of the vehicles produced groans of agony from the wretched passengers.[10]

Moodie could at least take some comfort in the fact that he was able, as the convoy passed through Wouw, to square matters with his commanding officer with respect to his disappearance on the night of the 8th, although this reunion was marred by the news that several of his friends and comrades had been killed or badly wounded during the fighting.

Since the ramifications of the prisoner exchange would drag on for some considerable time, it is as well to summarize them here before moving on to other matters. Initially, all seemed to be going well, and Graham sought to ensure that French prisoners were chosen for exchange who were either recommended by their countrymen serving in Bergen-op-Zoom and Antwerp, or else who were known to British officers involved in the operations. He himself stated that he would 'be very glad if Govt. would approve of Genl. Rey Gov. of St. Sebastian [sic] being exchang'd for M Genl. Cooke – as I promised him to try to get him released as soon as possible'.[11] Indeed, so confident was he of matters being quickly resolved that he assumed it would be 'unnecessary to send the B. op Zoom prisoners home in w'ch case arms & accoutrements w'd be necessary for them w'thout delay' so that they could again be employed in the field.[12]

From London, however, things were rather less clear-cut, and Bathurst was obliged to disabuse Graham of his assumption that matters could be swiftly resolved. The terms of the parole by which the released prisoners would not serve against France and its allies in Europe were entirely approved, but Bathurst was obliged to tell Graham that, after consultation with Allied ministers, it was not considered expedient to authorize the release of a commensurate number of French prisoners in exchange, meaning that the released prisoners would remain bound by the terms of their parole. To replace the men lost at Bergen-op-Zoom, Bathurst told Graham that:

> A Brigade of Provisional Battalions (Militia Volunteers) under the command of Major General Bailey is embarked, and will proceed to the Scheldt with the first change of wind. Upon their arrival you will be pleased to order the embarkation of all the British prisoners released, under the agreement of the 10th of March, on board of the Transports from which the Provisional Battalions will have landed;– and the vessels are to return immediately to this country.
>
> I embrace this opportunity of acquainting you that in addition to the Brigade before mentioned, which consists of about 2500 men, near 2000 Rank and File formed into Provisional Battalions of the Line, are already moving to embark for Holland.[13]

This was not quite the impressive reinforcement that it sounded, for the battalions formed from the Militia volunteers were a decidedly dubious entity. Originally envisaged as a reinforcement for Wellington, who had no great opinion of their merits but wanted every man he could get, neither officers nor men had seen anything by way of regular service and several of the senior officers owed their places to political clout rather than any military promise.[14] The 'Provisional Battalions of the Line' meanwhile, were a desperate attempt by the Duke of York, after much prodding by Bathurst, to scrape up available manpower from various regimental depots in Britain. These detachments were then to be used temporarily to reinforce three weak regular battalions – the 2/5th, 3/14th, and 2/22nd – to bring them up to 800 men apiece. Although the nuclei of these battalions were brought together at Colchester by the end of March under the supervision of Major General Wroth Acland, with an apparent view to forming them into a brigade under Major General William Eden, men were simply not available in the numbers that had been hoped for, and it proved impossible to get any of these battalions ready before the end of the war.[15]

In the meantime, Graham had protested in strong terms about the un-willingness of the authorities to make the exchange that would free his men from the terms of their parole. Rightly assuming that the real reason for Bathurst's decision was the pressure being exerted by the representatives of the other Allied powers, he responded to the news by a note of protest which was to be personally delivered to the Secretary of State by Lieutenant Colonel Jones, who was 'better acquainted with all the circumstances surrounding the Prisoners & the agreement, than any other person', and which concluded by expressing the 'hope that the statements & suggestions he can make, may induce your Lordship to bring the matter again under consideration'.[16]

Graham then followed up this theme in a long letter to Colonel Bunbury at Horse Guards, in which he stressed the disjointed state of those battalions that had lost large numbers of men as prisoners and which were as a result unable to muster anything like an effective strength. He recognized, however, that this 'circumstance will not weigh with the Russian ambassador – the only arguments that can induce him to relax must be founded on the little value to B'parte w'ch the release of men who have been confined for ten or twelve years in prison, & such in fairness ought to be sent in preference to men who have been lately captur'd'. Accordingly, Graham suggested that with this in mind 'it might at all events be worthwhile to try if a partial release would be approved to by the Allies, & accepted by the enemy'.[17]

Graham and Jones may well have been persuasive, but as it turned out it was events elsewhere that finally swung things in favour of an exchange, with news of the pro-Bourbon rising at Bordeaux, received towards the end of March, causing the redirection of the Brigade of Provisional Militia back to Wellington after all. Since it was also apparent by this juncture that the detachment battalions assembling at Colchester were nowhere near ready, Bathurst was left with no alternative but to agree to an exchange of prisoners that would release the bulk of Graham's men from their paroles. As he was informed in a letter of 1 April,

> The Government have determined to exchange Major General Cooke and all the officers and men belonging to the corps serving under your orders who were made prisoners at Bergen op Zoom with the exception of the Royal Scots. An Admiral and a sufficient number of French Prisoners (preferring those that have been confined the longest in this Country) will be sent to France without loss of time; and in the Selection of the officers every possible attention will be paid to the lists transmitted by you. Such of these French officers as have been well conducted will be included in the exchange. Tonnage goes to Holland sufficient to bring home to this country the whole of the Royal Scots.[18]

The reason for the exemption of the 4/1st was that it had already been decided to transfer this battalion to Canada, where it was free, thanks to Stanhope's wording of the parole agreement, to serve against the Americans without needing to be exchanged; since nearly 600 of the paroled men belonged to this unit, this reduced the number of Frenchmen being released to a total that would be more palatable to Britain's allies.

Graham thus eventually got his way over the parolees, being permanently deprived only of one battalion which would in any case, had the war gone on long enough, have been replaced by the three detachment battalions forming at Colchester. Nevertheless, by the time the exchange was authorized almost a month had passed during which, as we shall see in the next chapter, Graham was obliged to continue to conduct operations whilst deprived of around a quarter of his infantry.

If Bathurst did not respond as Graham might have wished with respect to the prisoner exchange, his reaction to the news of the defeat at Bergen-op-Zoom was altogether better suited to assuaging any doubts the general might have entertained as to how his failure would be received at home. In part, as was suggested in the Introduction to this work, Graham's despatch – speaking as it did of the problems caused by his lack of sufficient troops – may have stabbed at Bathurst's conscience since he was ultimately responsible for the size and composition of the force under Graham's command. Whilst Bathurst had certainly not withheld troops that could have gone to Holland, and had done his best to juggle the conflicting demands of multiple theatres of war, it is nevertheless easy to understand the Secretary of State taking the view that the less that was said about the causes of the defeat, the better for all concerned. In any case, Graham, and Stanhope as his emissary, also presented a series of additional justifications for the disaster, taking as their cue the line put forward by Carmichael Smyth that the attack itself had been successful and that it was only afterwards – and through the failings of subordinates – that things had gone wrong. In his official despatch, Graham was fairly circumspect, arguing only that 'the success of two of the columns in establishing themselves on the ramparts, with very trifling loss, must justify the having incurred the risk for the attainment of so important an object as the capture of such a fortress', blaming the subsequent confusion on the deaths of Skerrett and Gore, and glossing over Cooke's role in the disaster.[19]

In private, however, Graham was more explicit in attributing the defeat to the actions of the men on the spot, writing that, 'the attack must have succeeded had the orders been obeyed'. He also expanded upon his theme that the attack had failed through the use of insufficient troops, whilst at the same time seeking to demonstrate that it was carried out with all the means at his disposal. Having explained to Bathurst that he was induced to order the assault only because van Gorkum had produced a viable plan of attack – and making no mention of his encouraging the formulation of said plan, or of his allowing it to be altered by the addition of a fourth assaulting force – Graham went on to state that:

> It was necessary to carry into execution the plan almost as soon as it was determined on, to prevent the enemy from receiving information of the movements of the troops. It was not less so to watch Antwerp with increased vigilance. This prevented the concentration of as large a force as possible round Bergen-op-Zoom; but in truth, every account of the number and quality of the garrison led me to believe that if a footing could be gained on the rampart, success would be the result – there were near 4,000 men employed. The garrison was stated to be reduced to less than 2,000 two thirds of the worst quality. In all this uniform information I have certainly been grossly deceived.[20]

In this conception, then, the blame lay with bad intelligence regarding the nature of the garrison, although Graham naturally made no mention of the fact that the same man who had provided much of that intelligence – van Gorkum – had also cautioned him against attacking with so weak a force. Indeed, for all his contribution to the operation, van Gorkum was not mentioned by name at all in Graham's despatch, although those British officers who had been reported as having distinguished themselves – Proby, Rooke, Muttlebury, and Hogg, along with the late Lieutenant Colonels Clifton, Macdonald, and Mercer – all got a mention. Thanks to the fact that Cooke was the only senior officer in any fit state to make a report, all those named were those who had fought with him, and thus were predominately guardsmen. Whilst this is understandable enough in itself, the praise for the defeatist Proby, for whom Graham was also trying to procure an appointment as brigadier general, seems a particularly unfortunate inclusion when so many other, more distinguished, names were missing.[21]

Having made this case, however, and reinforced his point that orders were not properly followed, Graham ended his letter on a rather odd note that should really have called into question the logic being employed in the main argument. Having laboured the point that no further troops could be spared for the assault, Graham then rather let the cat out of the bag by informing Bathurst that 'we had considerable reinforcements at hand soon after daylight from the 2nd Division, who, I had the mortification to find, arrived too late'.[22] This should surely have begged the question, as it does now, of why those troops were not brought forward at an earlier hour and either employed in the assault or held in close readiness to support it.

Bathurst, of course, could not know that at least some of these troops had, in fact, remained motionless during the night along with 600 guardsmen, and could have been employed far earlier if orders had been given. To the modern reader, with all the facts at hand, it is hard to escape the conclusion that several hundred men could – had Graham given the orders earlier – been on hand to reinforce Cooke at dawn. In selling his argument to Bathurst, however, Graham had an excellent advocate in James Stanhope whose own account of events, as we have already seen, was decidedly partisan in favour of Graham and of the contribution made by the Guards, whilst blaming the failure on Skerrett – conveniently now dead – and on the misconduct of certain line battalions. With the added incentive of a promotion for himself riding on the outcome, Stanhope used every persuasive talent at his disposal to convince first Bathurst and then the Prince Regent that it would be entirely wrong to 'conceive that General Graham had squandered the lives of his men in any rash and impracticable undertaking, but that his reasons for trying it were good, his combinations succeeded and he was not to blame for the failure'. In response, Stanhope tells us that the Prince exclaimed that Graham had obtained more credit through this failed attack than in any of his victories, whilst Bathurst, either equally convinced or, more likely, aware of the need to pass off the failure in the best possible light, ensured that Stanhope received his brevet to lieutenant colonel 'as a public testimony of His R.H.'s approbation of General Graham's conduct'.[23] Whilst this was a generous gesture, it is interesting that Graham himself had told the Secretary of State that he could 'scarcely hope that on such an occasion as this any particular mark of favour can be shown to the Corps, otherwise I would recommend to Y'r L'dship's protection majors Muttlebury & Hog[g], Capt. Sir G. Hoste, Lts. Abbey & Spurling [sic] RE, & Capt. Mitchell of the RA'.[24]

The attempt to place the defeat in as positive a light as possible was also apparent in Bathurst's formal response to Graham's despatch, in which he informed the general that:

> I have the satisfaction to say that I am commanded by His Royal Highness to assure you that, however much he must regret the loss of so many brave officers and men, He is fully sensible of the daring spirit which dictated the enterprise, and the distinguished ability

which, with the strictest attention to the Directions given, would have ensured its success

Had that success been complete, the exploit would have resounded to the Honor [sic] of the British Arms, and would have largely contributed to the Defence of Holland, should the fortune of war oblige the allies to retreat from their present advanced position.[25]

With that, the question of blame for the defeat was effectively closed, and there were no moves, then or later, for any enquiry; neither, however, was there any disciplinary action against those, such as Muller, whose conduct Graham had questioned. So far as all parties were concerned, the thing was done and the matter now closed. This speedy acceptance of Graham's conduct, smacking as it does largely of a face-saving exercise, has, however, served severely to limit any objective analysis of what went wrong on the night of 8–9 January 1814.

Certainly, there were those within the defeated army who had their own ideas about why the attack failed, and who was to blame. Not since Whitelocke's disaster at Buenos Aires seven years previously had a British attack gone so catastrophically awry, and the comparison was explicitly made in the aftermath of the Bergen-op-Zoom disaster.[26] On that occasion, however, failure could readily be attributed to the failings of the general commanding, whereas here it was evident that the situation was far less clear-cut and it was therefore imperative for the troops under Graham's command – including those not directly connected with the assault – to account for the setback in such a light as to cast no dishonour on those involved.

Austin, still in hospital, heard all about the disaster from fellow patients and from his comrades in the 2/35th, and although his account of the fighting is as confused as one would expect considering its compilation from second- and third-hand gossip – amongst other things, he attributes Carleton's circuit along the ramparts to 'Lieut. Ralph, a brave officer of the 37th Regiment'[27] – it is nevertheless a good indicator of what Graham's junior officers thought of the defeat. In Austin's version of events, it is Cooke who is the villain of the piece, standing 'supinely inactive' along with the Guards, at a time when action was called for. Austin also picks up on the discord within the Right Attack, asserting that its division would have been avoided had 'the officer commanding the column communicated, to all regimental commanders, precise instructions [. . .] before entering the fortress'.[28] This is a valid point, but one that misses the fact that it was the officer commanding – Skerrett – who was primarily to blame for the disintegration of the column. This, however, was a secondary issue so far as Austin was concerned, and he made it clear that both officers and men 'attributed the whole blame of the failure to the want of an energetic leader' and that although Cooke's personal bravery could not be questioned, 'a strong and decided opinion was entertained as to his demerits as a leader of troops', as a result of which 'we were fairly out-generalled and disgracefully beaten'.[29]

The crucial point in all this was that there was never any question of the army blaming its commanding general for the defeat. Cooke, the man on the spot, had failed Graham, who 'with the greatest talent, had put the troops in the town, and, by some sad mistakes, they lost it'.[30] This view seemingly prevailed all the way through the ranks of the army, with Morris recording rather simplistically that the defeat was due to the troops stacking arms and getting drunk once they had possession of the ramparts, but presciently speculating that 'had the generals survived, we should have heard something more of the matter, but as they fell, it was hushed up'.[31]

No doubt it was a good thing for the morale of the troops as a whole that they retained every confidence in Graham as a commander, but, again, this transfer of all responsibility away from the man who had ordered the attack is perhaps just a little too easy and certainly serves to hamper an objective examination of what went wrong. A more detached analysis, based on all the accounts consulted in the preparation of this book, suggests a number of key failures, several of which can ultimately be traced back to Graham as commander of the British forces. Equally, some of the circumstances that have traditionally been presented as significant contributors to the defeat did not, on balanced reflection, play anything like as great a part in the disaster as the traditional accounts would have us believe.

Staying with that theme, a key point that requires reassessment is the role played by the False Attack. In many accounts, in particular those taking their cue from Stanhope and van Gorkum, it is stressed that this force attacked far too early and thus threw the whole plan out of kilter. Although confusion as to which accounts use local time and which British Army time will probably prevent an exact answer ever being arrived at, the balance of probability suggests that the False Attack was only early, if at all, by a few minutes: indeed, if, as seems to be the case, Sperling's version of events is based on local time then it was slightly late. The more significant failure of timekeeping was the major delay to the Left Attack caused first by the amount of time that it took the Guards to move up to their staging area, and then to the difficulties in passing through the 'Kijk in dem Pot' entrenched camp. It may well be significant here that the accounts that exaggerate the earliness of the False Attack most are those with a vested interest in drawing attention from this delay. Conversely, accounts critical of the fact that the False Attack was pressed home so vigorously that the troops were subsequently unavailable do have more validity, at least up to a point. With so few troops, it was never likely that much could be achieved against the Steenbergen Gate, and once the French had been drawn to that sector of the walls the task of the False Attack had been completed. By that stage, however, even if they still possessed a commander who had been briefed on their full role – which, with Ottley and Henry down, they did not – so few troops remained in a fit state for further action as to render the point moot. Stanhope estimated that even if the survivors had been brought back into the fight they would have contributed only 150 men: hardly enough for a decisive intervention.[32]

One last point surrounding the False Attack is that raised by Sperling, who believed that it was conceptually flawed from the outset and its diversionary role counter-productive. His contemporary account, already cited, merely observes that there was 'no time to be lost' for the Right Attack to penetrate the harbour area once the False Attack had revealed itself, but, when preparing his old letters for publication nearly sixty years later, the advantage of hindsight enabled him to elaborate on this point. Sperling now argued that had the False Attack not deliberately drawn the attention of the garrison upon itself by opening fire, it would have been possible for the Right Attack to penetrate the harbour area undetected and unopposed, and from there gain control of the rest of the southern ramparts and thus facilitate the entry of the other attacks.[33] This is all well and good up to a point, although even Sperling admits that for such a plan to have succeeded would have required Cooke and Proby to have arrived on time, but it surely assumes too much that the entire garrison would have remained supine throughout the movements proposed by Sperling. At some point, shots would have been fired and the game would have been up.

Sperling was not, however, the only participant in the operation to question the division of the attackers into so many distinct forces. Van Gorkum, as we have seen, strongly objected to the addition of what became the Centre Attack to his original plan and, in that it failed completely, was probably correct in doing so. On the other hand, it could equally be argued that the fact that one attack failed but two got in serves to reinforce the wisdom of employing multiple columns. Graham would certainly have been aware, for example, that at Badajoz two years previously it had been the success of two secondary attacks, after the main thrust had stalled, that allowed the British to fight their way into that fortress. There, however, there had been no false attack, and it does seem in retrospect that Graham at Bergen-op-Zoom would have been wiser either to dispense with that precaution and hope that three simultaneous real attacks would split the enemy forces sufficiently to allow a good chance of success, or else, if a False Attack were preferred, to mount only two strong real attacks in the expectation that both would be able to get in whilst the garrison was distracted. By mounting four attacks – three real and one false – Graham stretched his forces so thinly that the troops who did get in were insufficient to occupy the whole town.

There were, then, conceptual flaws in the plan of attack in the form in which it was put into practice, but these were not necessarily sufficient in themselves to guarantee failure. The ultimate reason for the French success in repelling the attackers was that they were able, despite inferior numbers, to achieve localized superiority of force where it mattered. This was initially more down to accident than design, for the concentration of nearly all the garrison at the Steenbergen Gate to meet the False Attack was undoubtedly a serious blunder that the British could have exploited if only they had had the troops to do so. Instead, however, the Left Attack was late, the Right Attack divided, and only Carleton's small party was able to take advantage of the French distraction. For things to have been otherwise would have required the Left Attack to have been on time, or for the Right Attack either to have remained as a single body or to have had sufficient troops to permit it both to send some along the ramparts and to secure the harbour area. The fact that neither of these things was possible can largely be laid down to rushed and poorly thought-out staff work.

From the outset, the whole operation was built on assumptions and misconceptions. Lack of intelligence, on both the state of the garrison and the movements of the French field armies – and, for that matter, the Allied field armies – led to false assumptions about how many troops would be required and how urgent the operation was. Clearly it was important to try to maintain surprise, but, equally, when planning for attacks along so many different axes, time had to be allowed to bring the attacking columns close enough to their objectives as to ensure a synchronized assault. In retrospect, it would have surely been worth delaying the operation by twenty-four hours in order to enable this to be done: something which, in addition, would have permitted a substantial strengthening of the assault columns by drawing on units like the 2/35th which, in the event, only arrived outside the walls in time to see the surviving guardsmen descending the ladders. Finally, such a delay would have permitted a more thorough briefing for the commanders involved, clearing up – one would hope – the confused arrangement in force in the northern sector, where far too much responsibility was placed on the shoulders of John Skerrett than any officer should have been asked to bear. The fault for all this, ultimately, was Graham's. However understandable his reasons for making the snap decision to attack, particularly bearing in mind the intelligence blackout in which he was operating, the fact remains that the decision, and the responsibility, were his.

To claim that the plan was a good one but that his commanders let him down is, then, really rather feeble. There were significant flaws in the plan, most notably the division of an already weak force into too many sub-formations, and in the lack of instruction as to how these sub-formations were to cooperate once they had gained the ramparts. In this regard, however, Graham considered himself blameless, telling Taylor that he was:

> satisfied that if I can blame myself for anything, it is for having placed more confidence than I ought in such young troops. At the same time I considered them much improved in steadiness by the Merxem campaign, and that they were less likely to run wild after plunder and wine than older soldiers.
>
> But above all, I could not reckon on their leaders behaving like subalterns carrying handfuls of men on without support or order to be uselessly sacrificed. It is quite heartbreaking to have had such a melancholy result, instead of that which would have been that of good conduct.[34]

Although Cooke's conduct, thanks to Proby's defeatist influence, hardly qualified him for Graham's criticism, it can be more reasonably applied to Carleton, Gore and Skerrett. Skerrett in particular merits the analogy, for he abandoned the responsibilities of a senior commander at an early stage, leaving Muller without orders whilst leading a quixotic attack that, if it needed making at all, could easily have been entrusted to a junior officer. This might be presented as support for Graham's argument that he was let down by others, but to do so overlooks the fact that it was Graham's orders that put these men in their various unenviable positions in the first place. If Skerrett and Cooke are to be castigated for failing to support their fellow commanders inside the fortress, so too must Graham himself be castigated for so completely abdicating responsibility for the attacking troops once they were within the ramparts. Ultimately, he had the chief command and it is simply not possible for a man in that position to be completely exonerated from responsibility for failure, whatever the mistakes of his subordinates.

In the final analysis, therefore, the decision to attack Bergen-op-Zoom was a gamble taken by Sir Thomas Graham. It was undoubtedly a risky operation – Cooke called it 'this bold and ambitious enterprise'[35] – but based on what Graham knew at the time he gave the orders the risk was probably a valid one. We might, with hindsight, join those participants who thought that the attack could have succeeded if only things had been done differently: if more troops had been available; if available troops had been concentrated; if commanders had been better briefed; if schedules had been followed. We might even, based on the conduct of the attacking troops once they gained the ramparts, argue that the enterprise was probably too bold and ambitious to succeed, at least with the numbers and commanders available. Nevertheless, what we cannot do, 200 years after the fact, is criticize Graham for choosing to gamble on an attack. Such decisions are what generals are paid for. Had the gamble paid off, the credit would have been Graham's; since it had failed, he now had to live with the consequences.

Chapter XIII

'We Are Making Little Progress Here'

WHILST GRAHAM WAS INITIALLY CONFIDENT that a rapid prisoner exchange would replace the greater part of the manpower losses sustained in the defeat at Bergen-op-Zoom, he was painfully aware that the debacle had left him dangerously short of senior officers. Not only was there a high proportion of field officers amongst the killed and wounded, but two general officers were dead and a third, for the moment at least, was a prisoner. Unless Bathurst intended to follow through his proposal to transfer the bulk of the forces from Holland to America, Graham told the Secretary of State that it was 'most urgent to have superior officers sent out'. His temporary solution to the command problem was, as he explained, not entirely to his satisfaction:

> I shall meanwhile give the charge of the 1st Divn. to M. Genl. Gibbs, the only other Gl. officer except M. Gl. Mackenzie now remaining. The Brigades will of course be commanded meanwhile by the senior officers of each, Gl. Gore's being probably broken up & thrown into the line Brigade of the 1st Divn. Were M. Gl. Mackenzie's health quite what it was, I sh'd wish these two officers to retain the two Div'ns but perhaps in the state he is still in from his accident it may not be considered advisable to leave him 2d in the Command of this Corps – if a superior officer sh'd be sent out I would beg leave to suggest Lieutenant Genl. [Sir Ronald] Ferguson an officer of the most try'd gallantry & judgement & of whose cordial cooperation I have had experience at Cadiz.[1]

As a result of this entreaty, Ferguson was indeed ordered to join Graham's army, as was Brigadier General Colin Halkett as a replacement brigade commander, although in the event neither officer would arrive in time to see active operations. On the other hand, Graham's staff was finally completed to his satisfaction by the arrival of Lieutenant Colonel Cathcart to take over from Trench as Deputy Quartermaster-General. The latter, indeed, had gone home on leave in late February, notwithstanding an avowed intention to serve on under Cathcart, and so the post was effectively vacant until Cathcart arrived in mid-March.[2]

For the time being, as well as merging the brigades previously under Skerrett and Gore, Graham also authorized the reorganization of the remaining line infantry of the First Division into two provisional battalions, effective as of 28 March. The First Provisional Battalion comprised the 4/1st, 2/69th, and 2/91st, and the Second the 2/21st, 2/37th, 2/44th, and 55th. In theory, this gave them all-ranks strengths of 1,022 and 1,225 respectively, but, as Graham pointed out, this 'included not only the sick and wounded, but all the most inefficient men in the Battalions'. Accordingly, effective strengths were barely half the cited figures.[3] Once the exchange of the paroled men had been completed this temporary measure was abandoned, with the exception that the 2/21st and 2/37th were still too weak to function independently – the former, in addition, having lost all its field officers at Bergen-op-Zoom – and so continued as a combined unit for the remainder of the war.[4] To command the brigade formed from these units, Graham appointed Robert Crawford, a former artilleryman who had more recently held commands in the Irish Militia and held brevet rank as a lieutenant colonel in the Army. Keen to serve in the line, he had obtained a captaincy in the 2/73rd, but, since he had extensive staff experience and twenty years of distinguished service, Graham plucked him from that battalion and gave him a brigade.[5]

Although the creation of provisional battalions enabled Graham to make better use of his remaining infantry, it became increasingly apparent that he would require additional support if the British troops were to play any further worthwhile role in the conflict. This, indeed, was also the wish of the British government, with Castlereagh urging the rest of the Cabinet to do their utmost to obtain the cooperation of the Crown Prince of Sweden in a renewed operation against Antwerp. As a result of this resolution, Herbert Taylor, who had only just arrived in London when the news of the Bergen-op-Zoom debacle came in, was asked to return to the continent and bring Graham up to date with the government's new thinking.[6]

Even without such prompting, Graham had already begun to look into the requirements of a siege operation against Antwerp, although he antici-pated that this would be no easy task. In any case, it would clearly be impossible without further troops and the likelihood of his being able to obtain any seemed slim. Saxe-Weimar was keen to follow Bülow into France, and Wallmoden's arrival to replace him remained uncertain. News did reach Graham on 14 March of Napoleon's defeat at Laon, and the consequent removal of any French threat to the Low Countries, but he nevertheless continued to worry about the wisdom of an advance against Antwerp so long as Bergen-op-Zoom remained in French hands in his rear. This smacks a little of wounded pride, and his complaint to Taylor that 'the value of Berg-op-zoom seems never to have been considered at home' has the ring of an after-the-fact justification for attacking the place.[7] In all events, Bizanet's garrison would remain quiescent for the remainder of the war, under blockade by the British and Dutch. Despite these reservations, and once it became clear that Bathurst no longer had any plans to break up the force in Holland, Graham nevertheless began negotiations with his allies with a view to obtaining assistance in a siege of Antwerp. As his opening gambit, Charles Hamilton Smith, previously engaged in monitoring the progress of the Belgian levies, was dispatched to Saxe-Weimar's headquarters.[8]

Smith was the obvious choice for such a mission, as he had already been liaising with Saxe-Weimar over the Saxon commander's supply and equipment problems – problems which, Graham reported with some exasperation, he – Graham – was being asked to solve by supplying Saxe-Weimar with British muskets which seemed a rather futile exercise when captured French ammunition was on its way for the Saxons to use in their existing muskets.[9] Smith's mission was now given extra urgency by the impending arrival in the Low Countries of a strong division of Saxon Landwehr under Generalleutnant Johann von Thielmann. This represented a sizeable increment to the Allied forces, and when Smith arrived at Tournai on 15 March he found Saxe-Weimar on the point of departing to review this new addition to his corps. However, just as Saxe-Weimar was about to leave, Generalmajor von Borstell, commanding those Prussian forces left behind in Belgium when Bülow marched south, arrived and Smith was asked to discuss his proposals with him, prior to meeting Saxe-Weimar that evening. This, Saxe-Weimar continued, would also enable him to confer first with his chief of staff, the well-connected Generalmajor Ludwig von Wolzogen.

Thus fobbed off, Smith passed on to Borstell Graham's proposal that Saxe-Weimar's corps would blockade Antwerp from the left bank of the Scheldt, and Graham's from the right whilst also masking Bergen-op-Zoom. Bergen was to be placed under formal siege once Wallmoden's troops arrived but, for now, all that could be done was to construct a series of redoubts designed to keep the garrison more firmly penned in.[10] That Graham could continue operations around Bergen-op-Zoom at all, Smith explained, was down to the arrival of a brigade of Dutch infantry, although both men agreed that the Dutch could be little relied upon. Borstell, in response, indicated that he was already *au fait* with Saxe-Weimar's intentions by putting forward a counter-proposal that Smith had already heard from Wolzogen on a prior occasion. This was to the effect that Graham should withdraw from Willemstad and Breda, which might now be considered secure, and make a shift to the left the better to mask Antwerp. Smith was uneasy about this, explaining that:

> the siege of Bergen op Zoom being resolved upon it did not belong to me to make further remarks upon the consequences of a measure which it was not the intention of the British Com'd in Chief to pursue; but allowing for the sake of argument that the British head-quarters were at Lier, I asked whether the total devastation of the north west of Brabant was of no consequence, whether the loss of your lines of operations, the consequent failure of provisions, of ammunition, of arms, not only for us but also for all the allied forces, would not be of immense detriment.

In other words, the British were not happy to leave large areas of Dutch territory open to the French: a stark contrast to the view espoused by Borstell, who freely admitted that if this plan were put into effect then the French might advance to the gates of Breda, but that it would not matter if they did. Smith agreed that it might be perceived that Bergen-op-Zoom and Antwerp were British objects, and that the whole lot would fall if Paris fell, so in that sense there was little point in arguing about priorities. But, as Smith pointed out, Borstell could offer him no assurances that Paris would fall – after all, if Blücher had beaten Napoleon at Laon as decisively as was claimed, why did he need Saxe-Weimar and Borstell to reinforce him? – and that the 'impression upon the public mind in the Netherlands' would be extremely harmful if the Allies did nothing to keep out the French. In the meantime, if Saxe-Weimar and Borstell did march into France, they needed to be aware that their doing so would force Graham to fall back onto the frontiers of Holland, 'and remain a spectator to the ruin of Belgium which must necessarily ensue because the French would burst forth upon Brussels, destroy the resources of the country & make it ever untenable for the allies should they be compelled to retreat in that direction'.[11]

For the moment, this was as far as Smith could get, but at dinner that night he was introduced to Thielmann, whom he described as being 'about 50 years of age, his countenance bears the marks of a vigorous intellect & decisive character – his uniform is loaded with stars and orders'. A Swedish staff officer was also present at the meal, 'and Swedish objects supported at the table', except by Thielmann who criticized the retention of that nation's forces in the rear. After the meal, Smith was joined by Wolzogen, who brought the British captain up to date with Saxon and Prussian intentions.

Having established that the British were still tied down around Bergen-op-Zoom, Wolzogen informed Smith that although it was not possible to cancel Saxe-Weimar's march southwards – indeed, Blücher thought him already on his way – nor did the Saxon general wish to 'withdraw without guarding, so far as it is in his power, the provinces of Belgium'. Unfortunately, what was in his power was not a great deal, beyond some light cavalry detachments watching Ostend and Thielmann's nine battalions at Tournai. The rest of the corps, less a brigade under Generalmajor von Gablenz, would first invest Maubeuge, albeit with the caveat that if the place did not fall in six days it was to be masked and the remaining troops would join Blücher. Gablenz, meanwhile, was to remain only until relieved by Wallmoden.

Since Wolzogen had raised the issue of Wallmoden's arrival, Smith took the opportunity to enquire if it were true that Wallmoden would be at Brussels by 17 March, but Wolzogen repeated what Saxe-Weimar had already told Smith, that he could not know because 'the Crown Prince was the most faithless unprincipled character in the world, who said & contradicted his own promises every moment, that with regard to him the affairs of the allies had a very suspicious appearance'. Wolzogen, however, had a proposal of his own to get the Crown Prince moving, telling Smith that 'England had paid him handsomely & that therefore England had a right to expect & was in fact bound to compel him to act'. Indeed, as Smith reported, Wolzogen:

> was particularly anxious I should urge with Yr. Exy. the necessity of forcing the Swedes to act. Not to enter France, if they did not like it, but at least to take upon themselves with the 20,000 national troops to cover the Netherlands & do something for their money, and the magnificent rewards they had obtained with the blood of the allies.

This view was reinforced by Saxe-Weimar himself, who, later that evening took Smith to one side, declaring him 'the only British officer to whom he could fully express his mind' and telling him that 'Ce Prince Royal de Suede est un homme sans principles', from whom he could obtain no firm word of Wallmoden's coming. Nevertheless, Saxe-Weimar proposed that he would in any case withdraw Gablenz, irrespective of whether or not Wallmoden appeared; Smith countered that this would uncover Brussels, but Saxe-Weimar claimed that the three Prussian Landwehr battalions left to hold Hertogenbosch might be brought up to replace him. Having earlier heard from the newly appointed Military Governor of Belgium, Karl von der Horst, that the Saxons would likely have already moved had Bülow not appropriated the magazine indented for their use at Mons, Smith realized that there was no point pressing the matter, and withdrew. The following day, he learnt from Wolzogen that the Prussian battalions were not under Saxe-Weimar's orders and so would be unlikely to move to replace Gablenz; they might in any case, in Wolzogen's opinion, be better employed in aiding in the blockade of Antwerp. The same morning, Smith watched as Borstell's brigade, the last element of Bülow's Prussians remaining in the Low Countries, marched south.

Graham was therefore forced to come to the same conclusion that Castlereagh had reached, namely that to be able to achieve anything constructive he would have to obtain the cooperation of the Crown Prince. Without troops from what remained of the Army of the North – essentially the Swedish contingent, Wallmoden's corps, and a few other miscellaneous Germans – there was no hope of being able to move against Antwerp. The Dutch were able to put increasing numbers of troops into the field, but they remained a dubious quantity so far as Graham was concerned, and in any case the bulk of them were not available to cooperate with the British. Taylor, on his return to the Continent, found that 'the Dutch Government, or rather the War Department, under its very inefficient chief General Bentinck, could not account for the application or distribution of any supplies from England', and that although there were in theory over 16,000 men under arms few were fully effective and their utility was further reduced by:

> the Dislike & Jealousy which the Prince of Orange betrays at any of the levies being brought forward separately and placed under the Command of any of the allied generals. This I am afraid was strongly manifested when the 3000 men were sent to Sir Thos. Graham, and there is reason to suspect that he wishes to keep all back until he has raised, equipped and disciplined a Corps d'Armée of which he may have distinct Command-in-Chief.[12]

The Prince's ambition was in line with his obvious intention of establishing himself as an important player in the post-war settlement, but it did little to aid the Allied cause in the meantime. In Taylor's opinion, it was necessary for an officer of rank and distinction, with 'experience in Business' to be sent to The Hague to oversee the efficient distribution of the arms and supplies and to inspect and report upon the preparation of the new levies. Graham, meanwhile, felt that it 'would add to the effectiveness of our brigades and divisions if I were allowed to mix some of the Dutch troops in the same way as the Portuguese are in L'd Wellington's army'. Although Graham's British battalions were no match for Wellington's, they were still an improvement on the Dutch levies and so 'it would still be an advantage for the Dutch troops to be employed in this manner'.[13] Nevertheless, Graham had the sense to realize that the Dutch would never agree to this and that Perponcher's brigade was the only close support he was likely to get. Whichever way things were considered, it all came down to the need to obtain the full cooperation of the Crown Prince of Sweden.

In the aftermath of his mission to Saxe-Weimar, which came on top of diligent liaison work in Belgium, Graham was keen that Smith receive a brevet promotion to major, both as a reward and as a means of increasing his prestige when dealing with Allied representatives. For the moment, however, he was sent to Swedish headquarters at Liége to draw the attention of the Crown Prince, and of the British plenipotentiary Edward Thornton, to 'the immense importance of covering Flanders with a sufficient force to secure it from the incursions of the Enemy'.[14] As a result of this renewed initiative, Graham at last heard from Wallmoden, who had finally received positive orders to unite his corps with the British. Unfortunately, as he was obliged to tell Graham, not all his troops were yet ready to march:

> I am sorry to say that the first detachment of troops Hanover is to send in the field, does not exceed 5000 men, of which 6 battalions of infantry at about 600 each; 2 Regiments of Hussars at about 450 each, and 3 troops of artillery (two horse & one foot) from the Russian German legion but paid by England, or now Hanover.
>
> Of the Hanoverian Troops only one battalion of Riflemen is now with me of about 4 to 500 strong. The whole of the infantry will amount to 4000 and about 1000 cavalry with 24 pieces of cannon Russian 6 Pounders.[15]

This was certainly bad news, but Graham seems to have read things in a worse light than Wallmoden had intended since he assumed that the corps was composed of only 5,000 men rather than the promised 8,000.[16] In fact, as a careful reading of Wallmoden's letter makes clear, he would have more like 10,000 men under his command once all the Hanoverians had joined. This was a sizeable reinforcement, and even 5,000 troops would provide a substantial increase to Graham's command and enable him to think more seriously about active operations again. Furthermore, Wallmoden had already sent on ahead the 3rd KGL Hussars, 1st and 2nd KGL Horse Artillery Troops, and the 2nd Rocket Troop, all of which joined Graham in early March.

Although it was clear that there was no likelihood of siege operations against Antwerp beginning in the immediate future, this did not stop Graham's troops trying to prepare the way. Since late February, the Second Division had been closely observing the French, and doing what it could to contain Carnot's garrison within their defences. With the weather continuing bad through into April, with thick fog, an icy wind and repeated falls of sleet even after the snow ceased, life was hard for the British troops on outpost duty, the more so since 'the villages we occupied had been abandoned by their inhabitants and destroyed by the Prussians'.[17] Because of this paucity of decent accommodation so far forwards, measures were set in force to improve the situation and make the main outpost at Brasschaat into a respectable advance-post. The position was based on a large square building that had once been a distillery, and which was now turned into a loopholed barracks. In order to accommodate a garrison of 300 men, an extensive entrenchment was also constructed, although Sperling was obliged to point out that this was 'of irregular shape, as the line of the garden fence has been followed'. However, as he went on to note, 'it is also palisaded, and otherwise strengthened, an adjoining wood supplying the material'.[18]

This was an impressive project, but even when Sperling described it on 22 March it was still incomplete and so McCready had therefore been most pleased to learn, three days before Sperling penned his description, that the 2/30th was to take up a new duty, providing cover for the battery that had been established on the Scheldt near the ruined Fort Frederick, to prevent water communication between Antwerp and the outlying French garrisons at Bergen-op-Zoom and Fort Batz. Graham's naval counterparts remained keen to see Batz taken, since its fall 'would open the river by means of the East Scheldt to a great flotilla w'thout w'ch I can scarcely think such a siege can be carried on'.[19] Since there was no other viable objective that could easily be attained with the forces available, Graham was now beginning to find himself in agreement with the admirals, although he continued to maintain that, ideally, Bergen-op-Zoom would need to be taken as well.

McCready, reaching the banks of the Scheldt on the morning of 20 March following a nightmarish march on icy roads through the darkness and fog, discovered when the murk finally cleared that there were now in fact two battery positions. The upper, where McCready found himself posted, was a defensive work containing a 6-pounder commanding the dyke running parallel to the river and a howitzer commanding the river bank itself: these precautions were necessitated by the proximity of the French further upstream at Fort Lillo. From this vantage point, the young volunteer was also able to see the remainder of the position:

> The remains of the old fort and two or three houses were close to
> us, and about a mile lower down the dyke was our battery of six long

twenty-four pounders, with its furnace for heating shot. In the contrary direction, and at about double the distance, was Lillo, with Liefenshoeck [*sic* – Fort Liefkenshoek] immediately opposite. Between them was a French line of battle ship and some craft at anchor. The river was here at least a mile in breath, and the enemy having opened the sluices, the whole country was under water. The forts and houses looked like islands which the roads and dykes connected with each other. Our advance, composed of riflemen, were on the banks towards Lillo at near a mile from us and about 300 yards from the French sentinels.[20]

That evening, the battery seemed to have proved itself a success, for the French were observed to be attempting to move some craft downstream but did not, apparently for fear of the British guns, attempt to pass below.[21]

Notwithstanding the French not having pushed any further downstream on the evening of 20 March, there was a not-unreasonable fear that they might now attempt a sortie by land to neutralize the British guns and re-open the Scheldt. Accordingly, the British infantry spent the night on the alert, twice falling in to repel what turned out to be false alarms. When the fog cleared on the morning of the 21st, however, it became apparent that the threat was not from the land but from the water: during the night, the French battleship – *l'Anversois*, of 74 guns – had come downstream and anchored close by the upper battery, which was now commanded by its broadside armament of heavy 36- and 24-pounder cannon. This clearly indicated serious intent on the part of the French, but since the ship's guns remained silent the troops were permitted to stand down and get some breakfast. Such complacency, however, was soon shown to be misplaced. McCready 'was just discussing an egg, when off went a broadside, down came the chimney in a shower of brick bats, and our poor egg-woman was cut in two by a round shot'.[22] Thereafter, the shots continued to fly thick and fast, to which the only reply was the single howitzer emplaced in the upper battery, directed by Lieutenant John Parker of the Royal Artillery who, as Graham reported, 'maintained this apparently unequal contest w'th the greatest gallantry for several Hours when the Ship & Brigs retir'd probably w'th considerable damage'.[23] Parker undoubtedly made a fine job of fending off the French warship, but it is only fairness to state that the eventual departure of *l'Anversois* was prompted not by the fire of a single howitzer alone, but by the additional employment of Congreve rockets, brought into action around noon.

This was the first time the new weapon had been employed under Graham's command, and it was quickly proven that the rockets were as infamously volatile here as in the other theatres where they had been employed. By this time, the 2/52nd had come up to reinforce the British outpost, and Shaw witnessed what happened when the 2nd Rocket Troop opened fire:

> The rocket that was discharged, hung for a few seconds above the ship, but returned with the same velocity, falling among some ice a few yards in the rear of the spot from whence it was discharged. Worst of all, too, the shell attached burst, and dispersed the numerous amateurs who congregated around.[24]

Thankfully, no harm was done to those ashore, and the threat of the rockets was enough to persuade the French captain to give up the attempt and get his ship out of harm's way. British casualties were remarkably light, considering the weight of shot in the broadside of *l'Anversois*, amounting to two men killed outright and four wounded of whom two later died.[25] Other than a single artilleryman, and McCready's unfortunate egg-seller who of course did not figure in the official return, these casualties came from the ranks of the 2/30th, including, amongst the mortally wounded, the battalion's veteran Drum-Major, Thomas Vipond. Lieutenant Colonel Hamilton, meanwhile, had a lucky escape after being near-missed by a round shot which – although the tale may have grown in the telling – was alleged to have passed under his drawn-up legs as he sat at his breakfast.[26] McCready, under fire for the first time, found the experience understandably terrifying, made worse by the fact that the infantry could make no effective reply to the French bombardment, but managed to retain his composure sufficiently to record that 'I saved my character and was hailed as a lad of pluck': an important consideration, when his only hope of winning a commission was through good conduct in action.[27]

With the city's river communications therefore cut for the time being, it was possible to think again about tightening the Allied grip on Antwerp yet further, but a consideration of the means needed to mount a formal siege remained daunting. Considering the extent of the French inundations on the east bank of the Scheldt, Graham was left with a very limited choice of approaches to the city, telling Bathurst that:

> The front of attack may by all accounts be so narrowed now by inundations as to confine them chiefly to the dykes – the progress of such attacks must of course be very slow. The Citadel however is an exception & may be liable to a more extended & regular attack, but it is much the strongest part of the works, & may have its garrison frequently renew'd.

Graham went on to state that although Carmichael Smyth had yet to complete his study as to the exact means required for the operation,

> I am confident however that the proportion of Battering train being suited for 20,000 men cannot be sufficient for a siege w'ch would require probably forty thousand to be employed in, taking in what is necessary to hold both sides of the River & this without the covering army towards the French frontier the force of w'h cannot well be estimated w'thout more knowledge of the enemy's means. I ought to add too that the quality of no part of the force likely to be employ'd can be reckoned good.[28]

This was a tall order since, even with Wallmoden's entire corps, Graham would have scarcely half that number of troops, and would need some of these to mask Bergen-op-Zoom and Fort Batz, as well as to cover the Scheldt battery.

One solution was to shift the focus of the assault to the other bank, and attack from the Tête de Flandres side, an idea on which Graham speculated in a letter to Bunbury at Horse Guards:

> Antwerp from the Tête de Flandres side, can only be approached by the Great Road & the Dykes of the Scheldt but much damage might be done by bombardment I imagine in spite of the inundation. We have not been able to ascertain to what extent it is in the Enemy's power to inundate round the town on this side. There is every reason to suppose, however, that by merely shutting the sluices at the town and thus damming back the water of the streams that pass thro' the town, much of the country on this side may be flooded, so at least to render the approaches difficult & to prevent the communications w'ch are so desirable between the different parts of an army employ'd in a siege.[29]

Such an operation would also expose the rear of the Allied forces on the west bank to any advance from the French frontier, since it would be impossible to provide a sufficient covering force in this quarter. In all events, though, it was clear to Graham that Britain would have to supply 'the whole burden of the material' demands of the siege, even if the Allies could be persuaded to supply troops. Taylor had been given to understand before leaving London that three more companies of artillery were to be sent, which Wood considered the bare minimum necessary. Graham speculated that sailors might be used in the batteries, which was all well and good, but his plans already called on Young's squadron to provide an extensive flotilla to work in the Scheldt and there were only so many sailors to be spared. There would also be a need for brick furnaces for heating shot, and 'in short, our means should be most ample in every thing'.

By the time that Graham put his thoughts about the siege of Antwerp down on paper, he had already sent Taylor to visit the Crown Prince at Liége, albeit with little expectation that any good would come of it. For a start, military realities meant that, on account of the 'extraordinary difficulties of the siege of Antwerp, now that there has been so much time for preparation, I should expect great hesitation from the Crown Prince in committing himself to an operation the success of which must be so doubtful'.[30] More significantly, however, Graham was now strongly of the opinion, having listened to Bülow and others decrying the Crown Prince's character over the course of the past four months, that the former French marshal was not to be counted upon. To support this stance, he forwarded to Bathurst a report that he had received from the intelligence agent Johnson in Brussels, containing an account of the Crown Prince's alleged views as expressed in a conversation with Louis XVIII's envoy, the Marquis de Chabannes.

The Crown Prince had apparently told Chabannes that he was a whole-hearted supporter of a Bourbon restoration, and was uniquely suited to bring success to their cause since the people of France trusted him and mistrusted the Allies who could therefore do nothing without him. He explained that he had 'rendered the greatest possible services to Europe, and the cause of the Allies', being 'at this moment occupied with plans of the greatest importance to the general Interest' as a result of which, thanks to orders already given to Wallmoden, he anticipated the prompt fall of Maastricht and Bergen-op-Zoom. In return, the Allies had failed to honour their agreements and taken away troops supposed to be under his command leaving him only his Swedes. He was nevertheless still willing to 'enter France and terminate the war', but only if his full command was restored to him; otherwise, he intended to return to Sweden. Most worrying for Graham, however, was the Crown Prince's opinion on the situation in the Low Countries. According to Johnson's source, he had stated that:

> I will in no case undertake the defence of the Netherlands altho'
> from my connections in the French Army I could do so with much
> effect. Maison was for eleven years my aide de camp; I have only to
> summon the Commdts. of the fortresses and they will every one
> surrender. I might have had Maestricht [sic] long since if I had
> wished it – such are the advantages the allies may obtain if they will
> act fairly. The Ministers of Britain and Russia have written to Hd.

Qtrs. on this subject, my movements will be guided by the answer to their despatches but I will in no case enter France, with Swedish troops alone, it would be beneath my character.[31]

This remarkable tirade was ended by an insistence that Chabannes keep the contents of the interview secret, 'for if the Swedes suspected that I was attached to the Bourbons, they would assassinate me'. Nevertheless, for all his duplicity and paranoia, this was the man on whom the final outcome of Britain's campaign now depended, for if Antwerp could yet be taken in what were now clearly the dying days of the war, the Bergen-op-Zoom debacle could be safely passed over and Britain's last remaining war aim achieved.

Taylor, for his part, accepted from the outset that he would 'have uphill work with HRH',[32] and this expectation was confirmed when he arrived at Liége on 25 March only to find that the Crown Prince was not there. Informed that he was now at Aix-la-Chapelle, Taylor resumed his journey in a foul temper, only to be overtaken on the road by a Swedish staff officer who had been sent to look for him and who directed him to the Crown Prince's head-quarters, which was now at Verviers. By the time Taylor arrived, it was late in the day, and so the interview took place on the morrow instead.[33] From Taylor's various accounts, it is clear that the Crown Prince did most of the talking, and that Taylor was able to coax only limited concessions from him, over and above what had already been agreed with respect to Wallmoden. The Crown Prince did accept the offer of the Allied command-in-chief in Belgium, albeit only conditionally, and was prepared to 'afford the immediate cooperation of 10,000 Swedes'. As he reported to Bathurst, Taylor thought that the Crown Prince would direct operations effectively enough, but remarked that he had 'never observed in the Conversation of any man such glaring evidence of Vanity, Conceit, and Egotism, and I really could not help at moments feeling disgusted by it, altho' disposed to give him full credit for distinguished talents'.[34]

Taylor was able to get rather more sense out of General Carl Löwenhielm, a soldier-diplomat on the Crown Prince's staff, who also took part in the meeting. Löwenhielm 'Admitted the Importance of the Reduction of Antwerp to the general Interests of the Allies, but observed that the scene of action for the Crown Prince & his Army ought to be France, and that he wished to find himself in the neighbourhood of Paris, where his presence is much required.' The Swede went on to point out that the Crown Prince was sacrificing much by being in the Low Countries at all when Sweden's own security was threatened by the Norwegians who 'had brought the war upon our frontiers', a point that the great man himself also raised in a tirade about the continued bad faith of the Allies and their breach of promise to him with respect to Norway, which he had been guaranteed by treaty but was now obliged to occupy by force. At length, and, one feels, after much flattery on Taylor's part, the Crown Prince agreed to the prosecution of siege operations against Antwerp. For him to direct them personally would be 'far beneath his talent & dignity' but that he would nevertheless 'feel happy to consider himself as having the General direction of this & other Operations in Brabant with the Command of the British, Dutch & other troops which may be collected for it'. Agreement having been reached, the Crown Prince offered the opinion that it would be necessary to capture Fort Lillo as a preliminary measure, and thereafter to attack from the direction of Malines and direct operations against the citadel rather than attempting to reduce the Tête-de-Flandres. If the town alone were attacked, he argued, even a successful conclusion would simply result in the garrison retiring into the citadel.[35]

In theory, then, agreement had been reached and Antwerp adopted as an objective by the Army of the North, to whose mercurial commander Graham had effectively subordinated himself. In practice, however, little of any practical import had changed and, for all the Crown Prince's promises, there was no immediate increase of the Allied forces. No doubt with such a result in mind, Bathurst had already instructed Clancarty to procure the services of 10,000 Dutch troops to take part in operations against Antwerp, to which proposal the Prince of Orange agreed as of 22 March. However, confusion still reigned as to who commanded what and where, and when Clancarty passed on Bathurst's proposal that, 'The regiments of Nassau and Frankfurt & the Prussian battalions lately placed in garrison at Breda might advantageously be formed into a Brigade, and become immediately a very efficient part of the Force', Orange was obliged to point out that the Frankfurters – all 200 of them – had gone home and had never been under his orders anyway, no more than had the Prussians, although he wished it was otherwise since they numbered 2,400 men. Nevertheless, Orange agreed that by taking the 400 Nassauers from Hertogenbosch and by adding three battalions of new levies, each about 950 strong and 'fine fellows properly equipped, tho' not in any very forward state of drill discipline', a total of 6,650 men could be assembled including the brigade already in the field under Perponcher. If the Prussian battalions were also available, this force could be raised to 9,250. Rather naively, again underlining his ignorance of military matters, Clancarty assured Taylor that although the Dutch troops 'would certainly not be in any forward state of military discipline, yet for entrenching work, & perhaps storming a breach, they would do as well as others'.[36] Unsurprisingly, a despondent Taylor, writing home to Bunbury on 29 March, felt that 'we are making little progress here and amidst all the calls for troops &c here I fear that the attempt on Antwerp will fall to the ground'.[37] By this time, however, events to the south-west meant that, yet again, Allied attention was diverted elsewhere.

A detailed examination of events in Belgium during the closing weeks of the war is really beyond the scope of this work, but the confused campaign that opened there in the last days of March 1814 is nevertheless important for its influence on Graham's dispositions during this time, and for its role in drawing away those Allied forces that might otherwise have cooperated against Antwerp. Yet again, poor intelligence and communications, and misreading of enemy intentions, led to the belief that a French counter-attack was on the cards when, in reality, such a move was the last thing that Maison had in mind. Fully aware how badly things were now going for his imperial master, the French commander elected to concentrate his remaining forces in order to extricate them from the Low Countries completely and get them back to France.

Graham first received news of the French movements on the morning of 28 March, in a despatch from Gablenz at Malines. This was nearly two days after the French had begun to move, and Graham was extremely displeased that he had been left in the dark so long. Anticipating that some or all of the French troops might be intended as a reinforcement for Antwerp, Graham ordered a concentration of his forces and, so as 'not to be embarass'd with the defence of the Scheldt Battery, the guns were remov'd from it'. Only later, with better intelligence now available, was Graham able to inform Bathurst that,

> Genl. Roguet with the Guards has gone [from Antwerp] to assist Genl. Maison at Ghent, & that the Saxons, Prussians & a part of Wallmoden's Corps w'ch was at Louvain have gone to attack the enemy. Meanwhile they have levied contributions & have sent conscripts from Flanders back into Antwerp & have shot 52 people at Ghent for rebellion. When this part of the garrison returns, it will be important to endeavour to ascertain whether it comes back increas'd, or diminish'd, in numbers. Wallmoden estimates the Corps under Maison only at from six to eight thousand men. Five thousand are suppos'd to have gone from Antwerp making them amount to 12 or 13 thousand – if they do not exceed this number I should hope Gl. Thielmann would give a good account of them as it was expected he would be able to assemble ab't 12,000 men as well.[38]

Graham could at least take some comfort from the fact that the new French moves had served to delay the transfer of Saxe-Weimar's corps from Flanders to France. The bombardment of Maubeuge had failed to bring about the surrender of that place, notwithstanding the efforts of Captain the Hon. Herbert Gardiner of the Royal Artillery who had been seconded to assist the Saxon gunners, but Saxe-Weimar had only moved off as far as Mons where he was now to remain for the foreseeable future. This calmed much of Graham's fears for Belgium, but he reminded Bathurst that 'there will be a very distressing kind of uncertainty about that most material point, since there will be nobody in fact who will have any superintendence over all the motley Corps that are likely to be employ'd in Brabant'.

Part of Graham's concern for Brabant was due to the fact that the new British liaison officer, intended to replace Smith, had not yet arrived. Major Charles Philippe de Bosset, a Swiss-born officer of de Roll's Regiment, had been selected for the job in late March, and only received his orders on the 25th. Having previously served in a similar capacity in Cephalonia, de Bosset was instructed 'that the Countries lying on the left bank of the Rhine which have been incorporated into France since the year 1792, are anxious to take up arms in the common cause' and that, as a result, 'various applications for assistance have been received by His Majesty's Government, and, particularly for supplies of arms and ammunition'. However, detailed intelligence was lacking as to what was going on and de Bosset was to endeavour to fill this gap. In particular, he was to 'make it a point of early attention to learn if the Flemings might not make themselves master of some port upon their Coast, and strengthen it so that supplies arriving from England might be landed with security and avoid the loss of time occasioned by their being sent through Holland'. Possession of such a port would also facilitate the investment of Antwerp, and de Bosset, whilst reporting directly to Bathurst, was therefore to keep Graham informed of all his doings.[39]

It was of course imperative for Britain to remain abreast of developments in the Low Countries, and, ideally, exert some influence upon them, and the delay in getting de Bosset into his new post meant that, although Smith continued with his own liaison duties in the interim, the Allies were able to act largely as they saw fit. This situation applied to the military as well as the civil sphere, with Graham expressing his certainty,

> from the manner in w'ch all the generals of the allies express
> themselves, that it is a general feeling that the reduction of Antwerp
> is a British object, & of no importance to the grand result of the war,
> & of course one cannot count much on the strict observance of any

agreement, where they may think a sacrifice of this minor object will contribute materially to success in the greater – in fact, they have so committed themselves by entering France without being in possession of any of the strong places on the Frontier, that they must at all hazards support their armies in the interior of France.[40]

Under these circumstances, Graham was increasingly developing the view that, with the course of the war moving onwards, it would be better to hand the blockades of Bergen-op-Zoom and Antwerp over to the Dutch, and the Hanoverians when they eventually came to the front, and 'move forward into Flanders to be more in the way of being useful'.[41] This, at least, would place British troops closer to the heart of affairs, perhaps enabling Graham to occupy one of the ports on the Flanders coast, in accordance with Bathurst's increasing focus on the Belgian provinces. No answer survives with Bathurst's views on this proposal.

By the beginning of April, Graham could at least inform the Secretary of State that Maison had withdrawn into France with his whole force, including Roguet's division, and that accordingly 'Antwerp must now remain w'th a much less effective garrison, as the Guards were the best troops in it, & certainly amounted to 4000 men. The reports of many of the inhabitants state the number of troops who have left the garrison as not less than 6000.' On the other hand, it was also clear that, in the course of the manoeuvring against Maison,

> Saxe-Weimar has in some degree laid hold of Genl. Wallmoden – first by calling him from Louvain onto Brussells [sic] w'thout any communication w'th me (w'ch however under the pressing circumstances I could not but approve of) & now, by putting him at the head of the united active force in the field – w'ch I am likewise very glad of for the moment, as I am sure he will do much more than the Duke of Saxe-Weimar. But I am apprehensive that the next step will be to send off at least as many of the Saxon troops beyond what was intended as Wallmoden's corps, or at least the part he has with the allies, consists of – thus imposing him of necessity, & me, to leave Wallmoden's Corps to defend the frontier.[42]

Thus, whilst the garrison of Antwerp was weakened, so too was the force that Graham could bring against it, and in the meantime it was clear for all to see that Britain could exert only the smallest influence over events in the Low Countries. Five days later, Bathurst would respond by placing Wallmoden's existing corps, and any future units that might be assigned to it, formally under Graham's command, but by then it was really too late to make any difference.[43]

Once the alarm as to French intentions during late March had subsided, Graham turned his attention once more to the lower reaches of the Scheldt, below Antwerp. Upon learning that Graham had been obliged to withdraw the guns from the Scheldt battery, Admiral Young had written to express his concerns that this left the Allied forces on South Beveland grievously exposed, and that if this island were to fall then it would be hard to sustain the Allied hold on the others. So worried was Young that the French might reinforce their foothold at Fort Batz and then assume the offensive, that he informed Graham that he had 'been under the necessity of calling two companies of Russians from Tholen, and to direct the officer commanding there to have the other two ready to send over should it be necessary to call for them'.[44] Under this pressure, and with no other immediate prospect of being able to achieve anything worthwhile in the absence of Allied assistance, Graham decided to resolve the situation once and for all by evicting the French from Fort Batz. Such an operation 'may be done w'th the assistance of the navy & the Russians w'th a small detachment from this Corps', and Graham further hoped, now the rivers were finally becoming navigable again as the worst of the ice melted, that it 'would not be a tedious business, & certainly cannot interfere w'th any arrangements which it may be proper to make for the attack on Antwerp, should circumstances make it advisable to undertake it'.[45]

In order to supplement the British and Russian seamen already on South Beveland under Captain Owen RN, Major General Gibbs was sent across at the head of a force composing the 2/35th and a composite light battalion commanded by the general's brother. This was formed by calling for a hundred volunteers from the ranks of the 2/52nd, and the same again from the four Rifle companies. Since these troops had had precious little to do in recent weeks, there was little trouble in finding men prepared to go. Indeed, Shaw of the 2/52nd, who had evidently grown bored of inactivity since his memoir for this period is otherwise composed solely of accounts of practical jokes played on fellow officers, was only able to obtain the post of adjutant to the detachment after securing the intervention of his brigade commander, Lieutenant Colonel Harris.[46] A detachment of the 2nd Rocket Troop was also included in the expedition. After a two-day delay at Tholen, Gibbs reached Goes on 5 April, and arrangements were quickly set in place for the attack to be mounted the following day.

Thus, on the morning of 6 April, the volunteers from the 2/52nd and Rifles drove in the enemy outposts, battery positions were established for the rockets, and the Russian detachment, leading the main advance, had already come under fire from the fort when a signal was received, relayed via Young's flagship anchored in the Scheldt. The news that it brought was momentous: Napoleon had abdicated, the war was over.

Epilogue

NEWS OF THE PEACE FIRST REACHED Graham on 9 April, via Wallmoden in Brussels. The provisional government in Paris had sent orders for all French commanders to conclude an armistice with the Allied forces opposing them, and Wallmoden was able to inform Graham that he was already in discussions with Maison aimed at reaching just such a settlement. For the commanders of the besieged and blockaded fortresses, the situation was rather more complex due to the lack of communication with France. Although the Crown Prince sent an emissary to Carnot in Antwerp, calling on the veteran governor not only to agree to an armistice but to declare openly for the Allies, the proposal was rebuffed and the emissary informed 'that Genl. Carnot had said that in consideration of the Prince Royal, he would evacuate Antwerp when ever he received orders to that effect from the Senate', but that 'there was not much chance of his doing more, & he could scarcely do less with the knowledge of all that had pass'd at Paris in the first days of this month'.[1] This was to be expected, but must have brought smiles to the lips of those who had been forced to listen to the Crown Prince's boasts of how his presence and influence would open the gates of the French strongholds. Less expected was the refusal of Bizanet at Bergen-op-Zoom even to accept Graham's message that hostilities had ceased, creating a fraught situation that was only eased when Carnot broke the deadlock by proposing an armistice.[2]

Once Carnot had opened negotiations, things became easier to organize but Bergen-op-Zoom remained a stumbling block since Carnot requested that the armistice terms allow him free communication with this and his other garrisons. Although feeling it 'impossible not to stop hostilities at a time where there is every reason to hope that the fate of these fortresses must soon be decided by negotiation which will establish the happiness of the world by a general peace', Graham also informed Carnot that he could not in conscience give up the advantageous position he held with respect to Bergen-op-Zoom and Fort Batz, and that any agreement on the former would require the consent of the Prince of Orange since there were Dutch troops as well as British involved in the blockade.[3] The end of hostilities had left Graham unable to remove the stain on his reputation left by the disaster at Bergen-op-Zoom, and all he could do now was to emphasize how close he had been to success had peace not intervened. Thus, although he might take a high hand with Carnot, and grumble to Bathurst about lost opportunities, he was honest enough with Taylor when bringing his former subordinate – now back in Britain – up to date with the situation:

> Events in France have succeeded one another so rapidly, and so much to every honest man's wish, that unless we should somehow be getting into a quarrel with the new King everything here will and must turn out satisfactorily.
>
> Yet it is not pleasant to be in the situation I am in. We had invested Batz, and I have reason to believe that Berg-op-Zoom [*sic*] could not last long. Yet it is impossible now to treat the French as enemies, seeing that Maison and the Duke of Saxe-Weimar dine together, and that all French soldiers wear the white cockade.[4]

In the meantime, having handed over the blockade of Bergen-op-Zoom to the Dutch and recalled Gibbs from South Beveland, Graham deployed his reorganized army – now with the First Division under Ferguson, the Second under Cooke, and a newly-created Reserve under Mackenzie – between Brasschaat and Lier whilst awaiting the progress of events in Paris, Antwerp, and London.[5]

In acting as he had, Graham had essentially come to the same conclusion as Bathurst, who, upon learning of the fall of Napoleon, sent instructions for Graham to open negotiations with the governors of Antwerp and the other remaining French posts, offering the option of withdrawing to France with safe conduct if they adhered to the new regime. If this offer was rejected, Graham was to 'adopt immediately the best means in your power to make known the above proceedings to the officers and soldiers which comprise the Garrison', thus hopefully forcing the hand of any senior officer who might wish to hold out. Just because France was in the process of bringing back the Bourbons it did not mean that it had become overnight a friendly power, and the thought of the lilies flying over Antwerp was little more appealing than the sight of the tricolour. It was thus with an eye to reasserting Britain's claim for primacy in deciding the fate of the great port that Bathurst, although raising no objection to the Dutch taking possession of Bergen-op-Zoom in their own right, instructed Graham that 'in case the Fortress of Antwerp should be delivered up to you, you will cause both the British and Dutch flags to be hoisted in unison above the walls'.[6] As would become increasingly apparent, however, Britain was not the only power keen to make a claim for the dominant part in deciding the fate of the Low Countries.

For all that their military forces were failing to cooperate, the British and the Dutch – or, rather, the British and the Prince of Orange, who was becoming quite the absolutist – were in essential agreement that the conclusion of a European peace should include the expansion of Dutch territory to encompass the Belgian provinces as well. The local British representatives were not pleased by bullish Dutch attempts to assert their dominance in Belgium in advance of any actual settlement, and nor was Britain entirely in agreement with the Prince of Orange's schemes for large territorial extensions southwards to incorporate Luxembourg and Jülich, but on the basic concept there was no argument. This stance was not, however, without its opponents, vociferous amongst whom were the Belgians themselves, who, though divided on what they did want for their future, saw no place for the Dutch in it. The Belgians, apart from a few notables, could be safely ignored, but less so the representations of the other Allied powers. Austria had no great interest in the Low Countries, being more concerned with the settlement of matters in Italy, but Prussia had its own ideas about the territorial settlement along the Rhine and the Maas. Russia, too, was taking a keener and keener interest in the fate of Holland, motivated partly by a desire to thwart the extension of British hegemony into continental Europe via a Dutch satellite and partly by the fact that it owed the equivalent of £6 million to Dutch bankers. Furthermore, whilst the Allied powers were in agreement that there would need to be a barrier against future French aggression into Holland, there was little concensus on what form it might take and no universal support for the incorporation of Belgium into the expanded Kingdom of the Netherlands envisaged by the Prince of Orange.[7]

As a result of these conflicting aims, it was by no means as simple to engineer an Anglo-Dutch occupation of Antwerp as Bathurst had hoped. Initially, the negotiations for an armistice went well, and Graham was quite happy to accept the terms agreed by Lieutenant Colonel Macdonald and Carnot's representative, Lieutenant-Colonel Huz.[8] In that they allowed the French free communication with their outlying garrisons, the terms brought forth a howl of protest from Admiral Young, who cautioned Graham to ensure that he must 'not let this Sans Culotte suppose we are not aware of his tricks'.[9] Since even Young was prepared to concede that a lasting peace was now practically a certainty, Graham found his interference – the Admiral had also written directly to Carnot – both irritating and futile. Nevertheless, he assured Carnot that the French had obtained advantageous terms only as a gesture of good faith on Graham's part.[10]

Once hostilities had been brought to a close, the actual mechanics of taking possession became rather simpler, although Graham now – when it had ceased to be of any use for him to be so – found himself suddenly elevated to the command of a large multi-national force. Not only was he assigned the Prussian Landwehr from Hertogenbosch – although these were soon redirected to Wesel – but he also found himself in nominal command of a Swedish division, and of the Brunswick contingent then marching up though Germany, as well as his own and Wallmoden's troops. At this late date, it was a decidedly empty honour.[11] The occupation of Antwerp would likewise prove to be a multi-national affair, delayed first by the late arrival of the Allied commissioner, and then of the French representative.[12] Bergen-op-Zoom was occupied by the Dutch on 3 May, and Forts Lillo and Liefkenshoek were likewise handed over, but it was two days more before Graham could finally report that his primary mission was complete:

> I have the honor [sic] to state to your Lordship that, agreeable to the terms of the Convention of Paris of the 23rd ulto. this Fortress with the Different Forts depending on it, was finally evacuated by the remaining French troops this morning.
>
> Major General Künigl, the Commissioner of the Allied Powers having signified to me his wish that, according to his instructions, British troops should occupy it; the 2nd Division under the command of Major General Cooke, & the 1st Brigade of the First Division were marched in, & after the different Guards were relieved, the new Garrison received the Commissioners with Military Honors [sic].
>
> The magistrates then assembled on the parade, & the Mayor, recommending Antwerp to the protection, & its future fate, to the powers of the Allies, presented the Keys of the Town to General Künigl, who received them in the name of the Allied Sovereigns.
>
> It is impossible to describe with what demonstrations of enthusiastic joy the inhabitants expressed their approbation of this interesting scene.
>
> All the Marine Establishments remain in the hands of the French. I have had the most satisfactory communications with the French Admiral Gourdon, commanding, & I have no doubt of the utmost harmony prevailing between the French & English of all descriptions during the time the town shall continue to be occupied by a British garrison.[13]

That evening, an illumination was staged, but Castlereagh had advised against the adding of any Dutch troops to the garrison and Graham therefore elected not to make any claims with respect to the hoisting of national flags. In conjunction with the fact that the fleet remained in French hands, this rendered it clear that, although there were redcoats behind the walls of Antwerp, Britain's position there was by no means secure.

Nor was Britain's position in Belgium any safer: indeed, it was yet more precarious and Graham had for some time been keen to establish a military presence there in order to maintain Anglo-Dutch interests in the face of Prussian encroachments. Until things were settled around Antwerp, military considerations had prevented the dispatch of any sizeable force, although reports from Brussels indicated that there was considerable disorder there, 'several affrays having taken place between the allied troops & the new levies of the Belgians in w'ch some lives have been lost & on many other acco'ts the presence of a Brit. Garrison was earnestly requested by the Governor & Mayor'.[14] On the conclusion of peace, Bathurst had cancelled de Bosset's role as emissary, and the Allies had appointed the Austrian Baron Vincent as their governor there. Nevertheless, the Prussians were increasing their military presence, pulling Bulow's corps back from France, and it became a matter of some import for the British to 'occupy Brussels and the fortified towns of Flanders &c. to relieve them from their present vexations and to raise their esteem for the British'.[15] Vincent had stressed that his role was 'to prepare, by every means in his power, the minds of the people for the cession of the Country to the Prince of Orange', and complained that the continued presence of the old military governor, Horst, was working against this.[16] Even as preparations were being made for the occupation of Antwerp, Graham had deliberately exempted the Guards and his cavalry so as to send them to Ghent and Ostend, but by the time that Antwerp was secure it was clear that the Prussians had beaten him to it.[17]

In response to Graham's report of the changed situation, he received new instructions from home, the very tone of which made it clear that things were coming to an end. The instructions came not direct from Bathurst, who was 'very much occupied', but via Bunbury, who told Graham that his master was 'very sorry to find that you have been prevented from occupying Brussels and Ostend', and that 'the cantonments which the troops of the different nations should take up' was for Castlereagh to settle in his negotiations at Paris:

> But if you should not hear from him (Lord Castlereagh) to a contrary effect by the 25th of this month, you will be so good as to

prepare the forces under your command to embark for England, leaving only a Garrison in Antwerp to the amount of about 4000 infantry, a large portion of artillery men, and the two regiments of German Hussars.[18]

Although Castlereagh's words were eventually able to win the concessions that Graham's arms could not, and British troops would ultimately take on a garrison role in the Belgian provinces preparatory to their incorporation into the Kingdom of the Netherlands, from this point onwards the story of Britain's involvement in European affairs shifts from a military narrative to a political one, and it is at this point that we must leave it.

Even as he sought to build on such gains as British arms had obtained in the Low Countries, Bathurst had been making plans for the dismemberment of Graham's army. One war might well be over, but there was another still to be won across the Atlantic and troops were needed to bring it to a conclusion. The 4/1st had gone even before the peace was concluded, and within days of the armistice being confirmed orders had gone out for the 33rd and 54th to embark for Cork along with as many rockets as could be shipped: the latter were for North America, whilst the infantry were needed in Ireland to free more effective units for service across the Atlantic.[19] In the event, the movement of the infantry was cancelled, but other peacetime concerns soon intervened to remove others of Graham's units. The 1st Royal Veteran Battalion was scheduled for disbandment as an economy measure and was to go home, although the 1st Foreign Veteran Battalion had come out to replace it, arriving on 30 March, and two companies of the Royal Wagon Train were likewise to be broken up. Bunbury also informed Graham that 'the Duke of York is anxious that the 55th should come to England on account of a Court Martial': the wretched Lieutenant Blake, who had been under arrest throughout his battalion's service in Holland, could at last be brought to trial. In due course, Blake would be found guilty and cashiered, but such justice was too late for Captain Clune. Too ill to accompany the 55th overseas, he remained behind sick at Harwich and eventually died in early April.[20]

In the same letter that he notified Graham that these units were to come home, Bunbury was also able to offer his congratulations that the general had been raised to the peerage as Lord Lynedoch. Ostensibly, the title had been earned though his service in the Peninsula and was awarded simultaneously with those bestowed upon Wellington's other chief subordinates, but was clearly also intended as recompense for the damage done to his reputation by his time in Holland. Even before his ennoblement, however, Graham had requested relief from his command, proposing Wallmoden as his obvious successor. He assured Bathurst that, 'as long as there was any prospect of military service I should not have thought of making this request, unless from inability to perform the duties on account of health, but as cold agrees with me much better than heat I have not that excuse to plead – but my private affairs very much require my attention'.[21] In the event, he remained in command until mid-July, although Ferguson replaced him for much of the second half of June whilst Graham visited Ostend and the French frontier. His permanent replacement was the Hereditary Prince of Orange, who had been made a lieutenant general in the British service and who also had command of his father's troops in Belgium.[22]

From the young prince's rag-tag corps, intended primarily to ensure a peaceful incorporation of Belgium into the Kingdom of the Netherlands, there would nevertheless grow the nucleus of the army that would face Napoleon during the Hundred Days, but with the political settlement still incomplete many of the same problems that had beset Graham would arise in that campaign. Wellington, however, would have the military strength and political clout to resolve matters in ways that his predecessor could never have hoped. Graham would play no part in the events of 1815, his active military career having ended with his return to Britain. Nevertheless, as Lord Lynedoch he remained the grand old man of the British Army, promoted to full general in 1821 and holding a series of increasingly prestigious regimental colonelcies. He was also instrumental in founding what became the United Service Club, and continued to take an interest in the lives of his one-time subordinates up until his death, at the age of ninety-six, on 18 December 1843.

About Graham the man there is little bad to say, and, indeed, about Graham the general most of the criticisms stem not from 1813 and 1814 but from his time in the Peninsula. Undoubtedly, his command in Holland was not without fault: his staff work was at times slap-dash, albeit in cases through the failings of others, and his style of command remained as impulsive as ever. On a tactical level, this was no bad thing and his personal interventions in the two attacks on Merxem – to order the 2/78th to charge on the first occasion, and to convert a faltering frontal assault into a flank attack on the second – both served to restore situations that might well have gone against him. On an operational level, however, his impulsiveness undoubtedly played a part in his decision to gamble on an attack at Bergen-op-Zoom, the failings of which have already been analysed. In his dealings with allies and colleagues, he remained as prickly as he had been in the

Peninsula, but this was tempered with a clear self-awareness so that his complaints, to Bathurst, Clancarty and others often contained an acceptance that he would have to make the best of things. A similar self-awareness, along with the need to remain with his headquarters, may also explain why Graham rarely attended important discussions in person, preferring instead to work through emissaries such as Taylor, Stanhope, and Carmichael Smyth, who had the diplomatic skills that he himself seemed to have lost with age. In the end, considering the restrictions that he had to work with, the campaign of 1813–14 was of more credit to him than otherwise, and the peerage that came after it helped restore – not that any restoration had ever been needed in the eyes of the Army – any damage done to Graham's reputation by Bergen-op-Zoom.

Amongst those who remained in the Low Countries after Graham's departure was the man who many in the ranks did blame for the Bergen-op-Zoom debacle, George Cooke. The contingent of Foot Guards was steadily reinforced, so that the Hundred Days saw the single brigade reorganized into two, forming the First Division of the army that fought at Quatre Bras and Waterloo. Cooke retained the command, but at the latter battle was badly wounded and lost his right arm. If anyone had ever doubted it, Cooke's conduct during the Hundred Days proved that he was a gallant soldier and a competent field commander, although it is interesting to note that he was not Wellington's preferred choice to head the First Division. But as Austin pointed out, 'there is a wide difference between exercising command, and directing the movement of troops, to that of acting under the directions of another': whatever his capabilities in the former capacity, Bergen-op-Zoom had clearly shown that Cooke was lacking in the latter.[23] After serving as Lieutenant Governor of Portsmouth, Cooke was promoted to lieutenant general in 1821 but saw no further service prior to his death in 1837. Unlike Cooke, Lord Proby was not with the Guards at Waterloo: although promoted to major general in June 1814 he soon went home on leave, which he eventually overstayed and was replaced by Major General Peregrine Maitland.[24] Succeeding his father as Earl of Carysfort in 1828, seniority carried Proby to the rank of full general by the time of his death in 1855 but he never saw active service again.

Samuel Gibbs also left the army before the end of the year, but in his case it was for another active appointment. Given a brigade command in the force operating against the American coast, he was entrusted by Pakenham with the direction of the main British assault on Jackson's lines outside New Orleans on 8 January 1815. As the ill-conceived attack went home, Gibbs's command rapidly lost cohesion under heavy fire and he found himself unable to rally them. Scarcely had he reported this to Pakenham than he was himself struck down by an American ball, dying the following day.[25] Seven days earlier, although he never knew it, his services in the war against France had been rewarded by the award of a KCB. Mackenzie, meanwhile, remained in the Low Countries through into 1815, and was still there when hostilities resumed. Unfit for an active post, he commanded the Seventh Brigade, composed only of the 2/25th and 2/37th, on garrison duties during the Hundred Days. Eventually raised to a baronetcy, he died in 1833.

Of all Graham's subordinates, the two who went on to greatest things after the brief campaign in Holland were James Carmichael Smyth and Herbert Taylor. Carmichael Smyth remained in the Low Countries after the peace, surveying the Scheldt fortresses, and was therefore ideally placed to serve Wellington during the Hundred Days in the same capacity as he had Graham eighteen months before; Sir George Wood, also the man on the spot, similarly progressed from commanding Graham's artillery to commanding Wellington's. Waterloo earned Carmichael Smyth a CB and an appointment as ADC to the Prince Regent, and in 1821 Wellington also secured him a baronetcy. During the 1820s he was employed surveying and reporting on fortifications in Europe and the colonies, becoming a major general and a personage of some import within the Board of Ordnance. The colonial experience eventually led to a second career as an administrator and governor, first in the Bahamas and then in Guiana, before a fever carried him off in 1838, aged fifty-nine. Maintaining lifelong contact with Jan van Gorkum, who remained in the Dutch Army and eventually rose to be a major general, in 1829 Carmichael Smyth produced a book discussing the applicability of a new topographical system that the Dutchman had developed.[26]

That book, interestingly, was dedicated to Herbert Taylor, who had also continued to display evidence of the talents that had impressed his superiors and subordinates alike during his service with Graham. Initially resuming his duties as Secretary to Queen Charlotte, he retained that post until her death in 1818. Two years later, he became Military Secretary at Horse Guards, serving until 1827 when he became Deputy Secretary at War and first ADC to George IV. Knighted in 1819, he became a lieutenant general in 1825 and Adjutant-General three years later. When the Duke of Clarence ascended the throne as William IV, he retained Taylor as first ADC, and also gave him the post of Secretary which he held throughout the new monarch's short reign. Upon William's death, Taylor retired from public life and died two years later, on 20 March 1839, aged eighty-three. An able diplomat and military administrator, it is perhaps a shame that his budding talents as a field commander never had a chance to develop. Nevertheless, he served his country far more effectively than many men of much greater renown.

The fate of Graham's more junior subordinates was equally mixed, as was that of the regiments in which they served. The 2/21st, 3/56th, and 2/91st followed the 1st Royal Veterans home to be disbanded as part of the peacetime reductions, but the rest of Graham's infantry were still on the continent in 1815. Few of them, however, fought at Quatre Bras and Waterloo. The 2/78th were in garrison, along with Mackenzie's two battalions, whilst the 2/35th and 54th formed part of the force covering the right flank at Hal. The 2/44th were at both battles though, part of Picton's Fifth Division, and the three Foot Guards battalions formed the nucleus of Cooke's First Division. Major General Adam's Third Brigade also contained men who had fought under Graham in the Rifle companies and the 2/52nd, although by now the riflemen had re-joined their battalions and the 2nd Battalion of the 52nd had been drafted into the 1st. The largest contingent of Graham's men to serve together were the four battalions of Halkett's Fifth Brigade – 2/30th, 33rd, 2/69th, and 2/73rd – who were badly cut up by French cavalry at Quatre Bras and helped hold the centre-right at Waterloo. The 2/69th lost their remaining colour at Quatre Bras, and at Waterloo the whole brigade came close to being broken in the final French assault, but enough of them held on long enough to be relieved. Morrice of the 2/69th was amongst those killed at Quatre Bras, and George Muttlebury again took over, commanding at Waterloo, for which he was made a CB. Harris of the 2/73rd was wounded in the fighting on the ridge, but recovered to die a lieutenant general and a peer. Hamilton of the 2/30th was wounded at Quatre Bras, and officer casualties were so heavy at Waterloo that the battalion came off the field under a junior captain, with young McCready, whose conduct in Holland had won him an ensigncy, the sole surviving officer in its Light Company. Elphinstone of the 33rd, meanwhile, survived both actions intact only to meet his end a quarter-century later amidst the ruins of the army that he commanded in the disastrous First Afghan War.[27]

Of the men whose memoirs have illuminated this account, Stanhope, Sperling and Shaw also survived Waterloo intact, but thereafter their fates were more varied. Stanhope's end was perhaps the most tragic, for although he began a new career in politics and entered into an extremely happy marriage, his young wife died giving birth to their second son, who also did not survive. Left devastated by his loss, and increasingly troubled by a wound he had taken at San Sebastián, he hanged himself two years later, on 5 March 1825, aged only thirty-six.[28] Sperling, by contrast, enjoyed a long and happy life after retiring on half pay in 1824. Having married in 1819, he survived until 1877. Charles Shaw also lived to a ripe old age, but whereas Sperling was happy to live the quiet life of a gentleman, Shaw embarked on a rather more adventurous career, fighting in the Portuguese Civil War between 1831 and 1834, and then commanding a brigade in the British Auxiliary Legion during the First Carlist War. Returning to Britain, he helped found the Greater Manchester Police and became a regular commentator on military matters. When he died in 1871, it was as Sir Charles Shaw, KTS.[29]

No such honours awaited Thomas Morris, but he was quite happy to relate, on penning his memoirs in 1845, that he had married and 'obtained a respectable position in civil society', which was more than a great many of those who fought in the ranks of Britain's infantry had the good fortune to achieve.[30] His brother William, meanwhile, remained with the regiment and went with it to India, eventually attaining a sergeant's stripes and siring a son who would continue the family tradition by serving with the 63rd in the Crimea: the three men published their combined memoirs in 1858, although William's deal only with his Indian service leaving his brother's account to stand as the sole record of their time under Gibbs and Graham.[31]

Of those memorialists unfortunate enough to have been wounded during the course of their time in Holland, neither Austin nor Moodie ever felt themselves to have been suitably recompensed for their sufferings. Moodie eventually made a full recovery from the musket shot that had struck him down, although for a time he lost the use of his right arm and was for two years in receipt of a pension as a result. His family having fallen into financial difficulty, in 1819 he joined a brother in attempting to make a new life in South Africa and remained there for a decade before returning to London where he married the author Susannah Strickland. In 1832 the couple emigrated to Canada, where Moodie, as an ex-officer, found himself serving with the Militia during the rebellion of 1837. Although husband and wife both had some literary success, albeit Susannah more so than her husband, times were hard and Moodie's health increasingly poor, so that the introduction to his final book, summing up his life story, is also a tirade against the circumstances into which he had fallen, and the means by which this had come about.[32] This work had some minor success, and with his wife's earnings was enough to keep him solvent until his death in 1869.

Austin, minus a leg, perhaps had more to be bitter about than Moodie, but his wound did not in itself prevent him continuing his military career and it was only after Waterloo, when the Army was again reduced, that he was obliged to retire. In his own words, 'wounded and cast aside, I devoted myself to the cultivation of natural science and literature', but such a summary omits to mention that he was in receipt of a wound pension sufficient not only to pay for this life of scientific enquiry, but also to enable him to marry. 1820 saw him also obtain an appointment, albeit a not very lucrative one, as Fort Major at Duncannon Fort in Ireland, which sinecure he retained for nearly half a century. In later years, however, the post was held *in absentia*, and Austin and his family resided in Bristol where he eventually died in 1881 aged eighty-seven, fondly remembered as 'Old Stick-Leg' by the great-nephew who would later edit his journals.[33]

Something of the same bitterness, perhaps, influenced the way Britain viewed the campaign in which Austin, Moodie and so many others had suffered. It would be hard to argue that the Sixth Coalition was ever a close and harmonious alliance, but the speed with which the former partners turned on one another after Napoleon's defeat is remarkable. Within months, squabbling over the spoils of victory seemed likely to lead to a renewal of hostilities that potentially set Britain and Austria, ironically now bound to Bourbon France, against Prussia and Russia. For all parties, as much was achieved by having troops on the ground as by diplomatic niceties and in this respect Britain could do little more than hang on to its gains in the Low Countries, where the remnants of Graham's former command were eventually reinforced rather than reduced.

Britain's efforts, however, were made on behalf of a power that was proving to be far less of the malleable client state than had blithely been assumed, for William of Orange, as Sovereign Prince and then, from March 1815, King of the United Netherlands, remained as independently minded as ever.[34] Nor, any longer, was his house bound to that of Hanover, for the dynastic connection that should have sealed the unequal partnership planned by Britain's politicians had vanished. A combination of Russian meddling, British domestic politics, and Charlotte's growing distaste for her husband-to-be once she had the chance to compare him with the scores of dashing princes who descended on London to celebrate the peace, led the Princess, after much indecision, to break off her engagement on 16 June.[35] She eventually married Prince Leopold of Saxe-Coburg-Saalfeld in May 1816, by which time her erstwhile fiancé had already wed the Grand Duchess Anna, sister of the Emperor of Russia.

By the time of the royal weddings, however, Britain had succeeded in ensuring that the bulk of the Low Countries, and all its vital ports, were in the hands of a power which, if not the desired client, was at least not French. The shock of the Hundred Days, and some judicious apportioning of Britain's share of the reparations in its aftermath, meant that the United Netherlands were rather better disposed to Britain than they had been in 1814.[36] Thus, in the long run, although it took another war to secure things,

Britain did eventually achieve the war aims that it had set out in 1813, and that it had sent Graham's army to Holland to help secure. True, only a portion of the Antwerp fleet passed into Dutch hands, the remainder reverting to France, but, for the time being at least, France was an ally and in any case it transpired that Napoleon's shipwrights, in their haste, had used unseasoned timber that gave the ships only a short life.

But if it took the events of the Hundred Days to secure Britain's objectives, Wellington was only able to do so by picking up where Graham had left off. Fortescue argued that it is impossible to understand the campaign of Waterloo without knowledge of Graham's campaign, and there is a definite truth in that, not least since many of the problems encountered by the British Army during the Hundred Days have their precursors in the events of 1813 and 1814 – often involving some of the same personalities.[37] That Britain was able, in 1815, to field an army based on Antwerp and Brussels, and incorporating troops from the Kingdom of the United Netherlands, indicates that Graham's campaign did not entirely fail in its objectives.

In many ways, the Dutch campaign of 1813–14 may fairly be compared with the attack on Bergen-op-Zoom that formed its military climax. Both were embarked upon at a rush, based on a perceived need to obtain a vital advantage before time ran out; both were crippled from the outset by inadequate means, and reinforced only when it was too late to make any difference; both, nevertheless, came extremely close to success. Cooke claimed that the Bergen-op-Zoom operation was a bold and ambitious enterprise, and, with all these parallels, we might well describe the campaign as a whole in the same terms. The grand strategy was, perhaps, overtly ambitious, but there was boldness aplenty by the men on the ground, and they won Britain more than Graham's forgotten campaign has been given credit for.

Appendix I

Proposed and Actual Strengths for Graham's Forces, December 1813

	Strength as per Bathurst Memo	Total Strength 25 December	Effective Strength 25 December
2/1st Foot Guards	800	761	696
2/Coldstream Guards	400	516	490
2/3rd (Scots) Foot Guards	400	546	509
2/25th (King's Own Borderers)	390	316	316
33rd (1st Yorks. West Riding)	600	530	502
2/35th (Sussex)	600	461	453
2/37th (North Hampshire)	500	298	279
2/44th (East Essex)	500	422	406
2/52nd (Oxfordshire Light Inf.)	300	197	191
54th (West Norfolk)	510	406	395
55th (Westmoreland)	400	356	340
3/56th (West Essex)	400	280	262
2/69th (South Lincolnshire)	500	487	487
2/73rd	560	450	402
3/95th Rifles	250	305	287
1st Royal Veteran Battalion.	500	461	459
2nd KGL Hussars[†]	480	451	480
Royal Artillery	615	787	650
Total	8,705	8,030	7,604

Bathurst's proposed strengths from memo of 21 November 1813, TNA, WO6/16, pp. 18–19. Actual strengths from Monthly Returns in TNA, WO17/1773 (figures for 2nd KGL Hussars from 25 January 1814 as regiment not included in December return).

† Listed in error as 3rd KGL Hussars in Bathurst's memo; see also Chapter II, n. 5.

Order of Battle for the First Advance on Antwerp, 10–16 January 1814

Commander-in-Chief: *General Sir Thomas Graham*

First Division: *Major General George Cooke*

Guards Brigade: *Colonel Lord Proby*
  2/1st Foot Guards
  2/Coldstream Guards
  2/3rd (Scots) Foot Guards

First Brigade: *Major General Herbert Taylor*
  2/44th (East Essex)
  55th (Westmoreland)
  2/69th (South Lincolnshire)

Divisional Artillery
  Rogers's Brigade (2nd Company, 3rd Battalion, RA)

Second Division: *Major General Kenneth Mackenzie*

Light Brigade: *Major General Samuel Gibbs*
  2/35th (Sussex)
  2/52nd (Oxfordshire Light Inf.)
  2/73rd
  Rifle Battalion

Second Brigade: *Colonel John Macleod*
  2/25th (King's Own Borderers)
  33rd (1st Yorks. West Riding)
  54th (West Norfolk)
  3/56th (West Essex)
  2/78th (Highland)

Divisional Artillery
  Fyers's Brigade (9th Company, 3rd Battalion, RA)[†]

Cavalry: *Lieutenant Colonel Baron Linsingen*
     2nd KGL Hussars

Left in Garrison
     2/21st (Royal North British Fusiliers)
     2/37th (North Hampshire)
     1st Royal Veteran Battalion

For most unit strengths, see Appendix I. Earliest strengths for 2/21st and 2/78th are from 25 January, being 282 (174 effective) and 315 (262 effective) respectively.

† Duncan, Francis, *History of the Royal Regiment of Artillery*. London: John Murray, 1873, Vol. I, p. 223, only gives Rogers's Brigade as present at Merxem, but Graham specifically notes that Fyers's was attached to the Second Division there, leading to the assignments conjectured in this order of battle.

Appendix III

Order of Battle for the Second Advance on Antwerp, 30 January–7 February 1814

Commander-in-Chief: *General Sir Thomas Graham*

First Division: *Major General George Cooke*

Guards Brigade: *Colonel Lord Proby*

2/1st Foot Guards	*(strength 708)*
2/Coldstream Guards	*(479)*
2/3rd (Scots) Foot Guards	*(499)*

First Brigade: *Major General John Skerrett*

2/44th (East Essex)	*(399)*
55th (Westmoreland)	*(295)*
2/69th (South Lincolnshire)	*(433)*
Flank Companies, 2/21st and 2/37th	*(264)*

Divisional Artillery

Rogers's Brigade (2nd Company, 3rd Battalion, RA)

Second Division: *Major General Samuel Gibbs*

Light Brigade: *Lieutenant Colonel William Harris*

2/25th (King's Own Borderers)	*(319)*
2/52nd (Oxfordshire) Light Infantry	*(185)*
54th (West Norfolk)	*(439)*
2/73rd	*(474)*
Rifle Battalion	*(255)*

Second Brigade: *Major General Herbert Taylor*

33rd (1st Yorks. West Riding)	*(502)*
2/35th (Sussex)	*(432)*
3/56th (West Essex)	*(255)*
2/78th (Highland)	*(262)*

Divisional Artillery

Fyers's Brigade (9th Company, 3rd Battalion, RA)

Cavalry: *Lieutenant Colonel Baron Linsingen*

2nd KGL Hussars   *(451, with 517 horses)*

Left in Garrison

     Centre Coys, 2/21st (Royal North British Fusiliers)   *(107)*

     Centre Coys, 2/37th (North Hampshire)   *(179)*

     1st Royal Veteran Battalion   *(330 + 131 detached)*

Strengths are effective rank and file, from Monthly Return of 25 January 1814 in TNA, WO17/1773.

Appendix IV

British Casualties in the Second Advance on Antwerp

Casualties at the Second Battle of Merxem, 2 February 1814[†]

	Killed		Wounded		Missing	
	Officers	ORs	Officers	ORs	Officers	ORs
Royal Artillery	0	0	1	2	0	0
2/1st Foot Guards	0	2	0	0	0	0
2/25th (King's Own Borderers)	0	0	1	12	0	0
33rd (1st Yorks. W. Riding)	0	0	0	3	0	0
2/35th (Sussex)	0	0	1	2	0	0
2/52nd (Oxfordshire) Lt Inf.	0	0	0	2	0	0
54th (West Norfolk)	0	2	4	53	0	0
3/56th (West Essex)	0	0	1	7	0	0
2/69th (S. Lincolnshire)	0	0	0	1	0	0
2/73rd	0	2	2	18	0	2
Rifle Battalion	0	0	4	31	0	0
Total	0	6	14	131	0	2

Casualties at the Bombardment of Antwerp, 3–6 February 1814[‡]

	Killed		Wounded		Missing	
	Officers	ORs	Officers	ORs	Officers	ORs
Royal Artillery	0	1	0	15	0	0
2/1st Foot Guards	0	0	0	1	0	0
2/Coldstream Guards	0	1	0	0	0	0
2/3rd (Scots) Foot Guards	0	1	0	1	0	0
2/25th (King's Own Borderers)	0	0	0	1	0	0
2/37th (N. Hampshire)	0	0	2	0	0	0
2/44th (East Essex)	0	0	2	6	0	0
54th (West Norfolk)	0	0	0	1	0	0
55th (Westmoreland)	0	0	0	1	0	0
2/69th (S. Lincolnshire)	0	0	0	3	0	0

	Killed		Wounded		Missing	
	Officers	*ORs*	*Officers*	*ORs*	*Officers*	*ORs*
2/73rd	0	0	0	2	0	0
2/78th (Highland)	0	0	0	19	0	0
Rifle Battalion	0	0	0	1	0	0
Sappers & Miners	0	0	0	2	0	0
Total	0	3	4	53	0	0

† Casualty Return, TNA, WO1/199, pp. 581–2.

‡ Casualty Return, TNA, WO1/199, p. 589. This return also records the loss of 16 horses killed and 9 wounded, as well as a further 12 that escaped during the firing, listed as missing.

Ordnance Employed in the Bombardment of Antwerp

On 3 February 1814

British Ordnance	Four 10-inch mortars
	Two 8-inch howitzers
	Six 24-pounders
Dutch Ordnance	Three 12-inch Gomers mortars
	Four 11-inch mortars
	Six 7½-inch mortars
Total	25 pieces

On 4 February 1814

British Ordnance	Four 10-inch mortars
	Two 8-inch howitzers
	Six 24-pounders
Dutch Ordnance	Three 12-inch Gomers mortars
	Two 7½-inch mortars
Total:	17 pieces

On 5 February 1814

British Ordnance	Two 10-inch mortars
	Two 8-inch howitzers
	Three 24-pounders
Dutch Ordnance	Three 12-inch Gomers mortars
	Six 7½-inch mortars (without beds)
Total	18 pieces

Detailed in Graham to Bathurst, 6 February 1814, TNA, WO1/199, pp. 569–78.

British Casualties at Bergen-op-Zoom, 8-9 March 1814

	Killed		Wounded		Missing	
	Officers	*ORs*	*Officers*	*ORs*	*Officers*	*ORs*
Royal Artillery	0	0	1	0	0	0
Royal Engineers	0	0	1	0	0	0
Sappers & Miners	1	7	0	11	0	9
2/1st Foot Guards	2	20	0	16	9	275
2/Coldstream Guards	0	2	1	6	0	33
2/3rd (Scots) Foot Guards	1	7	1	39	1	35
4/1st (Royal Scots)	3	38	5	70	17	519
2/21st (Royal N. Brit. Fusiliers)	0	37	9	76	0	98
33rd (1st Yorks. W. Riding)	0	36	10	57	0	49
2/37th (N. Hampshire)	1	70	5	44	0	79
2/44th (East Essex)	2	104	11	86	4	135
55th (Westmoreland)	0	5	6	31	7	62
2/69th (S. Lincolnshire)	1	8	4	23	2	89
2/91st	0	36	3	20	10	202
Total	11	370	57	479	50	1,585

The above figures come from 'Return of Killed Wounded and Missing of the Army under the Command of His Excellency General Sir Thomas Graham KB in the attack upon Bergen op Zoom by storm on the Night of the 8th and Morning of the 9th March 1814', TNA, WO1/200, p. 211. The accompanying 'List of Officers Killed Wounded and Missing', ibid., pp. 215–17, additionally lists 1 officer killed, 5 wounded and 2 missing from the staff of the army. Missing, in this context, equates to prisoners of war although when the final count was complete the total of prisoners came out at 1 major general, 4 lieutenant colonels, 2 majors, 20 captains, 62 subalterns, 4 surgeons, 93 sergeants and 1,872 rank and file, for a total of 2,058 all ranks. See 'State of English Prisoners included in the Capitulation', TNA, WO1/200, p. 223.

Appendix VII

British Forces in the Low Countries at the End of the War

Commander-in-Chief: *General Sir Thomas Graham*

First Division:	*Lieutenant General Sir Ronald Ferguson*	
Guards Brigade:	*Colonel Lord Proby*	
2/1st Foot Guards		*(strength 633)*
2/Coldstream Guards		*(499)*
2/3rd (Scots) Foot Guards		*(527)*
First Brigade:	*Lieutenant Colonel Robert Crawford*	
33rd (1st Yorks. West Riding)		*(486)*
54th (West Norfolk)		*(437)*
Provisional Battalion†		*(229)*

Divisional Artillery
Rogers's Brigade (2nd Company, 3rd Battalion, RA)

Second Division:	*Major General George Cooke*	
Second Brigade:	*Major General Samuel Gibbs*	
2/25th (King's Own Borderers)		*(296)*
2/44th (East Essex)		*(107)*
55th (Westmoreland)		*(233)*
2/73rd		*(473)*
Third Brigade:	*Brigadier General Colin Halkett*	
2/35th (Sussex)		*(473)*
3/56th (West Essex)		*(384)*
2/69th (South Lincolnshire)		*(210)*
2/91st		*(183)*

Divisional Artillery
Fyers's Brigade (9th Company, 3rd Battalion, RA)

Reserve: *Major General Kenneth Mackenzie*[‡]

    2/30th (Cambridgeshire)   *(430)*

    2/52nd (Oxfordshire) Light Infantry   *(248)*

    2/78th (Highland)   *(268)*

    2/81st   *(351)*

    Rifle Battalion   *(260)*

Cavalry: *No brigade commander*

    2nd KGL Hussars   *(417, with 512 horses)*

    3rd KGL Hussars   *(590, with 632 horses)*

In Garrison

    1st Royal Veteran Battalion   *(228 + 209 detached)*

    1st Foreign Veteran Battalion   *(167 + 301 detached)*

Unassigned Artillery: *Lieutenant Colonel Sir George Wood*

    Truscot's Brigade (5th Company, 3rd Battalion, RA)

    Tyler's Brigade (6th Company, 5th Battalion, RA)

    Hawker's Brigade (4th Company, 9th Battalion, RA)

    1st Troop, KGL Horse Artillery

    2nd Troop, KGL Horse Artillery

    2nd Rocket Troop, RHA

[†] 2/21st and 2/37th.

[‡] Mackenzie also had a squadron of hussars and four guns of the KGL horse artillery under his command, but it is not specified from which units these came.

Organisation as per Graham to Bathurst, 15 April 1814, TNA, WO1/200, pp. 553–7.
Unit strengths are effective rank and file, taken from Monthly Return of 25 April.
Effective strengths of other arms as follows:

    Royal Artillery (including KGL and RHA):   32 with headquarters, 1,285 detached, 1,370 horses

    Royal Wagon Train: 160 with headquarters, 64 detached, 327 horses

    Royal Sappers and Miners: 68

Notes

Introduction

1. Fortescue, Hon. J. W., *A History of the British Army*. London: Macmillan, 1899–1930, Vol. X, pp. 1–11, 33–54.
2. Anon., *British Minor Expeditions 1746 to 1814*. London: HMSO, 1884, pp. 80–8.
3. Brett-James, Antony, *General Graham, Lord Lynedoch*. London: Macmillan, 1959; Delavoye, Alex. M., *Life of Thomas Graham, Lord Lynedoch*. London: Richardson, 1880.
4. Leggiere, Michael V., *The Fall of Napoleon: The Allied Invasion of France, 1813–1814*. Cambridge: Cambridge University Press, 2007.
5. Renier, G. J., *Great Britain and the Establishment of the Kingdom of the Netherlands, 1813–1815: A Study in British Foreign Policy*. London: George Allen & Unwin, 1930.
6. Van Gorkum, Jan Egburtus (ed. L. J. F. Janssen), *De Bestorming der Vesting Bergen op Zoom, op den 8sten Maart 1814*. Leiden: Hooiberg & Zoon, 1862.

Chapter I 'Not at Present in a Fit State'

1. Unless otherwise referenced, political and strategic background in this chapter is taken primarily from Leggiere, *Fall of Napoleon*; Muir, Rory, *Britain and the Defeat of Napoleon 1807-1815*. New Haven and London: Yale, 1996; Renier, *Britain and Netherlands*.
2. Heathecote, T. A., 'Serjent Belle-Jambe', in Chandler, David (ed.), *Napoleon's Marshals*. London: Weidenfeld & Nicolson, 1998, pp. 18–40.
3. Chandler, David, *The Campaigns of Napoleon*. London: Macmillan, 1966, pp. 881–900, 1119–20.
4. Fortescue, *British Army*, Vol. IV, Part I, pp. 66–75, 80–133, 141–51, 220–324.
5. Longford, Elizabeth, *Wellington, The Years of the Sword*. London: Weidenfeld & Nicolson, 1969, p. 66.
6. Anon. *Minor Expeditions*, pp. 27–31.
7. Mackesy, Piers, *The Strategy of Overthrow 1798–1799*. London: Longman, 1974, *passim*.
8. James, W. M., *The Naval History of Great Britain During the French Revolutionary and Napoleonic Wars*: London: Richard Bentley, 1837. Vol. VI, p. 259. To this total must be added, in 1814, three sail of the line remaining of the old Dutch fleet, and a further nine French, including four of three decks and 110 guns, incomplete on the stocks.
9. Anon., *Minor Expeditions*, pp. 57–80.
10. Muir, *Britain and the Defeat of Napoleon*, pp. 280–1. Note that Muir states his belief that of the three aims in the second category, the independence of Holland would likely have been the first to be conceded in an early negotiated peace, if only because such a premature settlement would prevent the French being physically removed from former Dutch territory.
11. Heathecote, 'Serjent Belle-Jambe', pp. 32–7.
12. Bathurst to Wellington, 2 July 1813, Wellington, 2nd Duke of (ed.), *Supplementary*

Despatches, Correspondence, and Memoranda, of Field Marshal Arthur, Duke of Wellington. London: John Murray, 1858–62, Vol. VIII, pp. 46–7; see also Bamford, Andrew, '"Injurious to the Service Generally": Finding Manpower for Northern Europe 1813 & 1814', *JSAHR*, Vol. 90, No. 361 (Spring 2012), pp. 25–43.

13. Philippart, John, *The Royal Military Calendar. Containing the Services of Every General Officer in the British Army, from the Date of their First Commission.* London: A. J. Valpy, 1815, Vol. II, pp. 122–3.

14. Anon. *Letters from Germany and Holland, During the Years 1813–14; With a Detailed Account of the Operations of the British Army in those Countries, and of the Attacks Upon Antwerp and Bergen-op-Zoom, by the Troops under the Command of Gen. Sir T. Graham.* London: Thomas and George Underwood, 1820, pp. 1–2.

15. Londonderry, Lieut. General Charles William Vane, Marquis of, *Narrative of the War in Germany and France in 1813 and 1814.* London: Henry Colburn and Richard Bentley, 1830, pp. 85–6.

16. Bathurst to Gibbs, 30 June (1), Wellington, *Supplementary Despatches*, Vol. VIII, p. 47. The fact that Bathurst felt it necessary to send a copy of Gibbs's instructions to Wellington emphasizes how influential the latter was becoming in government circles.

17. Bathurst to Gibbs, 30 June (2), Ibid., p. 48.

18. Anon. *Letters from Germany and Holland*, pp. 2–4.

19. Morris, Thomas, *Recollections of Military Service, in 1813, 1814, & 1815, through Germany, Holland, and France, including some Details of the Battles of Quatre Bras and Waterloo.* London: James Madden, 1845, pp. 1–22.

20. Anon., *Letters from Germany and Holland*, pp. 5–11; Morris, *Recollections*, pp. 26–7, 30–3.

21. Gallaher, John G., *The Iron Marshal. A Biography of Louis N. Davout.* London: Greenhill, 2000, pp. 281–2.

22. Anon. *Letters from Germany and Holland*, pp. 15–16.

23. Morris, *Recollections*, p. 35.

24. Report by Gibbs accompanying Inspection Return of 12 October 1813, TNA, WO27/122, Part I.

25. Ibid.

26. Unit strengths all from Monthly Return of 25 July 1813, TNA, WO17/1773. This does show a higher figure for the 54th, but incorrectly includes men left at home, listed as 'On Command', who are not counted in subsequent returns.

27. Atkinson, C. T. *The Dorsetshire Regiment.* Oxford: Oxford University Press, 1947, Vol. II, pp. 108–108.

28. Morris, *Recollections*, p. 30.

29. Ibid., pp. 38–9.

30. Beamish, North Ludlow, *History of the King's German Legion.* London: Thomas and William Boone, 1837, Vol. II, p. 143.

31. Ibid., pp. 143–54.

32. Ibid., pp. 171–8.

33. Operational summary from Chandler, *Campaigns of Napoleon*, pp. 900–15; see also Leggiere, Michael V., *Napoleon and Berlin: The Napoleonic Wars in Prussia, 1813.* Norman: University of Oklahoma Press, 2002, pp. 141–211.

34. Morris, *Recollections*, pp. 40–2.

35. Ibid., pp. 43–4.

36. Beamish, *KGL*, Vol. II, pp. 192–8; Fortescue, *British Army*, Vol. IX, p. 387; Morris, *Recollections*, pp. 42–7. Strength of 3rd KGL Hussars from unit return for 25 August 1813, TNA, WO17/270, which shows 593 rank and file present for duty.

37. Morris, *Recollections*, pp. 47–50.

38. General Order of 17 October 1813, TNA, WO17/1773.

39. Smith, Digby, *1813: Leipzig – Napoleon and the Battle of the Nations*. London: Greenhill, 2001, pp. 208–13.

Chapter II 'An Essential Service'

1. Unless otherwise referenced, political background in this chapter is taken primarily from Schama, Simon, *Patriots and Liberators: Revolution in the Netherlands 1780–1813*. London: Collins, 1977.
2. Renier, *Britain and the Netherlands*, pp. 40–65.
3. Obituary in *The Gentleman's Magazine*, Jan–June 1838, pp. 93–4.
4. Renier, *Britain and the Netherlands*, pp. 124–7.
5. Memorandum of 21 November 1813, TNA, WO6/16, pp. 18–19. This document lists the 3rd KGL Hussars but this is evidently in error since the 3rd were in Germany with Wallmoden, and this is corrected to 2nd in subsequent documents. See also Appendix I.
6. York to Taylor, 6 January 1814, Taylor, Ernest (ed.), *The Taylor Papers: Being a Record of Certain Reminiscences, Letters, and Journals in the Life of Lieut.-Gen. Sir Herbert Taylor GCB, GCH*. London: Longmans Green, 1913, p. 117.
7. Graham to Wellington, 22 November 1813, Delavoye, *Thomas Graham*, pp. 697–8.
8. Oman, Sir Charles, *Wellington's Army 1809–1814*. London: Edward Arnold 1913, pp. 122–8. See also Brett-James, *General Graham*; Delavoye, *Thomas Graham, passim*.
9. Aitchison to Father, 19 June 1813, Thompson, W. F. K. (ed.), *An Ensign in the Peninsular War: The Letters of John Aitchison*. London: Michael Joseph, 1981, pp. 240–1.
10. Aitchison to Father, 3 July 1813, Ibid., pp. 250–1.
11. Aitchison to Father, 13 July 1813, Ibid., pp. 254–6.
12. Bathurst to Graham, 1 December 1813, Delavoye, *Thomas Graham*, pp. 698–9.
13. Philippart, *Royal Military Calendar*, Vol. II, pp. 35–6.
14. Hamilton, Lieutenant Gen. Sir F. W, *The Origin and Service of the First or Grenadier Guards*. London: John Murray, 1874, Vol. II, pp. 484–5.
15. Bathurst to Cooke, 27 November 1813 (1), TNA, WO1/199, pp. 1–4.
16. Bathurst to Cooke, 27 November 1813 (2), TNA, WO1/199, pp. 5–7.
17. Morris, *Recollections*, pp. 65–6.
18. Gibbs to Calvert, 26 November 1813, TNA, WO17/1773.
19. Bathurst to Gibbs, 27 November 1813, TNA, WO1/199, pp. 9–11.
20. Bathurst to Graham, 4 December 1813 (1), TNA, WO1/199, pp. 29–34.
21. Bathurst to Graham, 4 December 1813 (3 and 4), TNA, WO1/199, pp. 45–9.
22. Bathurst to Graham, 4 December 1813 (2), TNA, WO1/199, pp. 41–3.

Chapter III 'First Blasts of Patriotism'

1. Renier, *Britain and the Netherlands*, p. 124.
2. Philippart, *Royal Military Calendar*, Vol. II, pp. 123–5; Taylor, *Taylor Papers*, pp. 1–87.
3. Taylor to Bunbury, 9 January 1814, TNA, WO1/414, pp. 317–20.
4. Taylor to York, 3 December 1813, Taylor, *Taylor Papers*, pp. 89–92 (and, regarding Lord Yarmouth, editorial note on p. 98); Renier, *Britain and the Netherlands*, pp. 126–8.
5. Taylor to Bathurst, 2 December 1813, TNA, WO1/414, pp. 9–18.
6. Taylor to York, 3 December, 1813, in Taylor (ed), *Taylor Papers*, pp. 89–2.
7. Taylor to Bathurst, 3 December 1813, TNA, WO1/414, pp. 55–8.
8. Taylor to Bathurst, 2 December 1813, TNA, WO1/414, pp. 9–18.
9. Bathurst to Taylor, 7 December 1813 (1), TNA, WO6/16, pp. 24–6.
10. Memorandum of 24 November 1813, TNA, WO1/414, pp. 51–4.
11. 'Copy of the Paper to be Delivered to the Dutch Government at The Hague', 28 November 1814, TNA, WO1/414, pp. 39–47.

12. Bell to Croker, 21 and 24 November 1813, TNA, ADM1/3261.
13. Taylor to Bathurst, 4 December 1813, TNA, WO1/414, pp. 59–69, emphasis as original.
14. Taylor to York, 3 December, 1813, in Taylor, *Taylor Papers*, pp. 89–92; Taylor to Bathurst, 4 December 1813, TNA, WO1/414, pp. 59–69; Leggiere, *Fall of Napoleon*, pp. 100–1, 145–63.
15. Taylor to Bathurst, 4 December 1813, TNA, WO1/414, pp. 59–69.
16. 'Instructions for Lieut. Colonel Campbell Royal Marines', 4 December 1813, TNA, WO1/414, pp. 71–3.
17. Leggiere, *Fall of Napoleon*, pp. 145–67.
18. 'Memorandum of what passed at a meeting held at the Prince of Orange's, Hague, December 5th 1813', TNA, WO1/414, pp. 83–9.
19. Taylor to Bathurst, 5 December 1813, TNA, WO1/414, pp. 75–80.
20. Ibid.
21. Leggiere, *Fall of Napoleon*, pp. 148–67.
22. Taylor to Bathurst, 6 December 1813, TNA, WO1/414, pp. 91–3.
23. Taylor to York, 8 December 1813, Taylor, *Taylor Papers*, p. 94.
24. Cooke to Bathurst, 8 December 1813, TNA, WO1/199, pp. 69–71.
25. Bathurst to Cooke, 4 December 1813, TNA, WO1/199, pp. 21–5. Cooke acknowledged receipt of these instructions on 8 December.
26. Cooke to Taylor, 8 December 1813, TNA, WO1/414, pp. 101–8.
27. Taylor to Cooke, 8 December 1813, TNA, WO1/414, pp. 109–25.
28. Cooke to Bathurst, 8 December 1813, TNA, WO1/199, pp. 69–71.
29. Taylor to Bathurst, 9 December 1813 (1), and 10 December 1813, TNA, WO1/414, pp. 133–4, 145–52.
30. Taylor to Bathurst, 9 December 1813 (2), and 10 December 1813, TNA, WO1/414, pp. 137–40, 145–52.
31. Leggiere, *Fall of Napoleon*, pp. 166–8.
32. Leggiere, *Fall of Napoleon*, p. 168. Various exaggerated accounts of Benckendorff's coup, crediting the Russian with a variety of *ruses de guerre*, may be found in both contemporary and subsequent accounts: see Taylor to Bathurst, 11 December 1813, TNA, WO1/414, pp. 155–60 (passing on an account received from Lord Yarmouth); Austin, Brigadier General H. H. (ed.), *Old Stick Leg: Extracts from the Diaries of Major Thomas Austin*. London: Geoffrey Bles, 1926, p. 73; Morris, *Recollections*, p. 89.
33. Taylor to Bathurst, 11 December 1813, TNA, WO1/414, pp. 155–60. Byrne, Miles, *Memoirs of Miles Byrne*. Dublin: Maunsel & Co., 1907, Vol. II, p. 143 confirms that the Irishmen of 3/3éme Régiment Étranger were indeed withdrawn from Willemstad on 3 December.
34. Taylor to Bathurst, 11 and 12 December 1813, TNA, WO1/414, pp. 155–60, 165–7.
35. Cooke to Bathurst, 16 December 1813, TNA, WO1/199, pp. 77–9.
36. Graham to Bathurst, 16 December 1813 (1), TNA, WO1/199, pp. 145–8.

Chapter IV 'Experienced Troops Are So Much Wanted'

1. Graham to Bathurst, 8–13 December, TNA, WO1/199, pp. 89–143.
2. Austin, *Stick Leg*, pp. 13, 21–32.
3. Ibid., p. 34.
4. Graham to Bathurst, 3 January 1814, TNA, WO1/199, pp. 347–50.
5. Morris, *Recollections*, pp. 65–9; figures from Monthly Return, 25 December 1813, TNA, WO17/1773.
6. Glover, Gareth (ed.), *Eyewitness to the Peninsular War and the Battle of Waterloo: The Letters and Journals of Lieutenant Colonel the Honourable James Stanhope 1803 to 1825*. Barnsley: Pen & Sword, 2010, p. 125.

7. Austin, *Stick Leg*, p. 39.
8. Ibid., pp. 41–8.
9. Ibid., pp. 49–50.
10. Taylor to Bathurst, 17 and 19 December 1813, TNA, WO1/414, pp. 213–16, 245–50.
11. Austin, *Stick Leg*, p. 30.
12. Report of 1 October 1813, TNA, WO27/121, Part II.
13. Cope, Sir W. H., *The History of the Rifle Brigade (The Prince Consort's Own) Formerly the 95th*. London: Chatto and Windus, 1877, pp. 175–9. All unit strengths on landing are from Monthly Return of 25 December 1813, TNA, WO17/1773.
14. Shaw, Charles, *Personal Memoirs and Correspondence of Colonel Charles Shaw*. London: Henry Colburn: 1837, Vol. I, p. 8; see also Inspection Return accompanying Report by Major General McKenzie, 8 October 1813, TNA, WO27/122, Part I.
15. Battalion Return of 25 October 1813, TNA, WO17/263.
16. Battalion Return of 25 October 1813, TNA, WO17/262; Report by Major General Bingham, 4 October 1813, TNA, WO27/121, Part II.
17. Report by Major General Hawker, 26 October 1813, TNA, WO27/122, Part I.
18. Sutherland, Douglas, *Tried and Valiant: The Border Regiment 1702–1959*. London: Leo Cooper, 1972, p. 79.
19. James, Charles, *A Collection of the Charges, Opinions, and Sentences of General Courts Martial, as Published by Authority, From the Year 1795 to the Present Time*. London: T. Egerton, 1820, pp. 641–5; see also Prendergast, Harris, *The Law Relating to Officers in the Army*. London: Parker, Furnivall and Parker, 1855, pp. 204–5; Report by Major General Disney, 4 October, TNA, WO27/122, Part I.
20. Bamford, 'Injurious to the Service Generally', pp. 25–43.
21. Austin, *Stick Leg*, pp. 27–8.
22. Report by Major General Wilder, 4 November 1813, TNA, WO27/121, Part I.
23. Reports by Major General Disney, 1 and 2 October 1813, TNA, WO27/121, Part I.
24. Bathurst to Cooke, 4 December 1813; Cooke to Bathurst, 8 December 1813, TNA, WO1/199, pp. 21–5, 69–71.
25. Bathurst to Graham, 21 November 1813, in Delavoye, *Thomas Graham*, pp. 695–6.
26. Philippart, *Royal Military Calendar*, Vol. II, p. 41.
27. Smith, Sir Harry, *The Autobiography of Sir Harry Smith 1787–1819*. London: J. Murray, 1910, p. 118.
28. Smith, *Autobiography*, pp. 113–128; see also Oman, Sir Charles, *A History of the Peninsular War*. Oxford: Oxford University Press, 1902–30, Vol. VII, pp. 54–6 wherein some alternative accounts, none of them any more creditable to Skerrett, are discussed.
29. Oman, *Peninsular War*, Vol. IV, pp. 519–21; Vol. V, pp. 112–29.
30. 'Cantonments of the Army under General Sir Thomas Graham', 27 December 1813, TNA WO1/199, p. 245.
31. Graham to Bathurst, 21 and 25 December 1813, TNA, WO1/199, pp. 191–4, 227–30.
32. Torrens to Bunbury, 19 December 1813, TNA, WO1/198, p. 39.
33. Torrens to Bunbury, 23 December 1813, TNA WO1/198, pp. 47–50; see also Torrens to Bunbury, 30 December 1813, ibid., p. 55.
34. Graham to Bathurst, 21 December 1813, TNA, WO1/199, pp. 191–4.
35. Wallmoden to Graham, 18 January 1814, TNA, WO1/199, p. 509.
36. Graham to Bathurst, 16 December 1813 (2), TNA, WO1/199, pp. 149–52.
37. Graham to Bathurst, 19 December 1813, TNA, WO1/199, pp. 155–61.
38. Graham to Taylor, 19 December 1813, Taylor, *Taylor Papers*, pp. 104–5.
39. Carmichael Smyth to Mann, 2 December 1813, TNA, PRO30/35/6, pp. 1–2.
40. Sperling, John, *Letters of an Officer of the Corps of Royal Engineers from the British Army in Holland, Flanders, and France to his Father, from the Latter end of 1813 to 1816*. London: James Nisbet & Co., 1872, pp. vii–viii.

41. Carmichael Smyth to Mann, 31 December 1813, TNA, PRO30/35/6, pp. 2–6.
42. Glover, *Stanhope*, pp. 127–8, 129–30.
43. Austin, *Stick Leg*, p. 57.
44. Benckendorff to Cooke, 15 December 1813, TNA, WO1/199, pp. 187–90.
45. Graham to Bathurst, 21 December 1813 TNA, WO1/199, pp. 191–4.
46. Austin, *Stick Leg*, pp. 61–3.
47. 'Journal of Operations', Glover, *Stanhope*, p. 127.
48. Graham to Bathurst, 27 December 1813, TNA, WO1/199, pp. 277–80.
49. Bathurst to Graham, 9 December 1813, TNA, WO6/16, pp. 29–30.
50. Taylor to York, 17 December 1814, Taylor, *Taylor Papers*, pp. 101–2.
51. Taylor to Bathurst, 15 December 1813, TNA, WO1/414, pp. 169–76.
52. Muir, *Britain and the Defeat of Napoleon*, pp. 309–10.
53. Leggiere, *Fall of Napoleon*, pp. 174–5.
54. Diary entry of 17 December 1813, Taylor, *Taylor Papers*, p. 101; Taylor to York, 19 December 1813, ibid., pp. 102–3.
55. Taylor to Bathurst, 4 and 8 December and 16 December (1) 1813, TNA, WO1/414, pp. 59–69, 95–8, 189–98.
56. Bathurst to Graham, 13 and 14 December 1813, TNA, WO6/16, pp. 33–5, 37–8.
57. Taylor to Bathurst, 17 December 1813, TNA, WO1/414, pp. 213–16.
58. Graham to Bathurst, 21 December 1813, TNA, WO1/199, pp. 171–3.
59. Glover, *Stanhope*, p. 126.
60. Weil, Commandant [Maurice], trans. Greg Gorsuch, *La Campagne de 1814 (Campaign of 1814)*, www.napoleon-series.org/military/battles/1814/Weil/c_Weil Introduction.html, Chapter Four, Part I.
61. 'Information from Genl. Benckendorff to Genl. Cooke', 15 December 1813, TNA, WO1/199, pp. 187–90.
62. See, for example, Bülow to Graham, 20 December 1813 (translation), TNA, WO1/199, pp. 206–10.
63. Leggiere, *Fall of Napoleon*, pp. 175–81.
64. Bathurst to Taylor, 7 December 1813, Taylor, *Taylor Papers*, p. 100.
65. Taylor to York, 28 December 1813, Taylor, *Taylor Papers*, pp. 108–9.
66. Graham to Bathurst, 21 December 1813, TNA, WO1/199, pp. 191–4.
67. Leggiere, *Fall of Napoleon*, p. 183. Regarding Bülow's fears of a movement by Macdonald, see Taylor to York, 20 December 1813, Taylor, *Taylor Papers*, p. 103.
68. Diary entry of 23 December 1813, Taylor, *Taylor Papers*, p. 106.
69. Glover, *Stanhope*, p. 127.
70. Leggiere, *Fall of Napoleon*, pp. 183–4.
71. Clancarty to Graham, 22 December 1813, TNA, WO1/199, pp. 273–6.
72. Graham to Bathurst, 28 December 1813, TNA, WO1/199, pp. 285–8.
73. Taylor to York, 26 December 1813, Taylor, *Taylor Papers*, p. 108.
74. Graham to Bathurst, 26 December 1813, TNA, WO1/199, pp. 239–44.
75. Taylor to York, 26 December 1813, Taylor, *Taylor Papers*, p. 108.
76. Graham to Clancarty, 27 December 1813, TNA, WO1/199, pp. 289–92.
77. Carmichael Smyth to Mann, 31 December 1813, TNA, PRO30/35/6, pp. 2–6. No comment is made in this letter regarding the Breda fortifications, but Taylor's account has the engineer reporting that only 4,000–5,000 men would be needed to hold the place, and that the defences were strong – see Diary entry of 31 December 1813, Taylor, *Taylor Papers*, p. 112.
78. Graham to Clancarty, 29 December 1813, TNA, WO1/199, pp. 305–15.
79. Diary entry of 27 December 1813, Taylor, *Taylor Papers*, p. 108; see also Leggiere, *Fall of Napoleon*, pp. 184–7, 408–18.
80. Taylor to York, 1 January 1814, Taylor, *Taylor Papers*, pp. 112–15.

81. Delavoye, *Thomas Graham*, p. 702.
82. Journal of Operations', Glover, *Stanhope*, p. 130.
83. Graham to Clancarty, 27 December 1813, TNA, WO1/199, pp. 289–92.

Chapter V 'We Drove Them Before Us Like Sheep'

1. Graham to Bathurst, 3 January 1814, TNA, WO1/199, pp. 351–4.
2. Leggiere, *Fall of Napoleon*, pp. 410–12.
3. Renier, *Britain and the Netherlands*, pp. 87–98, 199–225; Muir, *Britain and the Defeat of Napoleon*, p. 313.
4. Chambers, James, *Charlotte and Leopold: The True Romance of the Prince Regent's Daughter*. London: Old Street, 2007, pp. 67–78; Renier, *Britain and the Netherlands*, pp. 163–73.
5. Prussian hopes are discussed in Leggiere, *Fall of Napoleon*, pp. 406–7; for proposals to maintain the separate crowns, see Chambers, *Charlotte and Leopold*, p. 82; Renier, *Britain and the Netherlands*, p. 197.
6. Graham to Bunbury, 15 January 1814 (1), TNA, WO1/199, pp. 459–64.
7. Taylor to York, 9 January 1814, Taylor, *Taylor Papers*, pp. 117–18.
8. 'Minute of Conference between Sir Thomas Graham and General Bülow January 8 1814', TNA, WO1/199, pp. 379–88.
9. Ibid.
10. Taylor to York, 9 January 1814, Taylor, *Taylor Papers*, pp. 117–18.
11. Anon., *British Minor Expeditions*, p. 82.
12. Sperling, *Letters*, p. 16.
13. Moodie, Dunbar, 'Narrative of the Campaign in Holland in 1814, with Details of the Attack on Bergen-op-Zoom', in *Memoirs of the Late War*. London: Henry Colburn and Richard Bentley, 1831, Vol. II, pp. 262–7.
14. Graham to Bathurst, 10 January 1814, TNA, WO1/199, unpaginated; Davidson, Major H. (ed.). *History and Services of the 78th Highlanders (Ross-shire Buffs) 1793–1881*. Edinburgh and London: W. & A. K. Johnston, 1901, Vol. I, pp. 95–122.
15. Report by Major General Gordon, 13 November 1813, TNA, WO27/122, Part I. Strength calculated from Monthly Return, 25 January 1814, TNA, WO17/1773, including allowance for men returned as dead during the previous month.
16. Graham to Bunbury, 15 January 1814 (1), TNA, WO1/199, pp. 459–64; Taylor to Bunbury, 9 January 1814, TNA, WO1/414, pp. 317–20; Taylor to York, 9 January 1814, Taylor, *Taylor Papers*, pp. 117–18.
17. For full order of battle, see Appendix II.
18. Austin, *Stick Leg*, pp. 75–8. Austin wrongly dates the forward movement as beginning on the evening of the 11th.
19. See, for example, Sperling, *Letters*, p. 18.
20. Morris, *Recollections*, pp. 84–5.
21. Ibid., p. 87.
22. Austin, *Stick Leg*, pp. 82–3.
23. 'Extract from a letter from a Non-Commissioned Officer of the 78th Regiment to his Wife, Dated Calmthout, 14th January 1814', Davidson, *78th Highlanders*, Vol. I, pp. 126–7.
24. Shaw, *Personal Memoirs*, Vol. I, p. 20.
25. Leggiere, *Fall of Napoleon*, pp. 421–4; Weil, *The Campaign of 1814*, Chapter Four, Part I.
26. 'Mem'm of Major Stanhope's message from Gl. Bülow 12th Jany at ½ past 1 pm', TNA, WO1/199, pp. 439–42; see also Glover, *Stanhope*, p. 131.
27. Anon. *Letters from Germany and Holland*, pp. 96–7.
28. Graham to Bathurst, 14 January 1814, TNA, WO1/199, pp. 389–92.

29. Graham to Bathurst, Private, 14 January 1814, TNA, WO1/199, pp. 397–408.
30. Carmichael Smyth to Mann, 14 January 1814, TNA, PRO30/35/6, pp. 7–11.
31. Glover, *Stanhope*, p. 131.
32. Taylor to York, 16 January 1814, Taylor, *Taylor Papers*, pp. 121–2.
33. Fortescue, *British Army*, Vol. X, p. 8; see also Leggiere, *Fall of Napoleon*, p. 421.
34. Anon., *Letters from Germany and Holland*, p. 96.
35. Cannon, Richard, *Historical Record of the Fifty-Sixth, or The West Essex Regiment of Foot: Containing an Account of the Formation of the Regiment in 1755, and of its Subsequent Services to 1844*. London: Parker, Furnivall and Parker, 1844.
36. Austin, *Stick Leg*, pp. 88–9.
37. Memorandum by Graham, 13 January 1814, TNA, WO1/199, p. 445.
38. Leggiere, *Fall of Napoleon*, pp. 426–7; Ambert to Lebrun, 14 January 1814, Weil, *The Campaign of 1814*, Chapter Four, Part II.
39. Glover, *Stanhope*, p. 131.
40. 'Extract from a latter from an Officer of the 78th Highlanders', Davidson, *78th Highlanders*, Vol. I, pp. 125–6.
41. Return of Casualties, 13 January 1814, TNA, WO1/199, p. 393.
42. 'Extract from a letter from a Non-Commissioned Officer', Davidson, *78th Highlanders*, Vol. I, pp. 126–7.
43. Stanhope to Mother, 14 January 1814, Glover, *Stanhope*, pp. 132–3.
44. Graham to Bathurst, 14 January 1814, TNA, WO1/199, pp. 389–92.
45. 'Extract from a latter from an Officer', *78th Highlanders*, Vol. I, pp. 125–6.
46. Graham to Bathurst, 15 January 1814, Private, TNA, WO1/199, pp. 451–8.
47. 'Extract from a letter from a Non-Commissioned Officer', Davidson, *78th Highlanders*, Vol. I, pp. 126–7. Both this incident, and that of the death of Buff, are corroborated in Glover, *Stanhope*, pp. 132–3.
48. Graham to Bathurst, 14 January 1814, Private, TNA, WO1/199, pp. 397–408.
49. Graham to Bathurst, 14 January 1814, TNA, WO1/199, pp. 389–2.
50. Return of Casualties, 13 January 1814, TNA, WO1/199, p. 393. One man was also returned as wounded by the Royal Artillery Drivers.
51. Ambert to Lebrun, 14 January 1814, Weil, *The Campaign of 1814*, Chapter Four, Part II.
52. Bülow to Graham, 13 January 1814 (translation), TNA, WO1/199, pp. 427–33.
53. Graham to Bathurst, 14 January 1814, Private, TNA, WO1/199, pp. 397–408.
54. Morris, *Recollections*, p. 88.
55. Shaw, *Personal Memoirs*, Vol. I, p. 22.
56. Graham to Bathurst, 27 January 1814, Private (2), TNA, WO1/199, pp. 549–52; see also Taylor to York, 14 January 1814, Taylor, *Taylor Papers*, pp. 119–20.

Chapter VI 'A Want of Bon Foi'

1. Graham to Bathurst, 14 January 1814, Private, TNA, WO1/199, pp. 397–408.
2. Davidson, *78th Highlanders*, Vol. I, pp. 123–4.
3. Austin, *Stick Leg*, pp. 97–8.
4. Leggiere, *Fall of Napoleon*, pp. 428–38.
5. Shaw, *Personal Memoirs*, Vol. I, p. 23.
6. Austin, *Stick Leg*, pp. 96–7.
7. Glover, *Stanhope*, pp. 132–3.
8. Austin, *Stick Leg*, pp. 99–100.
9. Graham to Bathurst, 15 January 1814, Private, TNA, WO1/199, pp. 451–8.
10. Graham to Bunbury, 15 January 1814 (2), TNA, WO1/199, pp. 467–9.
11. Graham to Bunbury, 15 January 1814 (1), TNA, WO1/199, pp. 459–64.
12. 'Campagne de l'armée Brittanique de 1814 dans les Pays Bas', TNA, PRO30/35/23, p. 1.

This is a handwritten manuscript by van Gorkum, apparently sent to Carmichael Smyth for the latter's comments when Gorkum was putting together his history of the campaign. See also Carmichael Smyth to Mann, 14 January 1814, TNA, PRO30/35/6, pp. 7–11.

13. Diary entries of 18 and 19 January 1814; Carmichael Smyth to Taylor, 21 January 1814, Taylor, *Taylor Papers*, pp. 124–5.
14. Van Gorkum, *Bergen op Zoom*, p. 5.
15. Glover, *Stanhope*, p. 133; Taylor to York, 14 January 1814, Taylor, *Taylor Papers*, pp. 119–20; Graham to Bathurst, 21 January 1814, TNA, WO1/199, pp. 477–9.
16. Anon. *Letters from Germany and Holland*, pp. 109–11.
17. Moodie, 'Narrative', pp. 268–9.
18. Diary entries of 16 and 17 January 1814, Taylor, *Taylor Papers*, p. 122.
19. Wellington to Graham, 17 January 1814, Gurwood, Lieut. Colonel (ed.), *The Dispatches of Field Marshal the Duke of Wellington, During his Various Campaigns in India, Denmark, Portugal, Spain, The Low Countries, and France*. London: John Murray, 1837–9, Vol. XI, pp. 460–1; Wellington to Cathcart, 18 January 1814, ibid., p. 464.
20. Graham to Gordon, 14 February 1814, Secret, TNA, WO1/199, pp. 651–6.
21. Graham to Bathurst, 15 February 1814, TNA, WO1/199, pp. 643–9.
22. Graham to Bathurst, 14 January 1814, Private, TNA, WO1/199, pp. 397–408.
23. Bathurst to Graham, 7 January 1814, TNA, WO6/16, pp. 49–54.
24. Cambridge to Taylor, 14 January 1814, Taylor, *Taylor Papers*, pp. 122–3.
25. Graham to Bathurst, 21 January 1814, TNA, WO1/199, pp. 477–9.
26. Returns of Provisions and Forage, 26 January 1814, TNA, WO1/199, pp. 511, 515.
27. Austin, *Stick Leg*, p. 108.
28. Sperling, *Letters*, p. 17.
29. Morris, *Recollections*, pp. 85–6.
30. Anon. *Letters from Germany and Holland*, pp. 115–18.
31. Austin, *Stick Leg*, p. 102; Shaw, *Personal Memoirs*, Vol. I, p. 21.
32. Glover, *Stanhope*, pp. 133–4.
33. Austin, *Stick Leg*, p. 110.
34. Sperling, *Letters*, pp. 4, 11–12.
35. Shaw, *Personal Memoirs*, Vol. I, p. 14.
36. Moodie, 'Narrative', pp. 267–8.
37. Ibid., p. 272.
38. Carmichael Smyth to Mann, 14 January 1814, TNA, PRO30/35/6, pp. 7–11.
39. The whole account of this conversation is taken from Taylor to Graham, 19 January, TNA, WO1/199, pp. 485–95. Since the two men conversed in French, Bülow's quoted speech is Taylor's translation from memory.
40. 'Minute of Conference with General Bülow', 20 January 1814, TNA, WO1/199, pp. 497–9; Taylor to York, 20 January 1814, Taylor, *Taylor Papers*, p. 125.
41. 'Minute of Conference with General Bülow', 20 January 1814, TNA, WO1/199, pp. 497–9.

Chapter VII 'A Fair Trial Against Antwerp'

1. Taylor to York, 23 January 1814, Taylor, *Taylor Papers*, pp. 126–7; Bülow to Graham, 26 and 27 January 1814, TNA, WO1/199, pp. 525–7, 541–2; Graham to Bülow, 27 January 1814, ibid., pp. 529–30. See also Leggiere, *Fall of Napoleon*, pp. 438–9.
2. Graham to Bathurst, 27 January 1814 (1), TNA, WO1/199, pp. 519–22; Taylor to York, 29 January 1814, Taylor, *Taylor Papers*, pp. 129–30; Leggiere, *Fall of Napoleon*, pp. 126–7.
3. 'Memorandum by Lieutenant Col. Smyth on returning from Breda 27th Jany. 1814',

TNA, WO1/199, pp. 533–40. Fort Pimentel, demolished in 1782, stood at Oosterweel on the Scheldt.

4. Graham to Bathurst, 27 January 1814 (1), TNA, WO1/199, pp. 519–22.
5. Graham to Bathurst, 27 January 1814 (2), TNA, WO1/199, pp. 549–52.
6. Austin, *Stick Leg*, p. 111.
7. Shaw, *Personal Recollections*, Vol. I, p. 24.
8. Taylor to York, 23 January 1814, Taylor, *Taylor Papers*, pp. 126–7. For full order of battle see Appendix III.
9. Sperling, *Letters*, p. 22.
10. Graham to Bathurst, 31 January 1814, TNA, WO1/199, pp. 561–5.
11. Ibid.
12. Taylor to Graham, 31 January 1814, TNA, WO1/199, pp. 565–8.
13. Diary entry of 31 January 1814, Taylor, *Taylor Papers*, pp. 132–3.
14. Taylor to York, 4 February 1814, Taylor, *Taylor Papers*, pp. 134–40.
15. Ibid., Taylor writes 'light companies', which makes no sense, but evidently meant 'flank companies' since Austin confirms that the Grenadiers were also brought up.
16. Austin, *Stick Leg*, pp. 124–7.
17. Ibid., pp. 127–8.
18. Graham to Cooke, 1 February 1814, Taylor, *Taylor Papers*, p. 133.
19. Anon., *Letter from Germany and Holland*, pp. 128–9; Taylor to York, 4 February 1814, Taylor, *Taylor Papers*, pp. 134–40.
20. 'Copy of the Disposition for the Attack on Merxem by General Sir Thomas Graham', 2 February 1814, TNA, PRO30/35/6, pp. 15–16.
21. Taylor to York, 29 January 1814, Taylor, *Taylor Papers*, pp. 129–30.
22. The following account is based largely on Taylor to York, 4 February 1814, Taylor, *Taylor Papers*, pp. 134–40, supplemented by Anon., *Letters from Germany and Holland*, pp. 122–30; Austin, *Stick Leg*, pp. 128–150, Morris, *Recollections*, pp. 92–7; Shaw, *Personal Recollections*, Vol. I, pp. 24–5. Graham's despatch (Graham to Bathurst, 6 February 1814, TNA, WO1/199, pp. 569–78) is little help on the progress of the fighting, although it does help confirm the details of how the Second Division was deployed.
23. Cope, *Rifle Brigade*, p. 177.
24. Morris, *Recollections*, p. 92.
25. Taylor to York, 4 February 1814, Taylor, *Taylor Papers*, pp. 134–40.
26. Muir, Howie, 'Order of Battle: Customary Battle-Array in Wellington's Peninsular Army', in Muir, Rory, et al., *Inside Wellington's Peninsular Army*. Barnsley: Pen & Sword, 2006.
27. For full casualty returns, see Appendix IV.
28. Morris, *Recollections*, pp. 93–4.
29. Austin, *Stick Leg*, p. 135.
30. Ibid., p. 28. The 56th were nicknamed 'Pompadours' in reference to their purple uniform facings.
31. Ibid., pp. 143–4.
32. Shaw, *Personal Recollections*, Vol. I, pp. 22–3.
33. P. W., 'The Duke of Clarence at Merkhem in 1814 (Communicated by an Officer Present)', *The United Service Journal and Naval and Military Magazine*, 1830, Part II, pp. 523–5.
34. Austin, *Stick Leg*, p. 88; see also Clarence to Liverpool, 6 February 1814, Taylor, *Taylor Papers*, p. 141.
35. Taylor to York, 4 February 1814, Taylor, *Taylor Papers*, pp. 134–40.

Chapter VIII 'Want of Means and of Time'

1. Byrne, *Memoirs*, Vol. II, pp. 147–8; see also Leggiere, *Fall of Napoleon*, p. 439.
2. Graham to Bathurst, 6 February 1814, TNA, WO1/199, pp. 569–78; see also Morillon, Marc, 'The Siege Mortars and Their Related Skills during the Napoleonic Era', at www.napoleon-series.org/military/organization/c_mortars.html.
3. Taylor to York, 4 February 1814, Taylor, *Taylor Papers*, pp. 134–40.
4. Carmichael Smyth to Mann, 5 February 1814, TNA, PRO30/35/6, pp. 12–14; see also Sperling, *Letters*, pp. 25–7.
5. Morris, *Recollections*, p. 98.
6. Sperling, *Letters*, p. 29.
7. Graham to Bathurst, 6 February 1814, TNA, WO1/199, pp. 569–78.
8. Taylor to Graham, 21 February 1814, TNA, WO1/199, pp. 699–700.
9. Taylor to York, 4 February 1814, Taylor, *Taylor Papers*, pp. 134–40.
10. 'Journal of Operations', Glover, *Stanhope*, p. 134.
11. Graham to Bathurst, 6 February 1814, TNA, WO1/199, pp. 569–78.
12. Glover, *Stanhope*, pp. 135–6.
13. Taylor to York, 4 February 1814, Taylor, *Taylor Papers*, pp. 134–40.
14. Graham to Bathurst, 6 February 1814, TNA, WO1/199, pp. 569–78.
15. Morris, *Recollections*, pp. 98–9.
16. Ibid., pp. 99–100.
17. Sperling, *Letters*, pp. 27–8.
18. Carmichael Smyth to Mann, 7 February 1814, TNA, PRO30/35/6, p. 18.
19. Connolly, T. W. J., *The History of the Corps of Royal Sappers and Miners*. London: Longman, Brown, Green and Longman, 1855, Vol. I, p. 207.
20. 'Journal of Operations', Glover, *Stanhope*, p. 135.
21. P. W., 'Duke of Clarence at Merkhem', p. 525; Austin, *Stick Leg*, pp. 155–6.
22. Return of Casualties, 3–5 February 1814, TNA, WO1/199, p. 589: Austin therefore has it wrong in naming the lieutenant as 'Stowards'. For details of all casualties, see Appendix IV.
23. Graham to Bathurst, 6 February 1814, TNA, WO1/199, pp. 569–78. See also Appendix V.
24. Byrne, *Memoirs*, Vol. II, p. 147.
25. Smith to Graham, 8 February 1814, TNA, WO1/199, pp. 601–2.
26. Taylor to York, 6 February 1814, Taylor, *Taylor Papers*, pp. 140–1.
27. Carmichael Smyth to Mann, 5 February 1814, TNA, PRO30/35/6, pp. 12–14.
28. Austin, *Stick Leg*, pp. 146–7.
29. Ibid., pp. 148–9.
30. Austin, *Stick Leg*, pp. 153–64.
31. Graham to Bathurst, 10 February 1814, TNA, WO1/199, pp. 597–600.
32. Monthly Return, 25 February 1814, TNA, WO17/1773: note that this figure is also artificially inflated by the sick in the newly arrived 4/1st, accounting for a fifth of the total number in hospital.
33. Graham to Bathurst, 10 February 1814, TNA, WO1/199, pp. 597–600.
34. Leggiere, *Fall of Napoleon*, pp. 440–1.
35. Table of Cantonments, 10 February 1814, TNA, WO1/199, p. 613.
36. Graham to Bathurst, Private, 10 February 1814 (1), TNA, WO1/199, pp. 617–20; Graham to Bathurst, 14 February 1814, ibid., pp. 629–31.
37. Graham to Bathurst, Private, 14 February 1814, TNA, WO1/199, pp. 633–6; see also Graham to Bathurst, 7 and 8 February 1814, TNA, WO6/16, pp. 60–2.
38. Elkington, James, 'Extracts from the Diary of Surgeon James Goodall Elkington during his Service with the 30th Regiment 11th March 1813–24th June 1817', Part I, *The XXX*, April 1911, p. 12.

39. Divall, Carole, *Redcoats Against Napoleon: The 30th Regiment During the Revolutionary and Napoleonic Wars*. Barnsley: Pen & Sword, 2009, pp. 130–1.
40. Divall, *Redcoats Against Napoleon*, p. 131; strength figure from Monthly Return, 25 February 1814, TNA, WO17/1773.
41. Inspection Return accompanying Report by Major General Hatton, 18 November 1813, TNA, WO27/122, Part I.
42. NAM 6807-209, 'Journal of Edward Nevil McCready', Chapters I–III.
43. 'Effective State of the Brigade of British Troops under the command of B. General Arthur Gore', 28 February 1814, TNA, WO1/200, p. 37; see also Graham to Bunbury, 25 March 1814, ibid., p. 347.
44. Graham to Bunbury, 2 April 1814, TNA, WO1/200, pp. 475–82; see also Inspection Report by Lieutenant General Ferguson, 25 April 1814, TNA, WO27/126 Part II.
45. Shaw, *Personal Memoirs*, Vol. I, p. 22.
46. Moodie, 'Narrative', pp. 273–7.
47. Bathurst to Graham, 28 January 1814, TNA, WO6/16, pp. 59–60; Graham to Bathurst 21 and 25 February 1814, TNA, WO1/199, pp. 659–62, 707–8; Croker to Young, 4 February 1814, ibid., pp. 715–18.
48. Monthly Return, 25 February 1814, TNA, WO17/1773.

Chapter IX 'We Might Get Hold of Bergen-op-Zoom'

1. Graham to Bathurst, Private, 10 February 1814 (1), TNA, WO1/199, pp. 617–20; Graham to Bunbury, 1 March 1814, TNA, WO1/200, pp. 17–24.
2. Graham to Bathurst, Private, 10 February 1814 (1), TNA, WO1/199, pp. 617–20.
3. Ibid.; see also Graham to Clancarty, 11 February 1814, TNA, WO1/199, pp. 637–8.
4. Clancarty to Graham, 12 February 1814, TNA, WO1/199, pp. 639–41.
5. Graham to Bathurst, 22 February 1814, TNA, WO1/199, pp. 663–4.
6. Graham to Bathurst, 25 February 1814, Private, TNA, WO1/199, pp. 719–22.
7. Renier, *Britain and the Netherlands*, pp. 136–7.
8. Bathurst to Graham, 12 January 1814, TNA, WO6/16, pp. 57–8.
9. Uythoven, Geert van, 'Nassauers in Netherlands Service', at www.livinghistory.co.uk/ 1800–1900/articles/xw_134.html; see also Clancarty to Taylor, 22 March, TNA, WO1/414, pp. 369–72.
10. Taylor to York, 21 February 1814, Taylor, *Taylor Papers*, pp. 145–6.
11. Graham to Bathurst, 22 February 1814, TNA, WO1/199, pp. 663–4.
12. NAM 6807-209, 'Journal of Edward Nevil McCready', Chapter III; Graham to Bathurst, Private, 7 March 1814, TNA, WO1/200, pp. 109–12.
13. Van Gorkum, *Bergen op Zoom*, pp. 5–6.
14. Graham to Bunbury, 1 March 1814, TNA, WO1/200, pp. 17–24; emphasis as original.
15. 'A list of the principal part of the cargoes of the four transports on shore and missing', 28 February 1814, TNA, WO1/200, p. 55; see also Graham to Bathurst, 1 March 1814, ibid., pp. 1–2; 'A list of Transports which sailed from Harwich the 18th Feb 1814 destined for Holland in charge of Lieutenant Tregarthen Agent of Transports', ibid., pp. 9–11.
16. For the full list of ordnance shipped, see Chapman to Goulburn, 17 December 1813, TNA, WO1/198, pp. 169–70.
17. Graham to Johnson, 19 February 1814, TNA, WO1/199, pp. 673–5, emphases as original; see also Johnson to Graham, 18 February 1814, Graham to Bathurst, 22 February 1814, ibid., pp. 671–2, pp. 667–70.
18. Van Gorkum, *Bergen op Zoom*, p. 6.
19. Fortescue, *British Army*, Vol. X, p. 38.
20. Graham to Bathurst, Private, 7 March 1814, TNA, WO1/200, pp. 109–12.
21. Bathurst to Graham, 28 February 1814, Delavoye, *Thomas Graham*, p. 714.

22. Delavoye, *Thomas Graham*, pp. 714–15.
23. Glover, *Stanhope*, p. 146. Stanhope states that 4,000 of Graham's line infantry – just over half – were to be withdrawn.
24. Leggiere, *Fall of Napoleon*, pp. 131, 140–4, 266–7.
25. Chandler, *Campaigns of Napoleon*, pp. 949–83; Muir, *Britain and the Defeat of Napoleon*, pp. 310–19.
26. Stanhope to Graham, 17 February 1814, TNA, WO1/199, pp. 403–4.
27. Glover, *Stanhope*, p. 138.
28. Graham to Bathurst, Private, 22 February 1814, TNA, WO1/199, pp. 677–680.
29. For Stanhope's lengthy account of his two meetings, and opinion of the Crown Prince's character, see Glover, *Stanhope*, pp. 138–45; a shorter précis, focussed on matters of more immediate import, can be found in Stanhope to Graham, 26 February 1814, TNA, WO1/200, pp. 31–42.
30. Stanhope to Graham, 26 February 1814, TNA, WO1/200, pp. 31–42.
31. Since the point is mentioned in Stanhope's report of 26 February, it also conclusively disproves the assertion made in Fortescue, *British Army*, Vol. X, p. 33, that his longer account of the conversation is embellished with after-the-fact knowledge.
32. Ibid.; see also Thornton to Graham 23 February 1814, TNA, WO1/200, p. 47.
33. Chandler, *Campaigns of Napoleon*, pp. 983–6.
34 . Saxe-Weimar to Graham, 28 February 1814, pp. 27–8.
35. Graham to Bathurst, 7 March 1814, TNA, WO1/200, pp. 85–6.
36. Graham to Bathurst, 14 February 1814, Private, TNA, WO1/199, pp. 633–6.
37. Graham to Trench, 25 February 1814, Private TNA, WO1/199, pp. 723–6; see also Graham to Bathurst, 25 February 1814, ibid., pp. 719–22.
38. Memorandum of 25 February 1814, TNA, WO1/199, pp. 747–9.
39. 'Plan for the Military Organisation of the Belgian Provinces', TNA, WO1/200, pp. 97–103; see also Graham to Bathurst, 7 March 1814, Johnson to Graham, 2 March 1814, ibid., pp. 85–6, 89–91.
40. Graham to Bunbury, 4 March 1814, TNA, WO1/200, pp. 71–4.
41. Ibid., pp. 67–8.
42. Shaw, *Personal Recollections*, Vol. I, p. 30.
43. Graham to Bunbury, 4 March 1814, TNA, WO1/200, pp. 71–4.
44. Carmichael Smyth to Mann, 10 March 1814, TNA, PRO30/35/6, pp. 19–24.
45. Graham to Bathurst, 7 March 1814, Private, TNA, WO1/200, pp. 109–12. This letter represents the most accurate indicator of Graham's views on the day that he decided upon the assault.
46. Ibid.
47. Ibid.
48. Glover, *Stanhope*, p. 146, emphasis as original.
49. Van Gorkum, *Bergen op Zoom*, p. 7; see also Carmichael Smyth to Mann, 10 March 1814, TNA, PRO30/35/6, pp. 19–24.
50. Graham to Bathurst, 7 March 1814, Private, TNA, WO1/200, pp. 109–112.
51. Bathurst to Graham, 8 and 9 March 1814, TNA, WO6/16, pp. 65–6, 67; Bunbury to Graham, 4 March 1814, ibid., pp. 64–5.
52. Some of these points are made in Brett-James, *General Graham*, p. 294, but the narrative remains overly preoccupied with Bathurst's withdrawal scheme.
53. Van Gorkum, *Bergen op Zoom*, p. 14.
54. Graham to Bathurst, Private, 11 March 1814, TNA, WO1/200, pp. 141–3.
55. Chandler, *Campaigns of Napoleon*, pp. 983–91.

Chapter X 'I Am in First'

1. The history of the lines is summarized, as background to discussion of their potential fate, in Vervloet, Jelier A. J., et al., 'Planning for the future: towards a sustainable design and land use of an ancient flooded military defence line', *Landscape and Urban Planning*, 70 (2005), pp. 153–63.

2. Rolt, Richard, *An Impartial Representation of the Conduct of the Several Powers of Europe, Engaged in the Late General War*. London: S. Birt, 1750, Vol. IV, pp. 441–53.

3. Van Gorkum, *Bergen op Zoom*, pp. 15–16.

4. Jones, Major General Sir John T., *Journal of Sieges Carried on by the Army under the Duke of Wellington*. London: John Weale, 1846, Vol. II, pp. 287–9.

5. Fortescue, *British Army*, Vol. X, pp. 34–6.

6. Van Gorkum, *Bergen op Zoom*, pp. 16–17.

7. Memoranda to Skerrett, Proby and Morrice, 8 March 1814, TNA, WO1/200, pp. 145–61, emphasis as original. This explains why some accounts, e.g. Glover, *Stanhope*, p. 147, refer to the Guards as forming the centre attack or column, which in turn turns the Right Attack into the left and the Centre Attack into the right.

8. Van Gorkum, *Bergen op Zoom*, pp. 17–18.

9. Memoranda to Skerrett, Proby, and Morrice, 8 March 1814, TNA, WO1/200, pp. 145–61; see also Glover, *Stanhope*, pp. 146–7.

10. Van Gorkum, *Bergen op Zoom*, pp. 16–17.

11. Carmichael Smyth to Mann, 10 March 1814, TNA, PRO30/35/6, pp. 19–24.

12. Fortescue, *British Army*, Vol. X, pp. 34–6.

13. Van Gorkum, *Bergen op Zoom*, p. 16: the Dutch foot of the period varied locally between 28 and 31 cm.

14. Sperling, *Letters*, p. 36.

15. Moodie, 'Narrative', pp. 277–8.

16. Ibid., pp. 279–80.

17. Ibid., pp. 282–3, 305.

18. Anon. *Letters from Germany and Holland*, pp. 157, 169–70.

19. Cannon, Richard, *Historical Record of the First or Royal Regiment of Foot: Containing an account of the Raising of the Regiment in the Reign of King James VI of Scotland and of its Subsequent Services to 1846*. London: Parker, Furnivall and Parker, 1847, p. 203.

20. Glover, *Stanhope*, pp. 146–50.

21. Anon., *Letters from Germany and Holland*, p. 169.

22. Memorandum to Skerrett, 8 March 1814, TNA, WO1/200, p. 145.

23. Graham to Bathurst, 10 March 1814, TNA, WO1/200, pp. 117–27; Glover, *Stanhope*, p. 147; van Gorkum, *Bergen op Zoom*, p. 53: note that no single account gives all of these timings, emphasizing the confusion that seems to have existed on this point.

24. Covering note by Graham accompanying duplicate copies of orders sent to Bathurst, 11 March 1814, TNA, WO1/200, p. 145. The time differential is noted in Cooke to Graham, 10 March 1814, TNA, WO1/200, pp. 129–33.

25. Memorandum to Skerrett, 8 March 1814, TNA, WO1/200, p. 145.

26. Glover, *Stanhope*, p. 147, emphasis as original.

27. Anon., *Letters from Germany and Holland*, p. 163; Glover, *Stanhope*, p. 147; Sperling, *Letters*, p. 40; van Gorkum, *Bergen op Zoom*, p. 56.

28. For details of all casualties, see Appendix VI.

29. Goff, Gerald L., *Historical Records of the 91st Argyllshire Highlanders, now the 1st Battalion Princess Louise's Argyll and Sutherland Highlanders, containing an Account of the Formation of the Regiment in 1794, and of its subsequent Services to 1881*. London: R. Bentley and Son, 1891, pp. 24, 324. Cahill remained with the 91st in his new rank, fought at Waterloo, and died in 1827 on Jamaica when serving as Adjutant.

30. This account of the False Attack is based primarily on Anon., *Letters from Germany*

and Holland, pp. 169–71; Fortescue, *British Army*, Vol. X, pp. 38–9; van Gorkum, *Bergen op Zoom*, pp. 56–7.

31. Memorandum to Skerrett, 8 March 1814, TNA, WO1/200, pp. 159–61.
32. Sperling, *Letters*, pp. 38–40.
33. Oman, *Peninsular War*, Vol. V, pp. 253–255; Carter, Thomas, *Historical Record of the Forty-Fourth or the East Essex Regiment of Foot*. London: W. O. Mitchell, 1864, pp. 72–5; Sperling, *Letters*, p. 38.
34. Carmichael Smyth to Mann, 10 March 1814, TNA, PRO30/35/6, pp. 19–24.
35. Sperling, *Letters*, pp. 40–1; note that Glover, *Stanhope*, has Carleton exclaim 'First in Badajoz, first in Bergen-op-Zoom', but Stanhope, of course, was not an eyewitness.
36. Moodie, 'Narrative', pp. 283–4.
37. Sperling, *Letters*, p. 41.
38. Moodie, 'Narrative', pp. 284–5.
39. Ibid., pp. 285–6.
40. Van Gorkum, *Bergen op Zoom*, p. 59.
41. Glover, *Stanhope*, p. 148.
42. Anon., *Letters from Germany and Holland*, pp. 165–6.
43. Van Gorkum, *Bergen op Zoom*, pp. 72, 76–7.
44. Fortescue, *British Army*, Vol. X, pp. 38–40.

Chapter XI 'Filled with Melancholy Forebodings'

1. Sperling, *Letters*, p. 42.
2. Graham to Taylor, 18 March 1814, Taylor, *Taylor Papers*, pp. 153–4.
3. Glover, *Stanhope*, p. 149.
4. This account of the Centre Attack is based primarily on Graham to Bathurst, 10 March 1814, TNA, WO1/200, pp. 117–27; Anon. *Letters from Germany and Holland*, pp. 171–2 (who wrongly asserts that it was the right wing of the 55th that was left behind); Glover, *Stanhope*, pp. 149–50; van Gorkum, *Bergen op Zoom*, pp. 60–1.
5. Sperling, *Letters*, pp. 42–3. Other sources mention Gore as still being alive later in the fighting, but since Sperling was an eyewitness, and is definite about his death at this point, I have followed his account.
6. Anon., *Letter from Germany and Holland*, pp. 166–9; Sperling, *Letters*, p. 43; Van Gorkum, *Bergen op Zoom*, p. 60.
7. Sperling, *Letters*, pp. 43–4.
8. Corporal Mueller, 1st Foot Guards, quoted in Brett-James, *General Graham*, p. 295.
9. Anon., *Letters from Germany and Holland*, p. 161.
10. Van Gorkum, *Bergen op Zoom*, p. 61.
11. This account of the entry of the Left Attack is based primarily on Cooke to Graham, 10 March 1814, TNA, WO1/200, pp. 129–33; Anon., *Letters from Germany and Holland*, pp. 158–63; Fortescue, *British Army*, Vol. X, p. 41; Hamilton, *Grenadier Guards*, Vol. II, pp. 488–90; Jones, *Sieges*, Vol. II, pp. 295–6; van Gorkum, *Bergen op Zoom*, pp. 61–3.
12. Jones, *Sieges*, Vol. II, p. 296.
13. Cooke to Graham, 10 March 1814, TNA, WO1/200, pp. 129–33.
14. Ibid.
15. Van Gorkum, *Bergen op Zoom*, pp. 64–6.
16. Ibid., pp. 64–70.
17. Cooke to Graham, 10 March 1814, TNA, WO1/200, pp. 129–33.
18. Jones, *Sieges*, Vol. II, p. 297.
19. Cooke to Graham, 10 March 1814, TNA, WO1/200, pp. 129–33.
20. Ibid.
21. Carmichael Smyth to Mann, 10 March 1814, TNA, PRO30/35/6, pp. 19–24.

22. Moodie, 'Narrative', pp. 286–9.
23. Van Gorkum, *Bergen op Zoom*, pp. 72–3; Fortescue, *British Army*, Vol. X, pp. 43–4.
24. Moodie, 'Narrative', pp. 289–90.
25. Ibid., pp. 291–2.
26. Sperling, *Letters*, p. 44.
27. Ibid., p. 45.
28. Van Wijk, Erny, 'Le 21ème à Bergen op Zoom' at www.histoire-empire.org/1814/ berg_op_zoom/berg_op_zoom_01.htm. Van Wijk has located records attesting to members of the 6/21ème being at Bergen-op-Zoom in early 1814, but is unclear if the troops present all belonged to this battalion or were the combined residue of this regiment, the bulk of which had been taken prisoner at Dresden.
29. Cooke to Graham, 10 March 1814, TNA, WO1/200, pp. 129–33.
30. Sperling, *Letters*, p. 45.
31. Van Gorkum, *Bergen op Zoom*, p. 80.
32. Moodie, 'Narrative', pp. 292–3.
33. Ibid., pp. 296–8.
34. Ibid., p. 299.
35. Graham to Bathurst, 11 March 1814, Private, TNA, WO1/200, pp. 141–3.
36. Anon., *Letters from Germany and Holland*, p. 182.
37. Glover, *Stanhope*, p. 148.
38. 'Letter from an Officer of Rank, Rosendaal [*sic*], March 9 1814', published in the *Edinburgh Evening Courant*, 21 March 1814.
39. Flatow, Major A. F., 'British Colours at Les Invalides', *JSAHR*, Vol. 27 (1949), pp. 138–9.
40. Anon., *Letters from Germany and Holland*, p. 182.
41. Parkinson to Graham of Fintry, 11 March 1814, Taylor, *Taylor Papers*, pp. 154–5.
42. Sperling, *Letters*, p. 46.
43. Cooke to Graham, 10 March 1814, TNA, WO1/200, pp. 129–33.
44. Sperling, *Letters*, pp. 46–7.
45. Cooke to Graham, 10 March 1814, TNA, WO1/200, pp. 129–33. See also Anon., *Letters from Germany and Holland*, pp. 183–5; Fortescue, *British Army*, Vol. X, pp. 49–50; Hamilton, *Grenadier Guards*, Vol. II, p. 491.
46. Van Gorkum, *Bergen op Zoom*, pp. 80–1.
47. Flatow, 'British Colours'.
48. Austin, *Stick Leg*, p. 181.
49. Ibid.; see also Timbs, John, *Wellingtoniana. Anecdotes, Maxims, and Characteristics of the Duke of Wellington*. London: Ingram, Cooke and Co., 1852, pp. 110–11.

Chapter XII 'Out-Generalled and Disgracefully Beaten'

1. NAM 6807-209, 'Journal of Edward Nevil McCready', Chapter III. Note, though, that McCready errs in asserting that these units were actually transferred to the First Division.
2. Carmichael Smyth to Mann, 10 March 1814, TNA, PRO30/35/6, pp. 19–24.
3. Van Gorkum, *Bergen op Zoom*, p. 82.
4. Account by Major Charles MacAlister, quoted in Austin, *Stick Leg*, pp. 148–9.
5. Moodie, 'Narrative', p. 302.
6. Glover, *Stanhope*, p. 151.
7. Graham to Bizanet, 9 March 1814, TNA, WO1/200, pp. 171–2; see also Graham to Bathurst, 15 March 1814, ibid., pp. 207–8.
8. Graham to Bizanet, 10 March 1814, TNA, WO1/200, pp. 171–2
9. Copy of exchange convention, TNA, WO1/200, pp. 179–186; see also Glover, *Stanhope*, pp. 150–1.
10. Moodie, 'Narrative', pp. 304–5.

11. Graham to Bunbury, 15 March 1814, Private, WO1/200, pp. 225–7.
12. Ibid., pp. 253–5.
13. Bathurst to Graham, 17 March 1814, TNA, WO6/16, pp. 69–71.
14. Burnham, Robert, 'Filling the Ranks: How Wellington Kept His Units up to Strength', in Muir, Rory, et al., *Inside Wellington's Peninsular Army*. Barnsley: Pen & Sword, 2006, pp. 201–25.
15. York to Bathurst, 14 March 1814, TNA, WO1/658, p. 455; Darling to Acland, 26 and 29 March 1814, TNA, WO3/61, pp. 4–5, 14; Darling to Eden, 5 April 1814, ibid., p. 31. See also Bamform, 'Injurious to the Service'.
16. Graham to Bathurst, 24 March 1814, TNA, WO1/200, pp. 339–40.
17. Graham to Bunbury, 25 March 1814, Private, TNA, WO1/200, pp. 367–8.
18. Bunbury to Graham, 1 April 1814, TNA, WO6/16 pp. 81–2.
19. Graham to Bathurst, 10 March 1814, TNA, WO1/200, pp. 117–27.
20. Graham to Bathurst, 11 March 1814, Private, TNA, WO1/200, pp. 141–3.
21. Graham to Bathurst, 10 March 1814, TNA, WO1/200, pp. 117–27.
22. Graham to Bathurst, 11 March 1814, Private, TNA, WO1/200, pp. 141–3.
23. Glover, *Stanhope*, pp. 151–2.
24. Graham to Bathurst, 11 March 1814, Private, TNA, WO1/200, pp. 163–4.
25. Bathurst to Graham, 14 March 1814, TNA, WO6/16, pp. 67–8.
26. In, for example, 'Letter from an Officer of Rank, Rosendaal [*sic*], March 9 1814', published in the *Edinburgh Evening Courant*, 21 March 1814.
27. Austin, *Stick Leg*, p. 179 – presumably Ensign William Ralph, who was lightly wounded during the attack and thus may well have been a fellow-patient of Austin's.
28. Ibid., p. 180.
29. Ibid., p. 186.
30. Shaw, *Personal Memoirs*, Vol. I, p. 30.
31. Morris, *Recollections*, p. 114.
32. Glover, *Stanhope*, pp. 149–50.
33. Sperling, *Letters*, p. 47.
34. Graham to Taylor, 18 March 1814, Taylor, *Taylor Papers*, pp. 153–4.
35. Cooke to Graham, 10 March 1814, TNA, WO1/200, pp. 129–33.

Chapter XIII 'We Are Making Little Progress Here'

1. Graham to Bathurst, 11 March 1814, Private, TNA, WO1/200, pp. 163–4, emphasis as original.
2. Graham to Bathurst, 22 and 25 February 1814, Private, TNA, WO1/199, pp. 677–80, 719–22.
3. Taylor to Bunbury, 2 April 1814, TNA, WO1/414, pp. 389–392; Carter, *Forty-Fourth*, p. 89; strengths and Graham's comment from 'State of the Undermentioned Corps Calmthout 24th March 1814', TNA, WO1/200, p. 219.
4. Graham to Bathurst, 15 April 1814, TNA, WO1/200, pp. 553–7; Inspection Report by Cooke, 21 May 1814, TNA, WO27/126, Part II.
5. Philippart, John, *The Royal Military Calendar or Army Service and Commission Book*. London: A. J. Valpy, 1820, Vol. V, pp. 391–9.
6. Diary Entry of 8 March 1814, Taylor, *Taylor Papers*, p. 152.
7. Graham to Taylor, 18 March 1814, Taylor, *Taylor Papers*, pp. 153–4.
8. Graham to Bathurst, 14 and 15 March 1814, Private, WO1/200, pp. 203–4, 253–5; Graham to Bunbury, 18 March 1814, ibid., pp. 273–6.
9. Graham to Bunbury, 14 March 1814, TNA, WO1/200, pp. 199–202.
10. Sperling, *Letters*, p. 55.
11. Smith to Graham, 17 March 1814, TNA, WO1/200, pp. 289–98. The whole account of Smith's meeting is taken from this source.

12. Taylor to Bunbury, 21, Private, TNA, WO1/414, pp. 321–2.
13. Graham to Bunbury, 25 March 1814, Private, TNA, WO1/200, pp. 367–8.
14. Graham to Bathurst, 19 March 1814, Private, TNA, WO1/200, pp. 281–3.
15. Wallmoden to Graham, 21 March 1814, TNA, WO1/200, pp. 327–8.
16. Graham to Bunbury, 22 March 1814, TNA, WO1/200, Private, pp. 331–4.
17. NAM 6807-209, 'Journal of Edward Nevil McCready', Chapter III.
18. Sperling, *Letters*, pp. 50–1.
19. Graham to Bunbury, 25 March 1814, Private, TNA, WO1/200, pp. 367–78, emphasis as original.
20. NAM 6807-209, 'Journal of Edward Nevil McCready', Chapter IV.
21. Elkington, 'Diary', Part II, *The XXX*, May 1911, p. 9.
22. NAM 6807-209, 'Journal of Edward Nevil McCready', Chapter IV.
23. Graham to Bathurst, 29 March 1814, TNA, WO1/200, pp. 393–4.
24. Shaw, *Personal Memoirs*, Vol. I, p. 31.
25. 'Return of Killed and wounded of the Army under the Command of His Excellency General Thomas Graham KB before Fort Lillo on the 21st March 1814', TNA, WO1/200, p. 401.
26. Divall, *Redcoats Against Napoleon*, pp. 136–7.
27. NAM 6807-209, 'Journal of Edward Nevil McCready', Chapter IV.
28. Graham to Bathurst, 25 March 1814, Private, TNA, WO1/200, pp. 351–4.
29. Ibid., pp. 367–78.
30. Ibid., pp. 351–4.
31. 'Minute of remarks and declarations said to have been made by the Prince Royal of Sweden in a conversation with the Marquis de Chabannes first aide-de-camp and Plenipotentiary of Louis 18 on the 19th March 1814', TNA, WO1/200, pp. 363–4.
32. Taylor to York, 22 March 1814, Taylor, *Taylor Papers*, p. 156.
33. Diary entries of 25 and 26 March 1814, Taylor, *Taylor Papers*, pp. 156–7.
34. Taylor to Bathurst, 28 March 1814, TNA, WO1/414, pp. 337–44.
35. Taylor to Castlereagh, 26 March 1814, TNA, WO1/414, pp. 345–62.
36. Clancarty to Taylor, 22 March 1814, TNA, WO1/414, pp. 369–72.
37. Taylor to Bunbury, 29 March 1814, TNA, WO1.414, pp. 373–6.
38. Graham to Bathurst, 29 March 1814, Private, TNA, WO1/200, pp. 405–12.
39. Bathurst to de Bosset, TNA, WO6/16, pp. 73–9.
40. Graham to Bathurst, 31 March 1814, TNA, WO1/199, pp. 751–4.
41. Graham to Bathurst, 5 April 1814, Private, TNA, WO1/200, pp. 479–82; see also Graham to Bunbury, 2 April 1814, Private, ibid., pp. 463–70.
42. Graham to Bathurst, 1 April 1814, Private, TNA, WO1/200, pp. 439–42.
43. Bathurst to Graham, 5 April 1814, TNA, WO6/16, p. 82.
44. Young to Graham, 29 March 1814, TNA, WO1/199, pp. 755–6.
45. Graham to Bathurst, 31 March 1814, TNA, WO1/199, pp. 751–4.
46. Shaw, *Personal Memoirs*, Vol. I, p. 31.

Epilogue

1. Graham to Bathurst, 11 April 1814, TNA, WO1/200, pp. 525–6; see also Wallmoden to Graham, 9 April 1814, ibid., pp. 521–3.
2. Carnot to Graham, 12 April 1814, TNA, WO1/200, pp. 541–2.
3. Graham to Carnot, 13 April 1814, TNA, WO1/200, pp. 545–7.
4. Graham to Taylor, 12 April 1814, Taylor, *Taylor Papers*, p. 162.
5. Graham to Bathurst, 15 April 1814, TNA, WO1/200, pp. 553–6; for the new order of battle, see Appendix VII.
6. Bathurst to Graham, 8 April 1814, TNA, WO6/16, pp. 83–4.
7. Renier, *Britain and the Netherlands*, pp. 181–90, 199–246, 294–9.

8. For armistice text, see TNA, WO1/200, pp. 585–7.
9. Young to Graham, 19 April 1814, TNA, WO1/200, pp. 95–6.
10. Graham to Carnot, 18 and 20 April 1814, TNA, WO1/200, pp. 589–90, 597–8; Graham to Bathurst, 21 April 1814, ibid., pp. 581–2; Young to Graham, 21 April 1814, ibid., pp. 599–600.
11. Graham to Bathurst, 26 April 1814, Private, and enclosures, TNA, WO1/200, pp. 621–38.
12. Graham to Bunbury, 29 April 1814, TNA, WO1/200, pp. 649–52; Graham to Bathurst, 3 May 1814, Private, ibid., pp. 661–4.
13. Graham to Bathurst, 5 May 1814, TNA, WO1/200, pp. 669–71.
14. Graham to Bathurst, 26 April 1814, TNA, WO1/200, pp. 617–19.
15. Bunbury to Lynedoch, 6 May 1814, TNA, WO16/6, pp. 88–90.
16. Graham to Bathurst, 26 April 1814, Private, TNA, WO1/200, pp. 621–30.
17. Graham to Bathurst, 3 May 1814, Private, TNA, WO1/200, pp. 661–4.
18. Bunbury to Lynedoch, 6 May 1814, TNA, WO16/6, pp. 90–1.
19. Bunbury to Graham, 15 April 1814, TNA, WO16/6, p. 85.
20. Bunbury to Lynedoch, 6 May 1814, TNA, WO16/6, pp. 88–90; see also James, *General Courts Martial*, pp. 641–5; Monthly Return for Holland, 25 December 1813, TNA, WO17/1773; Monthly Returns for 55th depot, TNA, WO17/278.
21. Graham to Bathurst, 26 April 1814, Private, TNA, WO1/200, pp. 621–30.
22. Ferguson to Bathurst, 13 June 1814, TNA, WO1/201, pp. 185–7; Lynedoch to Bathurst, 29 June 1814, ibid., pp. 9–11; Orange to Bathurst, 15 July 1814, ibid., pp. 233–4.
23. Austin, *Stick Leg*, p. 186.
24. Monthly Returns, TNA, WO17/1773.
25. Fortescue, *British Army*, Vol. X, pp. 163–71.
26. Carmichael Smyth, James, *Memoir upon the Topographical system of Colonel Van Gorkum: with Remarks and Reflections upon Various other Methods of Representing Ground*. London: T. Egerton, 1829.
27. Divall, *Redcoats Against Napoleon*, pp. 143–178; Dalton, Charles, *The Waterloo Roll Call*. London: Eyre and Spottiwoode, 1904, pp. 140–4, 149–52, 175–8, 185–8.
28. Glover, *Stanhope*, pp. 202–13.
29. KTS: Knight of the Order of the Tower and Sword of Valour, Loyalty and Merit (of Portugal).
30. Morris, *Recollections*, p. 319.
31. Morris, Thomas, et al.., *The Three Serjeants, or Phases of the Soldier's Life*. London: Effingham Wilson, 1858.
32. Moodie, Dunbar, *Scenes and Adventures as a Soldier and a Settler During Half a Century*. Montreal: John Lovell, 1866, pp. v–xvi.
33. Austin, *Stick Leg*, pp. 9–13, 195–205.
34. Renier, *Britain and the Netherlands*, pp. 340–2.
35. Chambers, *Charlotte and Leopold*, pp. 79–97.
36. Renier, *Britain and the Netherlands*, pp. 267–316.
37. Fortescue, *British Army*, Vol X, p. 405.

Bibliography

Manuscript Sources

The National Archives

Series ADM1, Admiralty, and Ministry of Defence, Navy Department: Correspondence and Papers
    ADM1/3261: Letters from Commandants at Chatham, 1813
Series PRO30/35: Sir James Carmichael Smyth Papers
    PRO30/35/6: Letters to Lieutenant General Mann December 1813–December 1818
    PRO30/35/23: Letters from Joannes Egbert Van Gorkum
Series WO1, War Office and Predecessors: Secretary-at-War, Secretary of State for War, and Commander-in-Chief, In-letters and Miscellaneous Papers
    WO1/198: Dutch Expedition (1813–1814): Various Departments (Commander-in-Chief, Treasury, Ordnance, Foreign Office Commissary-in-Chief)
    WO1/199–201: Dutch Expedition (1813–1814): Commander's Despatches
    WO1/414: Military Missions: Maj. Gen. Taylor's Mission to aid Dutch Army
    WO1/657–659: Commander-in-Chief: In-letters, October 1813–December 1814
Series WO3, Office of the Commander-in-Chief: Out-letters
    WO3/60–61: General Letters, September 1813–October 1814
Series WO6, War Department and successors: Secretary of State for War and Secretary of State for War and the Colonies, Out-letters
    WO6/16: Holland, Flanders, and France. 1813–1818
Series WO17, Office of the Commander in Chief: Monthly Returns to the Adjutant-General
    WO17/258: Foot Guards, 1813
    WO17/260–267: Regiments of Foot, 1813
    WO17/274–282: Regiments of Foot, 1814
    WO17/268: Veteran and Garrison Battalions and Unnumbered Corps, 1813
    WO17/270: King's German Legion, 1813
    WO17/1773: Germany, 1813–1814 [includes Holland]
Series WO27: Office of the Commander-in-Chief and War Office: Adjutant General and Army Council: Inspection Returns
    WO27/121–122: 1813 Second Half-Year
    WO27/126–127: 1814 First Half-Year
    WO27/129–130: 1814 Second Half-Year

The National Army Museum
    NAM 6807-209: Journal of Edward Nevil McCready

Printed Primary Sources

Anon., *Letters from Germany and Holland, During the Years 1813–14: With a Detailed Account of the Operations of the British Army in those Countries, and of the Attacks Upon Antwerp and Bergen-op-Zoom, by the Troops under the Command of Gen. Sir T. Graham*. London: Thomas and George Underwood, 1820

Austin, Brigadier General H. H. (ed.), *Old Stick Leg: Extracts from the Diaries of Major Thomas Austin*. London: Geoffrey Bles, 1926

Byrne, Miles, *Memoirs of Miles Byrne*. Dublin: Maunsel & Co., 1907

Elkington, James, 'Extracts from the Diary of Surgeon James Goodall Elkington during his Service with the 30th Regiment 11th March 1813–24th June 1817', *The XXX*, April 1911, pp. 12–13; May 1911, pp. 8–9

Glover, Gareth (ed.), *Eyewitness to the Peninsular War and the Battle of Waterloo: The Letters and Journals of Lieutenant Colonel the Honourable James Stanhope 1803 to 1825*. Barnsley: Pen & Sword, 2010

Gurwood, Lieut. Colonel (ed.), *The Dispatches of Field Marshal the Duke of Wellington, During his Various Campaigns in India, Denmark, Portugal, Spain, The Low Countries, and France*. London: John Murray, 1837–9

Londonderry, Lieut. General Charles William Vane, Marquis of [Sir Charles Stewart], *Narrative of the War in Germany and France in 1813 and 1814*. London: Henry Colburn and Richard Bentley, 1830

Moodie, Dunbar, 'Narrative of the Campaign in Holland in 1814, with Details of the Attack on Bergen-op-Zoom', in *Memoirs of the Late War*. London: Henry Colburn and Richard Bentley, 1831, Vol. II, pp. 259–314

——, *Scenes and Adventures as a Soldier and a Settler During Half a Century*. Montreal: John Lovell, 1866

Morris, Thomas, *Recollections of Military Service, in 1813, 1814, & 1815, through Germany, Holland, and France, including some Details of the Battles of Quatre Bras and Waterloo*. London: James Madden, 1845

——, et al., *The Three Serjeants, or Phases of the Soldier's Life*. London: Effingham Wilson, 1858

P. W., 'The Duke of Clarence at Merkhem in 1814 (Communicated by an Officer Present)', *The United Service Journal and Naval and Military Magazine*, 1830, Part II, pp. 523–5

Shaw, Charles, *Personal Memoirs and Correspondence of Colonel Charles Shaw*. London: Henry Colburn: 1837

Smith, Sir Harry, *The Autobiography of Sir Harry Smith 1787–1819*. London: J. Murray, 1910

Sperling, John, *Letters of an Officer of the Corps of Royal Engineers from the British Army in Holland, Flanders, and France to his Father, from the Latter end of 1813 to 1816*. London: James Nisbet & Co., 1872

Taylor, Ernest (ed.), *The Taylor Papers: Being a Record of Certain Reminiscences, Letters, and Journals in the Life of Lieut.-Gen. Sir Herbert Taylor GCB, GCH*. London: Longmans Green, 1913

Thompson, W. F. K. (ed.), *An Ensign in the Peninsular War: The Letters of John Aitchison*. London: Michael Joseph, 1981

Van Gorkum, Jan Egburtus (ed. L. J. F. Janssen), *De Bestorming der Vesting Bergen op Zoom, op den 8sten Maart 1814*. Leiden: Hooiberg & Zoon, 1862

Wellington, 2nd Duke of (ed.), *Supplementary Despatches, Correspondence, and Memoranda, of Field Marshal Arthur, Duke of Wellington*. London: John Murray, 1858–62

Secondary Sources

Anon., *British Minor Expeditions 1746 to 1814*. London: HMSO, 1884

Atkinson, C. T. *The Dorsetshire Regiment*. Oxford: Oxford University Press, 1947

Bamford, Andrew, '"Injurious to the Service Generally": Finding Manpower for Northern Europe 1813 & 1814', *JSAHR*, Vol. 90, No. 361 (Spring 2012), pp. 25–43

Beamish, North Ludlow, *History of the King's German Legion*. London: Thomas and William Boone, 1837

Brett-James, Antony, *General Graham, Lord Lynedoch*. London: Macmillan, 1959

Chambers, James, *Charlotte and Leopold: The True Romance of the Prince Regent's Daughter*. London: Old Street, 2007

Cannon, Richard, *Historical Record of the Fifty-Sixth, or The West Essex Regiment of Foot: Containing an Account of the Formation of the Regiment in 1755, and of its Subsequent Services to 1844*. London: Parker, Furnivall and Parker, 1844

———, *Historical Record of the First or Royal Regiment of Foot: Containing an account of the Raising of the Regiment in the Reign of King James VI of Scotland and of its Subsequent Services to 1846*. London: London: Parker, Furnivall and Parker, 1847

———, *Historical Record of the Seventy-Third Regiment: Containing an Account of the Formation of the Regiment from the Period of its Being Raised as the Second battalion of the Forty-Second Royal Highlanders in 1780 and of its Subsequent Services to 1851*. London: London: Parker, Furnivall and Parker, 1851

Carmichael Smyth, James, *Memoir upon the Topographical system of Colonel Van Gorkum: with Remarks and Reflections upon Various other Methods of Representing Ground*. London: T. Egerton, 1829

Carter, Thomas, *Historical Record of the Forty-Fourth or the East Essex Regiment of Foot*. London: W. O. Mitchell, 1864

Chandler, David, *The Campaigns of Napoleon*. London: Macmillan, 1966

——— (ed.), *Napoleon's Marshals*. London: Weidenfeld & Nicolson, 1998

Connolly, T. W. J., *The History of the Corps of Royal Sappers and Miners*. London: Longman, Brown, Green and Longman, 1855

Cope, Sir W. H., *The History of the Rifle Brigade (The Prince Consort's Own) Formerly the 95th*. London: Chatto and Windus, 1877

Dalton, Charles, *The Waterloo Roll Call*. London: Eyre and Spottiwoode, 1904

Davidson, Major H. (ed.). *History and Services of the 78th Highlanders (Ross-shire Buffs) 1793–1881*. Edinburgh and London: W. & A. K. Johnston, 1901

Delavoye, Alex. M., *Life of Thomas Graham, Lord Lynedoch*. London: Richardson, 1880

Divall, Carole, *Redcoats Against Napoleon: The 30th Regiment During the Revolutionary and Napoleonic Wars*. Barnsley: Pen & Sword, 2009

Duncan, Francis, *History of the Royal Regiment of Artillery*. London: John Murray, 1873

Flatow, Major A. F., 'British Colours at Les Invalides', *JSAHR*, Vol. 27 (1949), pp. 138–9

Fortescue, Hon. J. W., *A History of the British Army*. London: Macmillan, 1899–1930

Gallaher, John G., *The Iron Marshal: A Biography of Louis N. Davout*. London: Greenhill, 2000

Goff, Gerald L., *Historical Records of the 91st Argyllshire Highlanders, now the 1st Battalion Princess Louise's Argyll and Sutherland Highlanders: containing an Account of the Formation of the Regiment in 1794, and of its subsequent Services to 1881*. London: R. Bentley and Son, 1891

Groves, Lieut. Col. Percy, *History of the 91st Princess Louise's Argyllshire Highlanders Now the 1st Battalion Princess Louise's Argyll and Sutherland Highlanders*. Edinburgh: W. & A. K. Johnston, 1894

Hamilton, Lieutenant Gen. Sir F. W., *The Origin and Service of the First or Grenadier Guards*. London: John Murray, 1874

James, Charles, *A Collection of the Charges, Opinions, and Sentences of General Courts Martial, as Published by Authority, From the Year 1795 to the Present Time*. London: T. Egerton, 1820

James, W. M., *The Naval History of Great Britain During the French Revolutionary and Napoleonic Wars*. 6 vols, London: Richard Bentley, 1837

Jones, Major General Sir John T., *Journal of Sieges Carried on by the Army under the Duke of Wellington*. London: John Weale, 1846

Leggiere, Michael V., *Napoleon and Berlin: The Napoleonic Wars in Prussia, 1813*. Norman: University of Oklahoma Press, 2002

——, *The Fall of Napoleon: The Allied Invasion of France, 1813–1814*. Cambridge: Cambridge University Press, 2007

Longford, Elizabeth, *Wellington, The Years of the Sword*. London: Weidenfeld & Nicolson, 1969

Mackesy, Piers, *The Strategy of Overthrow 1798–1799*. London: Longman, 1974

Muir, Rory, *Britain and the Defeat of Napoleon 1807–1815*. New Haven and London: Yale, 1996

——, et al., *Inside Wellington's Peninsular Army*. Barnsley: Pen & Sword, 2006

Nicolas, Paul Harris, *Historical Record of the Royal Marine Forces*. London: Thomas and William Boone, 1845

Oman, Sir Charles, *A History of the Peninsular War*. Oxford: Oxford University Press, 1902–30, Vol. VII

——, *Wellington's Army 1809–1814*. London: Edward Arnold 1913

Philippart, John, *The Royal Military Calendar: Containing the Services of Every General Officer in the British Army, from the Date of their First Commission*. London: A. J. Valpy, 1815

——, *The Royal Military Calendar or Army Service and Commission Book*. London: A. J. Valpy, 1820

Prendergast, Harris, *The Law Relating to Officers in the Army*. London: Parker, Furnivall, and Parker, 1855

Renier, G. J., *Great Britain and the Establishment of the Kingdom of the Netherlands, 1813–1815: A Study in British Foreign Policy*. London: George Allen & Unwin, 1930

Rolt, Richard, *An Impartial Representation of the Conduct of the Several Powers of Europe, Engaged in the Late General War*. London: S. Birt, 1750

Schama, Simon, *Patriots and Liberators: Revolution in the Netherlands 1780–1813*. London: Collins, 1977

Smith, Digby, *1813: Leipzig – Napoleon and the Battle of the Nations*. London: Greenhill, 2001

Sutherland, Douglas, *Tried and Valiant: The Border Regiment 1702–1959*. London: Leo Cooper, 1972

Timbs, John, *Wellingtoniana: Anecdotes, Maxims, and Characteristics of the Duke of Wellington*. London: Ingram, Cooke and Co., 1852

Vervloet, Jelier A. J., et al., 'Planning for the future: towards a sustainable design and land use of an ancient flooded military defence line', *Landscape and Urban Planning*, 70 (2005), pp. 153–63

Zamoyski, Adam, *Rites of Peace: The Fall of Napoleon and the Congress of Vienna*. London: Harper Collins, 2007

Websites and Online Articles

Brown, Steve, 'British Regiments and the Men Who Led Them 1793–1815', at
www.napoleon-series.org/military/organization/Britain/Infantry/Regiments/c_Infantry
regimentsIntro.html

McGuigan, Ron, 'British Generals who Served in the Napoleonic Wars 1793–1815', at
www.napoleon-series.org/research/biographies/BritishGenerals/c_British
generals1.html

Morillon, Marc, 'The Siege Mortars and Their Related Skills during the Napoleonic Era', at
www.napoleon-series.org/military/organization/c_mortars.html

Uythoven, Geert van, 'Nassauers in Netherlands Service', at www.livinghistory.co.uk/
1800-1900/articles/xw_134.html

Van Wijk, Erny, 'Le 21ème à Bergen op Zoom', at www.histoire-empire.org/1814/
berg_op_zoom/berg_op_zoom_01.htm

Weil, Commandant [Maurice], trans. Greg Gorsuch, *La Campagne de 1814* (*The Campaign of 1814*), www.napoleon-series.org/military/battles/1814/Weil/c_Weil Introduction.html

Index

DISCOVER MORE ABOUT MILITARY HISTORY

Frontline Books is an imprint of Pen & Sword Books, which has more than 1500 titles in print covering all aspects of military history on land, sea and air. If you would like to receive more information and special offers on your preferred interests from time to time, along with our standard catalogue, please indicate your areas of interest below and return this card (no stamp required in the UK). Alternatively, register online at www.frontline-books.com. Thank you.

PLEASE NOTE: We do not sell data information to any third party companies

Mr/Mrs/Ms/Other.............. Name...

Address...

.... Postcode.....................

Email address..

If you wish to receive our email newsletter, please tick here ❑

PLEASE SELECT YOUR AREAS OF INTEREST

Ancient History	❑	Medieval History	❑	English Civil War	❑
Napoleonic	❑	Pre World War One	❑	World War One	❑
World War Two	❑	Post World War Two	❑	Falklands	❑
Aviation	❑	Maritime	❑	Battlefield Guides	❑
Regimental History	❑	Military Reference	❑	Military Biography	❑

Website: www.frontline-books.com • Email: info@frontline-books.com

Telephone: 01226 734555 • Fax: 01226 734438

Frontline Books
FREEPOST SF5
47 Church Street
BARNSLEY
South Yorkshire
S70 2BR